EVOLUTION AND THE PSYCHOLOGY OF THINKING

Current Issues in Thinking and Reasoning
Series editor: Kenneth J. Gilhooly

Current Issues in Thinking and Reasoning is a series of edited books which will reflect the state-of-the-art in areas of current and emerging interest in the psychological study of thinking processes. Each volume is tightly focused on a particular topic and consists of seven to ten chapters contributed by international experts. The editors of individual volumes are leading figures in their areas and provide an introductory overview. Example topics include, thinking and working memory, visual imagery in problem solving, evolutionary approaches to thinking, cognitive processes in planning, creative thinking, decision making processes, pathologies of thinking, individual differences, neuropsychological approaches and applications of thinking research.

Also available in this series:

Imagery, Language, and Visuo-spatial Thinking
Edited by Michel Denis, Robert H. Logie, Cesare Cornoldi, Manolo De Vega and Johannes Engelkamp

Working Memory and Thinking
Edited by Robert H. Logie and Kenneth Gilhooly

Evolution and the Psychology of Thinking

The Debate

edited by
David E. Over
University of Sunderland, UK

Ψ Psychology Press
Taylor & Francis Group

HOVE AND NEW YORK

First published in 2003
by Psychology Press Ltd
27 Church Road, Hove, East Sussex BN3 2FA

Simultaneously published in the USA and Canada
by Psychology Press Inc.
29 West 35th Street, New York, NY 10001

Psychology Press is a part of the Taylor & Francis Group

© 2003 Psychology Press

Typeset in Times by RefineCatch Limited, Bungay, Suffolk
Printed and bound in Great Britain by
MPG Books Ltd, Bodmin

British Library Cataloguing in Publication Data
A catalogue record for this book is available from the British Library

Library of Congress Cataloging in Publication Data
Evolution and the psychology of thinking : the debate / [edited by]
David E. Over.
    p.   cm.—(Current issues in thinking and reasoning)
Includes bibliographical references and index.
  ISBN 1–84169–285–9
  1. Cognitive psychology.   2. Genetic psychology.   I. Over, D. E.,
1946–   II. Current issues in thinking & reasoning.
  BF201.E94   2003
  155.7—dc21

                                            2002010079

            ISBN 1–84169–285–9

Contents

List of contributors   ix

Introduction: The evolutionary psychology of thinking   1
David E. Over

1.   **The allocation system: Using signal detection processes to regulate representations in a multimodular mind**   11
     Gary L. Brase
         Implications of a multimodular mind   11
         Primer on Signal Detection Theory   14
         The allocation system   16
         Misallocations and misrepresentations   18
         The structure of the allocation system   24
         Setting parameters in social situations   26
         Other implications   28
         References   29

2.   **Is there a faculty of deontic reasoning? A critical re-evaluation of abstract deontic versions of the Wason selection task**   33
     Laurence Fiddick
         Social Contract Theory   34
         The deontic alternative   37
         Abstract deontic rules are problematic for Social Contract Theory   39
         Is a social contract a permission or is a permission a social contract?   41

Emotions as a cue to interpretation   44
What is the significance of these results for the study of
    deontic reasoning?   49
Conclusion   57
References   58

3. **Evolutionary psychology's grain problem and the cognitive neuroscience
    of reasoning**   61
    Anthony P. Atkinson and Michael Wheeler
    Introduction   61
    The grain problem according to Sterelny and Griffiths   64
    The two-dimensional grain problem   69
    Levels of analysis   70
    Inferring adaptive problems from their solutions: The case
        of reasoning   73
    Inferring solutions from adaptive problems: The case of reasoning   78
    The pay-off   84
    A dispute dissolved?   86
    Conclusion   90
    References   91

4. **Specialized behaviour without specialized modules**   101
    Amit Almor
    Introduction   101
    Domain specificity in evolutionary psychology   102
    Evolutionary psychology and cheater detection   104
    Cheater detection—the empirical evidence   109
    A connectionist perspective   112
    Conclusion   118
    References   118

5. **From massive modularity to metarepresentation: The evolution of
    higher cognition**   121
    David E. Over
    Modularity arguments and deontic reasoning   123
    Modularity arguments and probabilistic reasoning   128
    Natural sampling   131
    Metarepresentation   136
    Conclusion   141
    References   141

6. **Probability judgement from the inside and out**   145
    Steven A. Sloman and David E. Over
    Base-rate neglect   148
    Conjunction fallacy   154
    Summary of studies   157

Types of probability judgement   158
More on the natural frequency hypothesis   161
Frames for probability judgement   163
Conclusion   166
References   167

7. **Evolutionary versus instrumental goals: How evolutionary psychology misconceives human rationality**   171
    Keith E. Stanovich and Richard F. West

Debates about the normative response in heuristics and biases tasks:
    Some examples   172
Dissociations between cognitive ability and the modal response in heuristics
    and biases tasks   178
Reconciling the two data patterns within a two-process view   181
Evolutionary rationality is not instrumental rationality   185
Where evolutionary psychology goes wrong   189
How evolutionary psychology goes wrong   197
The slippery notion of ecological rationality   206
The unacknowledged importance of the meme   209
Choosing the vehicle rather than the replicators: Evolutionary psychology
    without greedy reductionism   219
References   221

Author index   231
Subject index   240

List of contributors

Amit Almor, Department of Psychology, University of Southern California, Los Angeles, CA 90089-2520, USA

Anthony P. Atkinson, Psychology Department, King Alfred's College, Winchester, SO22 4NR, UK

Gary L. Brase, Division of Psychology, University of Sunderland, Sunderland, SR6 0DD, UK

Laurence Fiddick, ESRC Centre for Economic Learning and Social Evolution, University College London, London, EC1E 6BT, UK

David E. Over, Division of Psychology, University of Sunderland, Sunderland, SR6 0DD, UK

Steven A. Sloman, Department of Cognitive and Linguistic Sciences, Brown University, Providence, RI 02912, USA

Keith E. Stanovich, Department of Human Development and Applied Psychology, Ontario Institute for Studies in Education, University of Toronto, Toronto, Ontario, M5S 1V6, Canada

Richard F. West, Schools of Psychology, James Madison University, Harrisonburg, VA 22807, USA

Michael Wheeler, Department of Philosophy, University of Dundee, Dundee, DD1 4HN, UK

Introduction: The evolutionary psychology of thinking

David E. Over

Barkow, Cosmides, and Tooby (1992, p. 3) defined evolutionary psychology, in the collection of papers that did much to help launch the new subject, in the following terms:

> Evolutionary psychology is simply the psychology that is informed by the additional knowledge that evolutionary biology has to offer, in the expectation that understanding the process that designed the human mind will advance the discovery of its architecture. It unites modern evolutionary biology with the cognitive revolution in a way that has the potential to draw together all of the disparate branches of psychology into a single organised system of knowledge.

This definition gave little portent of the vigorous debate, sometimes with unproductive heat, that would flare up over evolutionary psychology (Archer, 2001a, 2001b; Buss, 2001; Campbell, 2001; Dunbar, 2001; Rose & Rose, 2001; Segal, 2001). Leading up to this debate were great advances in evolutionary biology, of obvious relevance to psychology, particularly in the study of the evolution of social behaviour (Hamilton, 1964a, 1964b) and of reciprocal altruism (Trivers, 1971). It is true that sociobiology had appeared before evolutionary psychology and been heavily criticized for its "vaulting ambition" (Kitcher, 1985). Sociobiology primed the critics, but it should have been clear that evolutionary psychology advanced beyond its forerunner, if only in not bypassing the human mind by trying to go straight from biology to human society and culture. (For introductions to the subject at a range of

1

levels, and from different points of view, see Badcock, 2000; Barrett, Dunbar, & Lycett, 2002; Buss, 1999; Evans & Zarate, 1999; Plotkin, 1997.) However, many prominent evolutionary psychologists (Buss, 1999; Pinker, 1994, 1997; Tooby & Cosmides, 1992) added to the above definition a bold, and highly contentious, new account of thinking and reasoning, and this has had a considerable impact on cognitive psychology.

The new account has been termed the Massive Modularity Hypothesis (Samuels, 1998; Sperber, 1994). Fodor (1983) argued strongly for the existence of content-specific mechanisms or modules in the mind, but these were for basic operations such as processing visual information. Fodor was mainly concerned to promote a dual process theory, in which there are also higher cognitive processes of thinking and reasoning that are not restricted to content-specific modules, but are general-purpose and content-independent. In contrast, Cosmides and Tooby (1994) criticized dual process theory and argued for the existence of what they preferred to call the multimodular mind. They compared the mind, in their model, to a Swiss army knife, which contains many special tools for specific jobs, like removing a stone from a horse's hoof, but supposedly no general-purpose blade (Cosmides & Tooby, 1994, p. 60). A critic has used a different image for this massive modularity, saying that this model implies that there is a "universal human jukebox of specialised psychological mechanisms that are played when pushed by environmental buttons" (Wilson, 1999).

Barkow et al. (1992) gave their book the subtitle "Evolutionary Psychology and the Generation of Culture". They had ambitious goals, like the sociobiologists before them, and held that evolutionary psychology could explain many significant social and cultural phenomena.

Consider what evolutionary psychologists have said about how mating strategies in men and women differ in certain respects. For example, men are supposed to place a higher value on the youth of possible mates than women do, while woman place a higher value on the material resources and social status of possible mates than men do (see Buss, 1999). These preferences are supposed to be explained by the biological differences between men and women in their investment in differing reproductive cells and in the gestation of a human child and lactation. Some evolutionary psychologists have wanted to use investigations of these, and other, contrasting values in men and women to explain, for instance, men's preference for pornography and women's for popular romantic fiction (Salmon & Symons, 2001). And, from this point, they hope to present a new perspective on the sexism in pornography and the sentimentality and snobbery of romantic fiction. In this way, evolutionary psychologists have tried not only to account for social phenomena, but also to have something relevant to contribute to the aesthetic and moral discussion of cultural products like popular novels.

Evolutionary psychology has much more of this claimed relevance if the

Massive Modularity Hypothesis is true. To continue with our example, suppose that mating preferences result from the type of evolved content-specific mechanisms described in the hypothesis. Then we can expect these preferences to be less influenced by education or upbringing than by whether one is a male or female, and the evolutionary account of these mechanisms will explain much. This is why evolutionary psychologists who want to say something important about cultural products endorse the massive modularity hypothesis (Salmon & Symons, 2001, pp. 22–27).

On the other hand, assume now that existing mating preferences in the societies most studied by evolutionary psychologists are mainly the result of a general-purpose learning mechanism. For example, suppose that women learn their mating preference for men with material resources as a result of growing up in societies where women have had little share of those resources. In this case, evolutionary psychology could not tell us much about these preferences, which would not follow directly from the biological facts of maternal investment in reproduction. Evolutionary psychologists with the greatest ambition of being relevant to, and even reforming, the study of society and culture require the truth of massive modularity in cognitive psychology. Opposed to this position, there is what Tooby and Cosmides (1992) called the Standard Social Science Model (SSSM). This presupposes that most significant social and cultural phenomena depend on a general learning ability and reasoning ability, which can produce vastly different societies and cultures in different historical circumstances.

Massive modularity cannot be dismissed as crude genetic determinism, even though some evolutionary psychologists invite this charge by calling the evolved content-specific mechanisms "instincts" (Pinker, 1994), but these are not usually held to be rigidly fixed from conception. It is rather that these cognitive mechanisms are canalized to a greater or lesser degree, and are the result of some degree of biological preparedness for content-specific learning (Cummins & Cummins, 1999). For example, we may have some evolved tendency to fear snakes more than flowers, as some monkeys do (Cook & Mineka, 1990), but this would show itself by our learning to fear snakes more easily and quickly than we can learn to fear flowers. Resulting from this biological preparedness for specific learning, many more people would always, or almost always, tend to fear snakes more than flowers. However, massive modularity, as usually stated, allows for the possibility that some people could learn, through special training, experience, or conditioning, to fear flowers more than snakes. They might even learn to fear some flowers more than some snakes known to be poisonous. (This does not necessarily require any technically advanced knowledge about allergies to the pollen in flowers. Some Native Americans could well have learned to prefer handling a copperhead snake to picking bunches of poison ivy flowers.) The question becomes how much biological preparedness there is for fearing snakes. If there is a great deal, then evolutionary psychology will not only be relevant to the study and treatment of snake phobias, but even to explaining why snakes have been used as symbols of evil in religion and literature. If there is very little, evolutionary psychology will not be of much relevance, even to the explanation of snake phobias. Between these extremes, there is obviously room for many views on the degree of biological preparedness for fearing snakes. Much more generally, there is plenty of space between massive modularity and the SSSM, let alone between pure genetic determinism and pure cultural determinism, for intermediate positions. One has only to think of all the different degrees of biological preparedness that could be proposed for each psychological mechanism in turn.

Massive modularity is a radical view and implies that the evolved cognitive mechanisms it refers to are highly canalized and result from a high degree of biological preparedness for content-specific learning. It is to the credit of evolutionary psychologists that they have tried to gather experimental evidence for massive modularity, and their experiments have had a highly stimulating effect on cognitive psychology. Massive modularity cannot be fairly or scientifically criticized until these experiments, and their theoretical underpinnings, are assessed in detail. If massive modularity is disconfirmed, evolutionary psychology will go on. There are certainly ways to practise evolutionary psychology, widely defined, without assuming massive modularity (for examples, see Bradshaw, 1997; Campbell, 1999; Dunbar, 2000; Heyes, 2000; Humphrey, 2000; Smith, Mulder, & Hill, 2001.) Even more broadly, there are psychologists who informally or vaguely use some of the basic terms of evolutionary psychology, particularly "adaptive". In fact, one sign of the influence of evolutionary psychology has been the way "adaptive" has become quite a vogue word in psychology. But then it can be used so loosely that it causes debates about how far these psychologists are committed to massive modularity, or even any evolutionary approach at all (Gigerenzer, Todd, & The ABC Research Group, 1999; Over, 2000a, 2000b; Todd, Fiddick, & Krauss, 2000). However, if the Massive Modularity Hypothesis is completely false, evolutionary psychology will not have striking implications, beyond psychology, for the study of society and culture. There is also the intermediate possibility, of course, that there will be good evidence for some evolved modular mechanisms for certain aspects of thinking and reasoning, but not for others.

This volume is an attempt to present a serious debate on the Massive Modularity Hypothesis. The first three chapters develop and extend the hypothesis, or seek to counter arguments against it. The other chapters are, to a greater or lesser extent, critical of massive modularity and of the experimental support that has been claimed for it.

There is a challenging question implicit in the negative metaphor of Wilson (1999). What account can be given of how the highly canalized psychological mechanisms, in the universal human jukebox, are pressed by environmental buttons? Samuels, Stich, and Tremoulet (1999) pointed out that there must be some way of determining which module in the massive modular mind is allocated to any given domain. In Chapter 1, Gary Brase uses Signal Detection Theory to address this problem of the allocation system for what he, like Cosmides and Tooby, prefers to call the multimodular mind. He suggests that the system will act to minimize two different kinds of error. For example, the evolved content-specific mechanism for identifying snakes as objects to fear might be incorrectly activated by a snake-like vine. This would be a false alarm in signal detection terminology. On the other hand, a camouflaged snake might be incorrectly seen as a vine. Brase also notes that the allocation system cannot be expected to work perfectly. This can easily be illustrated in the case of snakes. Even as the selection pressure on us tended to make us better at identifying snakes, the selection pressure on snakes tended to make us worse at identifying them.

In the single most influential paper in evolutionary cognitive psychology, Cosmides (1989) related certain forms of the selection task (Wason, 1966) to biological studies of reciprocal altruism. Using the experimental paradigm of the selection task, she argued that there is strong support for an evolved content-specific mechanism that identifies cheaters in social exchanges. A conditional that expresses an agreement in a social exchange is a type of deontic rule, for example, if people help us when we are in need then we must help them when they are in need. Given this rule, cheaters are those who accept help without ever reciprocating. Cosmides' view is apparently countered if there is a more general ability to understand deontic rules. In Chapter 2, Laurence Fiddick discusses conditional precautions, which are a type of nonsocial deontic rule (Mantelow & Over, 1990) about potential hazards (e.g. snakes), and abstract deontic rules with symbols in them for many different contents (Cheng & Holyoak, 1985). He argues that experiments on these do not go against Cosmides' original claims. He presents new evidence that there are separate-evolved, content-specific mechanisms for identifying and responding appropriately to cheaters and to hazards. The response to a cheater tends to be anger, whereas that to a hazard tends to be fear.

Sterelny and Griffiths (1999) argued that evolutionary psychology faces what they called the grain problem. This problem would seem to be particularly acute for those committed to massive modularity. We can ask, for instance, whether there really is just one module for identifying hazards in general. Perhaps there is a separate one for animals, or even for snakes, and another for potentially hazardous plants. Going "up" rather than "down", we could ask whether there actually are two separate modules for identifying cheaters and for recognizing hazards. Perhaps a cheater is, at an even more general level, a kind of "hazard". Are there coarse-grained or fine-grained modules to match coarse-grained or fine-grained adaptive problems? In

Chapter 3, Anthony Atkinson and Michael Wheeler explore this grain problem, arguing that it is even more serious than Sterelny and Griffiths indicate.
However, they conclude that evolutionary psychology can live with the problem, although it may not be possible to decide in the end, for example,
whether there are two fine-grained mechanisms for identifying cheaters and
hazards in a narrow sense or a higher coarse-grained one for more general
deontic reasoning.

Cosmides' stand on deontic reasoning has provoked or inspired much
comment. There are those who severely criticize it (Cheng & Holyoak, 1989),
those who have been influenced by it but have a more general analysis (Manktelow & Over, 1995), and those with a competing evolutionary account that is
still relatively content specific (Cummins, 1998). It is perfectly understandable
that this should be so. Far-reaching consequences are at stake, and not just in
the study of thinking and reasoning. Deontic rules range from the simplest
agreements to the highest level legal, moral, and political laws and principles.
If evolutionary psychology can explain much about deontic reasoning, then it
should be able to tell us a great deal about culture and society.

In Chapter 4, Amit Almor is critical of the massive modularity of current
evolutionary psychology, and especially of Cosmides' theory of deontic reasoning. He argues in favour of a highly flexible ability to assess social situations, going way beyond a mere capacity to pick out cheaters. Not even
cheating is a simple matter. No simple, inflexible mechanism for cheater
detection could, he holds, infer the costs and benefits of cheating people of
different relations to us in all the important circumstances of social life, and
of tolerating, or not tolerating, cheating by them. He critically examines the
claimed experimental support for Cosmides' theory, particularly the evidence
that supposedly comes from the social perspectives people are asked to take
on in some deontic selection tasks. On the theoretical side, he sketches a
connectionist account of deontic reasoning that is content general. His level
of explanation is extremely coarse grained, in the terminology of Atkinson
and Wheeler.

In my own chapter of the book (Chapter 5), I examine the logical structure
of the arguments used to try to support massive modularity. These modularity arguments are an attempt to identify an adaptive problem, and then to
show in an experiment that people can solve that specific problem and not
one that is of the same logical form but with a different, non-adaptive content. This is an original and stimulating way to argue for evolutionary conclusions but, in my view, the modularity arguments so far employed do not
achieve their purpose. The arguments used for deontic reasoning mistakenly
treat different logical forms as the same. The ones for probability judgement
actually establish the opposite of their intended conclusions, demonstrating
not that there is content-specific inference, but rather that there is content-
independent reasoning, about probability. I also conclude that very recent

work by Cosmides and Tooby (2000) on metarepresentation is a big step away from unqualified massive modularity and towards dual process theory.

Chapter 6, by Steven Sloman and myself, has further criticisms of the experiments on probability and provides additional experimental evidence for the existence of content-independent reasoning. Cosmides and Tooby (1996) claimed that people could solve probability problems when these are about frequencies but not when they are about single-case probabilities. Tversky and Kahneman (1983) were the first to get results of this kind, but they concluded that the frequency versions of the problems made the set and subset relations in them transparent, as they put it.

Their comments suggest that it is the simplicity of some content-independent set operations that explains why some frequency problems are so easy, and not a "sort of instinct" for frequency representations (Gigerenzer & Hoffrage, 1995). We argue that our results confirm Tversky and Kahneman's original suggestion.

In the final chapter of the book, Keith Stanovich and Richard West stress the importance of studying individual differences in thinking and reasoning, and the relevance of this study to the views some evolutionary psychologists have expressed about human rationality (Over, 2002). In their dual-process theory, they make a distinction between System 1 and System 2. System 1 contains content-specific modules on a short leash tied directly to what was in the interests of our genes in our evolutionary history (like fear of snakes). System 2 is responsible for content-independent reasoning, and is on a long leash to deal better with novelty and uncertainty in the world (such as whether some unfamiliar species of snake is really dangerous). According to Stanovich and West, there are individual differences in how effective System 2 is in overriding System 1. Such overriding can be rational for what they call the vehicle, that is, the whole individual, but not in the interests of the vehicle's genes. There is then, in their account, a difference between evolutionary rationality, defined by the genes' interests, and instrumental rationality, defined by the vehicle's, or individual's, interests. Much confusion, they argue, has been caused by a failure to make this vital distinction, and as a result of the use of apparently biological terms, like "ecological rationality", in an imprecise and even slippery way. Stanovich and West conclude with the pressing question of ". . . how to best advance human interests whether or not they coincide with genetic interests."

ACKNOWLEDGEMENTS

For comments on this book, I am indebted to Denise Cummins, Jonathan Evans, Ken Gilhooly, David Green, Ken Manktelow and Clare Saunders, as well as to all the contributors to it.

REFERENCES

Archer, J. (2001a). Evolving theories of behaviour. *The Psychologist, 14*, 414–419.

Archer, J. (2001b). Do not adjust your beliefs, there is fault in reality. Why do some psychologists have problems with evolutionary psychology? *The Psychologist, 14*, 430.

Badcock, C. (2000). *Evolutionary psychology: A critical introduction*. Cambridge: Polity Press.

Barkow, J.H., Cosmides, L., & Tooby, J. (Eds.) (1992). *The adapted mind: Evolutionary psychology and the generation of culture*. New York: Oxford University Press.

Barrett, L. Dunbar, R., & Lycett, J. (2002). *Human evolutionary psychology*. New York: Palgrave.

Bradshaw, J.L. (1997). *Human evolution: A neuropsychological approach*. Hove, UK: Psychology Press.

Buss, D. (1999). *Evolutionary psychology: The new science of the mind*. Boston, MA: Allyn & Bacon.

Buss, D. (2001). The design of the human mind. *The Psychologist, 14*, 424–425.

Campbell, A. (1999). Staying alive: Evolution, culture, and women's intrasexual aggression. *Behavioral and Brain Sciences, 22*, 203–252.

Campbell, A. (2001). Behaviour – Adapted? Adaptive? Useful? *The Psychologist, 14*, 426–427.

Cheng, P.W., & Holyoak, K.J. (1985). Pragmatic reasoning schemas. *Cognition, 17*, 391–416.

Cheng, P.W., & Holyoak, K.J. (1989). On the natural selection of reasoning theories. *Cognition, 33*, 285–313.

Cook, M., & Mineka, S. (1990). Selective associations in the observational conditioning of fear in rhesus monkeys. *Journal of Experimental Psychology: Animal Behavior Processes, 16*, 272–389.

Cosmides, L. (1989). The logic of social exchange: Has natural selection shaped how humans reason? Studies with the Wason selection task. *Cognition, 31*, 187–276.

Cosmides, L., & Tooby, J. (1994). Beyond intuition and instinct blindness: Toward an evolutionarily rigorous cognitive science. *Cognition, 50*, 41–77.

Cosmides, L., & Tooby, J. (1996). Are humans good intuitive statisticians after all? Rethinking some conclusions from the literature on judgment under uncertainty. *Cognition, 58*, 1–73.

Cosmides, L., & Tooby, J. (2000). Consider the source: The evolution of adaptations for decoupling and metarepresentations. In D. Sperber (Ed.), *Metarepresentations: A multidisciplinary perspective*. Oxford: Oxford University Press.

Cummins, D.D. (1998). Social roles and other minds: The evolutionary roots of higher cognition. In D.D. Cummins & C. Allen (Eds.), *The evolution of mind*. New York: Oxford University Press.

Cummins, D.D., & Cummins, R. (1999). Biological preparedness and evolutionary explanation. *Cognition, 73*, B37–B53.

Dunbar, R. (2000). Causal reasoning, mental rehearsal, and the evolution of primate cognition. In C. Heyes & L. Huber (Eds.), *The evolution of cognition*. Cambridge, MA: MIT Press.

Dunbar, R. (2001). Darwinising ourselves. *The Psychologist, 14*, 420–421.

Evans, D., & Zarate, O. (1999). *Evolutionary psychology*. Cambridge: Icon.

Fodor, J. (1983). *Modularity of mind*. Cambridge, MA: The MIT Press.

Gigerenzer, G., & Hoffrage, U. (1995). How to improve Bayesian reasoning without instruction: Frequency formats. *Psychological Review, 102*, 684–704.

Gigerenzer, G., Todd, P., & The ABC Research Group (1999). *Simple heuristics that make us smart*. New York: Oxford University Press.

Hamilton, W.D. (1964a). The genetical evolution of social behaviour, I. *Journal of Theoretical Biology, 7*, 1–16.

Hamilton, W.D. (1964b). The genetical evolution of social behaviour, II. *Journal of Theoretical Biology, 7*, 17–52.

Heyes, C. (2000). Evolutionary psychology in the round. In C. Heyes & L. Huber (Eds.), *The evolution of cognition*. Cambridge, MA: MIT Press.

Humphrey, N. (2000). The privatization of sensation. In C. Heyes & L. Huber (Eds.), *The evolution of cognition*. Cambridge, MA: MIT Press.

Kitcher, P. (1985). *Vaulting ambition: Sociobiology and the quest for human nature*. Cambridge, MA: MIT Press.

Manktelow, K.I., & Over, D.E. (1990). Deontic thought and the selection task. In K.J. Gilhooly, M. Keane, R.H. Logie, & G. Erdos (Eds.), *Lines of thinking* (Vol. 1). Chichester: Wiley.

Manktelow, K.I., & Over, D.E. (1995). Deontic reasoning. In S.E. Newstead & J.St.B.T. Evans (Eds.), *Perspectives on thinking and reasoning*. Hove, UK: Lawrence Erlbaum Associates Ltd.

Over, D.E. (2000a). Ecological rationality and its heuristics. *Thinking & Reasoning, 6*, 182–192.

Over, D.E. (2000b). Ecological issues: A Reply to Todd, Fiddick, & Krauss. *Thinking & Reasoning, 6*, 385–388.

Over, D.E. (2002). The rationality of evolutionary psychology. In J.L. Bermúdez and A. Millar (Eds.), *Reason and nature: Essays in the theory of rationality*. Oxford: Oxford University Press.

Pinker, S. (1994). *The language instinct*. New York: HarperCollins.

Pinker, S. (1997). *How the mind works*. New York: The Penguin Press.

Plotkin, H. (1997). *Evolution in mind: An introduction to evolutionary psychology*. London: Penguin.

Rose, H., & Rose, S. (2001). Much ado about very little. *The Psychologist, 14*, 428–429.

Salmon, C., & Symons, D. (2001). *Warrior lovers: Erotic fiction, evolution, and female sexuality*. London: Weidenfeld & Nicolson.

Samuels, R. (1998). Evolutionary psychology and the massive modularity hypothesis. *British Journal for the Philosophy of Science, 49*, 575–602.

Samuels, R., Stich, S., & Tremoulet, P.D. (1999). Rethinking rationality: From bleak implications to Darwinian modules. In E. LePore & Z. Pylyshyn (Eds.), *What is cognitive science?* Oxford: Blackwell.

Segal, L. (2001). Main agendas and hidden agendas. *The Psychologist, 14*, 422–423.

Smith, E.A., Mulder, M.B., & Hill, K. (2001). Controversies in the evolutionary social sciences: A guide for the perplexed. *Trends in Ecology & Evolution, 16*, 128–135.

Sperber, D. (1994). The modularity of thought and the epidemiology of representations. In L.A. Hirschfeld & S.A. Gelman (Eds.), *Mapping the mind: Domain specificity in cognition and culture*. Cambridge: Cambridge University Press.

Sterelny, K., & Griffiths, P.E. (1999). *Sex and death*. Chicago: Chicago University Press.

Todd, P.M., Fiddick, L., & Krauss, S. (2000). Ecological rationality and its contents. *Thinking & Reasoning, 6*, 375–384.

Tooby, J., & Cosmides, L. (1992). The psychological foundations of culture. In J.H. Barkow, L. Cosmides, & J. Tooby (Eds.), *The adapted mind: Evolutionary psychology and the generation of culture*. New York: Oxford University Press.

Trivers, R.L. (1971). The evolution of reciprocal altruism. *Quarterly Review of Biology, 46*, 35–57.

Tversky, A., & Kahneman, D. (1983). Extensional versus intuitive reasoning: The conjunction fallacy in probability judgment. *Psychological Review, 90*, 293–315.

Wason, P.C. (1966). Reasoning. In B.M. Foss (Ed.), *New horizons in psychology I*. Harmondsworth, UK: Penguin.

Wilson, D.S. (1999). Tasty slice – but where is the rest of the pie? *Evolution and Human Behavior, 20*, 279–287.

CHAPTER ONE

The allocation system: Using signal detection processes to regulate representations in a multimodular mind

Gary L. Brase
University of Sunderland, UK

IMPLICATIONS OF A MULTIMODULAR MIND

An aspect of evolutionary psychology that seems to distress a number of people is the degree of modularization it implies. The concept of a multi-modular mind can be difficult to accept. To be more precise, many sensible people readily accept that evolutionary theory is relevant to the study of the mind, and even that the evolutionary process is an important consideration in understanding how the mind was designed, but balk at the implication—drawn by most pre-eminent theorists in evolutionary psychology—that the mind is therefore composed of a large number of relatively specialized cognitive adaptations, or modules (Buss, 1995, 1999; Pinker, 1997; Tooby & Cosmides, 1992).

The reason for positing a large number of specialized mental abilities lies at the very foundations of evolutionary thinking. The evolutionary process must be enabled by a selection pressure—some aspect of the environment that poses a survival or reproductive problem for the species in question. Evolution happens by positive and negative feedback in relation to how well individuals (actually, genes that produce phenotypic traits that exist as part of individuals) solve that problem (assuming there is some variation in prob-lem solutions). Since we are talking about specific problems, the better solu-tions will be specific and tailored to that problem domain (see Cosmides & Tooby, 1987, 1994); one cannot have a single solution for problems as diverse as finding food, courting mates, learning a language, and bipedal locomotion.

Although there are debates about the nature of the processes and devices (Karmiloff-Smith, 1992; Sterelny, 1995), the mind must contain some form of specializations specific to these problem domains. Thus, it is proposed that there is a "learned taste-aversion" module, a "cheater detection" module, a "jealousy" module, a "theory of minds" module, "bluffing detection" and "double-cross detection" modules, and so on. (Tooby & Cosmides, 1992; also see Francis Steen's compendium for a tentative attempt at documenting the major categories of modules: http://cogweb.ucla.edu/EP/Adaptations.html.)

Although this process of module discovery appears to be ongoing, there already are concerns that evolutionary psychologists are creating a Frankensteinian mind. Some (Murphy & Stich, 2000; Samuels, 1998; Sperber, 1994) have referred to this evolutionary view of the mind as the "*Massive* Modularity" Hypothesis (italics added), an expression that seems to capture this concern quite well. Other, less restrained writers, have taken to calling evolutionary psychology "the new phrenology". Some of this discomfort is likely to be the result of the sheer magnitude of the transition from traditional psychological models to evolutionary approaches. Behaviourist models of the entire mind contain a small handful of extremely general associative modules. Early computational models of the mental abilities tend to have a similarly small number of modules (e.g. the Atkinson & Shiffrin (1968, 1971) model of memory, which, prior to later modifications, had three basic modules: sensory memory, short-term memory, and long-term memory). Even the model proposed by Fodor (1983), which in many ways introduced the idea of modularity, restricted itself to highly encapsulated modules at the interfaces between the external world and the (still general-purpose) central functions of the mind. In the context of these historical roots, the evolutionary vision of the mind is truly a radical step.

Another indication of the profound nature of this viewpoint shift is that some early critics of evolutionary approaches seemed to miss entirely the implications of multimodularity and criticized domain-specific abilities for not being able to explain phenomena outside that domain. Cosmides' theory on reasoning about social contracts was considered to be falsified if it failed to account for improved reasoning of any kind, with any other type of content:

> ... contrary to the prediction of social exchange theory, facilitation in the selection task can be readily obtained with unfamiliar regulations that do not involve social exchange, any type of "rationed benefit", or even any social situation at all.
>
> (Cheng & Holyoak, 1989, p. 299)

> We ourselves have found, however, that the facilitation effect [in selection tasks] is not only produced by conditionals relating benefits and costs as Cosmides describes.
>
> (Manktelow & Over, 1990, p. 156)

Intriguing as this theory is, it is incorrect as it stands, since, as several authors
have pointed out . . ., many of the best established facilitatory contexts do not
involve costs and benefits that are socially exchanged.

(Garnham & Oakhill, 1994, pp. 140–141)

Actually, the existence of a cognitive adaptation for dealing with social
exchanges in no way precludes the existence of other cognitive adaptations
for reasoning about other types of contents. In fact, it actually implies that
there *must* be other reasoning procedures, given any similar selection pressures over human evolutionary history that involved making inferences about
any other aspects of the world.

As some people grasp the "massiveness" of the multimodular mind
model, they have tried to dismiss the basic idea using an argument of incredu-
lity (see Samuels, 1998); claiming that the implications of multimodularity
are simply too outrageous to be true. Although this "too massive" objection
is a weak rhetorical argument (Dawkins, 1987), it does help to reveal some
points that do, deservedly, require serious attention. One of the most
important of these points is that the existence of a large number of modules
necessitates some form of coordinating superstructure; a regulation of the
modules that determines which modules are invoked at which times. In short,
a multimodular mind requires some procedural government of modules.

The government of a multimodular mind can be usefully viewed as being
a process just as much about the external world as it is about modules. The
primary task of this process is to categorize situations that arise in the
environment into the various domains in which particular inference
procedures (modules) are invoked. As pointed out by Samuels, Stich, and
Tremoulet (1999), "perhaps the most natural hypothesis is that there is a
mechanism in the mind (or maybe more than one) whose job it is to determine which of the many reasoning modules and heuristics that are available
in a Massive Modular mind get called on to deal with a given problem."
Samuels et al. call this device the "allocation mechanism". I shall adopt this
label, but with a modification: this allocation process is almost certainly a
multifaceted system and, as such, it is probably misleading to refer to it as a
mechanism (e.g. just as one does not usually refer to a "visual mechanism"
but rather the visual system). I will, therefore, refer to the *allocation system*.

This chapter will also use certain other conventions in terminology.
Cosmides and Tooby (1997, 2002) have used the term "multimodular" (as
opposed to massively modular) to describe the general structure of the mind
from an evolutionary viewpoint. Also, this chapter is concerned with the
information entering and being processed within this mental allocation system, and I will refer to the output of the allocation process as different
representations of information. That is, what the allocation system does is
impute specific representational forms onto environmental situations (based

on incoming information), so that each situation can be processed within a module suitable for such situations. (Admittedly, this description glosses over some complex processes, e.g. how representation, categorization, and the movement of these neurally instantiated representations to their appropriate modules, but it will have to suffice at this point.)

How does this allocation system work? In terms of a computational analysis (Marr, 1982), what is the computational problem that this system must solve? The situation that exists is a more-or-less continuous series of categorization tasks, all under situations of incomplete information, based on the properties of situations (cues) that are used as information (signals) for categorization. One of the most straightforward and widely used concep-tualizations for such perceptual cue/category relationships (in situations with incomplete information) is Signal Detection Theory (SDT). SDT has been applied across many situations in which a categorization decision must be made based on cues with less than perfect cue validity and other situations of incomplete information.

PRIMER ON SIGNAL DETECTION THEORY

Signal detection (SD) involves the perception of some information from the environment (the signal) and a decision process for categorizing that informa-tion as either being or not being the target signal (detection; Green & Swets, 1966). The issue in signal detection is not just whether the signal actually exists (it may or may not), but also whether observers detect it (they may or may not). Therefore, there are four possible states of affairs:

1. "Hit" (correct acceptance) = the signal is present, and it is detected.
2. "False alarm" (incorrect acceptance) = the signal is absent, but it is detected.
3. "Miss" (incorrect rejection) = the signal is present, but it is not detected.
4. "Correct rejection" = the signal is absent, and it is not detected.

So long as the information is incomplete in some way, due to limits in the sensitivity to the signal, environmental and/or neural noise, or infidelity of the signal itself, all four of these outcomes will be possible. In real-world settings there is nearly always some amount of insensitivity, noise, or corrup-tion in the signal, meaning there is always a distribution of ways the signal (or absence of a signal) may appear to an observer. An observer must therefore set a criterion (also called a cutting score, or C) for making decisions about whether the signal has occurred or not. As can be seen in Fig. 1.1, any given criterion results in errors (misses and false alarms); the task of the criterion generally is to minimize the effects of these errors, and a natural place to put

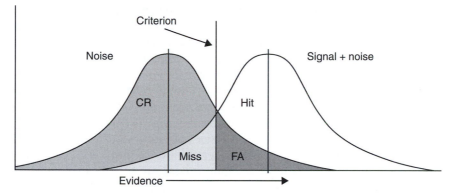

Figure 1.1 Generalized model of a signal detection situation. A judgement that there is only noise when there is, in fact, only noise (left-hand distribution) is a "Correct Rejection" (CR), whereas a judgement that there is a signal when there is actually a signal (right-hand distribution) is a "Hit". Errors can occur when either no signal is judged to exist even though a signal does exist (a "Miss") or a signal is judged to exist although there actually is no signal (a "False Alarm"; FA).

the criterion is at the point that minimizes both the miss rates and the false alarm rates. A criterion can be adaptively adjusted from this point, however, changing what is called the *criterion bias*, based on the relative costs of "miss" errors and "false alarm" errors. Placing the criterion in different locations changes the likelihood of these two errors, which are linked to one another in an inverse relationship (e.g. as in Neyman–Pearsonian statistical hypothesis testing theory, in which Type I and Type II errors are parallels to misses and false alarms).

It is important to note here that in most applications of Signal Detection Theory (SDT) the categorization itself is the crucial event that leads very directly to a decision and the end of the process. One reason for the focus on signal detection decisions as the end-points of the process is that most signal detection tasks are for fairly specific tasks. The topics most strongly associated with Signal Detection Theory are narrowly defined areas of decision making; from the original conception of Signal Detection Theory (identifying sonar objects as being either ships or nonships), to specific aspects of memory and attention (e.g. Posner, Snyder, & Davidson, 1980), to specific aspects of language (e.g. Katsuki, Speaks, Penner, & Bilger, 1984), taste and smell (e.g. Doty, 1992; Jamieson, 1981), and to jury decision making (Mowen & Linder, 1986). In each of these areas, the decision frame has already been constructed around a rather specific issue (also see Pastore & Scheirer, 1974, for a general discussion of Signal Detection Theory applications).

Even in understanding the behaviours of other animals, in which signal detection has also been useful, the animal signals have typically been signals of specific things (e.g. alarm calls, mate attraction, warning coloration, etc.;

e.g. Cheney & Seyfarth, 1990; Marler, 1996). Similarly, the detection of a signal has usually been directly linked to some specific behavioural response. Signal detection models in the animal world, however, more often involve the idea of detection errors that are caused not by random noise or insensitivity, but by other agents (i.e. other animals). Take, for example, the situation of a predator (say, a hawk) scanning the landscape for prey. A "hit" for the predator is a correct sighting of prey, and a "correct rejection" is a correct rejection of nonprey objects. The predator can be induced to commit miss errors, however, by prey that mimic the appearances of foul-tasting animals (Gould & Marler, 1987; one could also view this as a false alarm on the part of the predator, if considering the categorization dimension of "foul-tasting things to avoid"). Alternatively, some prey animals induce misses in predators by using camouflage with their surroundings so that the predators simply do not detect the prey's presence as such.

THE ALLOCATION SYSTEM

The ideas proposed herein are designed to outline an allocation system envisioned as a part of the multimodular mind generally (Fig. 1.2), but will, by necessity, focus on specific topical areas in describing and giving examples of this system's functioning. This focus is made for several reasons. First, specific areas (social relationships and judgements under uncertainty) have been loci of evolutionarily informed research, providing sufficient and relevant background research. Second, these are areas with particularly interesting properties: like the earlier predator/prey example, signals sent by other people may be intentionally made clearer or noisier to suit the sender's goals. Finally, I think it would be premature to attempt anything near a complete model of all aspects of the allocation system. At present, the goal is simply to develop a general framework.

The general form of the allocation task is to determine which type of representation is most appropriate for understanding a given situation, based on the perceived properties of that situation. In complex situations (such as most real-world settings), there are multiple cues to the nature of the situation, each of which is due to particular properties of that situation (analogous to multiple cues to visual depth; Holway & Boring, 1941). It is supposed, therefore, that the allocation system is structured to take advantage of these multiple cues by utilizing signal detection mechanisms for particular cues, each of which contributes—but is not alone sufficient—to trigger the allocation of a particular representation. So, for example, a social exchange situation (as described by Cosmides & Tooby, 1992), would involve all or some of the cues of another person's wanting something you possess, of them having something you want, of the relative values of both these items (and if their exchange would result in a net benefit for both parties), and how likely it is that you would receive what you want in the absence of action. Once represented as a social exchange, a similar signal detection procedure could be evoked by cues of deception or dishonesty; the much-discussed "cheater detection module". Other situations that could potentially be mentally represented may involve some—but not all—of these same situational cues (e.g. perceiving a threat involves another person wanting something you possess and cues as to the nil likelihood of them receiving it without any action but, critically, does not involve a reciprocal benefit for both parties). And, of course, other situations will additionally involve other detectable situational cues (e.g. a threat does not involve cues of a cost being implemented in the absence of the items being given over).

Some possible representations for social interaction situations include as a social exchange, a hazard, a threat, or as a sexual opportunity. Recent studies have provided evidence that these different representations not only exist but that specific social interactions can be categorized into different representations based on how people are induced to consider that interaction. Fiddick

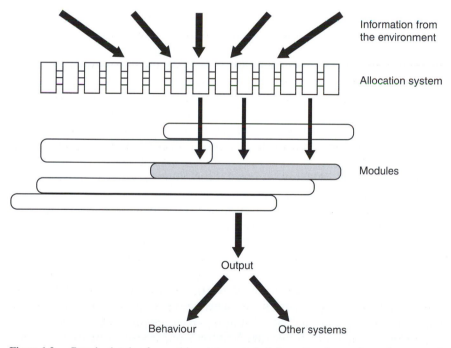

Figure 1.2   Rough sketch of a multimodular mind. Informational cues from the external environment are received by the multiple signal detection devices, operating in parallel and constituting the allocation system (rectangles). A particular combination of signals being detected will invoke a specific modular ability (elongated ovals), thereby fitting the environmental situation into a specific representation. The output of modular activities may take the form of either behaviour or information (signals) sent to other systems or modules.

(1998; Fiddick, Cosmides, & Tooby, 2000) has been able to induce research participants into representing ambiguous social interactions as social exchanges, threats, or precautions, demonstrating dissociations of these categories. Similarly, Brase and Miller (2001) found that a sexual harassment statement framed with a punitive consequence ("If you spend the night with me, then I won't eliminate your position") was judged by the majority of people (86 per cent) to be a threat. A sexual harassment statement in the same context but framed with a rewarding consequence ("If you spend the night with me, then I will give you a promotion") was judged by the majority of people (69 per cent) to be a social exchange.

How information is represented has also been a major topic of evolutionarily based research in the area of judgements under uncertainty. Although curious examples of frequency formats leading to facilitation in statistical judgements have been around for some time (Tversky & Kahneman, 1983), evolutionary explanations have helped to explain the reason for and nature of this effect (Cosmides & Tooby, 1996; Gigerenzer, 1991b). Specifically, it has been proposed that the human mind is designed by the evolutionary history of our species to be sensitive to the frequencies of events, as opposed to statements given in other numerical formats. Furthermore, these results have been taken even further by Brase, Cosmides, and Tooby (1998), who showed that our statistical judgement abilities are not just tuned to frequency formats (as opposed to, for example, single event probabilities), but also tuned to particular ways of parsing (or "individuating") the world. In short, the mind not only represents statistical information in frequencies, it preferentially represents that frequency information in terms of whole object, events, and locations (as opposed to aspects of objects, partial events, or idiosyncratic views of locations).

Samuels et al. (1999) also discussed the evolutionary views on judgements under uncertainty, leading them to propose the term "allocation" system that is adopted here. Their discussion led them to wrestle with an implication of this allocation system: the implied existence of misallocations.

MISALLOCATIONS AND MISREPRESENTATIONS

In terms of how the results of the allocation system are experienced, signal detection incidents of misses or false alarms—in social interactions—can be experienced as misinterpreted situations, social *faux pas*, and embarrassing misunderstandings (the fodder for hundreds of television situation comedy episodes). These same errors, when they occur in statistical judgement situations, have led to questions about the nature of human rationality (or irrationality). When information about a situation is misallocated by person X's allocation system it is misrepresented in person X's mind. From this it follows that the representation of that situation as held by others is missing in

X's mind. The result is that person X does not behave appropriately but commits a social error, or a statistical error, or some other type of error.

Samuels et al. (1999) talk about "misallocation" as a way to explain errors and apparent irrationality in reasoning. However, their insightful analysis is only a partial accounting of misallocation possibilities. Just as there are a large number of possible ways that a computer (or a car, or human organs, or any complex system) can manifest systematic errors, there are a number of ways that misallocation errors can come about. The following sections outline several ways in which misallocations, and subsequent misrepresentations, can occur.

Initial base-rate biases

Information will be allocated more frequently to representations that correspond to higher-frequency situations. (Note that here, as in subsequent sections, the term "bias" is being used in relation to signal detection theory and does not necessarily imply irrationality.) Indeed, certain representations appear to be more likely to be evoked than others, and these inequalities of representations can be general to all people, or specific to certain contexts (such as particular cultures). General base-rate biases can exist simply because the size and spread of distributions for various situation types are different. If events that evoke representation A are significantly more common than events that evoke representation B then, all other things being equal, there should be a bias towards selecting representation A in unclear situations (for example, there should be a bias to represent a small object flying overhead as a "bird" rather than a "bat", a bias to represent a doctor as male, and a bias to represent a couple as a pair of heterosexuals).

The idea that certain representations are more easily evoked than others has been recognized in social psychology for quite a while, under the label of "chronically accessible schemas" (Bargh & Pratto, 1986; Higgins, King, & Mavin, 1982). A chronically accessible schema is a particular way of representing events that is used by a person in a habitual manner, such as when a person represents all social events as being related to race relations (or politics, or sex, or ethnicity, or any other specific frame of reference). These schemata can be based on a combination of prior predispositions, objectively observed base-rates, and prior subjective representations of events (e.g. within a subjective Bayesian model).

The availability heuristic proposed by Tversky and Kahneman (1973) can also be understood as being a result of this base-rate bias. The availability heuristic is the use of one's phenomenal experience of how easy it is to recall a type of event occurring as a source of information for making probability judgements about that event. Systematic errors occur due to the availability heuristic, because subjective experiences of an event occurring do not always accurately reflect the actual prevalence of those events (for example, subject-ive experience appears to be influenced by exposures via television; O'Guinn & Shrum, 1997). Thus, people tend to overestimate the probability of plane crashes, terrorist acts, and school shootings, while underestimating the num-ber of heart failures, automobile accidents, and broken collarbones. If, how-ever, one takes into account the idea that the human mind is not designed to differentiate between electronic reports of exotic events in far-off locations and interpersonal communication about local events, then the availability heuristic is really a product of media technology corrupting an otherwise well-operating cognitive module. Specifically, the availability heuristic shows errors because initial base-rate settings are led to deviate from the true state of the world.

Context biases

Situational information can bias the allocation system towards one represen-tation, which can in some cases cause misrepresentations of specific aspects or particular incidents. For example, walking down a dark street in a seedy part of town provides contextual cues that could lead to a criterion bias in detecting signals for a threat representation of others' actions (e.g. if some-one crosses the street to help you and you initially represent them as coming to attack you). A retailer in a shop may have a bias towards interpreting situations as being social exchanges; a person in a singles bar may have a bias towards interpreting any social contact as a sexual overture. These context-sensitive criterion biases are overlayed on general base-rate biases.

There have been some interesting findings in social psychology that fit within the idea of situational information being used as cues that create context biases. One of these findings is the weapons effect, in which the mere presence of a weapon (usually a gun or a knife) leads participants to be more aggressive (Berkowitz, 1993; Berkowitz & LePage, 1967). Although there is no clear reason for people to become more aggressive because a weapon is present (and, indeed, an argument can be made for the reverse), there seems to be just such an effect. The weapons effect can be understood as a case of the weapon providing a context bias. A weapon, by definition, is a tool for aggressive purposes and the presence of such a tool therefore constitutes an environmental cue that aggressive behaviour is possible or anticipated. Sub-sequent aggressive behaviour could result from either counteraggression or defensive aggression. Another effect similar to the weapons effect has recently been documented: Payne (2001) found that priming white participants with images of black faces led to faster identification of guns and higher false-positive rates in identifying objects as guns.

A second set of relevant findings in social psychology is the general phe-nomenon of labelling effects. By telling someone that they have—or that others have—a particular characteristic (e.g. helpfulness, social deviance, discriminating taste), it is possible to increase the associated behaviours or the associated reactions to those characteristics (Cialdini, 2001). In these situations, the information given to the target person is specifically designed by the experimenter to create a context bias. Notably, these labelling effects are also notoriously short-lived; as soon as the target person is in a new situation the labelling effect tends to dissipate.

More recently, Cosmides, Tooby, Montaldi, and Thrall (1999) reported that the personalities of others were used as a context variable in reasoning about a social situation. Their participants were told that they would interact with one of two (fictional) persons, and they were given a character-defining story involving that person. The social interaction that participants engaged in was a social exchange setting, and the participants' task was to search the prior actions of the fictional person for any indications of "cheating" on social exchanges. For the fictional person who was characterized as exceptionally honest, her prior activities (where cheating could have occurred) were typically not scrutinized at all, whereas the prior actions of the not-as-honest fictional person were searched through in the same manner as in similar research tasks with no personality information.

Personality biases

People may have personality differences that thereby cause them to differ in their likelihood of forming various representations of situations. Some people are more fearful than others, some people are more attentive and concerned about precautions, and some people see a wider array of situations as involving sexual innuendo. Whereas it is not a radical step to claim that personality differences in extraversion, neuroticism or social deviance can have pervasive implications in terms of manifested behaviours, it may be quite interesting to consider the idea that these personality-based differences in behaviour can be understood as driven by biases in allocations to various situational representations. Thompson (1978) actually documented a relationship between individual difference variables (personality, age, and sex) and how people perceive social cues, using a signal detection theory framework (specifically, multiple linear regression analyses using the demographic variables was able to predict both sensitivity and response bias).

It is possible that at the extremes of these individual differences lie insights into some of the notoriously difficult-to-diagnose mental disorders. Paranoid personality disorder (a pervasive and unwarranted tendency to interpret the actions of others as deliberately demeaning, or threatening) can be well described as a severe criterion bias towards detecting threats. Obsessive–compulsive personality disorder (preoccupation with orderliness, perfectionism, and mental and interpersonal control, at expense of flexibility, openness, and efficiency) can be described as a severe bias towards detecting (and applying) precautions.

With some latitude, I will consider sex differences under personality. Sex differences have been a major topic in evolutionary psychology (Buss, 1999), probably because relevant predictions derived from evolutionary theory are clear, robust, and of some natural interest. In line with general evolutionary predictions and findings that men are more interested in sexual opportunities than women, Abbey (1982; see also Abbey, Ross, McDuffie, & McAuslan, 1996) found a difference between men and women in the representation of social interactions between the sexes. Both men and women in their study were shown the same videotape of a man and woman interacting, but men were significantly more likely to perceive that the woman was sexually interested in the man (i.e. the men were more likely to form a representation of the social interaction as involving sexual overtures).

Formulation errors

Samuels et al. (1999) coined the term "formulation errors" in reference to the particular misallocation phenomenon they noted: failures of certain forms of environmental inputs to register as the normatively appropriate representations. In particular, their discussion focused on statistical formats and the fact that frequency information seems to more effectively tap into intuitive statistical competencies than do single event probabilities. The formulation error is an error in that both frequency counts and probabilities convey information that is largely interchangeable within the context of many statistical tasks, yet the mind seems to be competent and rational only when the information is formulated in particular ways (Brase et al. 1998). Another example might be useful here: our visual system has a wonderful ability to maintain colour constancy under varying conditions of natural lighting (our perceptions of colours remain fairly constant regardless of if it is dawn, full light, dusk, sunset, etc.; Jameson & Hurvich, 1989; Lucassen & Walvaren, 1996). It is possible to perceive breakdowns of this colour constancy ability, however, by looking at colours under artificial lighting conditions (such as sodium vapour lamps). This phenomenon can similarly be described as a formulation error of the information fed into the visual system; this system was not designed over evolutionary history to be able to do things like maintain colour constancy under sodium vapour lamp illumination. Thus, there is an analogous set of implications: the visual system is in some ways very poorly designed (for some aspects of the modern visual world) and the statistical decision-making system is in some ways very poorly designed (for some aspects of modern probability expression). The key in both of these examples is that the visual or statistical incompetence derives from the fact that the relevant system is being called upon to perform an evolutionarily novel task.

Similarly, some other instances of apparent incompetence and irrationality (e.g. estimating the frequency of ----ing words versus the frequency of -----n-words; Tversky & Kahneman, 1973) can be understood as formulation errors (in this case, the fact that the human mind does not code the frequencies of *everything*, and some access to the frequency of linguistic morphemes such as "—ing" may be possible, whereas access to the frequency of "'n' in the sixth position of the word" is almost certainly not a part of our language abilities). Contrary to the implication that some readings of Samuels et al. (1999) might indicate, a multimodular mind is by no means perfectly competent (nor, obviously, is it perfect in performance) in the sense of being able to do anything in the world. Instead, it is satisfactorily competent in those things that it was designed to do.

Instigated errors

There is also the possibility of manipulation by the person who sends a signal out for others to receive. From this perspective, the signal sender may systematically alter his or her output in order to promote certain representations in the minds of others, and thus more effectively achieve their own desired outcome (Dawkins & Krebs, 1978). For example, a person may internally represent a situation as a threat ("If anyone touches my car I will beat them up"), but attempt to send out a message that is more palatable to others and more likely to achieve the desired result (e.g. as a precaution: "If you touch my car, I can't be responsible for what happens to you" or a social exchange: "If you don't touch my car, then I won't have to beat you up"). Another example might be someone who injects sexual overtures into interactions to get preferential treatment that would otherwise not be forthcoming (see, for example, Sarah Hrdy's work on female evolved strategies for resource extraction; Hrdy, 1997, 1999).

Intentional manipulation/suspension of allocation

Finally, there are many indications that the allocation system is not entirely transparent or beyond conscious control. The meta-awareness, and even willful control, of an allocation system can be argued as an explanation for how metaphors are both created and understood. A metaphor, on this account, is a way of understanding some aspect of the world that does not fit easily into some already established representational set by purposefully allocating it into some representation that is clearly not correct but useful in that the allocation into a representational framework allows further understanding of this aspect of the world. Along these lines, Gigerenzer (1991a) has proposed the idea of "Tools to Theories" metaphors; that the statistical techniques that psychologists use for research analysis purposes can be traced as the origin points for several theoretical accounts of mental processes (including, in the present case, Signal Detection Theory). Successful and popular metaphors are those that prove very useful in promoting a further understanding of the target phenomenon. This understanding of the world that metaphors can bring people, however, in no way guarantees that their understanding will be correct. Gentner and Gentner (1983), for example, found that the metaphors students used for understanding the nature of electricity (i.e. either electricity as running water or electricity as rats running through tubes) led to mis-representations of the true nature of electricity that were consistent with the particular metaphor used.

Another phenomenon that can be understood in terms of the functioning of the allocation system is the development of "abstract" representations of information. For example, higher mathematics, formal logic, and probability theory are all abstract systems of representation that do not appear to be naturally or intuitively present in the human mind (i.e. they require extensive training to acquire). The successful acquisition of these abstract represen-tational systems appears to be a process of more-or-less willful suspension of the usual allocation system processes. If one looks at how these abstract con-cepts are learned, it is possible to discern the development of this suspension process. Formal logic, for instance, is typically taught by beginning with statements that happen to be allocated and represented in such a way that the logically correct implications are usually drawn, but then the rules of formal logic are set out for how that implication should be derived. By successive modelling, students learn to apply the formal logic rules consciously instead of using the initial representational-based inferences. Some of the classically successful aids in learning formal logic are also based on this idea (e.g. Venn diagrams take the abstract formal logic and map it by metaphor onto a phys-ical representation of space). Finally, once the abstract representation has been successfully acquired, it is customarily necessary to invent some form of notation to communicate these abstract representations without falling back into more mentally convenient representational sets (e.g. $X \in Y \geq Z$).

THE STRUCTURE OF THE ALLOCATION SYSTEM

An implication of using signal detection processes for shunting situations into their correct mental representations is that a multimodular mind must therefore have multiple signal detection processes in place. Specifically, assume for the sake of argument that each signal detection process is designed to exactly categorize a situation or leave it uncategorized. In this case, there would be as many signal detection processes as there are modules. It is almost certain that this is not the true state of the allocation system; each representation is hypothesized to be evoked by multiple, converging signals, and there are also several ways of reducing the number of signal detection processes needed. Given, say, 10 signal detection processes, there are 2^{10} (1024) possible combinations of signals. It may also be the case that the correct rejection and miss outcomes of some signal detection processes lead to "default" categorizations. Regardless of these basic considerations, however, a lot of signal detection processes are required.

Having many signal detection processes is arguably not such a bad thing. Presumably these processes are operating in parallel with each other (see earlier discussion on multiple cues leading to allocation decisions), and more signal detection processes can yield a more reliable, accurate, and rapid government of modules. Furthermore, having a large number of signal detection processes involved leads to a robust design. The relative simplicity and redundancy of the signal detection process ensures that if a small number of the signal detection processes become corrupted (e.g. by stroke or head trauma), it is quite likely that some of the remaining signal detection processes can compensate for the loss. In other words, it is a somewhat fail-safe system in that the removal of a signal detection element (or even several) is not fatal for whole system. Another benefit of a large collection of relatively similar signal detection processes is that it provides a blueprint for the construction of the mechanisms during development (see Keil (1981, 1990, 1991) regarding the ontological repetition of modules, and Dawkins (1987) regarding simple rules for the development of body plans). The ability to construct a large component of the mental architecture from relatively few genetic directions in turn provides for great efficiency in genetic coding (e.g. pleiotropic DNA sequences). Finally, this in turn helps resolve a periodically emerging criticism regarding the relationship between genetic coding and the brain: how can only 30–5000 human genes (many of which must be committed to other parts of the body) provide a multimodularly detailed blueprint for billions of neurons in the brain? While many people have answered this criticism in general terms—that genes do not code for physical aspects in a one-to-one manner—the elaboration here has an added benefit of providing an explicit route by which a few genes can produce many neural structures.

There is one area of ambiguity regarding the structure of the allocation system and a multimodular mind that I will not go into much detail in trying to resolve, and that is the exact definition of a "module". There are a number of different definitions of a module, as well as a number of alternative names for what I have referred to here as modules (Darwinian algorithms, cognitive adaptations, instincts, mental organs; see Fodor, 1983, 2000; Tooby & Cosmides, 1992). Whole books have been written regarding how to best characterize human psychological adaptations (Bock & Cardew, 1997). The primary difficulty thus far appears to be that there is no one, single level at which all "modules" occur. Consider, for instance, vision. One might say that we have a module for vision, but it can also be argued that we have a whole array of modules for colour perception, motion detection, colour constancy, line orientation, face recognition, and so on. Going in the other direction, our ability to see is a fundamental subcomponent of other abilities that have themselves been called modules (e.g. evaluating physical attractiveness or inferring mental states from the actions of others). So is "vision" one module, a whole collection of modules, or a fraction of some other module? Until we develop a terminology system that clearly and validly distinguishes among the different levels of "lower-order" to "higher-order" cognitive abilities, we appear to be stuck with general terms that encompass all these various kinds of module. So, for example, the ability to engage in social exchanges, something that itself has been called an adaptation or a module, is actually an ability that invokes multiple "modules": a cheater-detection module, a cost-evaluation module, a benefit-evaluation module, a theory-of-minds module, and probably others (Cosmides & Tooby, 1992). Atkinson and Wheeler spend another whole chapter on this issue (see Chapter 3), and the present chapter will not delve any further into this issue. This chapter is actually only indirectly about modules, and more precisely is about the allocation of representations for information so that it can be directed to modules. Perhaps a better understanding of the allocation system can actually aid in our developing understanding of how to properly conceptualize modules.

Although I have taken an evolutionary, multimodular approach to the structure of the human mind, the task of representing incoming information as belonging to various categories so that it can be routed to appropriate cognitive processes is a task that nearly any conception of the human mind must properly address. If the choices for representations were not social exchanges, threats, hazards, and sexual opportunities, they could be induction and deduction, or deontic logic and descriptive logic, or information gain and expected utility. The allocation problem exists regardless of whether or not one's view of the mind ignores evolutionary considerations (e.g. the pragmatic reasoning schemas theory [Cheng & Holyoak, 1985, 1989] requires some allocation system), and the problem exists regardless of whether one adheres to the "massive" modularity thesis or to a much less aggressive view of modularity. The relative merits and validity of these different views are tremendously important issues, as they relate to the fundamental nature and structure of the human mind, but as such they are beyond this small chapter.

SETTING PARAMETERS IN SOCIAL SITUATIONS

Signal detection of objects in the physical world usually involves a mix of constant and variable (or "open") parameters. For example, detecting the letter "R" will involve about the same, fairly constant pattern of lines, curves, and spaces no matter where one is, who is around, or what time of day it is. The ease with which an "R" is detected does, however, change depending on whether the letter is embedded within a word (e.g. "WORD") or a nonword (e.g. "WYRZ"; this is known as the word superiority effect, see Reicher, 1969). Signal detection of social interaction types similarly involve both constant and variable parameters. Certain properties of a social exchange situation, for example, are constant across time, place, and person: items are intercontingently exchanged such that both parties experience a net benefit. A social exchange with one particular person at one point in time, however, is not entirely the same as a social exchange with a different person at a different time (Cosmides et al. 1999). One of the keys to effective representations of social interactions is an ability to facultatively adjust the signal detection parameters depending on the individuals with whom you are interacting. In other words, a key to effective social interactions is a memory for individuals. Our memory for individuals is, in fact, quite good (Farah, Wilson, Drain, & Tanaka, 1998), and this is a necessary prerequisite. The additional step taken here is that those memories for individuals are fed into the signal detection processes (e.g. in the modelling of the utilities of the possible outcomes), such that the signal detection parameters are adjusted to be reflective of that other person's traits. Specifically, it should be possible within the allocation system to adaptively adjust the criterion (cutting score) based on the particulars of a situation, to reflect the ambient costs and benefits of the possible outcomes of that situation. (Other aspects of the allocation system, such as the category distributions, may also be adjustable, but probably in an ontogenetic manner.)

One possible problem in this proposal is that we encounter hundreds of thousands of people in our daily lives. It would be impractical and computationally impossible to maintain signal detection parameters for every different individual. And, of course, we don't. One of the characteristics of the social world that the human mind constructs is that it is filled not just with people but with various categories of people. People are categorized according to their gender, their ethnicity, their race, their views, and other dimensions that are perceived to be relevant. The characteristics associated with each of these categories of people are stereotypes, and the use of stereotypes in the everyday world has serious implications in terms of prejudice and discrimination. These stereotypes, however, which could in this context be considered as template models of mental states for categories of individuals, also enable facultative adjustments to the process of categorizing social interactions into different representations. Recent research (Levin, 2000) has actually shown that people categorize new individuals (of a different race) as members of a racial group before they are categorized as individuals. Other research (Haselton & Buss, 2000) has explored the apparently significant extent to which people infer the wants, beliefs, and desires of others based just on the other person's sex. An open question is the extent to which it is possible to react to other individuals without tapping into some form of social categorization for that individual (i.e. whether or not there is a completely generic template model for considering individuals with no known gender, race, or other categorizable features).

OTHER IMPLICATIONS

There are some interesting implications of this allocation and representation system. The first two implications noted here are relevant for proponents of cultural relativism. First the bad news: this system broadly presumes a set of universal representational categories. It may be the case that certain specific representational categories will not exist in certain specific cultures (for various historical, social, or other reasons), but the system demands that there be a full set of categories from which the existing representational categories derive. In other words, the representational system is an element of human nature. So what is the good news? This system also provides a way for wide and superficially "fundamental" differences across cultures. The key is that there may be tremendous latitude in when and/or how the different representations are elicited. For instance, there may be a universal representation of a social exchange as the exchange of items that are differentially valued such that both parties realize a net gain, but the key element of what things are "valuable" and what things are not is apparently very open to social learning.

Another implication of this system is for the construction of human memory. It has been documented repeatedly over the years that human memory is far from veridical. We not only forget things that happened, but we remember things that did not happen (Bartlett, 1932/1967, Loftus, 1975, 1980, Roediger & McDermott, 2000). A vexing element of this research area is that people presumably see situations in a relatively veridical manner (i.e. without gross omissions and hallucinations), yet memories retrieved just a few hours after an event can be distorted. It almost appears that the way in which memories are stored even for brief periods is somehow defective. Consider, though, what happens to memories in the context of our allocation system. Once an event has been allocated a certain representation (for instance, as a threat), any deficient elements for that type of representation are sought out (are there weapons, menacing movements, escape routes?). Instead of simply perceiving the situation as one of billions of scenes from our lifetime, it is perceived representationally as a particular type of situation. Furthermore, different situations are assigned different representations, leading to both additions and omissions in memory that are systematic by representational type but almost chaotic if viewed in temporal order.

ACKNOWLEDGEMENTS

The preparation of this chapter benefited from discussions with, among others, David Over, Richard Heath, and Sandra Brase.

REFERENCES

Abbey, A. (1982). Sex differences in attributions for friendly behavior: Do males misperceive females' friendliness. *Journal of Personality and Social Psychology, 42*, 830–838.

Abbey, A., Ross, L.T., McDuffie, D., & McAuslan, P. (1996). Alcohol, misperception, and sexual assault: How and why are they linked? In D.M. Buss & N.M. Malamuth (Eds.), *Sex, power, conflict* (pp. 1138–1161). New York: Oxford University Press.

Atkinson, R.C., & Shiffrin, R.M. (1968). Human memory: A proposed system and its control processes. In K.W. Spence & J.T. Spence (Eds.), *The psychology of learning and motivation: Vol. 2. Advances in research and theory*. New York: Academic Press.

Atkinson, R.C., & Shiffrin, R.M. (1971). The control of short-term memory. *Scientific American, 225*, 82–90.

Bargh, J.A., & Pratto, F. (1986). Individual construct accessibility and perceptual selection. *Journal of Experimental Social Psychology, 22*, 293–311.

Bartlett, F.C. (1967). *Remembering*. Cambridge: Cambridge University Press. (Original work published 1932.)

Berkowitz, L. (1993). *Aggression*. New York: McGraw-Hill.

Berkowitz, L., & LePage, A. (1967). Weapons as aggression-eliciting stimuli. *Journal of Personality and Social Psychology, 7*, 202–207.

Bock, G.R., & Cardew, G. (1997). *Characterizing human psychological adaptations*. Symposium held at the Ciba Foundation on 29–31 October, 1996. Chichester, UK: John Wiley & Sons.

Brase, G.L., Cosmides, L., & Tooby, J. (1998). Individuals, counting, and statistical inference: The role of frequency and whole-object representations in judgment under uncertainty. *Journal of Experimental Psychology: General, 127*, 3–21.

Brase, G.L., & Miller, R.L. (2001). Sex differences in the perception of and reasoning about quid pro quo sexual harassment. *Psychology, Evolution, and Gender, 3*, 241–264.

Buss, D. (1995). Evolutionary psychology: A new paradigm for psychological science. *Psychological Inquiry, 6*, 1–30.

Buss, D.M. (1999). *Evolutionary psychology: The new science of the mind*. Boston, MA: Allyn and Bacon.

Cheney, D.L., & Seyfarth, R.M. (1990). *How monkeys see the world: Inside the mind of another species*. Chicago, IL: The University of Chicago Press.

Cheng, P.W., & Holyoak, K.J. (1985). Pragmatic reasoning schemas. *Cognitive Psychology, 17*, 391–416.

Cheng, P., & Holyoak, K. (1989). On the natural selection of reasoning theories. *Cognition, 33*, 285–313.

Cialdini, R.B. (2001). *Influence: Science and practice* (4th ed.). New York: Allyn and Bacon.

Cosmides, L., & Tooby, J. (1987). From evolution to behavior: Evolutionary psychology as the missing link. In J. Dupré (Ed.), *The latest on the best: Essays on evolution and optimality* (pp. 277–306). Cambridge, MA: MIT Press.

Cosmides, L., & Tooby, J. (1992). Cognitive adaptations for social exchange. In J.H. Barkow, L. Cosmides, & J. Tooby (Eds.), *The adapted mind: Evolutionary psychology and the generation of culture*. Oxford: Oxford University Press.

Cosmides, L., & Tooby, J. (1994). Origins of domain specificity: The evolution of functional organization. In L.A. Hirschfeld & S.A. Gelman (Eds.), *Mapping the mind: Domain specificity in cognition and culture* (pp. 85–116). New York: Cambridge University Press.

Cosmides, L., & Tooby J. (1996). Are humans good intuitive statisticians after all? Rethinking some conclusions from the literature on judgment under uncertainty. *Cognition, 58*, 1–73.

Cosmides, L., & Tooby, J. (1997). The multimodular nature of human intelligence. In A. Schiebel & J.W. Schopf (Eds.), *Origin and evolution of intelligence* (pp. 71–101). Sudbury, MA: Jones and Bartlett.

Cosmides, L., & Tooby, J. (2002). Unravelling the enigma of human intelligence: Evolutionary psychology and the multimodular mind. In R.J. Sternberg & J.C. Kaufman (Eds.), *The evolution of intelligence* (pp. 145–198). Mahwah, NJ: Lawrence Erlbaum Associates, Inc.

Cosmides, L., Tooby, J., Montaldi, A., & Thrall, N. (1999). *Character counts: Cheater detection is relaxed for honest individuals.* 11th Annual Meeting of the Human Behavior and Evolution Society, Salt Lake City, Utah, June 2–6, 1999.

Dawkins, R. (1987). *The blind watchmaker.* New York: W.W. Norton & Company, Inc.

Dawkins, R., & Krebs, J.R. (1978). Animal signals: Information or manipulation? In J.R. Krebs, & N.B. Davies (Eds.), *Behavioural ecology: An evolutionary approach.* Oxford: Blackwell.

Doty, R.L. (1992). Diagnostic tests and assessment. *Journal of Head Trauma Rehabilitation, 7,* 47–65.

Farah, M.J., Wilson, K.D., Drain, M., & Tanaka, J.N. (1998). What is "special" about face perception? *Psychological Review, 105,* 482–498.

Fiddick, L. (1998). *The deal and the danger: An evolutionary analysis of deontic reasoning.* Doctoral dissertation, University of California, Santa Barbara.

Fiddick, L., Cosmides, L., & Tooby, J. (2000). No interpretation without representation: The role of domain-specific representations and inferences in the Wason selection task. *Cognition, 77,* 1–79.

Fodor, J. (1983). *The modularity of mind.* Cambridge, MA: MIT Press.

Fodor, J. (2000). *The mind doesn't work that way: The scope and limits of computational psychology.* Cambridge, MA: MIT Press.

Garnham, A., & Oakhill, J.V. (1994). *Thinking and reasoning.* Oxford: Blackwell.

Gentner, D., & Gentner, D.R. (1983). Flowing waters or teeming crowds: Mental models of electricity. In D. Gentner & A.L. Stevens (Eds.), *Mental models* (pp. 99–129). Hillsdale, NJ: Lawrence Erlbaum Associates, Inc.

Gigerenzer, G. (1991a). From tools to theories – A heuristic of discovery in cognitive psychology. *Psychological Review, 98,* 254–267.

Gigerenzer, G. (1991b). How to make cognitive illusions disappear: Beyond heuristics and biases. *European Review of Social Psychology, 2,* 83–115.

Gould, J.L., & Marler, P. (1987). Learning by instinct. *Scientific American, 256,* 74–85.

Green, D.M., & Swets, J.A. (1966). *Signal detection theory and psychophysics.* New York: John Wiley.

Haselton, M.G., & Buss, D.M. (2000). Error management theory: A new perspective on biases in cross-sex mind reading. *Journal of Personality and Social Psychology, 78,* 81–91.

Higgins, E.T., King, G.A., & Mavin, G.H. (1982). Individual construct accessibility and subjective impressions and recall. *Journal of Personality and Social Psychology, 43,* 35–47.

Holway, A.H., & Boring, E.G. (1941). Determinants of apparent visual size with distance variant. *American Journal of Psychology, 51,* 21–37.

Hrdy, S.B. (1997). Raising Darwin's consciousness: Female sexuality and the prehominid origins of patriarchy. *Human Nature, 8,* 1–49.

Hrdy, S.B. (1999). *The woman that never evolved* (revised ed.). Cambridge, MA: Harvard University Press.

Jameson, D., & Hurvich, L.M. (1989). Essay concerning color constancy. *Annual Review of Psychology, 40,* 1–22.

Jamieson, D.G. (1981). Visual influence on taste sensitivity. *Perception and Psychophysics, 29,* 11–14.

Karmiloff-Smith, A. (1992). *Beyond modularity: A developmental perspective on cognitive science.* Cambridge, MA: MIT Press.

Katsuki, J., Speaks, C.E., Penner, S.B., & Bilger, R.C. (1984). Application of theory of signal detection to dichotic listening. *Journal of Speech and Hearing Research, 27,* 444–448.

Keil, F.C. (1981). Constraints on knowledge and cognitive development. *Psychological Review, 88,* 197–227.

Keil, F.C. (1990). Constraints on constraints: Surveying the epigenetic landscape. *Cognitive Science, 14,* 135–168.

Keil, F. (1991). The emergence of theoretical beliefs as constraints on concepts. In S. Carey & R. Gelman (Eds.), *The epigenesis of mind: Essays on biology and cognition.* Hillsdale, NJ: Lawrence Erlbaum Associates, Inc.

Levin, D.T. (2000). Race as a visual feature: Using visual search and perceptual discrimination tasks to understand face categories and the cross-race recognition deficit. *Journal of Experimental Psychology: General, 129,* 559–574.

Loftus, E.F. (1975). Leading questions and the eyewitness report. *Cognitive Psychology, 7,* 560–572.

Loftus, E.F. (1980). On the permanence of stored information in the human brain. *American Psychologist, 35,* 409–420.

Lucassen, M.P., & Walvaren, J. (1996). Color constancy under natural and artificial illumination. *Vision Research, 36,* 2699–2711.

Manktelow, K.I., & Over, D.E. (1990). Deontic thought and the selection task. In K.J. Gihooly, M.T.G. Keane, R.H. Logie, & G. Erdos (Eds.), *Lines of thinking* (Volume 1). Chichester: John Wiley & Sons.

Marler, P. (1996). The logical analysis of animal communication. In: L.D. Houck & L.C. Drickamer (Eds.), *Foundations of animal behavior: Classic papers with commentaries* (pp. 649–671). Chicago, IL: The University of Chicago Press.

Marr, D. (1982). *Vision: A computational investigation into the human representation and processing of visual information.* San Francisco: Freeman.

Mowen, J.C., & Linder, D.E. (1986). Discretionary aspects of jury decision making. In H.R. Arkes & K.R. Hammond (Eds.), *Judgment and decision making: An interdisciplinary reader* (pp. 593–612). Cambridge: Cambridge University Press.

Murphy, D., & Stich, S. (2000). Darwin in the madhouse: Evolutionary psychology and the classification of mental disorders. In P. Carruthers & A. Chamberlain (Eds.), *Evolution and the human mind: Modularity, language and meta-cognition.* Cambridge: Cambridge University Press.

O'Guinn, T.C., & Shrum, L.J. (1997). The role of television in the construction of consumer reality. *Journal of Consumer Research, 23,* 278–294.

Pastore, R.E., & Scheirer, C.J. (1974). Signal detection theory: Considerations for general application. *Psychological Bulletin, 81,* 945–958.

Payne, B.K. (2001). Prejudice and perception: The role of automatic and controlled processes in misperceiving a weapon. *Journal of Personality and Social Psychology, 81,* 181–192.

Pinker, S. (1997). *How the mind works.* New York: Norton.

Posner, M., Snyder, C.R., & Davidson, B.J. (1980). Attention and the detection of signals. *Journal of Experimental Psychology: General, 109,* 160–174.

Reicher, G.M. (1969). Perceptual recognition as a function of meaningfulness of stimuli material. *Journal of Experimental Psychology, 81,* 275–280.

Roediger, H.L., & McDermott, K.B. (2000). Distortions of memory. In E. Tulving & F.I.M. Craik (Eds.), *The Oxford handbook of memory* (pp. 149–162). New York: Oxford University Press.

Samuels, R. (1998). Evolutionary psychology and the massive modularity hypothesis. *The British Journal for the Philosophy of Science, 49,* 575–602.

Samuels, R., Stich, S., & Tremoulet, P. (1999). Rethinking rationality: From bleak implications to Darwinian modules. In E. Lepore & Z. Pylyshyn (Eds.), *What is cognitive science?* Oxford: Blackwell.

Sperber, D. (1994). The modularity of thought and the epidemiology of representations. In L.A. Hirschfeld & S.A. Gelman (Eds.), *Mapping the mind: Domain specificity in cognition and culture* (pp. 39–67). New York: Cambridge University Press. [Revised version in Sperber, D. (1996). *Explaining culture: A naturalistic approach.* Oxford, Blackwell.]

Sterelny, K. (1995). The adapted mind [book review]. *Biology and Philosophy*, *10*, 365–380.

Thompson, S.C. (1978). Detection of social cues: A signal detection theory analysis. *Personality & Social Psychology Bulletin*, *4*, 452–455.

Tooby, J., & Cosmides, L. (1992). The psychological foundations of culture. In J.H. Barkow, L. Cosmides, & J. Tooby (Eds.), *The adapted mind: Evolutionary psychology and the generation of culture* (pp. 19–136). New York: Oxford University Press.

Tversky, A., & Kahneman, D. (1973). Availability: A heuristic for judging frequency and probability. *Cognitive Psychology*, *5*, 207–232.

Tversky, A., & Kahneman, D. (1983). Extensional versus intuitive reasoning: The conjunction fallacy in probability judgment. *Psychological Review*, *90*, 293–315.

CHAPTER TWO

Is there a faculty of deontic reasoning? A critical re-evaluation of abstract deontic versions of the Wason selection task

Laurence Fiddick
Max Planck Institute for Human Development, Berlin, Germany

Undoubtedly one of the most important studies in evolutionary cognitive psychology is Cosmides' (1989) analysis of content effects on the Wason selection task in terms of adaptive cheater detection. However, in her landmark paper, Cosmides ventured beyond the confines of the selection task to argue for a bold new synthesis of evolutionary biology and cognitive psychology using Marr's (1982) concept of a computational theory as the bridge between these two disciplines. Following Marr's lead, Cosmides argued that cognitive psychology could not make progress unless it was informed by task analyses of the problems the mind was designed to solve. These task analyses would ultimately be supplied by evolutionary theory, which specializes in the study of natural design. Social Contract Theory, Cosmides' specific account of content effects on the Wason selection task, was merely one illustrative part of a larger programme, evolutionary psychology. Unfortunately, the double message of Cosmides' (1989) paper has generated a considerable amount of confusion as some appear to have confused Social Contract Theory as a general theory of reasoning whereas the true scope of the theory is much narrower. In this chapter I hope to dispel some of the confusion surrounding Social Contract Theory and, in the process, clarify where some of the difficulties facing the theory lie and where they do not.

Cosmides (1989) illustrated the benefits offered by an evolutionary perspective by making an example of the then puzzling literature on the Wason selection task. The Wason selection task was originally developed by Peter Wason (1968) as a test of people's ability to logically falsify a hypothesis. By then, the selection task had already generated a large literature, for while it is disarmingly simple, the selection task has proven to be notoriously difficult for subjects to solve. In the task, subjects are given a conditional rule of the form: "If P then Q", which applies to four cards with information on both sides. One side of each card states whether or not "P" is true, and on the other side of the card it states whether or not "Q" is true. Only one side of each card is showing (depicting the information "P", "not-P", "Q" and "not-Q") and the subjects' task is to determine which, if any, of the four cards they would need to turn over to determine if the rule has been violated. Since the rule is only logically violated when "P" is true and "Q" is false ("P & not-Q"), the solution is straightforward: Subjects need to turn over the "P" and "not-Q" cards since these cards, and only these cards, could potentially be instances of "P & not-Q". Yet, on standard versions of the task, typically fewer than 10 per cent of subjects solve it correctly.

This discrepancy between the apparent simplicity of the task and the overwhelming failure of subjects to solve it correctly has generated a large literature dedicated to figuring out what the source of the difficulty is and what, if anything, can be done to improve performance. Initially, some studies seemed to suggest that when more realistic rules are employed (Wason (1968) had employed the abstract rules such as: "If there is a D on one side of any card, then there is a 3 on its other side") performance on the task improves (e.g. Johnson-Laird, Legrenzi, & Legrenzi, 1972; Wason & Shapiro, 1971); however, later studies employing realistic rules failed to replicate the improvements (e.g. Manktelow & Evans, 1979). Later still there was some indication that prior experience with the rules was crucial to improved performance on the task (Griggs & Cox, 1982), although this interpretation has since been ruled out (Cosmides, 1989). Hence, by the early 1980s there was a confusing pattern of "content effects" whereby versions of the selection task employing some thematic contents but not others inexplicably enhanced performance on the selection task.

SOCIAL CONTRACT THEORY

It is in this context that Cosmides (1985, 1989) first proposed Social Contract Theory (SCT), formulated on the basis of an evolutionary task analysis of social cooperation—the computational theory of social exchange (Cosmides & Tooby, 1989). Drawing upon prior evolutionary task analyses of reciprocity suggesting that social cooperation among nonkin could evolve only if altruists could detect and punish/exclude cheaters (Axelrod, 1984; Axelrod & Hamilton, 1981; Trivers, 1971), the computational theory of social exchange (Cosmides & Tooby, 1989) hypothesizes that humans possess an evolved "look for cheaters" algorithm that is activated in situations involving the reciprocal exchange of benefits, that is, social exchange. In the Wason selection task, an offer to engage in social exchange can be expressed by a social contract rule of the form: "If you take the benefit then you must pay the cost", where a cheater is someone who "takes the benefit" but "doesn't pay the cost".[1] Previous studies demonstrating improved logical performance had, according to Cosmides (1989), unwittingly employed social contract rules and triggered the "look for cheaters" algorithm. This mental algorithm would then lead subjects to select the "benefit" ("P") and "no-cost" ("not-Q") cards and, thereby, fortuitously make the logically correct selection.

In support of this analysis, Cosmides (1989) constructed parallel versions of the selection task, one in which the context of the rule gave it the cost/benefit structure of a social contract and another lacking the cost/benefit interpretation. As predicted by SCT, subjects selected the logically correct "benefit" ("P") and "no-cost" ("not-Q") cards when the rule had the cost/benefit structure of a social contract, but failed to do so when it did not—a result that has subsequently been replicated in numerous experiments (Cosmides & Tooby, 1992; Gigerenzer & Hug, 1992; Platt & Griggs, 1993).

Cosmides (1989) presented SCT as an illustrative example of the results that can be achieved by adopting the evolutionary psychological framework, a metatheoretical framework for conducting all psychological research. Unfortunately, confusion quickly arose as to the precise scope of Cosmides' claims, with many seeming to interpret SCT—and not the evolutionary psychological framework—as a general theory of the mind, particularly reasoning, and not as a more restricted theory of social cooperation. If it were to be argued that Cosmides proposed a theory of reasoning, *tout court*, then that theory of reasoning would have to be the larger framework, evolutionary psychology, which argues for an adaptive, multimodular view of not only reasoning, but of all mental processes. Yet, the claim is routinely made that SCT, and not evolutionary psychology *per se*, is faulty or at best incomplete because it cannot account for instances of content effects on nonsocial contract versions of the selection task (Almor & Sloman, 1996; Cheng & Holyoak, 1989; Girotto, Blaye, & Farioli, 1989a; Manktelow & Over, 1990; Politzer & Nguyen-Xuan, 1992)[2] with reference often made to Cosmides'

---

[1] One constraint upon a well-formulated social contract is that the benefits of social cooperation outweigh the costs, $B > C$ (Trivers, 1971). This constraint is easily satisfied when $C = 0$, such that a social contract can be well-formed even when the "cost" is a costless requirement. See Appendix A.1 in Fiddick, Cosmides, and Tooby (2000) for further clarification.

[2] A peculiar corollary is the widely held view that Gigerenzer and Hug (1992) have proposed an alternative theory of deontic reasoning based upon a cheating option that is in some sense an alternative to SCT, where Gigerenzer and Hug's proposal remains viable even though SCT is falsified (e.g. Almor & Sloman, 2000; Girotto, 1991; Holyoak & Cheng, 1995). This error, I would suggest, is the result of a tendency to view SCT simply as a theory of content effects in reasoning, instead of as a functionalist theory of cooperation. The function of the "look for cheaters" algorithm is specified at the level of the computational theory, in this case the computational theory of social exchange (Cosmides & Tooby, 1989) from which Gigerenzer and Hug's (1992) theory is derived.

(1989) claim that "robust and replicable content effects are found only for rules that are standard social contracts". Invariably, this claim is taken as a prediction of SCT, specifically the prediction that people should be competent only at reasoning about social contracts. However, Cosmides was not making a prediction, as the full context of the claim (which is never given) makes clear:

> Previous results on the Wason selection task are consistent with a social contract interpretation (for a detailed review, see Cosmides, 1985). Robust and reliable content effects are found only for rules that relate terms that are recognizable as benefits and costs in the format of a standard social contract.
>
> (Cosmides 1989, pp. 199–200)

> Moreover, social contract theory explains the apparently contradictory litera-ture attempting to stalk the "elusive" content effect on the Wason selection task: robust and reliable content effects are found only for rules that are stand-ard social contracts – the only rules for which the predicted social contract response is also the logically falsifying response.
>
> (Cosmides, 1989, pp. 262)

As these quotes make perfectly clear, Cosmides was summarizing the past selection task literature, and not making a prediction about selection task performance in nonsocial contract domains. While there may be reasonable grounds for objecting to Cosmides' assessment of the selection task literature circa the late 1980s, SCT cannot be faulted for the failure of a prediction it does not make. Neither SCT, nor the larger evolutionary psychology frame-work, predicts that that logically correct performance cannot be elicited on nonsocial contract versions of the selection task. Yet many of the arguments against SCT have tended to focus on the theory's failure to account for enhanced reasoning on nonsocial contract rules.

Does reasoning about precautions falsify Social Contract Theory?

People do routinely solve certain nonsocial contract versions of the Wason selection task correctly. In particular, numerous studies have demonstrated enhanced levels of performance on precautionary versions of the Wason selection task (Cheng & Holyoak, 1989; Fiddick, 1998; Fiddick, Cosmides, & Tooby, 2000; Girotto, Gilly, Blaye, & Light, 1989b; Love & Kessler, 1995; Manktelow & Over, 1990). Whereas a social contract is a rule of the form: "If you take the benefit then you must pay the cost", a precaution is a rule of the form: "If the hazard exists then you must use protection", and all parties to this intellectual dispute agree that precautions do not fall within the scope of SCT (Cheng & Holyoak, 1989; Fiddick, 1998; Fiddick et al., 2000; Girotto et al., 1989a; Manktelow & Over, 1990; Politzer & Nguyen-Xuan, 1992).

In and of itself, these findings are damaging to SCT only to the extent that it is a general theory of reasoning, which it is not. Indeed, one of the most controversial aspects of SCT is the proposal that the reasoning mechanism involved is a module—a reasoning instinct—that is activated by a narrow range of contexts, in this case social relationships involving the exchange or regulation of benefits. It is the very domain-specificity of the proposed mechanism that places precautions beyond the scope of SCT (see Chapter 1). One should ask instead whether the evolutionary psychology framework, more generally, and not SCT specifically, can account for people's reasoning in nonsocial contract domains. With respect to precaution rules, Fiddick (1998; Fiddick et al., 2000), following Cosmides and Tooby (1992), has argued that people possess additional reasoning instincts for managing hazards. Hence, the real question with precautionary rules is not whether they fall within the domain of SCT—all sides agree that they do not—but whether people reason about social contracts and precautions using a common mental mechanism or whether these rules invoke distinct reasoning mechanisms (Fiddick, 1998).

The claim that enhanced performance on precaution problems argues against SCT merely begs the question for it assumes, but never demonstrates, that a common mental mechanism underlies reasoning about both social contracts and precautions. While it is true that both social contracts and precautions tend to elicit logically correct performance on the selection task, so do abstract rules with negated consequents[3] but few researchers feel compelled to argue that all three types of rules are handled by the same psychological mechanism (Sperber, Cara, & Girotto, 1995, being a notable exception). Likewise, few are tempted to argue that the logical similarity of responses elicited by abstract letter and number rules and nondeontic thematic rules suggests their psychological equivalence. Hence, the logical analysis of selection task performance provides a weak assay of people's understanding of rules. Still, social contracts and precautions, but not abstract rules with negated consequents, intuitively seem to be related types of rules and the observation that both types of rules elicit similar performance on the selection task is consistent with the proposal that a common reasoning faculty is operative.

THE DEONTIC ALTERNATIVE

What social contracts and precautions have in common is that they are both deontic rules, rules specifying actions that one is obligated or entitled to perform, and it is this feature of social contracts and precautions that is

---

[3] In a finding that has often been replicated, Evans and Lynch (1973) demonstrated that people routinely provide the correct logical answer to versions of the selection task employing abstract rules of the form: "If P then NOT Q".

widely held to account for enhanced performance when they are embedded in the Wason selection task (Cheng & Holyoak, 1985, 1989; Cummins, 1996a, 1996b; Girotto, 1991; Manktelow & Over, 1990, 1991, 1995). The most influential of these accounts is Cheng and Holyoak's (1985) Pragmatic Reasoning Schemas Theory (PRST). This proposes that people reason about practical real-world problems using abstract knowledge structures, pragmatic reasoning schemas, that are compiled from personal experiences with different problem domains. One problem domain that people have considerable experience with is rules regulating behaviour: permissions and obligations. A permission, for example, is a rule with the abstract form: "If the action is to be taken then the precondition must be satisfied". Experience with such rules leads to the construction of a *permission schema* composed of four production rules that guides inferences about them. The four rules of the permission schema are the following (Holyoak & Cheng, 1995, p. 291):

P1: If the action is to be taken, then the precondition must be satisfied.
P2: If the action is not to be taken, then the precondition need not be satisfied.
P3: If the precondition is satisfied, then the action may be taken.
P4 If the precondition is not satisfied, then the action must not be taken.

When the conditional rule employed in a selection task is a permission matching rule P1 of the permission schema: "If the action is to be taken then the precondition must be satisfied", the permission schema becomes activated. Logically correct performance follows as Rule P1 of the schema causes subjects to select the "action to be taken" ("P") card and Rule P4 causes subjects to select the "precondition is not satisfied" ("not-Q") card. Rules P2 and P3 indicate that it is irrelevant that the "action is not to be taken" ("not-P") and "precondition is satisfied" ("Q") cards, respectively. Therefore, the cards corresponding to these conditions need not to be selected. Like SCT, PRST also predicts that social contracts *qua* permission rules will elicit a high level of logically correct "P & not-Q" selections on the Wason selection task. However, unlike SCT, PRST also predicts that precautions, too, will elicit logically correct performance, since they also match the form of a permission rule.

In one of the key tests of the theory, Cheng and Holyoak (1985, Experiment 2) presented subjects with an abstract permission version of the selection task. The rule employed in this problem stated: "If one is to take action 'A', then one must first satisfy precondition 'P'", which matches Rule P1 of the permission schema. Performance with this rule was contrasted with performance on a version of the selection task employing the abstract, nondeontic conditional: "If a card has an 'A' on one side, then it must have a '4' on the other side", which fails to map on to permission schema. As predicted, 61 per cent of subjects correctly solved the abstract permission problem compared to only 19 per cent correct on the nondeontic problem. This finding has been challenged in studies claiming that the effect is vulnerable to minor alterations in the presentation of the problem (Jackson & Griggs, 1990) or changes in instructions (Noveck & O'Brien, 1996). However, these objections are either orthogonal to or predicted by the PRST, and the effect of these manipulations disappears when more carefully designed problems are employed (Girotto, Mazzocco, & Cherubini, 1992; Kroger, Cheng & Holyoak, 1993).

ABSTRACT DEONTIC RULES ARE PROBLEMATIC FOR SOCIAL CONTRACT THEORY

The demonstration that subjects can correctly solve abstract deontic versions of the Wason selection task is widely held to be amongst the most compelling evidence in support of PRST, yet in the debate between advocates of SCT and those of PRST, scant attention is paid to the deep difficulty that these rules pose to SCT. Yet the reason these rules pose a difficulty for SCT is straightforward. Subjects' ability to reason successfully about abstract deontic rules directly challenges the assumption that people rely upon more specialized reasoning mechanisms, be they a "look for cheaters" algorithm or procedures for managing hazards. Whereas social contracts and precautions require one to *assume* a common deontic schema, abstract deontic rules would appear to *directly map* onto the proposed schemas. Furthermore, advocates of SCT cannot simply propose an abstract deontic instinct without calling into question the rationale for distinct social contract and precaution mechanisms, since they would thereby be redundant.

Despite the obvious similarities between the abstract deontic rules employed in the selection task and the production rules in the proposed schemas, the importance of these findings depends upon whether subjects are reasoning with the abstract form of the rules as explicitly stated in the problem materials or whether they are reasoning with some other representation of the rules. PRST is only supported, and SCT flawed, to the extent that subjects do, in fact, map the abstract rules directly onto the hypothesized schemas. Although abstract deontic rules bear an obvious resemblance to the hypothesized production rules, it nevertheless remains an untested assumption that these rules are closer to the internal mental representation than are social contracts and precautions.

Cosmides (1989) has claimed that subjects interpret abstract permission rules as social contract rules, thereby triggering a search for cheaters as predicted by SCT. According to Cosmides (1989, p. 239) an abstract permission is implicitly a social contract because:

> . . . saying that one must fulfill or satisfy a precondition in order to be permitted to do something is just another way of saying that one must pay a cost or meet a

requirement . . . In addition, saying that someone is *permitted* to take action A linguistically marks "action A" as a rationed benefit: it implies that the person *wants* to take action A (your mother permits you to get ice cream, she does not "permit" you to be spanked), and it implies that the person doing the permitting has the power to forbid action A (emphasis in the original).

As Cosmides' (1989) analysis of abstract permission problems suggests, there are at least two ways to interpret people's reasoning about abstract permissions. Either people could be mentally representing abstract permissions in a manner very close to their surface form (as Rule P1 of the permission schema) and then invoking the appropriate schema; or they could be mentally representing the abstract permissions in a manner more distant from their surface form (as a social contract) and then invoking a "look for cheaters" algorithm. While the basic finding that people reason correctly with an abstract problem is impressive, it is not clear whether people are interpreting the rules as explicit permissions or implicit social contracts.

How do people interpret abstract deontic rules?

There are two possibilities to be considered: (1) people interpret the abstract permissions as explicitly stated in the problems and map them directly onto the deontic schemas postulated by PRST; or (2) people interpret the abstract permissions as implicit social contracts and thereby activate the "look for cheaters" algorithm postulated by SCT. One way to test between these possibilities is to use the following principle: the closer the surface form of a rule matches the representations processed by a cognitive mechanism, the more likely that mechanism will be invoked. For example, Jackson and Griggs (1990, Experiment 2) found that performance on abstract permission problems decreased when the cards representing "not-P" and "not-Q" used implicit negatives, for example, rather than stating "Has not taken action A", the "not-P" card read "Has taken action B". Kroger et al.'s (1993, p. 622) explanation for this result was that: "explicit negatives will make it easier to match the *not-q* case to Rule 4 of the permission schema. Accordingly, removing [this factor] should diminish facilitation for the abstract permission rule". By the same logic, given two equally abstract rules—both of which are hypothesized to feed into the same mechanism—that which elicits the greatest amount of facilitation should be closer to the form of representation processed by the underlying mechanism.

PRST and SCT propose that abstract permissions are mentally represented in different ways. PRST proposes that the abstract permission: "If one is to take action 'A', then one must first satisfy precondition 'P'", is mapped onto Rule P1 of the permission schema: "If the action is to be taken, then the precondition must be satisfied". SCT proposes that the abstract permission is mapped onto the representation of a social contract: "If the benefit is accepted, then the cost must be paid". Hence, SCT predicts that more of a transformation needs to be made in order to map the abstract permission onto the underlying mechanism, whereas PRST predicts the opposite— more of a transformation needs to be made to map the abstract social contract. The end result is that PRST predicts that performance on an abstract permission problem will be better than that observed on an abstract social contract problem. SCT predicts the opposite.

IS A SOCIAL CONTRACT A PERMISSION OR IS A PERMISSION A SOCIAL CONTRACT?

Past studies of abstract deontic versions of the selection task have featured abstract permissions (Cheng & Holyoak, 1985; Girotto et al., 1992; Jackson & Griggs, 1990; Kroger et al., 1993; Noveck & O'Brien, 1996), abstract obligations (Girotto et al., 1992; Jackson & Griggs, 1990; Noveck & O'Brien, 1996), and an abstract precaution (Cheng & Holyoak, 1989). There have been no published studies in which an abstract social contract rule was employed. Hence, it is difficult to judge the relative ease with which people reason about abstract permissions, on the one hand, and abstract social contracts on the other.

I attempted to fill this empirical gap by testing subjects on abstract social contract, permission, obligation and precaution versions of the Wason selection task. As outlined above, PRST predicts that people will perform better when reasoning about abstract permissions than when reasoning about abstract social contracts. SCT predicts the opposite. Similar predictions can be made with respect to abstract precautions and their corresponding abstract deontic rules. PRST predicts that people will perform better when reasoning about abstract permissions and obligations than when reasoning about a corresponding abstract precaution. The more domain-specific view of precautions proposed by Fiddick (1998; Fiddick et al., 2000) predicts the opposite: performance will be higher on abstract precaution problems than on abstract permission and obligation problems since abstract precautions are easier to input into the hypothesized hazard management mechanism. Hereafter, I shall refer to abstract precautions and social contracts collectively as *adaptive* rules, and abstract permissions and obligations as *deontic* rules. In summary, PRST predicts that performance will be higher on the deontic rules and the evolutionary psychology framework[4] predicts that performance will be higher on adaptive rules. I tested these contrasting

---

[4] Comprised, in this case, of SCT and additional account of precautions (Fiddick, 1998; Fiddick et al., 2000).

predictions by giving three groups of subjects, who were naïve to the selection task, abstract versions of the task.

The first group of 20 subjects received two abstract *deontic* versions of the selection task. These were Cheng and Holyoak's (1985, Experiment 2) abstract permission problem and Jackson and Griggs' (1990, Experiment 1) abstract obligation problem. The abstract permission problem featured the rule: "If one is to take action A, then one must first satisfy precondition P", whereas the abstract obligation problem featured the rule: "If situation I arises, then action A must be taken".

A second group of 20 subjects received two abstract *adaptive* versions of the selection task. These were a variant of Cheng and Holyoak's (1989) abstract precaution problem and an abstract social contract problem of my own design. The abstract precaution problem featured the rule: "If one is to take the dangerous action D, then one must have protection P", whereas the abstract social contract problem featured the rule: "If the benefit B is taken, then cost C must be paid". The abstract social contract problem was identical to the Cheng and Holyoak's abstract permission problem other than the change in rule and the necessary changes to the cards and supporting scenario that this required.

Finally, a third group of 20 subjects received two abstract *control* problems to assess baseline levels of performance on the selection task. Where others have contrasted performance on abstract deontic versions of the selection tasks with performance on abstract letter and number versions of the selection task (e.g. Cheng & Holyoak, 1985, Experiment 2; Girotto et al., 1992; Jackson & Griggs, 1990; Kroger et al., 1993; Noveck & O'Brien, 1996), I chose to devise control problems that more closely paralleled the deontic and adaptive versions of the task. Hence, this last group of subjects received selection tasks employing abstract rules that described people's actions. No modal verbs were employed, nor were subjects cued to adopt the perspective of an authority enforcing the rule, but they were still instructed to look for violations. In the abstract *action* problem, subjects read that, "The following rule describes people's behavior: 'If one takes action B, then one takes action A'." The rule in this task was designed to match the abstract permission. In the abstract *situation* problem, subjects read that "The following rule describes people's behavior: 'If situation I arises, then one takes action A'." The rule in this task was designed to match the abstract obligation.

Do people reason better with abstract deontic or abstract adaptive rules?

As predicted by the evolutionary psychology framework, performance was highest on the adaptive problems (Fig. 2.1) with 50 per cent of subjects correctly solving the precaution problem and 45 per cent correctly solving the

Abstract selection tasks

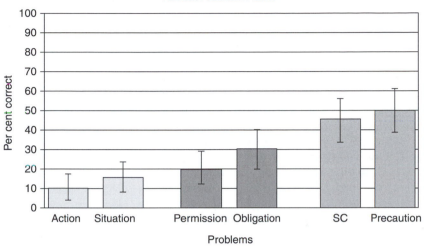

Figure 2.1 Percentage of correct responses on the abstract selection tasks. The error bars represent one standard deviation above and below the mean. SC, social contract.

social contract (SC) problem. Performance on the deontic problems was midway between that on the adaptive problems and the control problems: 30 per cent correct on the obligation problem and only 20 per cent correct on the permission problem. Performance was lowest on the control problems, 15 per cent on the situation problem and 10 per cent correct on the action problem. On average, subjects did significantly better on the adaptive problems than on the deontic problems. Summing performance across the adaptive problems and the deontic problems, the adaptive problems were correctly solved 48 per cent of the time, compared to 25 per cent for the deontic problems. While subjects performed significantly better on the adaptive problems than their matched controls,[5] there was no significant difference in performance between the deontic problems and their matched controls.[6]

The results of this experiment were in general agreement with the evolutionary psychology framework. Subjects appeared to find it easier to map abstract social contract and precaution rules onto the mechanisms postulated to underlie deontic reasoning. This suggests that the surface form of abstract social contracts and precautions is closer to the input conditions of the underlying mechanisms than is the surface form of abstract permissions and

---

[5] Abstract social contract versus action ($Z = 2.48$, $p < .01$, $h = .83$); abstract precaution versus action ($Z = 2.76$, $p < .005$, $h = .93$). All Z scores reported are the result of a test of proportions (Blalock, 1972). h is the effect size for a test of proportions: $h = .20$, small effect; $h = .50$, medium effect; $h = .80$, large effect (Cohen, 1977).

[6] Abstract permission versus action ($Z = 0.89$, $p > .10$, $h = .28$); abstract obligation versus situation ($Z = 1.14$, $p > .10$, $h = .36$).

obligations. Consequently, it is problematic to conclude that subjects in previous studies were mentally representing abstract permissions and obligations in a manner similar to their surface form. The purportedly strong evidence in favour of PRST is, at best, ambiguous in its support for the theory.

EMOTIONS AS A CUE TO INTERPRETATION

Although the previous experiment raised some doubt about whether people interpret abstract permissions and obligations explicitly as stated in the problem materials, it sheds no positive light on how people do, in fact, interpret these rules. The results provide little direct evidence in support of Cosmides' (1989) claim that people interpret abstract permissions as social contracts. Again, the cards that people select on the Wason selection task is a poor guide in determining how people interpret a rule. Consider, again, social contracts and conditionals with negated consequents. They both routinely elicit "P & not-Q" selections on the Wason selection task, but this provides little reason for believing that people are interpreting both types of rules in the same way. Hence, the fact that both abstract social contracts and abstract permissions elicit "P & not-Q" selection is no guarantee that people reason about both types of rules using the same mental mechanism. Although unlikely, people could be interpreting the abstract permissions as precautions, for example, which would also lead them to select the "P & not-Q" cards. Less ambiguous evidence is required to substantiate Cosmides' proposal.

Emotional reactions to rule violations can potentially provide an alternative means of categorizing deontic rules. Rozin, Lowery, Imada and Haidt (1999) have found that different moral codes are associated with different emotions. One of the methods they used was to give people descriptions of moral violations and have them select which facial expression a person would show if that person witnessed the violation. This same method could potentially be employed to assess how people interpret abstract permissions and obligations.

Indeed, Rozin et al.'s method can be used to dissociate social contracts from precautions. Using a modification of this method for the Wason selection task, I have found that people associate different emotions with violations of social contracts and precautions (Fiddick, unpublished). Subjects were presented with a rule embedded in a story, as with the Wason selection task. However, rather than instructing subjects to select cards representing potential violations, they were informed that the rule has been broken and their task was to indicate who, among an array of four people, saw the violation occur. The faces of the people varied in the emotions that they expressed. The results of this study indicated that people associate different types of rules with different emotions. In principle, the same method could easily be applied to abstract rules providing a converging line of evidence for the psychological equivalence of social contracts and permissions. Besides eliciting logically identical performance on the selection task, abstract social contracts and permissions might also elicit the same emotional reactions when they are violated.

The emotions associated with the rule violations were anger for social contracts and fear for precautions. This pattern of emotional reactions is readily explained from an evolutionary point of view. Consider first social contracts and anger. The goal in detecting cheaters, according to SCT, is to be able to punish or exclude them. It is this element of punishment that makes anger a suitable emotion to express, for as Lazarus (1991, p. 225) describes anger:

> I suggest that anger, in contrast with fright and anxiety, is potentiated by an appraisal that the demeaning offense *is best ameliorated by attack*; in effect, the individual *evaluates her coping potential of mounting an attack favorably*, which is also the innately given action tendency (emphasis added).

In short, anger is the emotion that is elicited when one seeks to punish others for a harmful wrongdoing. Consider, on the other hand, precautions and fear. According to the evolutionary analysis of precautions (Fiddick, 1998; Fiddick et al. 2000), the goal is to manage hazards. It is this element of avoiding or preventing injury that makes fear a suitable emotion, for as Lazarus (1991, p. 238) states: "In both fright and anxiety, the action tendency is avoidance or escape, in contrast with approach or attack". While violations of both social contracts and precautions may involve some form of loss or harm, the assignment of blame is an important component of cheater detection that is typically absent from hazard management. Likewise, blame is an important component of anger, but is absent from fear (Lazarus, 1991). In short, there are good functional grounds for predicting that anger will be associated with violations of social contracts and that fear will be associated with violations of precautions.

Moreover, this same line of argument suggests that there might be different types of precautions. There are grounds for distinguishing precautions against physical injury, from precautions against infections and social aggression. Whereas the threat of physical injury is typically associated with fear, the threat of infectious contamination is more closely associated with disgust. Similarly, Lazarus (1991) has argued that it might be best to distinguish between "fright" as elicited specifically by the threat of physical injury and "fear", which may include the threat of social aggression. Intuitively, these three types of hazards are quite distinct and may impose different computational demands, but whether there are characteristic differences in prudential reasoning about these three domains of hazards will have to remain an open question for future research. For now I will simply assume that precautionary rules employed in these studies are interpreted in terms of physical injury.

Instead, I investigated which emotions are associated with abstract permissions and obligations by devising some abstract adaptive and abstract deontic versions of the emotion selection task. I presented 21 subjects with four abstract versions of the emotion selection task. These included an abstract social contract task, an abstract precaution task, an abstract permission task, and an abstract obligation task. The tasks repeated the rules and stories employed in the Wason selection tasks in the previous experiment, but without the cards and their supporting statements. In their place were the pictures of four faces with each face depicting a different emotion. The four emotions were anger, disgust, fear, and happiness. The pictures were scanned, greyscale reproductions from Matsumoto and Ekman's (1988) Japanese and Caucasian Facial Expression of Emotion (JACFEE) slides, however, only Caucasian faces (of both sexes) were used. The accompanying story explained that "Recently someone observed the rule being broken. Indicate the person, who you think, saw the rule being broken".

What do PRST and the evolutionary framework predict for the deontic rules?

Although neither PRST nor SCT make explicit predictions about the emotional reactions that people will have in response to deontic rule violations, deducing the predictions that they would have to make given previous findings with adaptive rule violations is fairly straightforward (Fig. 2.2). Recall that violations of social contracts elicit angry reactions whereas violations of precautions elicit fearful reactions (indicated in the boxes in Fig. 2.2). According to PRST, permissions and obligations subsume both social contracts and precautions. This suggests two alternative predictions. The first alternative assumes that people mentally translate permission and obligations into social contracts and precautions before completing the task (this is depicted in Fig. 2.2 under the heading "PRST predicts"). Under this scenario, violations of permissions and obligations should elicit a mixture of anger and fear (the predicted emotions are given in italics). Some people will interpret the rules as social contracts and select the angry face, while others will interpret the rules as precautions and select the fear face. However, subjects may be more confused on the abstract obligation task because the antecedent, "situation I arises" suggests no clear interpretation as either a benefit or a danger. Should such confusion arise, one might predict a random pattern of responding on the abstract obligation task.

Indeed, subjects might fail to mentally translate either deontic rule into a social contract or precaution and instead try to complete the task on the basis of the abstract forms of the rules. Under this second alternative, PRST predicts that people will be confused, or otherwise unable to complete the task in any principled manner, and will select one of the four emotions at random for

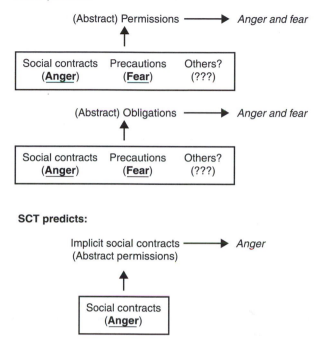

Figure 2.2 Emotions associated with abstract deontic rules according to PRST and SCT. Emotions that have previously been demonstrated to be associated with social contracts (anger) and precautions (fear) are underlined and in bold. Emotions predicted to be associated with abstract permissions and obligations are indicated in italics.

both the permission and the obligation rules, due to the very abstract nature of the rules. Since this basically amounts to random behaviour, I have not modelled this option in Fig. 2.2.

PRST cannot, however, argue that people will have a default tendency to associate abstract permissions with anger. Not only would this concede Cosmides' (1989) claim that people interpret abstract permissions as though they were social contracts, but it would also weaken the claim that precautions are readily interpreted as permissions since these rules would then evoke different emotions—a distinction that would not appear to be warranted by PRST.

SCT predicts a different pattern of performance (see Fig. 2.2 "SCT predicts"). According to Cosmides' analysis of abstract permissions, people interpret these rules as social contracts, so there should be a clear preference for selecting the angry face. However, SCT offers no clear predictions for performance with an abstract obligation, nor does a theory of hazard management (Fiddick, 1998; Fiddick et al., 2000). The problem, suggested above, is that the abstract obligation offers no clear interpretation as either a social contract or a precaution.

What did subjects do?

In a replication of previous findings, a majority of subjects selected the angry face for the abstract social contract problem (67 per cent of selections) and the fear face for the abstract precaution problem (86 per cent of selections, Fig. 2.3). The interesting question, though, is what emotions subjects selected for the abstract deontic rules. Did they select a mixture of emotions as pre-dicted by PRST or did they select a single emotion—anger—as predicted by SCT, at least with respect to the permission rule? The modal response of the subjects was to select the angry face for both the abstract permission problem (43 per cent of selections) *and* the abstract obligation problem (48 per cent of selections). The next most frequent selections were the disgust face for the abstract permission (29 per cent of selections) and the fear face for the abstract obligation (24 per cent of selections). The remaining emotions were selected by less than 20 per cent of the subjects for both deontic rules.

This experiment provides additional support for SCT's account of abstract permission rules. Not only did the emotions selected on the abstract permission problem match that predicted by SCT, but the percentage of sub-jects selecting the angry face for the abstract permission problem was slightly lower than that observed on the abstract social contract problem. This is precisely the pattern that would be expected if people interpreted the abstract permission as an implicit social contract. Given that the abstract social

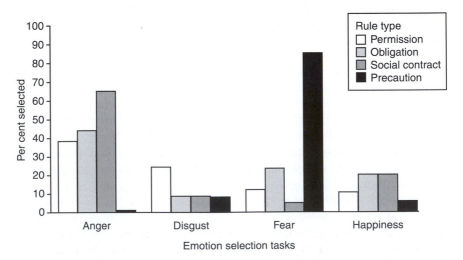

Figure 2.3 Percentage of participants selecting an emotion for each of the emotion selection tasks.

contract is a better exemplar of a social contract than the abstract permission, the former should elicit a clearer pattern of emotion selections than the latter.

Neither of PRST's alternative set of predictions was supported. Subjects were not guessing when they completed the deontic problems (ruling out the second alternative, performance would be random) and they showed a clear preference for selecting the anger face for both deontic rules (ruling out the first alternative, a bimodal response pattern for both rules).

Although the results of this experiment disconfirm PRST and lend support to Cosmides' (1989) claim that people interpret abstract permission rules as social contracts, it is not clear whether Cosmides' analysis is entirely correct. The problem is that a slightly higher percentage of participants selected the angry face on the abstract obligation problem than was observed on the abstract permission problem, but the abstract obligation lacks precisely those features that Cosmides invoked to interpret the permission as a social contract. For example, while it might be plausible to suggest that one is "permitted" to do things one considers a benefit, it is less straightforward to assume that a "situation arising", and presumably beyond one's control, is a benefit that obliges one to take an action. This is not to deny that participants are interpreting the abstract permission rule as a social contract. I merely wish to suggest that participants might be interpreting both the abstract permission and the abstract obligation as social contracts for some reason other than the one provided by Cosmides.

One possible alternative explanation is a cultural bias in the West to interpret rights and duties in contractual terms (Shweder, Mahapatra, & Miller, 1987). Given rules stating vague permissions and obligations, the subjects in this study, who were all highly educated Westerners, might invoke a default cultural bias to interpret deontic rules in contractual terms. Such a bias would lead a sizeable proportion of subjects to view both abstract permissions and abstract obligations as contracts.

WHAT IS THE SIGNIFICANCE OF THESE RESULTS FOR THE STUDY OF DEONTIC REASONING?

While there are major differences in theoretical explanations of deontic reasoning (Almor & Sloman, 1996; Cheng & Holyoak, 1985; Cosmides, 1989; Cummins, 1996a; Manktelow & Over, 1991; Oaksford & Chater, 1994; Sperber et al., 1995), recent studies on abstract deontic rules have done little to assess the relative merits of these different positions. For the most part, these studies have either focused on theoretically trivial manipulations, such as whether "not-P" and "not-Q" are stated explicitly or implicitly on the cards (Girotto et al., 1992; Jackson & Griggs, 1990; Kroger et al., 1993); or they have focused on manipulations already known to have an effect on reasoning about deontic rules, such as whether one is instructed to look for violations of an existing rule or instructed to look for violations in order to establish the rule's existence (Noveck & O'Brien, 1996; cf. Gigerenzer & Hug, 1992). In general, these studies appear to have been motivated by an attempt to either undermine or support what is taken to be some of the best evidence in favour of PRST, but without, thereby, advancing any alternative account of deontic reasoning. No studies that I am aware of have attempted to use abstract rules to decide among rival accounts of deontic reasoning. This is an oversight because the demonstration that people reason correctly on abstract deontic versions of the selection task is highly problematic for some rival accounts of deontic reasoning.

The findings presented here do not simply end with a negative verdict against PRST, they also give positive support for a specific class of deontic reasoning theories. The abstract social contract and abstract permission rules that I have employed here are considered to be paraphrases by all who accept the psychological reality of deontic reasoning, so the question inevitably arises: Which version is paraphrastic and which version is primitive? Of course, neither rule may be psychologically primitive—both may be tokens of some other type of rule—but until an alternative candidate is proposed, the current state of the field can be roughly divided in two. On the one side there are those who assume that deontic concepts are psychologically primitive (Cheng & Holyoak, 1985; Cummins, 1996a) and on the other there are those who assume that deontic concepts can be further decomposed into costs and benefits or other more specific terms (Cosmides, 1989; Manktelow & Over, 1991; Oaksford & Chater, 1994). The results presented here would appear to support the latter position, but not everyone accepts the psychological reality of deontic reasoning—at least not as evidenced by the Wason selection task.

Nondeontic accounts of abstract deontic rules

Some researchers have questioned the need to postulate domain-specific reasoning mechanisms to account for people's reasoning on abstract deontic versions of the Wason selection task (Almor & Sloman, 1996; Sperber et al., 1995). These researchers would not necessarily deny that people possess a deontic reasoning competence, only that it has not been demonstrated by people's performance on the selection task. To bolster these claims, they have presented evidence that it is possible to elicit high levels of "P & not-Q" selections on abstract nondeontic versions of the selection task. Given that the interpretation of the results that I have adopted here assumes that some more specialized forms of reasoning underlie performance on abstract deontic versions of the selection task, it is worth considering these claims in more detail.

Almor and Sloman (1996), for example, have demonstrated enhanced levels of "P & not-Q" selections with abstract nondeontic versions of the Wason selection task employing rules such as: "If a large object is stored, then a large container must be used". Almor and Sloman (1996, 2000) interpret their results as being problematic for the deontic reasoning theories because it undermines what they take to be a prediction of the theories, that only deontic rules will elicit high levels of "P & not-Q" selections. As foreshadowed in my discussion of SCT and precautions, this is not a general prediction made by SCT, nor is it a prediction made by other theories of deontic reasoning. As is the case with SCT and precautions, the error is in taking the aims and claims of the deontic theorists out of context. The theory's claims were largely retrodictive in attempting to account for the differences between those rules that *had* and those rules that *had not* elicited high levels of normatively correct performance on the Wason selection task—a distinction that had roughly corresponded to the difference between deontic and nondeontic rules when the theories were proposed.

No deontic theory has proposed that nondeontic rules would always fail to elicit correct performance on the selection task. Any number of theoretically trivial manipulations, such as negating the consequent or explicitly prompting subjects to look for instances of "P & not-Q", could conceivably improve performance on nondeontic versions of the selection task. The real question is whether or not people reason differently about deontic and nondeontic rules regardless of whether nondeontic rules elicit "P & Q" selections or "P & not-Q" selections. Of course, logically different performance on the selection task constitutes *prima facie* evidence for different reasoning processes, but even so there is no guarantee that different reasoning processes are at play. Indeed, the "matching bias" explanation for the effect of negated consequents proposes that there really is no difference in subjects' reasoning (or lack thereof) despite the logical difference in performance with standard conditionals. Subjects are simply ignoring the negation and selecting the same cards that they would with non-negated consequents, with performance guided in both cases by the topic of the rule (Evans, 1989). What is required to undermine the deontic theories is not simply to demonstrate logically identical performance on both deontic and nondeontic versions of the selection task, but to provide a convincing argument that performance on both versions of the task is guided by the same principles.

Almor and Sloman's (1996, p. 379) proposed explanation is that:

> According to our intuitions—the same intuitions that have guided us in constructing the problems we used—people's performance in the selection task is governed by their beliefs about the dependence relations in the problem. This

belief causes them to form probabilistic expectations that they can test as they select cards.

But it borders on a tautology to claim that in a test of *conditional* reasoning beliefs about dependence relations governs subjects' performance. Nor does it provide any further insight to note that when subjects' selections conform to the normative interpretation of the rule as the material conditional that relevant expectations are those that "happen to have a structure like conditional implication" (Almor & Sloman, 1996, p. 375). Other than demonstrating that people can solve nondeontic versions of the selection task at levels comparable to those found with deontic versions, Almor and Sloman provide no independent confirmation or argument that people do have these expectations when solving both deontic and nondeontic versions of the selection task.

A more promising line of explanation is provided by Sperber et al.'s (1995; see also Liberman & Klar, 1996; Love & Kessler, 1995) Relevance Theory account of the selection task. Sperber et al. present a detailed account of the principles guiding performance on both deontic and nondeontic versions of the selection task. The key to enhanced performance on all versions of the selection task is whether or not the conversational pragmatics of the task: (1) make violating instances of "P & not-Q" manifest (although not necessarily explicitly); and (2) highlight the relevance of detecting violations.

The device that they employ to elicit correct performance on nondeontic versions of the task is to place the conditional rule in the context of a denial. When it has been alleged that "P & not-Q" is true, one can deny the claim by stating: "If P then Q", which is logically equivalent to claiming "It is not the case that P & not-Q". Most importantly for present concerns, Sperber et al. (1995, Experiment 4, The Machine Problem) demonstrated this with an abstract letter and number task. In one condition of their experiment it was alleged that a machine has mistakenly produced cards with the features "6-on-the-front & not-E-on-the-back". A repairman then fixed the machine, denying that the machine is still malfunctioning by stating: "If a card has a 6 on the front, it has an E on the back". As predicted, subjects performed well, with 57 per cent correctly solving the task. Further strengthening their claims to have isolated the relevant variables, when they systematically removed elements of the scenario that highlighted violating instances of "P & not-Q" and the relevance of detecting violations, they observed that performance decreased accordingly.

Although providing an elegant and convincing demonstration of their proposal with respect to nondeontic versions of the selection task, this experiment does not in itself provide a convincing demonstration that the same principles are at play in deontic versions of the selection task. While the deontic theories agree with Sperber et al.'s analysis in suggesting that there is some practical utility to detecting deontic rule violations,[7] they part ways with the Relevance Theory account over the assumption that the context needs to highlight violating instances. The question is really how much structure must be supplied by the scenario and, conversely, how much can be supplied by knowledge structures in the mind of the reasoner. The deontic theories assume that a large amount of the relevant structure is built in to the mind of the reasoner, while the Relevance Theories assume that the supporting scenario supplies almost all of this structure.

Consider, in this light, Cheng and Holyoak's (1989, p. 289) abstract precaution scenario, a close variant of which was employed in the experiments reported here:

> Suppose you are responsible for ensuring whether people who are about to engage in certain hazardous activities have taken the precautionary measures necessary for protecting them from harmful effects inherent in those activities. The precautions take the general form: *If one is to take the hazardous activity H, then one must have protection P,* where H is any hazardous activity and P is the appropriate protection for the particular activity.

While it is apparent from this scenario that there would be some practical utility to detecting violations of the rule, neither the rule nor the surrounding context highlights "P & not-Q" as violations of the rule. Contrast this with Sperber et al.'s "machine problem" where the story stated that: "the machine has printed cards it should not have printed. On the back of the cards with a 6, the machine has not always printed an E: sometimes it has printed an A instead of an E" (Sperber et al. 1995, p. 75). High levels of violation detection result in both cases, but it requires more coaxing on the part of the experimenter in the case of nondeontic versions of the selection task.

Expanding upon Sperber et al.'s own metaphor, it would appear that it is possible to cook up nondeontic versions of the selection task that elicit high levels of violation detection by following their proposed recipe, but following such a strict recipe is not required in the case of deontic versions of the task. When the supporting devices employed by the Sperber et al.'s (1995) "relevant" versions of the selection task are removed, the deontic content effect still persists (Fiddick et al., 2000). Moreover, many of these relevance cues are generally absent from abstract deontic versions of the selection task, so it is not surprising that Relevance Theoretic accounts of the selection task (e.g. Liberman & Klar, 1996; Love & Kessler, 1995; Sperber et al., 1995) have

---

[7] Strictly seaking, Sperber et al. (1995) argue that the detection of violations has to have some degree of "cognitive effect". However, this concept of cognitive effect is rather vaguely defined and does not seem to rule out cognitive effects derived from detecting other outcomes like mutual cooperation (see Fiddick et al., 2000, for further discussion).

virtually ignored abstract deontic versions of the task in their account of the "deontic content" effect.[8] Hence it would appear that there is a genuine deontic content effect worth accounting for. Subjects are competent at detecting deontic rule violations over a wide range of pragmatic contexts, whereas with nondeontic versions of the selection task, various *ad hoc* contextual elements need to be incorporated before substantial levels of violation detection are elicited.

The brittleness of the Relevance Theories is further underlined by the emotion study presented here. There are, as I have suggested above, good evolutionary grounds for predicting that anger will be associated with violations of social contracts and fear will be associated with violations of precautions. The evolutionary analysis of deontic reasoning was, therefore, able to provide some guidance beyond the Wason selection task, but it is not clear if or how the Relevance Theoretic perspective can provide any guidance in making predictions for the emotion study. The finding that different emotions are associated with social contracts and precautions not only reinforces the view that social contracts and precautions are psychologically distinct, but it further suggests that the psychology of cooperation and hazards is far richer than the simple dichotomy of "reasoning" versus "interpretation" favoured by the Relevance Theorists.

The modular view of mind espoused by evolutionary psychology does not only entail domain-specificity, for example, the psychological dissociation between social contracts and precautions. It also suggests the "vertical", as opposed to "horizontal", organization of the mind in which special-purpose representations, inferences, memories, and even emotions are all integrated to bring about adaptive functioning (Fodor, 1983; Gigerenzer, 1995; Tooby & Cosmides, 1990). In putting the disparate pieces of the functional puzzle together, a considerable degree of constraint is placed upon enumeration of psychological adaptations, potentially solving evolutionary psychology's "grain problem" (see Chapter 3). Hence, the parallel dissociation between social contracts and precautions in terms of both elicited emotions, as presented here, and reasoning processes, as studied previously (Fiddick, 1998, unpublished; Fiddick et al., 2000), suggests that the proposed characterization of these rules and the adaptive problems they map onto is couched at the right grain of analysis.

In contrast, while the Relevance Theoretic approach is not only plausible but may even have some rigour in the context of one highly constrained task, such as the selection task, these accounts threaten to degenerate into the trivial claim that people act on the basis of their representation of the materials provided as additional methodologies demonstrate systematic

---

[8] For a more extended defence of SCT against the relevance theoretic accounts of the selection task, see Fiddick et al. (2000).

dissociations in the psychology of cooperation and hazards. Hence, nonevolutionary accounts of reasoning are likewise susceptible to the grain problem.

The constraints of vertical integration also come to the fore in the assessment of some other deontic theories that I have not directly addressed so far: Cummins' (1996a, 1999) Dominance Theory and assorted Decision Theoretic accounts of deontic reasoning (Kirby, 1994; Manktelow & Over, 1991, 1995; Oaksford & Chater, 1994).

Dominance Theory and deontic reasoning

Aligned on the side of PRST is Cummins' (1996a, 1999) Dominance Theory. Where PRST claims that permissions and obligations are rules imposed by an authority for a social purpose, Cummins gives the theory an evolutionary gloss by proposing that social living within dominance hierarchies has shaped the human mind (and that of other species as well) for reasoning about the "social code"—rules imposed and enforced by high-ranking individuals to maintain their priority of access to fitness-enhancing resources. In contrast to PRST, which proposes that deontic reasoning schemas are compiled from extensive ontogenetic experience with social rules and regulations, Dominance Theory hypothesizes that the deontic concepts of permission, obligation and prohibition are innately built-in to the human mind, enabling fast-track learning of the rules and regulations of one's community. Cummins' proposal highlights the diversity of opinion found within the evolutionary psychology community, even within a narrowly restricted topic such as deontic reasoning. Besides tracing deontic reasoning to a different set of selection pressures than does SCT, Cummins also places a greater emphasis on a comparative approach than is found within Cosmides and Tooby's programme.

Given the close affinities between Dominance Theory and PRST, the former suffers the same problems as the latter in accounting for the findings presented here. Namely, the theory has a difficult time accounting for why subjects perform better on the abstract adaptive problems than the abstract deontic problems. However, it is the results of the emotion study that pose the greatest difficulty for Dominance Theory as it is presently formulated. While Dominance Theory gives a reasonable account of people's reasoning about social contracts—rules regulating access to benefits—reasoning about precautions deviates from the theory in two respects. First, the dissociation in emotions evoked by violations of social contracts and precautions is not predicted by Dominance Theory given that it, like PRST, treats social contracts and precautions as psychologically equivalent rules—deontic rules pure and simple. Second and more specifically, the emotion study suggests that people are less prone to punish violations of precautions than violations of social contracts. This is evidenced by their tendency to get angry, a prelude to punishing the transgressor, when social contracts are violated but not when precautions are violated. Hence, it is unlikely that enforcement of the "social code" motivates people's reasoning about precautions quite like Dominance Theory predicts. The theory would be more consistent, it would seem, if it abandoned the claim that deontic reasoning is a unified phenomenon encompassing both social contracts and precautions, and concentrated on social contracts alone.

Decision-theoretic accounts of deontic reasoning

Allied with SCT, at least with respect to abstract deontic rules, are various decision-theoretic accounts of deontic reasoning (Kirby, 1994; Manktelow & Over, 1991, 1995; Oaksford & Chater, 1994). Like SCT, these theories stress the importance of perceived costs and benefits and, hence, are similarly challenged to explain why subjects succeed in their reasoning about abstract deontic rules when it is not readily apparent how detecting violations of these rules would increase one's subjective utility. While Cosmides' (1989) interpretation of abstract permissions in terms of social contracts provides a common defence for both these decision-theoretic accounts and SCT and these theories, thereby, derive some support from the abstract selection task study presented here, these utilitarian theories find little support in the emotion study. Like Dominance Theory, the decision-theoretic approach is generally taken to apply uniformly to both social contracts and precautions (Manktelow & Over, 1991, 1995), but as the results of the emotion study demonstrate, social contracts and precautions are clearly dissociable in terms of their associated emotions. This suggests a psychological differentiation of these rules not captured by the decision theoretic approach.

While the results of the emotion study suggest that social contracts and precautions should be distinguished, the opposite conclusion is suggested by Manktelow and Over's (1990, 1991, 1995) semantic analysis of deontic statements. Borrowing the methods and results of analytic philosophy, Manktelow and Over have asked "what it means to say" that one "may" or "must" perform an act. They conclude that any proper semantic analysis of deontic statements must ultimately refer to people's preferences/perceived utilities and on these grounds there is no distinction between social contracts and precautions. In either case, we prefer that the rules are not violated and so we say that "If one does X, then one MUST do Y", whereas when we are indifferent to the outcome we say "one MAY do Y". How is vertical integration possible when the emotions pull one way and semantic intuitions pull the other?

One way of resolving this impasse is to consider the design constraints that the various psychological faculties are subject to. Whereas the emotions are functionally integrated with cognition and motivation (Lazarus, 1991) suggesting a richness of psychological articulation, our linguistic abilities, which I am assuming semantics to be a part of, are under a strong design constraint to be economical, for example, information has to pass through a serial channel bottleneck (Pinker & Bloom, 1990), suggesting that the semantic system might be impoverished in comparison (although this representational poverty may be compensated for by pre- and postcommunicative inference, see Sperber & Wilson, 1995). The upshot is that the semantic system might, simply for communicative purposes, group things like social contracts and precautions (not to mention *necessity* and *possibility*, which also share the modal operators "must" and "may") that the rest of the mind distinguishes. Although we may have easier cognitive access to the semantic system, it may provide only a rough map of the mind's design.

CONCLUSION

Despite frequent pronouncements of its demise, SCT remains a viable theory of people's reasoning about social exchange. Over the past decade there have been refinements in the predictions of the theory, especially with respect to performance on the Wason selection task (Gigerenzer & Hug, 1992), but these changes have been within the spirit of the core theory—the computational theory of social exchange (Cosmides & Tooby, 1989). The theory has, unfortunately, had its fate too closely tied to findings from the Wason selection task. This narrow focus on a single method has distorted the intellectual debate about social cooperation. It has provided a false sense of psychological cohesion between social cooperation and hazards due to the logical analysis of selection task performance under which both social contracts and precautions are interpreted as eliciting the same pattern of responding. It has also encouraged alternative accounts of cheater detection based solely on methodological artifacts limited to the selection task. Moreover, it has obscured other facets of the psychology of social cooperation and hazards, such as associated emotions. Yet there is also much we have learned from using the selection task. What is called for is not an abandonment of the selection task as some have called for (Sperber et al., 1995), but converging lines of evidence from different methods and the second experiment reported here is, I hope, a step in that direction.

ACKNOWLEDGEMENTS

I would like to thank Jörn Schultz and Stefan Krauss for their help in translating the problems and conducting the experiments and Denise Cummins, David Over and Melissa Rutherford for helpful comments. I would also like to acknowledge the generous support of the ESRC Centre for Economic Learning and Social Evolution, University College London, where I was a fellow while writing this chapter.

REFERENCES

Almor, A., & Sloman, S. (1996). Is deontic reasoning special? *Psychological Review, 103*, 374–380.

Almor, A., & Sloman, S. (2000). Reasoning versus text processing in the Wason selection task: A nondeontic perspective on perspective effects. *Memory & Cognition, 28*, 1060–1070.

Axelrod, R. (1984). *The evolution of cooperation*. New York: Basic Books.

Axelrod, R., & Hamilton, W. D. (1981). The evolution of cooperation. *Science, 211*, 1390–1396.

Blalock, H. (1972). *Social statistics* (2nd ed.). New York: McGraw Hill.

Cheng, P., & Holyoak, K. (1985). Pragmatic reasoning schemas. *Cognitive Psychology, 17*, 391–416.

Cheng, P., & Holyoak, K. (1989). On the natural selection of reasoning theories. *Cognition, 33*, 285–313.

Cohen, J. (1977). *Statistical power analysis for the behavioral sciences* (revised Ed.). New York: Academic.

Cosmides, L. (1985). *Deduction or Darwinian algorithm?: An explanation of the "elusive" content effect on the Wason selection task*. Doctoral dissertation, Harvard University. University Microfilms 86–02206.

Cosmides, L. (1989). The logic of social exchange: Has natural selection shaped how humans reason? Studies with the Wason selection task. *Cognition, 31*, 187–276.

Cosmides, L., & Tooby, J. (1989). Evolutionary psychology and the generation of culture, part II. Case study: A computational theory of social exchange. *Ethology and Sociobiology, 10*, 51–97.

Cosmides, L., & Tooby, J. (1992). Cognitive adaptations for social exchange. In J. Barkow, L. Cosmides, & J. Tooby (Eds.), *The adapted mind* (pp. 163–228). New York: Oxford University Press.

Cummins, D.D. (1996a). Evidence for the innateness of deontic reasoning. *Mind & Language, 11*, 160–190.

Cummins, D.D. (1996b). Evidence of deontic reasoning in 3- and 4-year-olds. *Memory & Cognition, 24*, 823–829.

Cummins, D.D. (1999). Cheater detection is modified by social rank. The impact of dominance on the evolution of cognitive functions. *Evolution & Human Behaviour, 20*, 229–248.

Evans, J.St.B.T. (1989). *Bias in human reasoning: Causes and consequences*. Hove, UK: Lawrence Erlbaum Associates Ltd.

Evans, J.St.B.T., & Lynch, J. (1973). Matching bias in the selection task. *British Journal of Psychology, 64*, 391–397.

Fiddick, L. (1998). *The deal and the danger: An evolutionary analysis of deontic reasoning*. Unpublished doctoral dissertation. University of California, Santa Barbara.

Fiddick, L. (under review). Domains of deontic reasoning: Resolving the discrepancy between the cognitive and moral reasoning literatures.

Fiddick, L., Cosmides, L., & Tooby, J. (2000). No interpretation without representation: The role of domain-specific representations and inferences in the Wason selection task. *Cognition, 77*, 1–79.

Fodor, J. (1983). *The modularity of mind*. Cambridge, MA: MIT Press.

Gigerenzer, G. (1995). The taming of content: Some thoughts about domains and modules. *Thinking and Reasoning, 1*, 324–333.

Gigerenzer, G., & Hug, K. (1992). Domain specific reasoning: Social contracts, cheating, and perspective change. *Cognition, 43*, 127–171.

Girotto, V. (1991). Reasoning on deontic rules: The pragmatic reasoning schemas approach. *Intellectica, 11*, 15–52.

Girotto, V., Blaye, A., & Farioli, F. (1989a). A reason to reason: Pragmatic basis of children's search for counterexamples. *Cahiers de Psychologie Cognitive, 9*, 297–321.

Girotto, V., Gilly, M., Blaye, A., & Light, P. (1989b). Children's performance in the selection task: Plausibility and familiarity. *British Journal of Experimental Psychology, 80*, 79–95.

Girotto, V., Mazzocco, A., & Cherubini, P. (1992). Judgements of deontic relevance in reasoning: A reply to Jackson and Griggs. *Quarterly Journal of Experimental Psychology, 45A*, 547–574.

Griggs, R., & Cox, J. (1982). The elusive thematic-materials effect in Wason's selection task. *British Journal of Psychology, 73*, 407–420.

Holyoak, K., & Cheng, P. (1995). Pragmatic reasoning with a point of view. *Thinking and Reasoning, 1*, 289–313.

Jackson, S., & Griggs, R. (1990). The elusive pragmatic reasoning schemas effect. *Quarterly Journal of Experimental Psychology, 42A*, 353–373.

Johnson-Laird, P., Legrenzi, P., & Legrenzi, M. (1972). Reasoning and a sense of reality. *British Journal of Psychology, 63*, 395–400.

Kirby, K. (1994). Probabilities and utilities of fictional outcomes in Wason's four-card selection task. *Cognition, 51*, 1–28.

Kroger, K., Cheng, P., & Holyoak, K. (1993). Evoking the permission schema: The impact of explicit negation and a violation-checking context. *Quarterly Journal of Experimental Psychology, 46A*, 615–635.

Lazarus, R. (1991). *Emotion and adaptation*. Oxford: Oxford University Press.

Liberman, N., & Klar, Y. (1996). Hypothesis testing in Wason's selection task: Social exchange cheating detection or task understanding. *Cognition, 58*, 127–156.

Love, R., & Kessler, C. (1995). Focusing in Wason's selection task: Content and instruction effects. *Thinking and Reasoning, 1*, 153–182.

Manktelow, K., & Evans, J.St.B.T. (1979). Facilitation of reasoning by realism: Effect or non-effect? *British Journal of Psychology, 70*, 477–488.

Manktelow, K., & Over, D. (1990). Deontic thought and the selection task. In K. Gilhooly, M. Keane, R. Logie, & G. Erdos (Eds.), *Lines of thought: Reflections of the psychology of thinking* (pp. 153–164). London: Wiley.

Manktelow, K., & Over, D. (1991). Social roles and utilities in reasoning with deontic conditionals. *Cognition, 39*, 85–105.

Manktelow, K., & Over, D. (1995). Deontic reasoning. In S. Newstead & J.St.B.T. Evans (Eds.), *Perspectives on thinking and reasoning: Essays in honour of Peter Wason* (pp. 91–114). Hove, UK: Lawrence Erlbaum Associates Ltd.

Matsumoto, D., & Ekman, P. (1988). *Japanese and Caucasian facial expressions of emotion (JACFEE) and neutral faces (JACNeuF)* [slides]. San Francisco: Intercultural and Emotion Research Laboratory, Department of Psychology, San Francisco State University.

Noveck, I., & O'Brien, D. (1996). To what extent do pragmatic reasoning schemas affect performance on Wason's selection task? *Quarterly Journal of Experimental Psychology, 49A*, 463–489.

Oaksford, M., & Chater, N. (1994). A rational analysis of the selection task as optimal data selection. *Psychological Review, 101*, 608–631.

Pinker, S., & Bloom, P. (1990). Natural language and natural selection. *Behavioral and Brain Sciences, 13*, 707–784.

Platt, R., & Griggs, R. (1993). Darwinian algorithms and the Wason selection task: A factorial analysis of social contract selection task problems. *Cognition, 48*, 163–192.

Politzer, G., & Nguyen-Xuan, A. (1992). Reasoning about conditional promises and warnings: Darwinian algorithms, mental models, relevance judgments or pragmatic schemas? *Quarterly Journal of Experimental Psychology, 44A*, 401–421.

Rozin, P., Lowery, L., Imada, S., & Haidt, J. (1999). The CAD triad hypothesis: A mapping between three moral emotions (contempt, anger, disgust) and three moral codes (community, autonomy, divinity). *Journal of Personality and Social Psychology, 76*, 574–586.

Shweder, R., Mahapatra, M., & Miller, J. (1987). Culture and moral development. In J. Kagan &

S. Lamb (Eds.), *The emergence of moral concepts in early childhood* (pp. 1–83). Chicago, IL: University of Chicago Press.

Sperber, D., Cara, F., & Girotto, V. (1995). Relevance theory explains the selection task. *Cognition, 57*, 31–95.

Sperber, D., & Wilson, D. (1995). *Relevance: Communication and cognition* (2nd ed.). Cambridge, MA: Blackwell.

Tooby, J., & Cosmides, L. (1990). The past explains the present: Emotional adaptations and the structure of ancestral environments. *Ethology and Sociobiology, 11*, 375–424.

Trivers, R. (1971). The evolution of reciprocal altruism. *Quarterly Review of Biology, 46*, 35–57.

Wason, P. (1968). Reasoning about a rule. *Quarterly Journal of Experimental Psychology, 20*, 273–281.

Wason, P., & Shapiro, D. (1971). Natural and contrived experience in a reasoning problem. *Quarterly Journal of Experimental Psychology, 23*, 63–71.

CHAPTER THREE

Evolutionary psychology's grain problem and the cognitive neuroscience of reasoning

Anthony P. Atkinson
King Alfred's College, Winchester, UK

Michael Wheeler
University of Dundee, UK

INTRODUCTION

In its most general form, evolutionary psychology is simply psychology that is properly grounded in evolutionary biology. But most research that falls under the banner of evolutionary psychology might be given a more specific gloss, as the Darwinian adaptationist programme applied to the mind/brain. How does this idea work?[1]

Viewed through the lens of Darwinian theory, organisms are (for the most part) integrated collections of adaptations, where adaptations are phenotypic traits that are evolved responses to adaptive problems, and where adaptive problems are selection pressures—recurring environmental conditions that influence reproductive success, or fitness, of individual organisms. Adaptations, then, contribute (or once contributed) to the reproductive success of the organisms that have them. Fitness maximization *per se* is not a goal of individual organisms, however. Organisms cannot seek directly to maximize their fitness, since what counts as fitness-promoting behaviour in one situation or for one individual is not likely to be so in another situation or for another individual (Cosmides & Tooby, 1987; Symons, 1992). Rather, thanks

---

[1] It is not our intention here to engage directly with the basic line of reasoning and argument that grounds evolutionary psychology, but what we do wish to do requires that we first briefly summarize its main features (see Atkinson & Wheeler, unpublished; Bloom, 1999; Cummins & Cummins, 1999; Samuels, 1998, 2000; Wheeler & Atkinson, 2001, for reviews and critical analyses).

to their specific adaptations, individual organisms have correspondingly specific goals that are tied to particular aspects of their physical and social environments, and to the lives they lead in those environments, and which affect, directly or indirectly, their reproductive success. In other words, organisms maximize their fitness by solving many specific adaptive problems. Evolutionary psychology "simply" applies this well-established Darwinian reasoning to the human brain. Thus conceived, the brain is an integrated collection of psychological mechanisms that evolved because their behavioural effects tended to help maintain or increase the fitness of organisms whose brains contained those mechanisms. The human brain is thus viewed as a system of psychological adaptations, a system shaped by natural selection to solve many specific adaptive problems.

Of course, adaptive problems (psychological or otherwise) are not set in stone: the goal posts often move, because while certain environmental conditions, such as sunlight coming from above (Ramachandran, 1988), will remain constant for aeons, other such conditions will change across evolutionary time. Against this background, a key claim often made by evolutionary psychologists is that the adaptive problem to which some psychological mechanism is an evolved response must be specified by reference to a certain ancestral environment, what is often called the organism's "environment of evolutionary adaptedness", or EEA. For humans, this claim is typically unpacked via the following argument: Given the slow pace of evolutionary change, the last time any significant modifications could have been made, by selection, to the functional architecture of the human brain, was during the Pleistocene era. The Pleistocene is thus the most significant part of the human EEA. Put crudely, the thought is that we have ancient hunter–gatherer minds inhabiting twenty-first-century environments.

A major task facing the evolutionary psychologist is therefore to show just *how* modern human behaviour is produced by psychological adaptations to ancestral environments. For present purposes, however, a rather different issue is to the fore. Several prominent evolutionary psychologists have argued that, on the basis of the kind of evolutionary reasoning sketched out above, we should expect the mind's information-processing architecture to consist in myriad domain-specific devices rather than a relatively small number of domain-general devices (Baron-Cohen, 1995; Buss, 1999; Cosmides & Tooby, 1987, 1992, 1994a, 1994b; Gigerenzer, 1997; Pinker, 1994, 1997; Sperber, 1996; Symons, 1992; Tooby & Cosmides, 1992, 1995, 2000). As we have explained elsewhere (Atkinson & Wheeler, unpublished; Wheeler & Atkinson, 2001), these arguments depend on the idea that domains are to be defined in terms of adaptive problems. So a feature of our cognitive architecture will be maximally domain-specific just when it is dedicated to solving one particular adaptive problem, and maximally domain-general just when it can contribute to the solution of any adaptive problem whatsoever. The evolutionary–psychological claim, then, is that since the brain's functional architecture is a system of psychological adaptations that reflect the vast range of adaptive problems that our hunter–gatherer ancestors faced, it must be a multifarious suite of innately specified, domain-specific devices (often called modules). This, in short, is the "Massive Modularity Hypothesis" (MMH) (Samuels, 1998, 2000; Sperber, 1996).

While the MMH is both widely endorsed within evolutionary psychology and championed vigorously by some leading theorists, not all who are broadly sympathetic to the overall evolutionary–psychological enterprise are ardent advocates of the idea (Cummins & Cummins, 1999; Shapiro & Epstein, 1998). And the MMH has certainly attracted a good deal of critical fire from outside the discipline. That combination of pre-eminence and controversy has motivated several detailed critical examinations of the core concepts and arguments of the MMH (e.g. Atkinson & Wheeler, unpublished; Samuels, 1998, 2000; Wheeler & Atkinson, 2001), to which can be added the present chapter.

In their recent book on the philosophy of biology, Sterelny and Griffiths (1999) devote two chapters to evolutionary psychology. Within these two chapters, they devote little more than a couple of pages to the presentation of a problem that they see as posing a significant threat to the viability of an explanatory programme predicated on the MMH. Evolutionary psychology, Sterelny and Griffiths argue, faces a "grain problem". In essence, their conception of this problem is that attempts to identify evolved, domain-specific modules require one to fix a single level of description at which the selection pressures in play are specified, but that the process of fixing that level will often be arbitrary. In the next section, we elucidate Sterelny and Griffiths' view of evolutionary psychology's grain problem, showing that their account in fact contains two threats to evolutionary psychology, not just one. Having suggested that one of these problems is the more worrying for evolutionary psychology, we turn, in the third section, to our own vision of the grain problem. We reveal a second dimension to the difficulty that Sterelny and Griffiths do not notice (or at any rate, do not make explicit), and that transforms the grain problem into a far more serious challenge to evolutionary psychology than is present in their narrower interpretation. In the subsequent five sections, we present a detailed examination of the interdisciplinary, multi-level approach to the study of cognition offered by evolutionarily inspired cognitive neuroscience, using research on social cognition and reasoning as a case study. In doing this we show that evolutionary psychologists can and do live with the two-dimensional grain problem.

THE GRAIN PROBLEM ACCORDING TO STERELNY
AND GRIFFITHS

Sterelny and Griffiths (1999) identify a problem for evolutionary psychology (in fact, it seems, for Darwinian selective reasoning in general), which comes into view when one combines the following two observations: (1) at a fairly gross level of description, a range of coarse-grained adaptive problems can be distinguished that might include obtaining sustenance, avoiding predators, selecting mates, reproducing, and caring for offspring; and (2) many such coarse-grained adaptive problems may also be appropriately described as hierarchically organized complexes of progressively finer-grained adaptive problems. Consider, for example, a problem for animals that live in complex social environments, namely, that of predicting the behaviour of conspecifics and adjusting one's own behaviour accordingly, a solution for which, in humans at least, is the ability to "mindread". What might appear to be a unitary problem at a coarse-grained level of description can nevertheless be decomposed into a set of more specific problems. Candidate component problems include: interpreting movements in terms of goals and desires, attributing perceptual states to others, attributing shared attention and knowledge, and attributing mental states (Baron-Cohen, 1995; Leslie, 1994). And each of these more specific problems might themselves be decomposed into yet finer-grained problems: attributing perceptual states, for example, might involve the separable abilities to detect eyes and to track their gaze. Or consider mate selection. Sterelny and Griffiths (1999, p. 328) ask, rhetorically, "Is the problem of mate choice a single problem or a mosaic of many distinct problems?" Is choosing a mate a single adaptive problem, or is it a set of related problems, such as: choosing someone of the opposite sex, someone who shows good reproductive prospects, and someone who shows signs of being a good parent? Or at a yet finer-grained level of description, is the problem of choosing someone with good reproductive prospects a single problem or a set of related problems, such as choosing someone who is young, who is healthy, of high status, etc.? (See also Sterelny, 1995.) The implied outcome of this rhetorical interrogation is, of course, that there is no final answer to any of the questions posed, and that this indeterminacy is a feature of evolutionary scenarios in general (or, at least, of significantly many of them), rather than just a local nuisance specific to mate choice. If this is correct, then the dilemma facing the evolutionary theorist is not merely that adaptive problems are, typically, hierarchical and nested. Rather, the full dilemma is that, since no particular level in a selective hierarchy—or, as one might say, no individual descriptive "grain"—takes explanatory precedence over any other, any decision to promote a single descriptive grain as the one at which the selection pressures in operation ought to be specified is simply arbitrary. This is the difficulty that Sterelny and Griffiths dub the "grain problem'.[2] (For now we shall use the term "grain problem" to indicate the grain problem as Sterelny and Griffiths see it. In the next section, however, we shall argue that this is in fact a limited version of the real grain problem.)

But how, exactly, does the fact that attempts to specify adaptive problems are encumbered by a plurality of equally viable descriptive grains come to constitute a problem for evolutionary psychology? Here, with a few clarificatory bells and whistles, is what Sterelny and Griffiths (1999, pp. 328–329) say:

> The grain problem in evolutionary psychology challenges the idea that adaptations [in this context, cognitive devices] are explained by the [adaptive] problem to which the adapted trait [some single cognitive device] is a solution. If (but only if) there is a single cognitive device that guides an organism's behavior with respect to issues of mate choice [for example], then mate choice is a single domain, and these [more specific problems] are all different aspects of the same problem. It is not the existence of a single problem confronting the organism that explains the module [the single cognitive device], but the existence of the module that explains why we think of mate choice as a single problem.

What are we to make of this short explication of the threat posed by the grain problem? As far as we can tell, the target passage is consistent with two different interpretations of that threat, which are not clearly distinguished by Sterelny and Griffiths. Moreover, these distinct interpretations actually constitute alternative, rather than complementary, arguments against evolutionary psychology. The difference between the two possible interpretations here turns on how we unpack the two key points made in the target passage, namely that:

(1) The grain problem challenges the view that cognitive devices (as adapted traits) are explained by the adaptive problem to which those devices are a solution.

(2) Evolutionary psychologists will be in a position to say with certainty why some, but not other, related adaptive problems can be grouped together as a single problem, only in those cases where it is possible antecedently to identify a distinct cognitive device subserving a distinct type of behaviour.

Here is the first interpretation: In point (1), Sterelny and Griffiths claim that the grain problem threatens to undermine the principle that an adapted trait

---

[2] The grain problem ought not to be mistaken for an apparently similar problem, that of trying to isolate, at a given lower level of description, just that subset of adaptive problems that actually impinge (or once impinged) on the organism in question, from the mass of possible adaptive problems at that lower level which together might constitute a single adaptive problem at a higher level. For further discussion of this point, see Atkinson and Wheeler (unpublished).

is, in some sense, explained by the adaptive problem to which that trait is a solution. This principle must surely be an essential plank of any genuinely Darwinian enterprise, and so must be a non-negotiable feature of the evolutionary–psychological treatment of cognitive devices. But how, exactly, is it threatened by the grain problem? Sterelny and Griffiths are disappointingly quiet on this point, but the answer may depend on what commitments we inherit when we endorse the claim that adapted traits are explained by their associated adaptive problems. On one understanding of those commitments, evolutionary psychologists not only require there to be some robust and principled method for identifying the unique adaptive problem to which some adapted trait constitutes an evolutionary solution, they also need that method to be, in a certain sense, independent of our identification of the phenotypic feature that constitutes the trait to be explained. What is meant by "independent" here is captured by the following thought: The way in which we specify an adaptive problem must not appeal essentially to the particular phenotypic trait that, ultimately, we intend to explain as the evolved solution to that problem, because if we have no option but to appeal to the evolutionary solution in the specification of the adaptive problem, then (so the argument goes) we are building into our explanation the very thing that we are trying to explain, and that is no explanation at all.

What we have identified as point (2) in Sterelny and Griffiths' exposition of the grain problem states that there is only one principled strategy by which the evolutionary psychologist might pin-down the grain at which to specify an adaptive problem. That strategy is first to identify a distinct cognitive device (the adapted trait) subserving a distinct type of behaviour, and then to use that knowledge to constrain the choice of grain. Given the independence criterion, however, point (2) emerges as nothing more than a powerful illustration of the disastrous failure of evolutionary psychology to solve the grain problem. Why? Because the proposed strategy contravenes the independence criterion, and so (under this interpretation) marks the failure of the evolutionary psychologist to respect the adaptationist principle that evolved traits are explained by the adaptive problems to which they are solutions. Thus if the independence criterion (or something like it) does figure in the correct unpacking of point (1) in Sterelny and Griffiths' exposition, then that fact demands a pessimistic reading of point (2). (On the plus side, it also provides a much-needed explanation for why the second point comes hard on the heels of the first.) In effect, then, on this first interpretation of Sterelny and Griffiths' analysis, evolutionary psychologists face a dilemma: If they relinquish their commitment to the independence criterion, then they can no longer hold claim to a non-negotiable principle of Darwinian explanation. But if, on the other hand, they hold fast to that prior explanatory principle, then they have to accept that in many cases there may be no nonarbitrary way of pinning down the choice of grain at which to specify adaptive problems, and thus no nonarbitrary way of explaining evolved traits in terms of the adaptive problems for which they are solutions.

A second interpretation of the passage in question comes into view if, in fact, Sterelny and Griffiths do not intend the independence criterion to be required by the view that adapted traits must be explained by their associated adaptive problems. If an adaptive problem can rightly be said to explain an adapted trait, even though that problem can be singled out only by specifying that trait, then, at first sight anyway, point (2) becomes not an observation that simply illustrates the rout of evolutionary psychology by the grain problem, but rather an initially plausible response to the grain problem, and more specifically to the threat identified in point (1). In other words, on this interpretation, the grain problem is taken to threaten the principle that an adapted trait is explained by its associated adaptive problem simply because it suggests that the choice of grain at which the adaptive problem might be specified is often arbitrary. But without the background presence of the independence criterion, the antecedent identification of a distinct cognitive device subserving a distinct type of behaviour might legitimately be thought to meet this challenge by non-arbitrarily constraining the choice of grain.

This way of understanding Sterelny and Griffiths' argument is wholly in tune with the fact that they follow-up the target passage reproduced above by immediately giving several weighty arguments for why (they think) evolutionary psychology has wedded itself prematurely to the idea of a massively modular theory of higher-level cognition, and thus for why (they think) the search for distinct cognitive devices subserving distinct types of behaviour is doomed to fail (Sterelny & Griffiths, 1999, pp. 329–332). In other words, having proposed a possible response to the grain problem, Sterelny and Griffiths immediately mount a secondary offensive to tell us why that response won't work.

We shall summarize one of Sterelny and Griffiths' second-wave arguments against evolved modularity—partly to illustrate their position but also because, as we shall see in a moment, the conclusion of that argument is telling. It is an undeniable fact that our psychological architecture has evolved in a social environment. Such socially embedded evolution is inherently interactive, in that one individual's adaptive solution is another's adaptive problem. This leads to a co-evolutionary arms race, in which each of the competing strategies in the population (say, cheating and cheater detection), always in pursuit of the evolutionary advantage, periodically transforms itself and hence the selective environment of the other, in a series of adaptations and counteradaptations. But this means, Sterelny and Griffiths claim, that our evolved psychological mechanisms cannot be modules—that is, innate domain-specific mechanisms that are hard-wired to solve long-enduring adaptive problems—simply because, in the co-evolutionary arms races that characterize social environments, there are "no stable problems . . .

to which natural selection can grind out a solution. The 'adaptive problem' is always being transformed in an arms race" (Sterelny & Griffiths, 1999, p. 331).

So, on the first interpretation of Sterelny and Griffiths' position, the grain problem is decisive, since even if distinct cognitive devices subserving distinct types of behaviour were there to be found (something which the secondary offensive calls into doubt), the appeal to the antecedent identification of such devices would fall foul of the independence criterion. On the second interpretation, the antecedent identification of distinct cognitive devices would, in principle, enable us to solve the grain problem. In this instance, the case against evolutionary psychology is completed by the secondary offensive, which aims to provide good reasons to think that such devices are simply not there to be found. But which of these options is the correct interpretation?

In our view, the exegetical waters here are far from clear. However, one way to approach the matter is to take a step back and to ask whether or not adaptationist explanation, *in any form*, really is committed to the independence criterion. This move highlights a further tension in Sterelny and Griffiths' argument. In constructing the interactive-social-evolution argument against evolved modularity (described above), Sterelny and Griffiths depend on the claim that evolutionary psychologists adopt a view of adaptation as being essentially a process of accommodation to a pre-existing environment or set of adaptive problems. Such a view of adaptation is at least strongly suggestive of the independence criterion. In contrast, and on the basis of their account of social evolution, Sterelny and Griffiths (1999, pp. 331–332) promote a notion of adaptation as transformation, concluding that "cognitive adaptation often transforms the environment rather than being an accommodation to it. So there will be real troubles in store for a methodology of discovering the mechanisms of the mind that proceeds by first trying to discover the problems that it must solve, and then testing for the presence of the solutions". But is evolutionary psychology inextricably bound to the allegedly problematic view of adaptation as accommodation? The crucial point here is that while there seems to be no room for the independence criterion in the view of adaptation that Sterelny and Griffiths promote, still they do not suggest that explanations in terms of adaptation as transformation are anything other than solidly Darwinian–adaptationist in character. But this means that even if, in practice, evolutionary psychologists do tend to adopt an independence-criterion-friendly view of adaptation as accommodation, they nevertheless could, in principle, avail themselves of the adaptation-as-transformation view, without being duty-bound to give back their copy of the "Descent of Man". So even if it is true that adaptation must often be conceived as transformation rather than accommodation, evolutionary psychology, as a Darwinian theoretical endeavour, can continue intact. Our conclusion, then, is that it is the second interpretation of Sterelny and Griffiths' argument that has the intellectual legs here, precisely because it does not make the apparently unreasonable assumption that evolutionary psychology is, in principle, wedded to the independence criterion.

THE TWO-DIMENSIONAL GRAIN PROBLEM

Notwithstanding the fact that Sterelny and Griffiths harbour grave doubts concerning the massively modular view of mind, their position (on our favoured interpretation) seems to be that if those doubts were to be allayed, then the appeal to the antecedent identification of distinct cognitive devices would constitute a general solution to the grain problem. In contrast, our view is that it would not.

The difficulty for the devices-first strategy becomes clear once one realizes that there will regularly be a second dimension to the grain problem—one that goes unnoticed by Sterelny and Griffiths. The fact is that it is not just adaptive problems that often form the kind of nested hierarchy that makes choosing a level of descriptive grain arbitrary; so do the parts of organisms that are potential solutions to adaptive problems. For example, Lewontin (1978, p. 161) asks: "Is the leg a unit in evolution, so that the adaptive function of the leg can be inferred? If so, what about a part of the leg, say the foot, or a single toe, or one bone of a toe?" This difficulty of matching phenotypic characters with adaptive problems is perhaps even greater in psychology, given the complexity of the brain. Take the human visual system, for example. Are the large-scale neural pathways, such as the ventral stream from occipital to temporal cortex and the dorsal stream from occipital to parietal cortex (Baizer, Ungerleider, & Desimone, 1991; Goodale, 1997; Goodale & Milner, 1992; Milner & Goodale, 1995; Ungerleider & Mishkin, 1982), properly called adaptations, that is, units in evolution appropriately described as having adaptive functions? Or at a lower level of description, what about the 30 or so functionally distinct areas of visual cortex (Maunsell & Newsome, 1987; Ts'o & Roe, 1995; Van Essen, 1985; Van Essen & Deyoe, 1995)? Or at still lower levels, smaller-scale neural circuits, or even individual neurons— are they units in evolution appropriately described as having adaptive functions? We can ask the same question about the perceptual and cognitive systems identified by cognitive psychologists, such as those that underpin object recognition, face recognition and expression recognition (Ellis & Young, 1996; Young, 1998). These systems are individuated by their information-processing functions rather than by any particular anatomical location or brain circuitry, as are, in some cases, their constituent subsystems. Which, if any, of these cognitive devices might constitute solutions to distinct adaptive problems?

These observations open the door to what we might call the "two-dimensional grain problem", which can be glossed as the difficulty of matching phenotypic features with selection pressures, given that selection pressures are hierarchical and nested (the grain problem according to Sterelny and Griffiths), coupled with the mirror difficulty of matching selection pressures with phenotypic features, given that phenotypic features are hierarchical and nested. The explanatory space has the following geography. If we can fix the level at which we describe selection pressures, then we can search for features of the organism's phenotype whose functions are (or once were) direct responses to those selection pressures. This would be a case of fixing the adaptive problem to infer the phenotypic solution from that problem. Conversely, if we can fix the level at which we describe features of an organism's phenotype, then we can ask whether there were any selection pressures in the organism's EEA to which those features would have been direct responses. This would be a case of fixing the phenotypic solution in order to infer the adaptive problem from that solution, and corresponds to the devices-first strategy. Unfortunately, where the two-dimensional grain problem manifests itself, there will be no satisfactory way to make either of these options available, because whichever level-fixing decision one takes, to get an explanation going, that decision will be arbitrary.

At present, the signs are not good for evolutionary psychology in its battle with the grain problem. But now it is time for a more positive analysis, because despite all the doom and gloom of our discussion up to now, our view is that evolutionary psychology is not impaled on even the more potent, two-dimensional form of that difficulty. In the remaining sections we shall try to make this claim stick. (Henceforth we will default to using "the grain problem" as shorthand for the two-dimensional grain problem. Where we think there is room for confusion, we will refer to the one-dimensional grain problem and the two-dimensional grain problem.)

LEVELS OF ANALYSIS

Mainstream evolutionary–psychological theorizing is predicated on Marr's (1982) well-known conceptual framework for analysing an information-processing system (Cosmides & Tooby, 1987, 1994a, 1994b). Famously, Marr proposed three distinct levels of analysis. (In the interests of keeping things clear, we note that a Marrian level of analysis is not the same thing as a level of descriptive grain.) As Marr's tripartite framework is central to our account, in what follows, of evolutionary–psychological theorizing about social reasoning, we here briefly summarize that framework, as it applies within evolutionary psychology. (For a more detailed consideration of Marr's levels of analysis and how they feature in evolutionary–psychological theorizing generally, see Atkinson & Wheeler, unpublished.)

The backbone of evolutionary–psychological theorizing is what Marr called the computational level of analysis—or, as we prefer, the ecological level (Sterelny, 1990). This is the level at which information-processing capacities are broadly characterized in terms of what a system can do, without any commitment as to the processes or mechanisms that enable the system to do those things. The rationale of this level of analysis is that, to understand how a system works—that is, in order to construct detailed theories about the mechanisms and processes that underpin and explain its observable behaviour—we must first understand what problems that system can solve and how it can solve them. This involves specifying cognitive capacities relative to the environment or background in which those capacities are displayed. Evolutionary psychologists working at this level draw upon knowledge of the design principles and practices of natural selection to provide a framework that informs and constrains their theories of the underlying psychological architecture.

At the second, algorithmic level, possible algorithms by which the system under investigation might solve a given information-processing problem are specified, along with descriptions of the type of representation required for the input and output.

The third level of analysis, the level of hardware implementation, concerns the physical realization of those algorithms and representations (e.g. in neural structures and processes).

There is an important difference between ecological-level theories on the one hand, and algorithmic- and implementational-level theories on the other. (We are here going beyond Marr's own account of these levels of analysis, although our intention is to elucidate rather than extend Marr's idea.) Ecological-level theories are concerned with capacities and properties of whole systems; paradigmatically, although, as we shall see, not exclusively, they are concerned with the way in which the behavioural responses and psychological capacities of whole organisms are related to the organism's EEA.[3]

Algorithmic- and implementational-level theories, in contrast, are concerned with parts of systems (their information-processing components and relevant inputs and outputs). This distinction between wholes and their parts is significant because whole systems will have capacities that their parts do not have (see Bechtel & Richardson, 1993, and Bechtel, 1994a, for detailed discussion of this general point). Moreover, there is an important sense

---

[3] We say that the ecological level is paradigmatically but not exclusively concerned with whole organisms because: (1) the parts of whole systems (e.g. the organs of organisms), when viewed at a lower level of description or organization, can themselves be considered as whole systems (systems that will often, in turn, be decomposable into yet smaller subsystems); and (2) on our favoured interpretation of Marr's view, each of the three levels of analysis can be applied at different levels of organization (Atkinson & Wheeler, unpublished; Bechtel, 1994b; McClamrock, 1991). Thus, on this view, it is possible for parts of whole organisms (or perhaps even groups of whole organisms) to be the subject of ecological-level analyses.

in which system-level characterizations are able to "ride free" of their subsystem-level explanations. Within the ecological level, there is no necessary commitment as to the functional architecture of the system; ecological-level theories can be neutral with respect to mechanism. Theories at the algorithmic and implementational levels, on the other hand, are proffered as accounts of, and thus presuppose, ecological-level phenomena. (Or at any rate, to be psychologically relevant, algorithmic- and implementational-level theories should be proffered as accounts of ecological-level phenomena. This was Marr's (1982) point in arguing for the utility, and indeed necessity, of the ecological level for psychology.)

With this Marrian framework in place, we can understand the overall explanatory enterprise of evolutionary psychology as being the search for answers to two general and distinct kinds of question, which are nevertheless interconnected:

(1)   Working within the ecological level, evolutionary psychologists want to know how psychological capacities are related to adaptive problems. Given a psychological capacity, they will ask what selection pressures in the organism's EEA (if any) might have led to the evolution of that capacity. Given an adaptive problem, they will ask what psychological capacities might be solutions to that problem.

(2)   Moving between the ecological level on the one hand, and the algorithmic and implementational levels on the other, evolutionary psychologists want to know how adaptive problems and psychological capacities are related to features of the brain's information-processing architecture. Given a psychological capacity, they will ask whether there is a feature, or set of related features, of the psychological architecture underpinning that capacity. Given a feature, or set of related features, of the psychological architecture, they will ask what psychological capacities might those features underpin, and for what adaptive problem, or set of related adaptive problems, those features might have evolved to solve.

Notice that within each of these two general kinds of question, there are two main sorts of inference employed by evolutionary psychologists, and by adaptationists generally. These are: (1) inferring adaptive problems from phenotypic solutions; and (2) inferring phenotypic solutions from adaptive problems. In the next two sections, we draw on recent work in the evolutionary cognitive neuroscience of social cognition and reasoning to show how these two kinds of inference play their part in enabling evolutionary psychology to absorb the grain problem.[4] Note, however, that the picture we are

---

[4] Sterelny and Griffiths (1999) themselves examine these two sorts of inference and the problems with each (see also Griffiths, 1996, 1997, 2001), but do not marry this examination with

about to paint of two kinds of inference constituting two separate explanatory paths is an idealized one. We paint an idealized picture for ease of
exposition but, as we will elaborate later, the reader should bear in mind that
these two inferential paths—from problems to solutions, and from solutions
to problems—in fact work together to constitute a unified explanatory project, and that, in practice, any one researcher's explanatory endeavours may
sometimes involve both kinds of inference.

INFERRING ADAPTIVE PROBLEMS FROM THEIR SOLUTIONS: THE CASE OF REASONING

What psychological mechanisms underlie our ability to reason and make
decisions? The burgeoning search for the information-processing and neural
substrates of reasoning and decision-making abilities in humans and other
primates is beginning to show fruit. By way of illustration, we here concen-
trate on the neural substrate of social reasoning. Our aim is to highlight the
way in which cognitive neuroscientists have appealed to evolutionary theory
to help them make sense of the cognitive architecture underpinning social
reasoning. That is, in this section we wish to illustrate the approach to
evolutionary–psychological explanation that begins with proposals concerning how specific neural structures and processes underpin certain psychological capacities (in this case, those related to social cognition) and ends up
by positing an adaptive problem or set of related adaptive problems for which
those capacities and their architectural substrates are evolved solutions (Fig.
3.1). Our approach in what follows is briefly to survey the literature on the
neural basis of social cognition, with particular reference to social reasoning,
while keeping firmly in mind questions of the following sort: Why is the brain
structured and organized this way? What are the various mechanisms for?
How did they evolve? These are the sort of questions whose answers require
appeal to selection pressures in ancestral environments, that is, to adaptive
problems. We end this section by detailing one such attempt to provide a
general answer to these sorts of questions in relation to social cognition,
namely, the Machiavellian intelligence hypothesis.

Recent research has shown that three of the most important areas of the
brain for social cognition are the frontal lobes, especially the ventromedial
prefrontal cortex, the amygdala, and the superior temporal sulcus. We shall
briefly discuss what has so far been revealed about the roles that each of these
areas play in social cognition, before going on to summarize the Machiavellian intelligence hypothesis.

---

their discussion of the (one-dimensional) grain problem. The account we develop here is also to
be distinguished from Cosmides and Tooby's writings on various strategies in evolutionary–
psychological explanation (Cosmides & Tooby, 2000; Cosmides, Tooby, & Barkow, 1992; Tooby
& Cosmides, 1992, 1995, 2000)—see Atkinson and Wheeler (unpublished) for details.

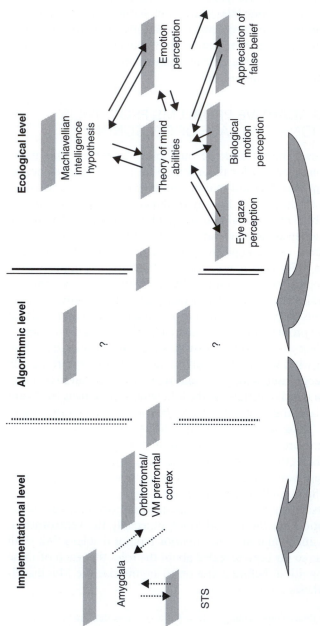

Figure 3.1 Levels of analysis from the bottom up. Explanatory paths followed when inferring adaptive problems from phenotypic solutions, illustrated with the case of social reasoning (see text). Arrows represent directions of theorizing, except for the dotted arrows on the left, which represent actual neural connections between the amygdala, STS, and VMPFC. The transitions represented by the thick arrows across the vertical dividing-lines indicate moves between theorizing within Marr's (1982) implementational, algorithmic, and ecological levels of analysis. The solid vertical lines between the ecological level and the algorithmic and implementational levels indicates a change from theorizing about components of organisms (especially of their brains) to theorizing about those whole organisms themselves. The darker right-to-left arrows at the bottom indicate the iterative, continuously evolving nature of theorizing in evolutionary cognitive neuroscience (see text). (The initial inspiration for this figures came from Buss, 1999, p. 40.)

The frontal lobes are critically involved in many higher cognitive capacities, such as those that enable us to behave in an organized way, to plan actions, to make decisions, and to decide what to attend to (for reviews see Damasio, 1994; Duncan, 1986, 1995; Luria, 1966; Miller, 2000; Milner, 1982; Passingham, 1993; Shallice, 1988). Certain memory abilities also involve the frontal lobes: several regions of prefrontal cortex are involved in episodic memory (Henson, Shallice, & Dolan, 1999; Lepage, Ghaffer, Nyberg, & Tulving, 2000), and dorsolateral prefrontal cortex is critically involved in working memory (Goldman-Rakic, 1990, 1992; Milner, Petrides, & Smith, 1985). Not all higher cognitive capacities are dependent on the frontal lobes, however, for we know that frontal lobe lesions do not produce marked decrements in performance on standard intelligence tests (Black, 1976; Hebb, 1939; Milner, 1964). But what is most relevant for present purposes is the importance of the frontal lobes in social cognition, and in particular, the subdivision known as the ventromedial prefrontal cortex (VMPFC). (This area includes a significant part of the cortex behind the eyes, that is, part of orbitofrontal cortex or OFC. Hence the two terms are sometimes used interchangeably.)

VMPFC is particularly involved in social reasoning and decision making (for reviews see Adolphs, 1999; Adolphs, Tranel, Bechara, Damasio, & Damasio, 1996; Allison, Puce, & McCarthy, 2000; Barton & Dunbar, 1997; Bechara, Damasio, & Damasio, 2000; Brothers, 1990, 1997; Damasio, 1994; Raleigh et al., 1996; Stone, 2000; Tranel, Bechara, & Damasio, 2000). For instance, work by Bechara, Damasio and colleagues (Adolphs, 1999; Adolphs et al., 1996; Bechara et al., 2000; Damasio, 1994) has shown that lesions to VMPFC selectively impair decision-making that depends on associations with emotional experience (e.g. gambles based on hunches) and performance on social contract versions of the Wason selection task. These authors conclude that the VMPFC plays a vital role "in linking perceptual representations of stimuli with representations of their emotional and social significance" (Adolphs, 1999, p. 474; see especially Damasio, 1994).

The ventromedial or orbitofrontal region is also implicated in certain aspects of "theory of mind", that is, in some of the cluster of abilities involved in explaining and predicting behaviour by attributing mental states. For example, Stone, Baron-Cohen, and Knight's (1998) patients, who had bilateral OFC damage, exhibited performance within the normal range on first- and second-order false belief tasks, but were nevertheless significantly impaired in their performance on subtler forms of social reasoning involving mental state attributions, such as recognizing a *faux pas* in a story. Rowe, Bullock, Polkey, and Morris's (2001) study suggests that performance on first- and second-order false belief tasks might be compromised by more general but unilateral frontal lesions (their patients' brain damage was limited to either left or right frontal cortex but varied in both extent and exact location). There is also the tentative finding by Stuss, Gallup, and Alexander

(2001), whose patients had lesions in the region of VMPFC/OFC, especially in the right hemisphere. These patients were impaired on a task that required them to infer that they were being deceived by the experimental assistant; in contrast, patients with lesions throughout the frontal lobes, but particularly in the right hemisphere, were impaired on a task that required them to infer visual experience in others.

The amygdala has a multifaceted role in social cognition (Adolphs, 1999; Aggleton, 2000; Baron-Cohen et al., 2000; Brothers, 1990; Emery & Amaral, 1999; Kling & Brothers, 1992), as well as in other capacities, such as associative learning (Bechara et al., 1995; Davis, 1992; La Bar, Le Doux, Spencer, & Phelps, 1995; Le Doux, 1995, 1998; Rolls, 1999; Weiskrantz, 1956). Lesion-based neuropsychological experiments, functional brain-imaging and other neurophysiological measures all converge on the finding that the amygdala plays a key role in the processing of emotional signals, especially those related to fear and in some cases anger, resulting in the triggering of appropriate physiological and behavioural responses (Adolphs et al., 1999b; Allman & Brothers, 1994; Broks et al., 1998; Calder et al., 1998; Le Doux, 1995, 1998; Morris et al., 1996, 1998; Scott et al., 1997; Tranel, 1997; Young et al., 1995; Young, Hellawell, Van De Wal, & Johnson, 1996). A word of caution here, however: The jury is still out on whether the role of the amygdala in humans (and in other primates) is specific to stimuli related to social threat or to threat and danger in general (Adolphs, 1999; Adolphs, Russell, & Tranel, 1999a; Adolphs & Tranel, 1999; Adolphs, Tranel, & Damasio, 1998; Allman & Brothers, 1994; Brothers, 1992; Kling & Brothers, 1992; Le Doux, 1995, 1998). Indeed, some authors propose that the amygdala is not so much involved in dealing with threats but rather in dealing with situations of distress (Blair, Morris, Frith, Perrett, & Dolan, 1999) or stimulus ambiguity (Whalen, 1999).

The amygdala, especially the left amygdala, is also implicated as part of a neural circuit underpinning theory of mind abilities (Baron-Cohen, 1995; Baron-Cohen et al., 2000; Fine, Lumsden, & Blair, 2001; Stone, 2000). In particular, research so far has shown that the amygdala is involved in: (1) processing information about biological motion (Bonda, Petrides, Ostry, & Evans, 1996; Brothers et al., 1990), especially in enabling us to attribute social meaning to moving stimuli (Heberlein et al., 1998); (2) the perception of eye gaze (Kawashima et al., 1999; Young et al., 1995; although see Broks et al., 1998 for a word of caution), allowing us, for example, to judge someone's mental state from eye gaze alone (Baron-Cohen et al., 1999); and (3) the ability to appreciate that people can have false beliefs and the related ability to deploy knowledge about mental states in order to understand jokes and nonliteral speech such as sarcasm and metaphor (Fine et al., 2001).

The superior temporal sulcus (STS) has also been implicated as an important structure in theory of mind abilities (Frith & Frith, 1999), again especially via its involvement in the perception of eye gaze and of biological motion (Abell et al., 1999; Emery, 2000; Hietanen & Perrett, 1996; Perrett et al., 1985, 1989, 1991), including motion of the head, mouth, hands, and whole body, and even of implied biological motion (see Allison et al., 2000; Carey, Perrett, & Oram, 1997; Jellema & Perrett, 2001, for reviews). Indeed, the STS both sends projections to the amygdala and receives projections from it (Amaral, Price, Pitkanen, & Carmichael, 1992), which goes some way to explaining the shared functions of these structures. Moreover, the amygdala is reciprocally connected to the orbitofrontal/ventromedial region (Amaral et al., 1992). So the VMPFC, amygdala, and STS together form a system for social cognition, including social reasoning.[5]

It is now time to step back from the details of the neurological underpinnings of social cognition and to consider, as some evolutionary psychologists and neuroscientists do, those questions with which we began this section. We can here summarize these questions as follows: How and why did our many specialized cognitive abilities evolve? And in particular, how and why did the specialized circuitry for social reasoning evolve? As indicated in Fig. 4.1, one popular suggestion is the social or Machiavellian intelligence hypothesis (Byrne & Whiten, 1988, 1991, 1992; Dunbar, 1998; Whiten & Byrne, 1997).

The general idea of the Machiavellian intelligence hypothesis is that group living sets up an environment in which each individual is out to get the best or most he or she can by using strategies of social manipulation, but without causing such disruption that his membership in the group is jeopardized. This hypothesis began with Humphrey's (1976) observation that primates appear to have more intelligence than they need for their everyday tasks of feeding and ranging, and his subsequent suggestion that the social complexity inherent in many primate groups would have been a significant selection pressure acting to increase primate intelligence. This idea has since gained credence from the finding that average social group size and neocortex size are positively correlated across species: the bigger the social groupings, the bigger is the neocortex relative to the rest of the brain (Aiello & Dunbar, 1993; Dunbar, 1992, 1995; Sawaguchi & Kudo, 1990). When we turn to the question of dedicated psychological mechanisms for social reasoning, the Machiavellian hypothesis predicts that the many specialized cognitive abilities of primates evolved via an arms race in which individuals competed with each other, and formed alliances with some to compete with others, using increasingly sophisticated social strategies. The hypothesis thus predicts psychological

---

[5] The overall neurocomputational basis of social cognition is likely to be more complex than this, however, involving these three neural structures in ways not surveyed here, and probably also certain other parts of the brain. See, for example, Damasio's (1994, 1999) ideas about the role of somatosensory cortex in social cognition, and the exciting work on "mirror neurons" and how they might be involved in certain theory of mind abilities (Gallese, 2000a, 2000b; Gallese & Goldman, 1998; Rizzolatti, Fadiga, Fogassi, & Gallese, 1999).

mechanisms specialized for prosocial behaviour such as cooperation and altruism, as well as for coercion and deception, and mechanisms for predicting behaviour and for "reading" the mental states of conspecifics. These psychological capacities have been operationalized, and their presence in children and nonhuman primates tested by means of tasks probing, for example, self-recognition and self-directed actions, gaze following and joint visual attention, cooperative problem-solving, joint role comprehension, understanding of false beliefs, and several forms of tactical deception and intentional teaching (for reviews and critical discussion see Baron-Cohen, 1995, 1999; Byrne, 1995; Byrne & Whiten, 1988, 1992; Heyes, 1998; Povinelli, 1999; Povinelli & Preuss, 1995; Povinelli & Prince, 1998; Premack & Woodruff, 1978; Tomasello & Call, 1997; Whiten, 1991, 1999; Whiten & Byrne, 1988, 1997).

Our discussion of this work on social reasoning illustrates how theorizing in the cognitive and brain sciences involves a sophisticated methodology in which the theorist moves back and forth between the ecological and subecological levels of analysis. In adopting the strategy of inferring problems from solutions, the explanatory endeavours begin at the ecological level, whether explicitly or not. Working within that level of analysis (see the right-hand side of Fig. 3.1), investigators take a psychological capacity (e.g. theory of mind abilities) and break it down into a set of subcapacities (e.g. the perception of eye gaze and of biological motion, and the appreciation of false belief). They might then continue to decompose each of these subcapacities into yet more specific subcapacities, and so on. At each stage of this decompositional analysis, the postulated subcapacities may be revised, supplemented with additional subcapacities, or replaced by alternatives, in the light of relevant evidence. The next stage in this inferential strategy is to switch to the algorithmic or implementational levels, or both, and ask, for each capacity identified at the ecological level, whether there are in fact any such features of the psychological architecture underpinning the identified capacity. Once some such architectural features have been identified (e.g. the interrelated roles of the amygdala, STS and VMPFC in social reasoning), the investigator can switch back to the ecological level and ask what selection pressures in the organism's EEA (if any) might have led to the selection of those features that underpin the capacity in question (e.g. the pressures grouped together under the Machiavellian intelligence hypothesis).

INFERRING SOLUTIONS FROM ADAPTIVE PROBLEMS: THE CASE OF REASONING

Evolutionary cognitive psychologists and neuroscientists not only infer adaptive problems from psychological capacities; they also infer psychological capacities from adaptive problems. For example, in investigating reasoning and decision-making abilities, one might start from a higher-level theory whose essence is that many of the most serious adaptive challenges for primates took place during social interactions with conspecifics. One might start, for instance, with the Machiavellian intelligence hypothesis (Fig. 3.2). One might then propose that certain specific pressures in the social environments of primates, including the human EEA, selected for certain psychological mechanisms that enabled our ancestors to make decisions concerning who to form alliances with, who to share precious food and other resources with, who to avoid for fear of being beaten up, who to groom, who to mate with, and so forth.

On the basis of some such account of the likely selection pressures for social decision-making, evolutionary psychologists would (or at any rate, should) then embark on a two-part search for candidate solutions to those adaptive problems. First, they would remain at the ecological level of analysis, and search for psychological capacities that might have been direct responses to those selection pressures in the organism's ancestors. Having identified a list of specific adaptive problems and candidate solutions to those problems, they would then drop to the algorithmic or implementational levels, or both, and search for underlying architectural features in that organism that subserve or underpin those capacities. This will involve an "engineering analysis": constructing and testing plausible arguments about how individual phenotypic features function as well-engineered adaptive devices (see Dawkins, 1986; Lewontin, 1978; Tooby & Cosmides, 1992; Williams, 1966). It should also involve, but often does not, comparative testing of these hypothesized adaptations (Griffiths, 1996, 1997, 2001), that is, analysing the historical development of these phenotypic features across related species.

There are several good examples of theories of human reasoning and decision-making explicitly motivated by and grounded in considerations of ancestral selection pressures. We shall now briefly introduce two of them— social contract theory and hazard management or precaution theory—in order to illustrate how evolutionary psychologists have engaged in this two-part search for candidate solutions (psychological mechanisms) to adaptive problems (likely selection pressures). We discuss a third theory in a later section.

Social Contract Theory

Social Contract Theory is concerned with deontic reasoning, that is, reasoning about obligations, permissions, and prohibitions. Its particular focus is with reasoning in situations of social exchange—situations in which individuals exchange resources and favours (Cosmides, 1989; Cosmides & Tooby, 1989, 1992, 1997; Fiddick, 1998; Fiddick, Cosmides, & Tooby, 2000; Gigerenzer & Hug, 1992). The primary proponents of this theory, Cosmides

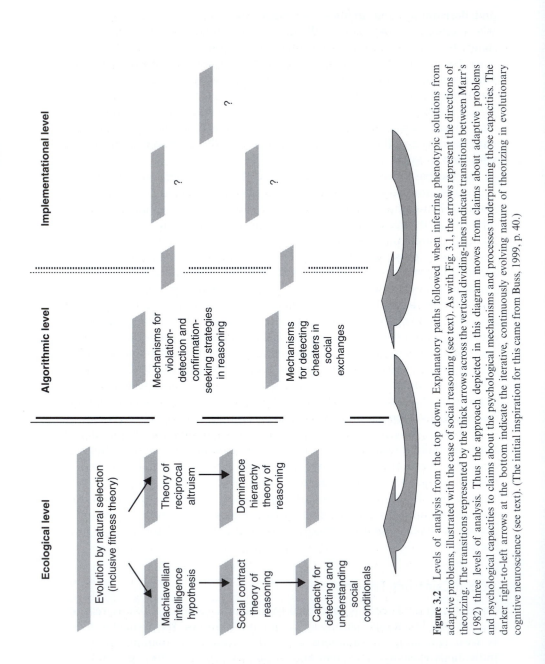

Figure 3.2 Levels of analysis from the top down. Explanatory paths followed when inferring phenotypic solutions from adaptive problems, illustrated with the case of social reasoning (see text). As with Fig. 3.1, the arrows represent the directions of theorizing. The transitions represented by the thick arrows across the vertical dividing-lines indicate transitions between Marr's (1982) three levels of analysis. Thus the approach depicted in this diagram moves from claims about adaptive problems and psychological capacities to claims about the psychological mechanisms and processes underpinning those capacities. The darker right-to-left arrows at the bottom indicate the iterative, continuously evolving nature of theorizing in evolutionary cognitive neuroscience (see text). (The initial inspiration for this came from Buss, 1999, p. 40.)

and Tooby, began by drawing upon some ideas and general observations about human social interaction from evolutionary biology, game theory and economics, to derive some conclusions about the selection pressures likely to have shaped social reasoning. One idea they focused upon was that much human social behaviour involves bestowing benefits or inflicting costs on others (helping or hurting them), and that these acts are performed conditionally. For example, people will generally aid a nonrelative only if they themselves received help from that person in the past, or if there is good reason to believe that that person will reciprocate the good deed in the future. This idea is the essence of the theory of reciprocal altruism (Axelrod & Hamilton, 1981; Trivers, 1971), according to which psychological mechanisms supporting altruistic behaviour towards non-relatives can evolve as long as the benefits bestowed on others are reciprocated. So under these lights, human interaction is saturated with social conditionals, that is, with what Cosmides and Tooby describe as "statements or behaviours that express an intention to make one's behaviour contingent upon that of another" (Cosmides & Tooby, 1997, p. 140).

So social contract theory is derived principally from the more general theory of reciprocal altruism. Continuing down the hierarchy of levels of theorizing, Cosmides and Tooby derived a specific evolutionary hypothesis from social contract theory, namely, that an important selection pressure in the human EEA was one that selected "for cognitive designs that can detect and understand social conditionals reliably, precisely and economically" (Cosmides & Tooby, 1997, p. 140). But given that this selection pressure is still at a fairly high level of description, it is of more use in informing ecological-level theories about the general kinds of cognitive capacities involved in social reasoning and decision-making than it is in informing theories of the underlying cognitive machinery. Finer-grained selection pressures are required to inform detailed dissection of psychological mechanisms, insofar as having these finer-grained selection pressures to hand allows the evolutionary psychologist to draw up a list of design features that those mechanisms must embody. In our example of the evolutionary psychology of reasoning, it is at this stage in the explanatory enterprise that the concept of social exchange comes to the fore. Cosmides and Tooby reasoned that social exchanges or contracts are an important category of social conditional, and further, that detecting cheaters is an important adaptive problem for those engaging in social exchange. Cheaters in this context are those who break a social contract, that is, those who accept a benefit without paying an appropriate cost, such as someone who receives a favour but does not return it.

So we now have a reasonably specific adaptive problem that was arrived at by decomposing a general or high-level selection pressure into more specific or lower-level pressures. The pressure for forming social contracts and the concomitant pressure for detecting cheaters were derived from the pressure for reliable, precise and economical detection and understanding of social conditionals in general. Famously, Cosmides and Tooby went on to propose that the human cognitive architecture contains mechanisms specialized for detecting cheaters in social exchange, and to test this idea using variations on the Wason selection task (see especially Cosmides, 1989; Cosmides & Tooby, 1989, 1992, 1997; see also Gigerenzer & Hug, 1992). But the important matter for present purposes is that Cosmides and Tooby proposed some specific design features of the psychological architecture underlying social exchange by examining what evolutionary biology and game theory had to say about these selection pressures. They (Cosmides & Tooby, 1992) derived a "partial list" of design features at the algorithmic level of analysis that must be embodied by the psychological mechanisms of a species engaging in social exchange. This list includes algorithms for: assessing costs and benefits, regardless of the goods or services exchanged; recognizing other individuals; remembering one's interactions with others; communicating one's values, needs, and desires to others; and recognizing someone else's values, needs, and desires.

One might continue along this explanatory path by decomposing each of these fairly broadly defined algorithms into more specific ones. For example, the ability to remember one's past interactions with others might involve, *inter alia*, algorithms for remembering whether people were previously cooperators or cheaters, and for remembering and updating records of who owes what to whom. To take another example, person recognition might involve the operation of algorithms for face and voice recognition, and for storing, organizing, and retrieving semantic and episodic knowledge about people.

Once the evolutionary psychologist has arrived at some such specific hypotheses about the information-processing architecture underlying the psychological capacities in question, these hypotheses must, of course, be tested, by using behavioural experiments (e.g. those employing the Wason selection task). The next major step in the explanatory enterprise, which can also serve to test these algorithmic-level hypotheses, is to search for the neural substrates of these postulated features of the cognitive architecture. Clearly, then, it is in this next step in the explanatory enterprise that a link with the discussion of the previous section emerges. In terms of our idealized account, evolutionary psychologists who infer phenotypic solutions from adaptive problems will eventually be concerned with just those findings with which theorists who adopt the converse inferential strategy begin, namely, data concerning the neural substrate of psychological capacities.

We shall shortly mention some (admittedly initial and tentative) neuro-psychological evidence for social contract theory. As that evidence also involves a second and complementary theory of deontic reasoning, we shall first need to introduce that second theory.

Social contract theory explanations of patterns of performance on conditional reasoning tasks are not exclusive, despite implications to that effect in the early literature (Cosmides, 1989). Cheng and Holyoak (1989) and Manktelow and Over (1990) showed that precaution rules, which lack the cost/benefit structure of a social contract—such as "If you clear up spilt blood then you must wear rubber gloves"—also facilitate conditional reasoning. Cheng and Holyoak (1989) used such results as ammunition against social contract theory and evolutionary psychology more generally, whereas Manktelow and Over (1990) were only showing that the initial statement of social contract theory was too strong. Subsequently, Cosmides, Tooby, and Fiddick (Cosmides & Tooby, 1997; Fiddick, 1998; Fiddick et al., 2000) ran with Manktelow and Over's view that social contract theory can explain some but not all instances of facilitation on conditional reasoning tasks, and gave it a more detailed evolutionary twist by developing the complementary hazard management or precaution theory.[6] The central idea of hazard management theory is that, since the ability to avoid hazards (predators, poisonous creatures, cliffs, etc.) would have been of significant evolutionary advantage to our ancestors, we should expect to find within the human cognitive architecture a system specialized for reasoning about hazards and precautions. Moreover, on this view, the hazard management system should be separate from the social contract system, since hazard avoidance and social exchange involve different selection pressures and different computational requirements.

The operation of a system specialized for reasoning about precautions has been tested by presenting subjects with a form of the Wason selection task that utilizes precaution rules (Fiddick, 1998; Fiddick et al., 2000). Fiddick et al. (2000, p. 17) characterize precaution rules as being of the form: "If a valued entity is subjected to a hazard, then taking an appropriate precaution lowers the risk of harm". Notice, then, that it is not just the person doing the reasoning who might be subjected to a hazard and thus be the recipient of a precaution; precautions can apply to anything of value to the reasoner, such as one's children or other genetic relatives, one's mate, or even one's possessions. Hazard management theory proposes that precaution rules are a separate class of deontic rules that delineate a distinct adaptive domain. Accordingly, hazard management theory makes at least the following two

---

[6] Manktelow and Over (1990), who can be credited with the discovery of precaution rules facilitating reasoning (Cosmides & Tooby, 1992, p. 205), inferred this idea from the simple assumption that people have some basic ability at practical reasoning (rather than a more specific ability at detecting cheaters in social contracts). So hazard management theory did not first arise via the line of theorizing we are focusing on in this section, that is, as involving the inference of a cognitive solution from an adaptive problem. Nevertheless, in the hands of Fiddick, Cosmides and Tooby, one can see how hazard management theory now fits that standard evolutionary–psychological mould.

predictions. First, the majority of subjects given precaution rule versions of the Wason selection task should perform well, that is, choose the "P" and "not-Q" cards, which in this case correspond to "subject to a hazard" and "did not take the precaution", respectively. The results of several experiments confirm this prediction (see Fiddick, 1998; Fiddick et al., 2000; Stone, Cosmides, Tooby, Kroll, & Knight, 2002; Stone, Cosmides, & Tooby, 1996).

A second prediction—and it is here that the complementary work on hazard management and social contract theory finally promises to "bottom out" in the brain—is that it should be possible to find experimental and neuropsychological dissociations between two types of task, one of which depends on the hypothesized hazard management system, the other on the hypothesized social contract system. Some such dissociations have been reported: Fiddick and colleagues (Fiddick, 1998; Fiddick, Cosmides, & Tooby, 1995; Fiddick, Cosmides, & Tooby, 2000, unpublished) have demonstrated experimentally induced double dissociations of the social contract and precaution versions of the Wason selection task, using a priming paradigm, and Stone and colleagues (Stone et al., 1996, 2002) report a case of a subject with bilateral limbic system damage who is impaired at detecting violations of social contract rules but who retains a normal ability to detect violations of precaution rules.

THE PAY-OFF

At this stage in the proceedings, we would dearly like to be in a position to illustrate, using developed and detailed examples, the substantial meeting and theoretical integration of the two general inferential strategies we have been considering, namely, inferring adaptive problems from phenotypic solutions and inferring phenotypic solutions from adaptive problems. Regrettably, we cannot. It is early days in the evolutionary cognitive neuroscience of reasoning and such an integration has not as yet established itself in the literature. We are nevertheless hopeful that it will. In the meantime, what we can do is say what the methodological reflections of last two sections tell us about the prospects for evolutionary psychology in the face of the grain problem.

We have illustrated, with reference to work in the cognitive neuroscience of reasoning, a sophisticated explanatory strategy in which the theorist moves within and between levels of description and levels of analysis. We suggest that once the explanatory endeavours of evolutionary psychologists are seen under these lights, any worry that progress in evolutionary psychology is stymied by the grain problem turns out to be unfounded. Here is why.

The picture that we have painted so far, of two separate explanatory paths is, as we forewarned, an idealized one. At times we gave the impression that different researchers will adopt different approaches: inferring psychological capacities and mechanisms from adaptive problems, or inferring adaptive problems from psychological capacities and mechanisms. But in reality, and as we indicated in our two diagrams, the two approaches are complementary and many researchers will adopt both approaches, sometimes at the same sitting. Moreover, ideally there is a dynamic and mutually constraining relationship between these two approaches. Theorists who are attempting to infer an adaptive problem from a phenotypic solution will benefit from what their colleagues in psychology, anthropology and evolutionary biology have to say about the likely selection pressures on our ancestors that are relevant to the phenotypic solution in question. And theorists who are attempting to infer a phenotypic solution from an adaptive problem will benefit from what their colleagues in psychology and neuroscience have to say about the features of our psychological architecture that might be relevant to the adaptive problem in question.

As a result of this mutual guidance and constraint, theories at each level of analysis codevelop, both within a given level of description and especially between levels of description (cf. Churchland's (1986) account of the "co-evolution" of theories at different levels of description). In other words, theories at a given level of description concerning the adaptive function, the algorithms, inputs and outputs, and the neural hardware relevant to some psychological capacity are informed and constrained by theories about the adaptive function, the algorithms, inputs and outputs, and the neural hardware relevant to that psychological capacity at various other levels of description. Importantly, we suggest, this recurring reciprocal feedback between theories at different levels of analysis and description has the effect of neutralizing the grain problem. Recall that the two-dimensional grain problem genuinely threatens the evolutionary–psychological enterprise of explaining adapted traits in terms of adaptive problems. The essence of this threat is that, in many cases, both the choice of grain at which to specify adaptive problems, and the choice of grain at which to specify adapted traits, appear to be arbitrary. But given that, as we have now argued, the very methodology of evolutionary theorizing about the mind/brain means that there will often be equally legitimate stories to be told about a given psychological capacity at different levels of description, the pressure to single out a unique level of description at which adaptive problems and phenotypic traits (including cognitive devices) must be described simply dissipates. And once this fact is recognized, the grain problem ceases to be a serious in-principle difficulty.

At this point one might raise the worry that this multilevel explanatory enterprise places no clear restrictions on what counts as a good evolutionary–psychological explanation, such that evolutionary psychologists are free to avail themselves of whatever level of description, or combination of levels of description, will happen to tell a cogent story. But this worry can be met, for implicit in the methodology as we have described it is a means for constraining the choice between sets of levels and thus the boundaries of evolutionary–psychological explanation. In general terms, an overall, multilevel account of a given psychological capacity is constrained by the requirement that the component theories at each of the different levels must ultimately be consistent with, and indeed interlock with, each other. But more specifically, mutual guidance and constraint between theories at different levels, and between the differently directed inferential strategies at work in evolutionary psychology, should (one might think) narrow down the range of possible and acceptable theories, and thus take us closer to nature's real joints. (These points are developed in more detail in Atkinson & Wheeler, unpublished.)

A DISPUTE DISSOLVED?

In the remainder of this chapter we shall identify some consequences of the foregoing discussion by investigating one more research programme in which the strategy of inferring architectural solutions from adaptive problems gets played out. We shall then have on the table three theories of deontic reasoning, two of which are complementary and together appear in dispute with the third. However, once we place this supposed disagreement in the context of the kind of multilevel evolutionary–psychological explanation that (we have argued) is resistant to the grain problem, the air of conflict appears to subside.

In contrast to the combination of social contract and hazard management theories, Dominance Hierarchy Theory proposes a single system specialized for all forms of deontic reasoning (Cummins, 1996a, 1996b, 1998, 1999, 2000). Cummins observes that when we reason about deontic rules, we overwhelmingly adopt a violation-detection strategy, whereas when we reason about indicative rules (i.e. descriptions of the world, about what is true or false), we adopt a confirmation-seeking strategy. She argues that this difference in reasoning strategies is fundamental, and that we should expect it to be reflected in the cognitive architecture. We adopt a violation-detection strategy and are thereby proficient deontic reasoners, Cummins argues, thanks to a domain-specific system that evolved as the result of selection pressures related to dominance hierarchies (although see Chater & Oaksford, 1996 for a counterargument).

Dominance hierarchies are characterized by competition and cooperation amongst conspecifics for limited resources (food, mates, etc.). An animal's position within a dominance hierarchy is highly correlated with access to those resources: the higher the rank, the greater the share and control over the available resources. Moreover, rank depends crucially on skilful social interaction and manipulation, especially the ability to form and maintain alliances. Cummins' idea is that a significant component of this set of skills is adeptness in social reasoning, especially of the deontic variety. Reasoning effectively about what oneself and others are obliged to do is central to success in forming and maintaining alliances, and in fulfilling other social contracts, especially when those obligations are reciprocal. Moving up in the world depends on trading favours. And reasoning effectively about what one-self and others are permitted and forbidden to do allows higher-ranking individuals to detect lower-ranking transgressors (so they can be warned or punished) and lower-ranking individuals to avoid transgressions, or to engage in deceptive transgression (thus avoiding threatening encounters and pun-ishment). So moving up in the world also depends on following the law, and on breaking the law while not being seen.

Cummins (1996a, 1996b) cites a variety of evidence in support of her claim that the human cognitive architecture includes an evolved system spe-cialized for deontic reasoning. Numerous studies of reasoning in nonhuman primates show a "social content effect", that is, these animals make various sorts of inferences much more readily in social tasks, such as kin and domin-ance rank discriminations (Cheney & Seyfarth, 1990; Dasser, 1985), than they do in nonsocial, object-oriented tasks (Gillian, 1981; McGonigle & Chalmers, 1977). Developmental studies show that: (1) children are consider-ably more accomplished at deontic reasoning than they are at indicative rea-soning; (2) like adults, children tend to adopt violation-seeking strategies for deontic rules and confirmation-seeking strategies for indicative rules; and (3) this differential ability is established early in life, around 3 to 4 years of age (Cummins, 1996c; Harris & Nunez, 1996; Nunez & Harris, 1998). And there is some cross-cultural evidence for the indicative–deontic distinction, includ-ing indirect evidence from members of preliterate societies (see Cummins, 1996b for a review).

Cummins also cites neuropsychological studies in humans and monkeys that show evidence of a selective deficit of deontic reasoning. As we noted earlier, lesions to frontal cortex, especially VMPFC, can result in severe impairments in social behaviour and reasoning, such as reduced inhibitions, an inability to organize and plan future actions, impairments in making decisions that depend on associations with emotional experience (e.g. gambles based on hunches), and a lack of concern for oneself and others (see Adolphs, 1999; Adolphs et al., 1996; Bechara et al., 2000; Damasio, 1994 for reviews). Results of this kind lead Cummins to claim that damage to prefrontal cortices "impacts most severely on the capacity to respond effec-tively to the social rules that underlie the dominance hierarchy" (Cummins, 1996b, p. 176).

In Cummins' work, then, we again see an example of an evolutionary psychologist using the inferential strategy of reasoning from adaptive prob-lems to psychological solutions. At the ecological level of analysis, she began by deriving dominance hierarchy theory from the general claim that the social complexity inherent in many primate groups would have been a significant selection pressure acting to increase primate intelligence (roughly, the Machiavellian intelligence hypothesis). That theory makes certain claims about adaptive problems related to dominance hierarchies, from which Cummins inferred a psychological capacity that plausibly plays a significant role in solving those adaptive problems, namely, adopting a violation-detection strategy in deontic reasoning. She then dropped to the subecological levels of analysis to propose a mind/brain mechanism that underpins that capacity, namely, a deontic reasoning system, and garnered a variety of converging evidence for such a system (at least a significant part of which is supposed be located within the frontal lobes).[7]

So how many distinct psychological mechanisms or modules underpin deontic reasoning? As we have seen, Cummins argues that a single mechanism underpins deontic reasoning, whereas Fiddick, Cosmides and Tooby argue for two separate systems, one for social contracts, the other for hazard management. Cummins' argument is based on the claim that the relevant selection pressures confronting our ancestors selected for the ability to reason about permissions, obligations and prohibitions within dominance hierarchies. Hence, on her view, all deontic reasoning, including that about hazards or precautions, is restricted to the social realm.[8] The arguments of Fiddick, Cosmides, and Tooby, in contrast, are based on the claim that there were two separate sets of pressures, both selecting for deontic reasoning abilities: one for the ability to reason about precautions (allowing our ancestors

---

[7] Here we see that Cummins has moved more-or-less straight from the ecological level of analysis to the implementational level, thus skipping explicit theorizing at the algorithmic level. Such skipping of algorithmic-level theorizing is quite common in these early days of cognitive neuroscience. This is no more so than in the cognitive neuroscience of reasoning, where there is a marked paucity of formal models and simulations of domain-specific reasoning abilities such as those that we have been discussing. An exception, of course, is the large body of work on formalizing and modelling higher-level (and sometimes more domain-general) theories of reasoning, such as the Prisoner's Dilemma (see Axelrod, 1984; Axelrod & Hamilton, 1981; Emshoff, 1970; Hayashi, 1995; Messick & Liebrand, 1993; Nauta & Hoeksta, 1995; Watanabe & Yamagishi, 1999). The ecological rationality programme (Gigerenzer, Todd, & the ABC Research Group, 1999) might also be regarded as a notable exception. This programme proposes a variety of "simple heuristics" ("fast and frugal" procedures that exploit the structure of environments to produce ecologically useful inferences and decisions) as the algorithmic underpinnings of many of our reasoning and decision-making abilities. We should nevertheless note that ecological-level theorizing for those pursuing the ecological rationality programme does not focus solely, or even primarily, on adaptive problems in ancestral environments. On their view, ecological rationality has a wider purview than evolutionary psychology (the latter being grounded in the former), encompassing decision making in modern as well as ancestral environments (see Over, 2000a, 2000b; Todd, Fiddick & Krauss, 2000, for discussion).

[8] Others have also argued that deontic reasoning is inherently social, although not in terms of dominance hierarchy theory. For example, Manktelow and Over (1991) argue that how one represents a deontic rule, and thus how one reasons about that rule, depends on the social role one adopts with respect to it, i.e. whether one represents the utilities associated with the agent who lays down the rule or with the actor whose behaviour is its target.

to avoid hazards), the other for the ability to reason about social contracts (allowing our ancestors to trade favours and goods, and to detect cheaters). With respect to deontic reasoning, then, the social realm for Fiddick, Cosmides, and Tooby is more restricted than it is for Cummins; it is reasoning about social contracts that is crucial to Fiddick, Cosmides, and Tooby's view, not reasoning within dominance hierarchies (which might subsume some or all reasoning about social contracts), or social reasoning in general (which would subsume reasoning about social contracts).

Certainly the neuropsychological data do not yet allow us to decide between dominance hierarchy theory and social contract plus hazard management theories. The neuropsychological study of reasoning is still in its infancy; there is as yet insufficient evidence to make any firm conclusions about how specific types of social behaviour and reasoning map on to specific brain regions. For instance, it is an open question as to whether selective impairment on social contract versions of the Wason selection task after VMPFC lesions (Adolphs et al., 1996) result because VMPFC forms a crucial part of a system specialized for reasoning about social contracts or for reasoning about dominance hierarchies (which would include reasoning about social contracts). That being said, there is at least one study that provides more direct support for Cummins' theory over Social Contract Theory, which turns on the difference between the two theories with respect to social rank: Dominance Hierarchy Theory predicts social reasoning to be affected by rank whereas Social Contract Theory does not make this prediction. Work by Raleigh and colleagues (Raleigh et al., 1996) has shown that the density of serotonin receptors in the orbitofrontal cortex of monkeys varies according to rank, and that social behaviour and rank are affected by manipulation of serotonin neurotransmission. (See Cummins, 1996a, 1996b, 1998, 1999, 2000, for further evidence and arguments for Dominance Hierarchy Theory as against Social Contract Theory. And see Fiddick, 1998 for a counterargument, which centres on the claim that, *pace* Cummins, all deontic reasoning—specifically, reasoning about precautions—is not intrinsically social reasoning.)

While the empirical adequacy of these theories is undoubtedly crucial, the main point that we wish to highlight here is this: The interdisciplinary, multi-level explanatory enterprise that we have outlined in the wake of the grain problem, brings to the fore the possibility that the positions of Cummins on the one hand, and of Cosmides, Tooby, and Fiddick on the other, may not be in competition after all. For it is plausible that these two sets of theories are pitched at different levels of description, and are thus potentially compatible. Specifically, Cummins' Dominance Hierarchy Theory is pitched at a higher level than social contract and hazard management theories, proposing higher-level selection pressures and corresponding psychological mechanisms. So consider, for example, how one might get from Cummins' position to that of Fiddick, Cosmides, and Tooby. One might first seek to decompose the higher-level selection pressure for deontic reasoning within dominance hierarchies into more specific selection pressures at a lower level of description. One might also decompose the ability to adopt a violation-detection strategy in deontic reasoning into more specific or lower-level psychological capacities. The second step in this continuation of Cummins' work would then be to identify the more specific psychological mechanisms at lower levels of description that together compose the larger deontic reasoning system, and whose joint operation underpins the adoption of a violation-detection strategy in deontic reasoning tasks. Interestingly, Cummins herself is open to this move, at times implying the possibility that a single deontic reasoning system might itself be decomposed into subsystems (see, for example, Cummins, 1996b, p. 177). Once all this has been done, it is at least conceivable that the subsystems of the larger deontic reasoning system that one ends up with are something like the subsystems proposed by Fiddick, Cosmides, and Tooby. Of course, arriving at that position would first require one to revise Cummins' initial claim that the selection pressures for deontic reasoning are specific to dominance hierarchies (i.e. the claim that all deontic reasoning is inherently social). Indeed, the main unresolved issue blocking a reconciliation of these two positions is whether reasoning about nonsocial precautions engages a deontic reasoning mechanism (as Cosmides, Tooby, and Fiddick claim), or not (as Cummins claims). The resolution of this particular disagreement is an empirical matter. Be that as it may, our point is that the multilevel explanatory enterprise allows us to see how a reconciliation might proceed.[9]

CONCLUSION

Our take-home message is this. The grain problem is even more serious than Sterelny and Griffiths' account suggests. Nevertheless, that problem is not a

---

[9] Although we do not pursue the matter in detail here, the foregoing discussion provides support for a more general conclusion that we have argued for in detail elsewhere (Atkinson and Wheeler, under review; Wheeler and Atkinson, 2001). In many cases at least, there will be no stage at which one could provide a definitive answer to the question of whether a psychological capacity is domain-specific or domain-general, because that would require one to fix a unique level of description, from which judgements about domain specificity or domain generality could be made, and the regular failure to fix such a level of description is just what is suggested by the theoretical endeavours that we have been illustrating. If this is right, then regardless of whether the two positions on deontic reasoning highlighted in the main text are compatible, it may well be that at no point in the continuing evolutionary–psychological enterprise could one provide a definitive answer to the question of whether deontic reasoning is domain-specific in the sense suggested by Cummins, or whether it is instead a function of more domain-general abilities. Similarly, at no point could one say definitively, as Cosmides, Tooby, and Fiddick are wont to do, that social contract reasoning and precaution reasoning constitute two distinct domain-specific abilities rather than two facets of a higher-level, more domain-general ability.

silver bullet for evolutionary psychology. So as far as this particular threat is concerned, the explanatory credentials of a truly interdisciplinary, scientific, and evolutionary approach to the human mind remain in good shape.

ACKNOWLEDGEMENTS

A.P.A. was supported by a Leverhulme Trust Research Fellowship and a grant from the McDonnell Project in Philosophy and the Neurosciences (http://www.sfu.ca/neurophilosophy/) while this chapter was written. Our thanks to Ralph Adolphs and David Over for comments.

REFERENCES

Abell, F., Krams, M., Ashburner, J., Passingham, R., Friston, K., Frackowiak, R., Happe, F., Frith, C., & Frith, U. (1999). The neuroanatomy of autism: A voxel-based whole brain analysis of structural scans. *Neuroreport, 10,* 1647–1651.

Adolphs, R. (1999). Social cognition and the human brain. *Trends in Cognitive Sciences, 3,* 469–479.

Adolphs, R., Russell, J.A., & Tranel, D. (1999a). A role for the human amygdala in recognizing emotional arousal from unpleasant stimuli. *Psychological Science, 10,* 167–171.

Adolphs, R., & Tranel, D. (1999). Preferences for visual stimuli following amygdala damage. *Journal of Cognitive Neuroscience, 11,* 610–616.

Adolphs, R., Tranel, D., Bechara, A., Damasio, H., & Damasio, A.R. (1996). Neuropsychological approaches to reasoning and decision-making. In A.R. Damasio, H. Damasio, & Y. Christen (Eds.), *Neurobiology of decision-making* (pp. 157–179). Berlin: Springer-Verlag.

Adolphs, R., Tranel, D., & Damasio, A.R. (1998). The human amygdala in social judgment. *Nature, 393,* 470–474.

Adolphs, R., Tranel, D., Hamann, S., Young, A.W., Calder, A.J., Phelps, E.A., Anderson, A., Lee, G.P., & Damasio, A.R. (1999b). Recognition of facial emotion in nine individuals with bilateral amygdala damage. *Neuropsychologia, 37,* 1111–1117.

Aggleton, J.P. (Ed.) (2000). *The amygdala: A functional analysis.* Oxford: Oxford University Press.

Aiello, L.C., & Dunbar, R.I.M. (1993). Neocortex size, group size and the evolution of language. *Behavioral and Brain Sciences, 34,* 184–193.

Allison, T., Puce, A., & McCarthy, G. (2000). Social perception from visual cues: Role of the STS region. *Trends in Cognitive Sciences, 4,* 267–278.

Allman, J., & Brothers, L. (1994). Faces, fear and the amygdala. *Nature, 372,* 613–614.

Amaral, D.G., Price, J.L., Pitkanen, A., & Carmichael, S.T. (1992). Anatomical organisation of the primate amygdaloid complex. In J.P. Aggleton (Ed.), *The amygdala: Neurobiological aspects of emotion, memory and mental dysfunction* (pp. 1–66). New York: Wiley-Liss.

Atkinson, A.P., & Wheeler, M. (under review). The grain of domains: The evolutionary–psychological case against domain-general cognition.

Axelrod, R. (1984). *The evolution of cooperation.* New York: Basic Books.

Axelrod, R., & Hamilton, W. (1981). The evolution of cooperation. *Science, 211,* 1390–1396.

Baizer, J.S., Ungerleider, L.G., & Desimone, R. (1991). Organization of visual inputs to the inferior temporal and posterior parietal cortex in macaques. *Journal of Neuroscience, 11,* 168–190.

Baron-Cohen, S. (1995). *Mindblindness: An essay on autism and theory of mind.* Cambridge, MA: MIT Press/Bradford Books.

Baron-Cohen, S. (1999). The evolution of a theory of mind. In M.C. Corballis & S.E.G. Lea (Eds.), *The descent of mind: Psychological perspectives on hominid evolution* (pp. 261–277). Oxford: Oxford University Press.

Baron-Cohen, S., Ring, H., Wheelwright, S., Bullmore, E., Brammer, M., Simmons, A., & Williams, S. (1999). Social intelligence in the normal and autistic brain: An fMRI study. *European Journal of Neuroscience, 11*, 1891–1898.

Baron-Cohen, S., Ring, H.A., Bullmore, E.T., Wheelwright, S., Ashwin, C., & Williams, S.C.R. (2000). The amygdala theory of autism. *Neuroscience and Biobehavioral Reviews, 24*, 355–364.

Barton, R.A., & Dunbar, R.I.M. (1997). Evolution of the social brain. In A. Whiten & R.W. Byrne (Eds.), *Machiavellian intelligence II: Extensions and evaluations* (pp. 240–263). Cambridge: Cambridge University Press.

Bechara, A., Damasio, H., & Damasio, A.R. (2000). Emotion, decision making and the orbitofrontal cortex. *Cerebral Cortex, 10*, 295–307.

Bechara, A., Tranel, D., Damasio, H., Adolphs, R., Roackland, C., & Damasio, A.R. (1995). Double dissociation of conditioning and declarative knowledge relative to the amygdala and hippocampus in humans. *Science, 269*, 1115–1118.

Bechtel, W. (1994a). Biological and social constraints on cognitive processes: The need for dynamical interactions between levels of inquiry. In M. Matthen & R.X. Ware (Eds.), *Biology and society: Reflections on methodology. (Canadian Journal of Philosophy Supplementary Vol. 20)* (pp. 133–164). Calgary: University of Calgary Press.

Bechtel, W. (1994b). Levels of description and explanation in cognitive science. *Minds and Machines, 4*, 1–25.

Bechtel, W., & Richardson, R.C. (1993). *Discovering complexity: Decomposition and localization as strategies in scientific research.* Princeton, NJ: Princeton University Press.

Black, F.W. (1976). Cognitive deficits in patients with unilateral war-related frontal lobe lesions. *Journal of Clinical Psychology, 32*, 366–372.

Blair, R.J., Morris, J.S., Frith, C.D., Perrett, D.I., & Dolan, R.J. (1999). Dissociable neural responses to facial expressions of sadness and anger. *Brain, 122*, 883–893.

Bloom, P. (1999). The evolution of certain novel human capacities. In M.C. Corballis & S.E.G. Lea (Eds.), *The descent of mind: Psychological perspectives on hominid evolution.* Oxford: Oxford University Press.

Bonda, E., Petrides, M., Ostry, D., & Evans, A. (1996). Specific involvement of human parietal systems and the amygdala in the perception of biological motion. *Journal of Neuroscience, 16*, 3737–3744.

Broks, P., Young, A.W., Maratos, E.J., Coffey, P.J., Calder, A.J., Isaac, C.L., Mayes, A.R., Hodges, J.R., Montaldi, D., Cezayirli, E., Roberts, N., & Hadley, D. (1998). Face processing impairments after encephalitis: amygdala damage and recognition of fear. *Neuropsychologia, 36*, 59–70.

Brothers, L. (1990). The social brain: A project for integrating primate behavior and neurophysiology in a new domain. *Concepts in Neuroscience, 1*, 27–51.

Brothers, L. (1992). Perception of social acts in primates: Cognition and neurobiology. *Seminars in the Neurosciences, 4*, 409–414.

Brothers, L. (1997). *Friday's footprint.* New York: Oxford University Press.

Brothers, L., Ring, B., & Kling, A. (1990). Response of neurons in the macaque amygdala to complex social stimuli. *Behavioural Brain Research, 41*, 199–213.

Buss, D.M. (1999). *Evolutionary psychology: The new science of the mind.* Boston: Allyn & Bacon.

Byrne, R.W. (1995). *The thinking ape: Evolutionary origins of intelligence.* Oxford: Oxford University Press.

Byrne, R.W., & Whiten, A. (1988). *Machiavellian intelligence: Social expertise and the evolution of intellect in monkeys, apes and humans.* Oxford: Clarendon Press.

Byrne, R.W., & Whiten, A. (1991). Computation and mindreading in primate tactical deception. In A. Whiten (Ed.), *Natural theories of mind: Evolution, development and simulation of everyday mindreading* (pp. 127–141). Oxford: Basil Blackwell.

Byrne, R.W., & Whiten, A. (1992). Cognitive evolution in primates: Evidence from tactical deception. *Man, 27,* 609–627.

Calder, A.J., Young, A.W., Rowland, D., Perrett, D.I., Hodges, J.R., & Etcoff, N.L. (1996). Facial emotion recognition after bilateral amygdala damage: Differentially severe impairment of fear. *Cognitive Neuropsychology, 13,* 699–745.

Carey, D.P., Perrett, D.I., & Oram, M.W. (1997). Recognizing, understanding and reproducing actions. In F. Boller & J. Grafman (Eds.), *Handbook of neuropsychology* (Vol. 11, in Section 16: Action and cognition, M. Jeannerod, Ed.). Amsterdam: Elsevier.

Chater, N., & Oaksford, M. (1996). Deontic reasoning, modules and innateness: A second look. *Mind and Language, 11,* 191–202.

Cheney, D.L., & Seyfarth, R.M. (1990). *How monkeys see the world.* Chicago: Chicago University Press.

Cheng, P.W., & Holyoak, K.J. (1989). On the natural selection of reasoning theories. *Cognition, 33,* 284–313.

Churchland, P.S. (1986). *Neurophilosophy: Toward a unified science of the mind/brain.* Cambridge, MA: MIT Press/Bradford Books.

Cosmides, L. (1989). The logic of social exchange: Has natural selection shaped how humans reason? Studies with the Wason selection task. *Cognition, 31,* 187–276.

Cosmides, L., & Tooby, J. (1987). From evolution to behavior: Evolutionary psychology as the missing link. In J. Dupre (Ed.), *The latest on the best: Essays on evolution and optimality* (pp. 227–306). Cambridge, MA: MIT Press.

Cosmides, L., & Tooby, J. (1989). Evolutionary psychology and the generation of culture, part II. Case study: A computational theory of social exchange. *Ethology and Sociobiology, 10,* 51–97.

Cosmides, L., & Tooby, J. (1992). Cognitive adaptations for social exchange. In J.H. Barkow, L. Cosmides, & J. Tooby (Eds.), *The adapted mind: Evolutionary psychology and the generation of culture* (pp. 163–228). New York: Oxford University Press.

Cosmides, L., & Tooby, J. (1994a). Beyond intuition and instinct blindness: toward an evolutionarily rigorous cognitive science. *Cognition, 50,* 41–77.

Cosmides, L., & Tooby, J. (1994b). Origins of domain specificity: The evolution of functional organization. In L.A. Hirschfeld & S.A. Gelman (Eds.), *Mapping the mind: Domain specificity in cognition and culture* (pp. 85–116). Cambridge: Cambridge University Press.

Cosmides, L., & Tooby, J. (1997). Dissecting the computational architecture of social inference mechanisms. *Ciba Foundation Symposium, 208,* 132–156.

Cosmides, L., & Tooby, J. (2000). Evolution: Introduction. In M.S. Gazzaniga (Ed.), *The new cognitive neurosciences* (2nd ed.). Cambridge, MA: MIT Press/Bradford Books.

Cosmides, L., Tooby, J., & Barkow, J.H. (1992). Introduction: Evolutionary psychology and conceptual integration. In J.H. Barkow, L. Cosmides, & J. Tooby (Eds.), *The adapted mind: Evolutionary psychology and the generation of culture* (pp. 9–13). New York: Oxford University Press.

Cummins, D.D. (1996a). Dominance hierarchies and the evolution of human reasoning. *Minds and Machines, 6,* 463–480.

Cummins, D.D. (1996b). Evidence for the innateness of deontic reasoning. *Mind and Language, 11,* 160–190.

Cummins, D.D. (1996c). Evidence of deontic reasoning in 3- and 4-year-old children. *Memory and Cognition, 24,* 823–829.

Cummins, D.D. (1998). Social norms and other minds: The evolutionary roots of higher cognition. In D.D. Cummins & C. Allen (Eds.), *The evolution of mind* (pp. 30–50). New York: Oxford University Press.

Cummins, D.D. (1999). Cheater detection is modified by social rank: The impact of dominance on the evolution of cognitive functions. *Evolution and Human Behavior, 20*, 229–248.

Cummins, D.D. (2000). How the social environment shaped the evolution of mind. *Synthese, 122*, 3–28.

Cummins, D. D., & Cummins, R. (1999). Biological preparedness and evolutionary explanation. *Cognition, 73*, B37-B53.

Damasio, A.R. (1994). *Descartes' error: Emotion, reason and the human brain.* New York: Putnam/Picador.

Damasio, A. (1999). *The feeling of what happens: Body, emotion and the making of consciousness.* London: William Heinemann.

Dasser, V. (1985). Cognitive complexity in primate social relationships. In R.A. Hinde, A.N. Perret-Clemont, & J. Stevenson-Hinde (Eds.), *Social relationships and cognitive development.* Oxford: Clarendon Press.

Davis, M. (1992). The role of the amygdala in conditioned fear. In J.P. Aggleton (Ed.), *The amygdala: Neurological aspects of emotion, memory and mental dysfunction* (pp. 255–306). New York: Wiley-Liss.

Dawkins, R. (1986). *The blind watchmaker.* London: Longman/Penguin.

Dunbar, R.I.M. (1992). Neocortex size as a constraint on group size in primates. *Journal of Human Evolution, 20*, 469–493.

Dunbar, R.I.M. (1995). Neocortex size and group size in primates: A test of the hypothesis. *Journal of Human Evolution, 28*, 287–296.

Dunbar, R.I.M. (1998). The social brain hypothesis. *Evolutionary Anthropology, 6*, 178–190.

Duncan, J. (1986). Disorganisation of behaviour after frontal lobe damage. *Cognitive Neuropsychology, 3*, 271–290.

Duncan, J. (1995). Attention, intelligence, and the frontal lobes. In M.S. Gazzaniga (Ed.), *The cognitive neurosciences* (pp. 721–733). Cambridge, MA: MIT Press/Bradford Books.

Ellis, A.W., & Young, A.W. (1996). *Human cognitive neuropsychology: A textbook with readings* (2nd ed.). Hove, UK: Psychology Press.

Emery, N.J. (2000). The eyes have it: the neuroethology, function and evolution of social gaze. *Neuroscience and Biobehavioral Reviews, 24*, 581–604.

Emery, N.J., & Amaral, D.G. (1999). The role of the primate amygdala in social cognition. In R.D. Lane & L. Nadel (Eds.), *Cognitive neuroscience of emotion* (pp. 156–191). New York: Oxford University Press.

Emshoff, J.R. (1970). A computer simulation model of the Prisoner's Dilemma. *Behavioral Science, 15*, 304–317.

Fiddick, L. (1998). *The deal and the danger: An evolutionary analysis of deontic reasoning.* Unpublished PhD thesis. University of California, Santa Barbara.

Fiddick, L., Cosmides, L., & Tooby, J. (1995). *Are there really separate reasoning mechanisms for social contracts and precautions?* Paper presented at the Seventh Annual Meeting of the Human Behavior and Evolution Society, University of California, Santa Barbara.

Fiddick, L., Cosmides, L., & Tooby, J. (2000). No interpretation without representation: The role of domain-specific representations and inferences in the Wason selection task. *Cognition, 77*, 1–79.

Fiddick, L., Cosmides, L., & Tooby, J. (under review). Does the mind distinguish between social contracts and precautions? Dissociating cognitive adaptations through inference priming.

Fine, C., Lumsden, J., & Blair, R.J.R. (2001). Dissociation between 'theory of mind' and executive functions in a patient with early left amygdala damage. *Brain, 124*, 287–298.

Frith, C.D., & Frith, U. (1999). Interacting minds – a biological basis. *Science, 286*, 1692–1695.

Gallese, V. (2000a). The acting subject: Towards the neural basis of social cognition. In T. Metzinger (Ed.), *Neural correlates of consciousness: Empirical and conceptual questions* (pp. 325–333). Cambridge, MA: MIT Press.

Gallese, V. (2000b). The inner sense of action: Agency and motor representation. *Journal of Consciousness Studies, 7*, 23–40.

Gallese, V., & Goldman, A. (1998). Mirror neurons and the simulation theory of mind-reading. *Trends in Cognitive Sciences, 2*, 493–500.

Gigerenzer, G. (1997). The modularity of social cognition. In A. Whiten & R.W. Byrne (Eds.), *Machiavellian intelligence II: Extensions and evaluations* (pp. 264–288). Cambridge: Cambridge University Press.

Gigerenzer, G., & Hug, K. (1992). Domain-specific reasoning: Social contracts, cheating, and perspective change. *Cognition, 43*, 127–171.

Gigerenzer, G., Todd, P.M., & the ABC Research Group (1999). *Simple heuristics that make us smart.* New York: Oxford University Press.

Gillian, D.J. (1981). Reasoning in the chimpanzee: II. Transitive inference. *Journal of Experimental Psychology: Animal Behavioral Processes, 7*, 150–164.

Goldman-Rakic, P.S. (1990). Cellular and circuit basis of working memory in prefrontal cortex of nonhuman primates. *Progress in Brain Research, 85*, 325–336.

Goldman-Rakic, P.S. (1992). Working memory and the mind. *Scientific American, 267*, 111–117.

Goodale, M.A. (1997). Visual routes to perception and action in the cerebral cortex. In M. Jeannerod (Ed.), *Handbook of neuropsychology* (Vol. 11, pp. 91–109). Amsterdam: Elsevier.

Goodale, M.A., & Milner, A.D. (1992). Separate visual pathways for perception and action. *Trends in Neurosciences, 15*, 20–25.

Griffiths, P.E. (1996). The historical turn in the study of adaptation. *British Journal for the Philosophy of Science, 47*, 511–532.

Griffiths, P.E. (1997). *What emotions really are: The problem of psychological categories.* Chicago: University of Chicago Press.

Griffiths, P.E. (2001). From adaptive heuristic to phylogenetic perspective: Some lessons from the evolutionary psychology of emotion. In H.R. Holcomb (Ed.), *Conceptual challenges in evolutionary psychology: Innovative research strategies.* Dordrecht: Kluwer.

Harris, P., & Nunez, M. (1996). Understanding of permission rules by pre-school children. *Child Development, 67*, 1572–1591.

Hayashi, N. (1995). Emergence of cooperation in one-shot prisoner's dilemmas and the role of trust. *Japanese Journal of Psychology, 66*, 184–190.

Hebb, D.O. (1939). Intelligence in man after large removals of cerebral tissue: Report of four left frontal lobe cases. *Journal of General Psychology, 21*, 73–87.

Heberlein, A.S., Adolphs, R., Tranel, D., Kemmerer, D., Anderson, S., & Damasio, A.R. (1998). Impaired attribution of social meanings to abstract dynamic visual patterns following damage to the amygdala. *Society of Neuroscience Abstracts, 24*, 1176.

Henson, R.N.A., Shallice, T., & Dolan, R.J. (1999). Right prefrontal cortex and episodic memory retrieval: A functional MRI test of the monitoring process. *Brain, 122*, 1367–1381.

Heyes, C.M. (1998). Theory of mind in nonhuman primates. *Behavioral and Brain Sciences, 21*, 101–148.

Hietanen, J.K., & Perrett, D.I. (1996). Motion sensitive cells in the macaque superior temporal polysensory area: Response discrimination between self-generated and externally generated pattern motion. *Behavioural Brain Research, 76*, 155–167.

Humphrey, N. (1976). The social function of intellect. In P.P.G. Bateson & R.A. Hinde (Eds.), *Growing points in ethology* (pp. 303–317). Cambridge: Cambridge University Press.

Jellema, T., & Perrett, D.I. (2001). Coding of visible and hidden actions. In W. Prinz & B. Hommel (Eds.), *Attention and performance XIX.* Oxford: Oxford University Press.

Kawashima, R., Sugiura, M., Kato, T., Nakamura, A., Hatano, K., Ito, K., Fukuda, H., Kojima, S., & Nakamura, K. (1999). The human amygdala plays an important role in gaze monitoring. A PET study. *Brain, 122*, 779–783.

Kling, A.S., & Brothers, L.A. (1992). The amygdala and social behavior. In J.P. Aggleton (Ed.),

The amygdala: Neurological aspects of emotion, memory and mental dysfunction (pp. 353–377). New York: Wiley-Liss.

La Bar, K.S., Le Doux, J.E., Spencer, D.D., & Phelps, E.A. (1995). Impaired fear conditioning following unilateral temporal lobectomy in humans. *Journal of Neuroscience, 15*, 6846–6855.

Le Doux, J.E. (1995). Emotion: Clues from the brain. *Annual Review of Psychology, 46*, 209–235.

Le Doux, J. (1998). *The emotional brain: The mysterious underpinnings of emotional life.* New York: Simon & Schuster.

Lepage, M., Ghaffer, O., Nyberg, L., & Tulving, E. (2000). Prefrontal cortex and episodic memory retrieval mode. *Proceedings of the National Academy of Sciences, 97*, 506–511.

Leslie, A.M. (1994). ToMM, ToBY, and agency: Core architecture and domain specificity. In L.A. Hirschfeld & S.A. Gelman (Eds.), *Mapping the mind: Domain specificity in cognition and culture* (pp. 119–148). Cambridge: Cambridge University Press.

Lewontin, R.C. (1978). Adaptation. *Scientific American, 239*, 156–169.

Luria, A.R. (1966). *Higher cortical functions in man.* New York: Basic Books.

Manktelow, K.I., & Over, D.E. (1990). Deontic thought and the selection task. In K.J. Gilhooly, M.T.G. Keane, R.H. Logie, & G. Erdos (Eds.), *Lines of thinking: Reflections on the psychology of thinking* (Vol. 1, pp. 153–164). London: Wiley.

Manktelow, K.I., & Over, D.E. (1991). Social roles and utilities in reasoning with deontic conditionals. *Cognition, 39*, 85–105.

Marr, D. (1982). *Vision.* New York: W.H. Freeman.

Maunsell, J.H.R., & Newsome, W.T. (1987). Visual processing in monkey extrastriate cortex. *Annual Review of Neuroscience, 10*, 363–401.

McClamrock, R. (1991). Marr's three levels: A re-evaluation. *Minds and Machines, 1*, 185–196.

McGonigle, B.O., & Chalmers, M. (1977). Are monkeys logical? *Nature, 267*, 694–696.

Messick, D.M., & Liebrand, W.B. (1993). Computer simulations of the relation between individual heuristics and global cooperation in Prisoner's Dilemmas. *Social Science Computer Review, 11*, 301–312.

Miller, E.K. (2000). The prefrontal cortex and cognitive control. *Nature Reviews: Neuroscience, 1*, 59–65.

Milner, A.D., & Goodale, M.A. (1995). *The visual brain in action.* Oxford: Oxford University Press.

Milner, B. (1964). Some effects of frontal lobectomy in man. In J.M. Warren & K. Akert (Eds.), *The frontal granular cortex and behavior* (pp. 313–334). New York: McGraw-Hill.

Milner, B. (1982). Some cognitive effects of frontal lobe lesions in man. In D.E. Broadbent & L. Weiskrantz (Eds.), *The neuropsychology of cognitive function* (pp. 211–226). London: The Royal Society.

Milner, B., Petrides, M., & Smith, M.L. (1985). Frontal lobes and the temporal organization of memory. *Human Neurobiology, 4*, 137–142.

Morris, J.S., Friston, K.J., Buchel, C., Frith, C.D., Young, A.W., Calder, A.J., & Dolan, R.J. (1998). A neuromodulatory role for the human amygdala in processing emotional facial expressions. *Brain, 121*, 47–57.

Morris, J.S., Frith, C.D., Perrett, D.I., Rowland, D., Young, A.W., Calder, A.J., & Dolan, R.J. (1996). A differential neural response in the human amygdala to fearful and happy facial expressions. *Nature, 383*, 812–815.

Nauta, D., & Hoeksta, J. (1995). Effective choice in the single-shot Prisoner's Dilemma tournament. *Theory and Decision, 39*, 1–30.

Nunez, M., & Harris, P.L. (1998). Psychological and deontic concepts: Separate domains or intimate connection? *Mind and Language, 13*, 153–170.

Over, D.E. (2000a). Ecological rationality and its heuristics. *Thinking and Reasoning, 6*, 182–192.

Over, D.E. (2000b). Ecological issues: A reply to Todd, Fiddick, & Krauss. *Thinking and Reasoning, 6*, 385–388.

Passingham, R.E. (1993). *The frontal lobes and voluntary action.* Oxford: Oxford University Press.

Perrett, D.I., Harries, M.H., Bevan, R., Thomas, S., Benson, P.J., Mistlin, A.J., Chitty, A.J., Hietanen, J.K., & Ortega, J.E. (1989). Frameworks of analysis for the neural representation of animate objects and actions. *Journal of Experimental Biology*, *146*, 87–113.

Perrett, D.I., Oram, M.W., Harries, M.H., Bevan, R., Hietanen, J.K., Benson, P.J., & Thomas, S. (1991). Viewer-centred and object-centred coding of heads in the macaque temporal cortex. *Experimental Brain Research*, *86*, 159–173.

Perrett, D.I., Smith, P.A., Mistlin, A.J., Chitty, A.J., Head, A.S., Potter, D.D., Broennimann, R., Milner, A.D., & Jeeves, M.A. (1985). Visual analysis of body movements by neurones in the temporal cortex of the macaque monkey: A preliminary report. *Behavioural Brain Research*, *16*, 153–170.

Pinker, S. (1994). *The language instinct*. London: Allen Lane/Penguin.

Pinker, S. (1997). *How the mind works*. London: Allen Lane/Penguin.

Povinelli, D.J. (1999). Social understanding in chimpanzees: New evidence from a longitudinal approach. In P.D. Zelazo, J.W. Astington, et al. (Eds.), *Developing theories of intention: Social understanding and self-control* (pp. 195–225). Mahwah, NJ: Lawrence Erlbaum Associates, Inc.

Povinelli, D.J., & Preuss, T.M. (1995). Theory of mind: Evolutionary history of a cognitive specialization. *Trends in Neurosciences*, *18*, 418–424.

Povinelli, D.J., & Prince, C.G. (1998). When self met other. In M.D. Ferrari & R.J. Sternberg (Eds.), *Self-awareness: Its nature and development* (pp. 37–107). New York: Guilford Press.

Premack, D., & Woodruff, G. (1978). Does a chimpanzee have a theory of mind? *Behavioral and Brain Sciences*, *1*, 515–526.

Raleigh, M., McGuire, M., Melega, W., Cherry, S., Huang, S.-C., & Phelps, M. (1996). Neural mechanisms supporting successful social decisions in Simians. In A.R. Damasio, H. Damasio, & Y. Christen (Eds.), *Neurobiology of decision-making* (pp. 63–82). Berlin: Springer-Verlag.

Ramachandran, V.S. (1988). Perception of shape from shading. *Nature*, *331*, 163–166.

Rizzolatti, G., Fadiga, L., Fogassi, L., & Gallese, V. (1999). Resonance behaviors and mirror neurons. *Archives Italiennes de Biologie*, *137*, 85–100.

Rolls, E.T. (1999). *The brain and emotion*. Oxford: Oxford University Press.

Rowe, A.D., Bullock, P.R., Polkey, C.E., & Morris, R.G. (2001). 'Theory of mind' impairments and their relationship to executive functioning following frontal lobe lesions. *Brain*, *124*, 600–616.

Samuels, R. (1998). Evolutionary psychology and the massive modularity hypothesis. *British Journal for the Philosophy of Science*, *49*, 575–602.

Samuels, R. (2000). Massively modular minds: evolutionary psychology and cognitive architecture. In P. Carruthers & A. Chamberlain (Eds.), *Evolution and the human mind: Modularity, language and meta-cognition* (pp. 13–46). Cambridge: Cambridge University Press.

Sawaguchi, T., & Kudo, H. (1990). Neocortical development and social structure in primates. *Primates*, *31*, 283–290.

Scott, S., Young, A.W., Calder, A.J., Hellawell, D.J., Aggleton, J.P., & Johnson, M. (1997). Impaired auditory recognition of fear and anger following bilateral amygdala lesions. *Nature*, *385*, 254–257.

Shallice, T. (1988). *From neuropsychology to mental structure*. Cambridge: Cambridge University Press.

Shapiro, L. and Epstein, W. (1998). Evolutionary theory meets cognitive psychology: A more selective perspective. *Mind and Language*, *13*, 171–194.

Sperber, D. (1996). *Explaining culture: A naturalistic approach*. Oxford: Basil Blackwell.

Sterelny, K. (1990). *The representational theory of mind: An introduction*. Oxford: Basil Blackwell.

Sterelny, K. (1995). Review of *The Adapted Mind*. *Biology and Philosophy*, *10*, 255–285.

Sterelny, K., & Griffiths, P.E. (1999). *Sex and death: An introduction to philosophy of biology*. Chicago: University of Chicago Press.

Stone, V., Cosmides, L., Tooby, J., Kroll, R., & Knight, N. (2002). Selective impairment of reasoning about social exchange in a patient with bilateral limbic system damage. *Proceedings of the National Academy of Sciences, 99*, 11531–11536.

Stone, V.E. (2000). The role of the frontal lobes and the amygdala in theory of mind. In S. Baron-Cohen, H. Tager-Flusberg, & D.J. Cohen (Eds.), *Understanding other minds: Perspectives from developmental cognitive neuroscience* (2nd ed., pp. 253–273). Oxford: Oxford University Press.

Stone, V.E., Baron-Cohen, S., & Knight, R.T. (1998). Frontal lobe contributions to theory of mind. *Journal of Cognitive Neuroscience, 10*, 640–656.

Stone, V.E., Cosmides, L., & Tooby, J. (1996). *Selective impairment of cheater detection: Neurological evidence for adaptive specialization*. Paper presented at the 8th Annual Meeting of the Human Behavior and Evolution Society, Northwestern University, Evanston, IL.

Stuss, D.T., Gallup, G.G., & Alexander, M.P. (2001). The frontal lobes are necessary for 'theory of mind'. *Brain, 124*, 279–286.

Symons, D. (1992). On the use and misuse of Darwinism in the study of human behavior. In J.H. Barkow, L. Cosmides, & J. Tooby (Eds.), *The adapted mind: Evolutionary psychology and the generation of culture* (pp. 137–159). New York: Oxford University Press.

Todd, P.M., Fiddick, L., & Krauss, S. (2000). Ecological rationality and its contents. *Thinking and Reasoning, 6*, 375–384.

Tomasello, M., & Call, J. (1997). *Primate cognition*. New York: Oxford University Press.

Tooby, J., & Cosmides, L. (1992). The psychological foundations of culture. In J.H. Barkow, L. Cosmides, & J. Tooby (Eds.), *The adapted mind: Evolutionary psychology and the generation of culture* (pp. 19–136). New York: Oxford University Press.

Tooby, J., & Cosmides, L. (1995). Mapping the evolved functional organization of mind and brain. In M.S. Gazzaniga (Ed.), *The cognitive neurosciences* (pp. 1185–1197). Cambridge, MA: MIT Press/Bradford Books.

Tooby, J., & Cosmides, L. (2000). Toward mapping the evolved functional organization of mind and brain. In M.S. Gazzaniga (Ed.), *The new cognitive neurosciences* (2nd ed.). Cambridge, MA: MIT Press/Bradford Books.

Tranel, D. (1997). Emotional processing and the human amygdala. *Trends in Cognitive Sciences, 1*, 46–47.

Tranel, D., Bechara, A., & Damasio, A.R. (2000). Decision making and the somatic marker hypothesis. In M.S. Gazzaniga (Ed.), *The new cognitive neurosciences* (2nd ed.). Cambridge, MA: MIT Press/Bradford Books.

Trivers, R. (1971). The evolution of reciprocal altruism. *Quarterly Review of Biology, 4*, 35–57.

Ts'o, D.Y., & Roe, A.W. (1995). Functional compartments in visual cortex: Segregation and interaction. In M.S. Gazzaniga (Ed.), *The cognitive neurosciences* (pp. 325–337). Cambridge, MA: MIT Press/Bradford Books.

Ungerleider, L.G., & Mishkin, M. (1982). Two cortical visual systems. In D.J. Ingle, M.A. Goodale, & R.J.W. Mansfield (Eds.), *Analysis of visual behavior* (pp. 549–586). Cambridge, MA: MIT Press.

Van Essen, D., & Deyoe, E. (1995). Concurrent processing in the primate visual cortex. In M.S. Gazzaniga (Ed.), *The cognitive neurosciences* (pp. 383–400). Cambridge, MA: MIT Press/Bradford Books.

Van Essen, D.C. (1985). Functional organization of primate visual cortex. In A. Peters & E.G. Jones (Eds.), *Cerebral cortex, Vol. 3: Visual cortex* (pp. 259–329). New York: Plenum Press.

Watanabe, Y., & Yamagishi, T. (1999). Emergence of strategies in a selective play environment with geographic mobility: A computer simulation. In M. Foddy, M. Smithson, et al. (Eds.), *Resolving social dilemmas: Dynamic, structural, and intergroup aspects* (pp. 55–66). Philadelphia, PA: Psychology Press.

Weiskrantz, L. (1956). Behavioral changes associated with ablations of the amygdaloid complex in monkeys. *Journal of Comparative Physiology and Psychology*, *49*, 381–391.

Whalen, P. (1999). Fear, vigilance, and ambiguity: Initial neuroimaging studies of the human amygdala. *Current Directions in Psychological Science*, *7*, 177–187.

Wheeler, M., & Atkinson, A.P. (2001). Domains, brains, and evolution. In D.M. Walsh & A. O'Hear (Eds.), *Evolution, naturalism and mind* (pp. 239–266). Cambridge: Cambridge University Press.

Whiten, A. (Ed.) (1991). *Natural theories of mind: Evolution, development and simulation of everyday mindreading*. Oxford: Basil Blackwell.

Whiten, A. (1999). The evolution of deep social mind in humans. In M.C. Corballis & S.E.G. Lea (Eds.), *The descent of mind: Psychological perspectives on hominid evolution* (pp. 173–193). Oxford: Oxford University Press.

Whiten, A., & Byrne, R.W. (1988). Tactical deception in primates. *Behavioral and Brain Sciences*, *11*, 233–273.

Whiten, A., & Byrne, R.W. (1997). *Machiavellian intelligence II: Extensions and evaluations*. Cambridge: Cambridge University Press.

Williams, G.C. (1966). *Adaptation and natural selection: A critique of some current evolutionary thought*. Princeton, NJ: Princeton University Press.

Young, A.W. (1998). *Face and mind*. Oxford: Oxford University Press.

Young, A.W., Aggleton, J.P., Hellawell, D.J., Johnson, M., Broks, P., & Hanley, J.R. (1995). Face processing impairments after amygdalotomy. *Brain*, *118*, 15–24.

Young, A.W., Hellawell, D.J., Van De Wal, C., & Johnson, M. (1996). Facial expression processing after amygdalotomy. *Neuropsychologia*, *34*, 31–39.

CHAPTER FOUR

Specialized behaviour without specialized modules

Amit Almor
Department of Psychology, University of Southern California,
Los Angeles, USA

INTRODUCTION

Evolutionary psychology has received much attention recently both within the scientific world and in the popular media (Dennett, 1995; Pinker, 1997). The reason for the high interest in this new field is not hard to understand. Evolutionary psychology, if correct, has the potential to provide a scientific explanation of what makes us the way we are, think, feel, and act the way we do, and most importantly, how we have come to be this way. As a discipline, evolutionary psychology is based on the application of the tools developed by evolutionary biologists to the study of psychological mechanisms. The under-lying premise is that just as a certain biological structure in a specific organ-ism could be understood as a solution to an adaptive problem in the environment of that organism, so could a human mental mechanism be understood as a solution to an adaptive problem faced by humans or their humanoid ancestors in their relevant environment (Tooby & Cosmides, 1992). Evolutionary psychologists further believe that identifying the adap-tive context of mental mechanisms could shed light not only on how they emerged but also on how they work (Cosmides, 1989; Pinker, 1997). Indeed, there are some areas in which the contribution of this evolutionary logic to psychology is clearly evident. The study of several aspects of sexuality, emo-tions, and perception has made significant progress by considering the adap-tive context in which the related mental and brain mechanisms evolved (Shepard, 1994; Solomon et al., 2000; Symons, 1979; Tooby & Cosmides,

1990a, 1990b). In other areas of psychology, however, most notably in the area of thinking and reasoning, the value of evolutionary psychology is marred by overly strong claims that are often made on the basis of questionable empirical evidence. One of the most contentious claims made by some evolutionary psychologists in this area is that taking evolution seriously necessarily entails a view of the mind as consisting of specialized domain-specific modules, each of which provides the solution to an individual adaptive problem (Cosmides, 1989). In the present chapter, I will argue that it is unwarranted to make an *a priori* commitment to highly domain-specific mechanisms without first giving sufficient consideration to the adaptive value of domain-general mechanisms. I will further argue that the evolutionary rationale for the emergence of general mechanisms is as good as any argument previously made in favour of domain-specific mechanisms and that, consequently, the domain specificity of studied behaviours should be considered an empirical question. To support my argument I will demonstrate that in the most central area where empirical evidence has been claimed to support domain specificity—social reasoning and cheater detection (Cosmides, 1989; Gigerenzer & Hug, 1992)—the empirical evidence is weak and could be also explained by a more general mechanism. Finally, I will propose such a general mechanism that is based on connectionist principles. Although this mechanism relies mostly on domain-independent principles, it allows for the emergence of seemingly domain-specific behaviours when operating on particular kinds of inputs. In conclusion, I would suggest that evolutionary psychology is better off without an *a priori* commitment to a large number of specialized mental modules. Overall, the present work is not aimed as a general critique of the use of evolutionary arguments in psychological theories but only against the widespread belief that such arguments necessarily lead to a view of the mind as consisting of a large number of domain-specialized modules (Cosmides, 1989).

DOMAIN SPECIFICITY IN EVOLUTIONARY PSYCHOLOGY

The application of evolutionary principles to the study of any complex biological system involves several steps. The preliminary and possibly most important step is the identification of the adaptive problem the system under study may have evolved to solve (Plotkin, 1998; Tooby & Cosmides, 1992). This step entails certain assumptions about the specific environment of the organism under study, as well as the challenges that this environment may have presented the organism with at the time the system under study had evolved. An important aspect of identifying the adaptive problem relevant to a given biological system is that, frequently, there is not one but several related adaptive problems that *together* may have affected natural selection.

For example, whereas it is plausible to assume that the need to forage consti-
tuted an initial adaptive problem that selected for locomotion ability, it would
be a mistake not to consider the fact that the evolution of locomotion ability
was in many cases affected by the existence of predators. Biological locomotion that has evolved mainly to address the foraging problem would not have
the same characteristics as a locomotion system that has also evolved to
address the problem of outrunning predators. There is, of course, no *a priori*
reason to expect that locomotion should address both foraging and predator
avoidance in all species. Indeed, many species have evolved separate solutions
to the two problems and do not rely on locomotion to evade predators.
However, the fact that in some species locomotion has evolved as a solution
to both problems highlights the importance of considering the range of possibly relevant adaptive problems when examining any given system. Similarly,
a given adaptation could be addressed by more than one biological system.
Thus, for example, predator avoidance could be addressed by locomotion,
camouflage, toxicity, deception, and so on. Considering as much of the adaptive context as possible is especially important when the system in question is
known in advance to be flexible and well adapted to solve a wide range of
tasks. Brains are arguably one of the most flexible biological systems in that
they show remarkable plasticity, a high degree of dependency on environmental input in the course of development, and overall are well adapted to
deal with a remarkably diverse range of tasks. Granted, brains are not equi-
potential general-purpose computational machines but the degree to which
various brain mechanisms are adapted to deal with various problems, and
consequently the likelihood that various brain mechanisms evolved to deal
with certain adaptive problems and not others, is an empirical question. It is
thus quite remarkable that many evolutionary psychologists (most notably
Tooby, Cosmides, and their colleagues), whose ultimate goal is to explain how
the brain processes information, would abandon the practice from biology of
examining as much of the adaptive context as possible and assume, *a priori*,
that the brain consists of many specialized mechanisms each of which has
developed in response to an *individual* adaptive problem, even when it is likely
that there were other closely related adaptive problems. The logic of the
motivation provided by these evolutionary psychologists (Cosmides & Tooby,
1997) for making this *a priori* assumption can be summarized as follows:

Much research in social sciences has failed to recognize the important role
biological biases play in learning and has instead assumed that a few general-
purpose learning principles can explain all cognitive processes.

   This so-called Standard Social Science Model is wrong.

   Therefore, the correct way to construct theories of cognition is to *a priori*
assume that any behaviour of interest is generated by a special-purpose
mechanism that has evolved to address one adaptive problem but not others.

*

This argument is obviously wrong. The Standard Social Science Model is quite probably false but there may still not be a single brain mechanism that has evolved to solve only one adaptive problem. The point here is not that there are or are not brain mechanisms that are specialized to solve individual adaptive problems but simply that there is no way of knowing in advance. Discerning whether a certain psychological mechanism is highly specialized to solve a specific adaptive problem requires a careful examination of both the theoretical considerations and the relevant empirical evidence in the context of *all* the possibly relevant adaptive problems. As will be explained in more detail below, the failure to consider the broader adaptive context of human behaviour represents the most serious shortcoming of evolutionary psychology theories of thinking and reasoning.

EVOLUTIONARY PSYCHOLOGY AND CHEATER DETECTION

The application of evolutionary analysis to psychological processes rests on several premises that are relatively uncontroversial (Plotkin, 1998). The first premise is that the process of natural selection is "genocentric" in that the entities whose replication drives this process are the genes and not the individuals that carry them or the species these individuals belong to (Dawkins, 1989). Due to the nature of natural selection, genetic changes that increase the reproductive success of the individuals who carry them will tend to spread through a species for as long as they confer their reproductive advantage. Genetic changes can occur for a variety of reasons but only those changes that, at the bottom line, confer a reproductive advantage or are bundled with other changes that confer a reproductive advantage, will tend to spread. The emphasis on the gene as the unit whose replication drives the process of natural selection is important because it provides the key to understanding why various forms of altruism, especially those involving kin, are consistent with natural selection. A gene that induces behaviour in an individual that increases the likelihood of the gene's successful replication will tend to spread through the population even if this spread is achieved by other individuals (Axelrod, 1984, 1997; Skyrms, 1996). Thus, altruistic behaviour is consistent with natural selection if it improves the replication odds of the underlying genes, even if it decreases the survival odds of the altruistic individual. For example, parental altruism could be expected in cases when the genes of a parent have better odds to replicate and spread if the parent acts altruistically and invests effort in its offspring than if the parent acts selfishly and invests the same effort in itself. This "genocentric" logic can also explain cooperation behaviour between individuals. Cooperation could be generally described as an agreement whereby the cooperating parties pay some cost by making a certain effort or by taking a certain risk in exchange to obtaining some benefit. Such cooperative behaviour is observed in many species and is consistent with natural selection for as long as, at the bottom line, it increases the replication odds of the underlying genes.

It is important to note that none of this means that a certain genetic change will either spread to the entire population of a species or disappear altogether. In many cases, further spread of a certain property would result in reduced reproductive success of all the individuals sharing the property, which would lead in turn to a reduction in the number of individuals having this property. However, once the number of individuals sharing the property goes down below a certain threshold, the property can become advantageous again. Such situation can result in an "evolutionary equilibrium" wherein only a certain part of a species' population has a certain property (Skyrms, 1996). Thus, certain genetically determined behaviours can spread to only a certain part of a species' population and the proportion of individuals who do and don't exhibit this behaviour can remain stable. For example, if individuals of a certain species are generally able to cooperate then cheating behaviour, namely taking an unfair advantage of a cooperation with another individual (either by not paying the perquisite cost or by taking an unfair part of the benefit), may become a genetically determined behaviour that will spread to only a part of the population. This is because the advantage conferred by cheating, which depends on the relative costs and benefits of cooperating and cheating, may be related to the number of cheaters in the population such that if the likelihood of being cheated goes beyond a certain threshold (i.e. there are too many cheaters), cheating becomes disadvantageous. However, as long as cheating is not very common it remains an advantageous behaviour (see Skyrms, 1996, for a detailed computational illustration of these issues).

A related point is that natural selection rarely results in changes that are present to exactly the same extent in all members of the species. This variability in the properties of individuals from the same species can be due to genetic differences (e.g. a gene that hasn't spread to the entire population, interaction between various genes, etc.) or due to environmental factors that modulate the expression of the genes. Differences between individuals not only affect the individuals' own reproduction success but also their value for the reproduction success of their conspecies. A strong individual not only has a better chance of surviving longer than a weak individual, and thus have more reproduction opportunities and possibly better cared-for offspring, but can also increase the reproduction success of its mates and its allies. This means that the ability to discern certain properties of conspecies could confer a reproductive advantage. Thus, genetic changes that lead to an improved ability to detect important properties of conspecies who are potential partners for some activity (e.g. mating, cooperation, etc.) are likely to spread through a population. For example, because the ability to detect the fertility of a potential mate can increase an individual's reproduction success, a genetic change resulting in an improved ability to recognize a mate's fertility is prone to spread in a population of a species. The speed and likelihood of such spread would probably depend, among other things, on the cost of mating in the species. When there are few mating opportunities, a missed opportunity to have offspring due to a mate's infertility could have a significant adverse effect on the reproductive success of an individual. The ability to estimate fertility in a potential mate in such circumstances is more likely to spread than when mating opportunities are abundant and a single mating is relatively costless. This can vary between species and even between males and females of the same species (Cronin, 1991; Symons, 1979).

Based on these relatively uncontroversial premises, evolutionary psychologists Cosmides and Tooby argued that significant parts of high level human cognition is based on specialized mechanisms that provide genetically encoded solutions to highly specific adaptive problems (Cosmides, 1989; Cosmides & Tooby, 1992, 1997). The flagship example they used, which is often cited as the paradigmatic example of evolutionary psychology in action, is cheater detection. Based on the principles described above, Cosmides and Tooby have argued that the conditions during the Pleistocene period in human evolution, when significant aspects of human high level cognition probably evolved, made cooperation a highly valuable behaviour, possibly necessary for survival. Consequently, cheating behaviour could have become very advantageous and thus spread to significant parts of the population. This spread in turn allowed the ability to detect cheaters to also become an advantageous behaviour that consequently spread through the population. This theory thus states that cheater detection is a genetically based behaviour that may have evolved a long time ago but still governs the way we reason about situations that trigger it. The basic claims of this theory, namely that cooperation, cheating, and cheater detection ability are likely to have evolved in this order, are supported by several computational investigations of the spread of different strategies to solve various model cooperation problems, such as the Prisoner's Dilemma (Skyrms, 1996). Both the theoretical arguments and the computational investigations make several simplifying assumptions that raise several problems.

Problem 1: Circumstantial variability

The major problem in the evolutionary psychology theory of cheater detection is the leap from an argument for why it is likely that humans have evolved to be effective cheater detectors to the conclusion that this ability must be the product of domain-specific mechanisms. Indeed, there is little doubt that humans have a substantial genetic endowment that underlies much social behaviour and that the human ability to cheat and detect cheaters owes to this genetic endowment. This does not entail, however, that cheating and cheater-detection behaviours are caused by a mental organ that has evolved for just this purpose. A close examination of the evolutionary argument for specialized cheater detection reveals several problems. First, although cheating and cheater detection may seem relatively simple notions, their evolutionary context is rather complex. Recall that the evolutionary rationale for cooperation, cheating, and cheater detection was in all cases the increased reproduction advantage conferred by these behaviours to the underlying genes. In reality, it is not clear that cheating or cheater detection would be advantageous in all cases or even in most cases. Instead, it is more likely that cheating and cheater detection would have variable effect on reproduction success depending on many factors. Some examples for such factors are kin relation between the cooperating parties (both cheating and cheater detection should be less likely among kin), the power relation between the cooperating individuals (the cost and benefit of cheating and of detecting a cheater would be different depending on the relative strength and social status of the involved individuals), and the sexes of the cooperating individuals (males and females may face different risks and subsequently may gain differently from cheating and/or from detecting cheaters). Thus, even when only considering cheating and cheater-detection behaviours, evolutionary analysis favours a complex and flexible mechanism that should be capable of weighing in the complex costs and benefits of cheating and detecting cheaters under a wide range of variable social circumstances. When the broader context of other adaptive challenges in the social domain, such as mating, parenting, and sibling relations, is also considered, it becomes unclear why a complex cost/benefit mechanism would be restricted to cheating or cheater detection. Most actions in the social context could be assigned costs and benefits in terms of their expected effect on reproduction success and there seem to be no *a priori* reason to assume that the weighing of these costs and benefits is achieved through a different mechanism in each possible scenario. Obviously, one could argue that while there may be some cost/benefit mechanism that is not specific to individual social problems, the generation of the costs and benefits that are the inputs to the general mechanism is. Note, however, that this is already a very different story than the specialized domain-specific mechanisms favoured by Cosmides and Tooby in that it allows much broader information to affect supposedly specific behaviours such as cheating and cheater detection. Importantly, such a story, which is compatible with several existing theories of social reasoning (Manktelow & Over, 1995; Oaksford & Chater, 1996; Over & Manktelow, 1993), also assumes that subjective utilities and costs, and not cheating or cheater detection, are the important elements of decision making in social contexts and thus also for the natural selection processes that shaped this decision-making ability. Such a general mechanism, whose scope covers at least the social domain, is not informationally encapsulated in that its operation is affected by information from many external sources. It therefore does not meet the criteria for a specialized mental module that was established in Fodor's influential "The modularity of mind" (Fodor, 1983), and is thus not compatible with Tooby and Cosmides's notion of specialized modules.

Problem 2: Historical variability

The inherent complexity in determining the adaptive value of cheating and cheater detection in any given circumstances raises another related concern, which is the historical variability in the physical and social characteristics of the environment in which humans evolved. Indeed, human evolution has taken place under fairly diverse and constantly changing contexts (Diamond, 1997). The adaptive value of cheating and detecting cheaters is likely to have been quite different in those periods and places where most of the human population consisted of small groups than in those periods and places where humans lived in large groups. Cheating or punishing a cheater in the first kind of circumstances may not have been advantageous because the effort of each individual would have been crucial to the survival of all the individuals in the group including the cheater. In the latter kind of circumstances, however, cheating may have been more advantageous and punishing cheaters (for example by excluding them from future cooperation) may not have had much adverse effect on the punishers. Similarly, differences in resource availability may also have contributed to fluctuations in the adaptive value of cheating and cheater detection. This historical variability in the parameters of the relevant adaptive problem poses a problem for any theory that argues that a highly specialized mechanism has evolved to address this problem.

One way of extending the argument for specialized mechanisms to address the implications of historical variability is to postulate that humans may have evolved different cheating propensities and different cheater-detection abilities in different periods. Clearly, differences in the physical environments of different races have affected the process of natural selection in humans, as is apparent by the fact that different races have developed different skin pigmentation in response to regional differences in solar radiation. It is also likely that not only differences in the physical but also in the social environment of different human societies have had an effect on the process of natural selection. This is suggested by racial differences in germ resistance and lactose tolerance, which have arguably resulted from differences in societal structure in different regions (Diamond, 1997). Thus, if cheating and cheater detection are the result of specialized mental and brain mechanisms, and indeed if different physical and social environments render cheating and cheater detection more or less advantageous, we should expect racial diversity in cheating tendency and in cheater detection ability according to the social history and geographical origin. Given, however, that to date there is no evidence for racial differences in cheating or cheater-detection behaviours, the possibility that they result from a mechanism that was fine-tuned to deal with the specialized problem of cooperation in a specific historical context seems unlikely.

One other possible way to extend the specialized mechanism view to address historical variability is by arguing that, through natural selection, the relevant environmental parameters may have entered the mechanism of cheater detection such that its operation is modulated by social and physical environmental conditions such as group size and resource availability. Note, however, that again, this indicates that cheater detection must be a complex and flexible mechanism that would be very hard to delineate from other closely related and equally complex mechanisms.

Given the circumstantial and historical variability in the adaptive value of cheating and cheater detection it seems plausible that a flexible mechanism that would be powerful enough to solve a range of adaptive problems could have spread in early humans and, importantly, survived subsequent changes in the physical and social environmental conditions. A highly specialized mechanism may have been a better solution to the adaptive problem presented by cooperation in a specific period under specific conditions but is not likely to have remained very effective when conditions changed. Such a highly specific mechanism would therefore be very likely to be selected out of the human endowment when conditions change and the behaviour it generates starts decreasing reproductive success. A more flexible mechanism, however, would not be likely to disappear as conditions change. More specifically, a reasoning mechanism that relies on the broader notions of cost and utility could have provided good adaptive solutions to a range of adaptive problems both in the social and nonsocial domains. Also, once such a mechanism has become part of the human genetic endowment it is likely to remain part of it.

In summary, theoretical considerations seem to favour a model of cognition based on cognitive mechanisms that are more general than specialized in that they allow for a high degree of flexibility in the range of problems they address as well as in the solutions they provide for individual problems under different conditions. Most importantly, these theoretical considerations show clearly that there are simply no evolutionary grounds for assuming *a priori* that mental mechanisms are highly specialized for individual problems in specific domains. Instead, domain specialization should be considered an empirical question. The next section reviews some of the central empirical evidence for domain specialization.

CHEATER DETECTION—THE EMPIRICAL EVIDENCE

To date, most of the empirical evidence supporting specialized cheater detection comes from a single task—the Wason four-card selection task (Wason,

1966). This task has a long history in psychology, where it has been used extensively to study the effect of context and experience on reasoning. Specifically, much research with the selection task concentrated on distinguishing between domains in which reasoning seems to operate differently. It should not be surprising, therefore, that the selection task has had an important role in research that seeks to demonstrate reasoning behaviour that is specialized to problems in specific domains. In the original version of the Wason selection task, participants are required to decide how to test the truthfulness of an arbitrary rule of the form "if P then Q"[1] like the following vowel-even number rule: "If a card has a vowel on one side then it must have an even number on the other side". They are shown four cards and are told that each card represents a single combination of P and Q values. Their task is to decide which cards to turn over to test the rule. Because participants can only see one side of each card (i.e. "A", "4", "B", "7" in the vowel-even number problem), they have to judge, according to what is on the visible side, whether the invisible side may be useful for testing the rule. The general finding is that with many abstract problems, like the arbitrary vowel-even number problem, people tend to select only the P card (i.e. the card with the letter "A"), or both the P and Q cards (i.e. the card with the letter "A" and the card with the number "4") (Cox & Griggs, 1982; Wason & Shapiro, 1971). However, in some domains, the predominant selection is P & ~Q (Cheng & Holyoak, 1985; Cox & Griggs, 1982). For example, in the day-off problem used by Gigerenzer and Hug (1992), in which participants are required to test whether a rule set by a company, "If an employee gets a day off during the week then that employee must have worked at the weekend", is violated by employees, most participants select the P and ~Q cards ("An employee who gets a day off during the week", and "An employee who did not work at the weekend").

The sharp difference between response patterns in different domains has been argued to provide evidence for domain specialized reasoning (Cheng & Holyoak, 1985; Cosmides, 1989; Gigerenzer & Hug, 1992). Most relevantly here, it had been observed that many of the domains in which the majority of people select the P and ~Q cards include some kind of social relation that should be respected yet could be violated. In these domains, it has been argued, people interpret the selection task as detecting a violation of a conventional rule, and thus pick the two cards that may represent such a violation. In this view, domains in which the P or the P & Q selections are predominant elicit a different reasoning mechanism that does not involve violation detection.

Recent research, however, has shown that a predominant P & ~Q selection can be elicited in a range of domains where card selection could not be

---

[1] Variable names appear in capitals and variable values appear in lower case.

construed as detecting a violation of a social relation (Almor & Sloman, 1996; Sperber, Cara, & Girotto, 1995). For example, Almor and Sloman (1996) showed that people's selection performance in domains such as containment, force dynamics, prize winning, and quality control is indistinguishable from their performance on problems that could be construed as involving violation detection. Thus, the distinction between problems that lead to a high proportion of P & ~Q selections and problems that do not cannot be based solely on whether the problem involves violation detection. Obviously, the finding that selection responses in violation detection tasks are similar to selection responses in other domains means very little. It certainly does not mean that cheater detection cannot engage a specialized reasoning mechanism that happens to yield behaviour that is analogous to the behaviour yielded by other reasoning mechanisms. The major significance of finding similar selection patterns in violation and nonviolation contexts is simply in showing that selection responses do not provide empirical evidence for specialized reasoning. This squarely counters claims made by evolutionary psychologists that strong and replicable P & ~Q selection responses are an indicator of violation detection scenarios.

Another property that has been argued to be unique to cheater-detection reasoning is its dependency on the perspective from which the possible cheating is examined. The major finding in experiments that purport to demonstrate perspective effects is that the participants make card selections according to the perspective they are cued into and not according to the formal structure of the rule as stated in the problem (Fairley, Manktelow, & Over, 1999; Gigerenzer & Hug, 1992; Manktelow & Over, 1991). For example, using the day-off rule ("If an employee gets a day off during the week then that employee must have worked at the weekend"), Gigerenzer and Hug observed that when cued into the perspective of the company most participants selected the "Did not work at the weekend" (~Q) and "Got a day off during the week" (P) cards, but when cued into the perspective of an employee wishing to check whether the company is not keeping its part of the deal, many participants selected the "Worked at the weekend" (Q), and "Did not get a day off during the week" (~P) cards. According to Gigerenzer and Hug, these perspective-dependent selection patterns are unique to contexts that allow cheating and therefore provide further empirical evidence for the existence of specialized cheater-detection mechanism.

Recent research, however, has found perspective effects in contexts that do not involve any cheating or cheater detection (Fairley et al., 1999; Staller, Sloman, & Ben-Zeev, 2000). Other research has further investigated the nature of perspective-based reasoning and found it to be no different than any other interpretive process that is involved in text comprehension. More specifically, Almor and Sloman (2000) asked participants to recall the rule from a previously read perspective reversal problem and found that people tended to recall a rule that was compatible with the perspective they were cued into rather than the rule that actually appeared in the problem. Almor and Sloman subsequently concluded that the perspective effects reported by Gigerenzer and Hug are better understood as the product of domain-general text interpretation that is sensitive to knowledge from many different domains, including perspective. Finally, Fairley, Manktelow, and Over (1999) have further shown that the interpretive processing involved in perspective-based reasoning generalizes to causal conditionals and could be explained both in the social and causal domain by one general reasoning mechanism that could be described in the nondomain specific terms of mental models theory (Johnson-Laird, 1983). As before, showing that perspective-based behaviour can be found in noncheating contexts, or showing that it could be the product of a general, nonspecialized mechanism does not necessarily mean that there isn't a specialized cheater detection mechanism; it only shows that an important part of the empirical evidence in support of specialized cheater detection is in fact compatible with a nonspecialized view of reasoning.

The discussion so far has shown that specialized mental mechanisms are not a logical consequence of following evolutionary analysis and that some of the most important empirical evidence for domain specialization is inconclusive. The next and final section of this chapter will outline an alternative framework that is based on connectionist principles that are, to a large extent, domain general.

A CONNECTIONIST PERSPECTIVE

Human reasoning is not the only area within cognitive psychology where claims for domain specialization have been made and debated. In psycholinguistics, debates about specialization and modularity have been going on for many years, especially in the area of lexical processing (Pinker, 1999; Seidenberg, 1997). Whereas some researchers believe that most, if not all, lexical processes could be explained on the basis of relatively domain-general learning principles, other researchers argue that a full consideration of all available evidence necessitates domain-specific knowledge (Pinker, 1999). Crucial evidence for and against specialized modules has come from the use of connectionist models. These models, which generally embody powerful domain-general learning principles, allow a detailed examination of the relation between theory and observed behaviour. In the area of lexical processing, for example, a close examination of the performance of connectionist models has shown that behaviours that were previously considered to provide clear evidence for the existence of domain-specific mechanisms could in fact emerge from domain general mechanisms (Seidenberg, 1997). Consequently, most researchers in the field agree that domain-general connectionist-like mechanisms underlie at least some areas of lexical processing. The remaining debate is about whether there are other lexical processes that could not be understood as the product of connectionist-like mechanisms and therefore require assuming other, domain-specific, mechanisms. In the course of the debate on the nature of lexical processes, several important properties of connectionist models have been identified. These properties characterize the operation of domain-general experience-based processes and could be there-fore generalized from connectionist models of lexical processing to con-nectionist models in other domains even if the specific details of these domains are quite different. Although no specific connectionist model will be described here, some of the properties of connectionist models will be drawn upon in the following discussion in an attempt to ascertain whether domain-general experience-based mechanisms could yield seemingly domain-specific behaviour.

Regulars, irregulars, and connectionist models

One question that spawned considerable debate in the literature on lexical processing concerns the proper explanation of the differences and similarities between so-called "regular" and "irregular" phenomena (Marchman, 1997; Pinker, 1999; Plunkett & Juola, 1999). For example, inflectional morphology, namely the process of applying inflections such as the past tense to the verbs' base form, seems to operate in two distinct ways. Regular inflections seem to be rule governed in the sense that they are not sensitive to the properties of individual lexical items. In contrast, irregular inflections seem to be related to the phonological properties of specific stems and the inflected forms. For example, in English, the past tense form of most verbs could be derived by applying the default rule "add -ed" to the base form of the verbs, but there are certain "irregular" verbs whose past tense form is related to the base form via an idiosyncratic mapping. Furthermore, the irregular verbs but not the regular verbs are organized in neighbourhoods of similarly sounding verbs that share the same idiosyncratic mappings from base to inflected form (Pinker, 1999). Also, the ease of learning irregular past tense forms as well as the likelihood of making errors in their production are sensitive to the fre-quency of the verb but the learning ease of regularly inflected verbs and the likelihood of making errors using them are not (Pinker, 1999). Finally, irregu-larly inflected verbs tend to occur with higher frequency in the language whereas regular verbs occur with either high or low frequency in the language (Pinker, 1999). These differences have motivated an influential view of the underlying lexical mechanisms according to which irregular verbs are pro-cessed via a connectionist-like experience-based memory system and regu-larly inflected verbs are processed primarily through a rule-based mechanism (Pinker, 1999). In addition to the memory system and the rule application mechanism, this theory also stipulates a blocking mechanism that blocks the application of the default rule when the memory system produces an inflected form. The proponents of this theory consider the rule mechanism and the blocking mechanism to be specialized and domain specific in the same sense that Tooby and Cosmides consider cheater detection to be specialized and domain specific. It will thus be useful to consider how connectionist models have challenged the specialized mechanisms view in the area of inflectional morphology, leading instead to a view according to which one connectionist-like memory system that is not domain specific underlies the processing of both regular and irregular inflections. It should be noted here that whereas early connectionist models of inflectional morphology have been correctly criticized for making many unrealistic assumptions and making false predictions (Pinker & Prince, 1988; Prince & Pinker, 1988), more recent work has employed more realistic assumptions about the representation of the input and has consequently led to empirical predictions that have been confirmed (Plunkett & Juola, 1999; Plunkett & Marchman, 1996). The purpose of the present discussion is not to take sides in the argument about the nature of inflectional morphology but instead to examine whether, correct or not, observations about connectionist models of inflectional morphology could be useful in debates about domain specialization in reasoning.

In many connectionist models of the production of the English past tense, the same network handles both regular and irregular forms by mapping an input base form to an output inflected form. The internal representations that allow these models to perform this mapping are the product of applying general learning principles that are sensitive to various statistical properties of the relations between the base and inflected forms. Importantly, the same principles govern the learning of regular mappings and irregular mappings. The only difference between regular verbs and irregular verbs therefore lies in the statistical distributions of both kinds of verbs and not in the mental mechanism that underlies their processing. The statistical differences between regular and irregular verbs could be understood in terms of the properties of the internal representations created by the model during the process of learning. These internal representations could be thought of as mappings from the multidimensional space of the phonological features of words' base forms into the multidimensional space of the phonological features of inflected forms. The base forms of regularly inflected verbs are distributed through large parts of the input space but in a rather sparse manner in the sense that they do not tend to cluster in neighbourhoods of similarly sounding verbs that share the same idiosyncratic mapping to inflected forms (Plunkett & Marchman, 1993). Instead of being mapped to inflected forms through different neighbourhood-specific mappings, all these sparsely distributed base forms are mapped similarly. In contrast, the base forms of irregularly inflected verbs tend to cluster in neighbourhoods of similarly sounding base forms that share the same idiosyncratic mapping to the inflected form. These differences in the distributional properties of regular and irregular verbs can give rise, in the right kind of model, to different patterns of performance with the two kinds of verbs without there being any specialized rule-based or blocking mechanisms. The important factor determining the performance of the model is the nature of the underlying representation in terms of its neighbourhood structure. Neighbourhoods can vary from being highly regular in the sense that the same mapping is shared by many sparsely distributed input patterns to being highly irregular in the sense that a mapping is shared by only a small number of similar input patterns (Marchman, 1997).

A connectionist model of reasoning that shares some of the important design features of models of morphological inflection could be hypothesized here. Such a hypothetical model can, for example, learn to map various physical and social input features of an observed situation, to conclusion and action output features. Importantly for this exercise, the input and output features in the model will represent information from many domains. With experience, such a model can be expected to form input to output mappings of both the "regular" and "irregular" kinds. The regular mappings will be characterized by being easy to apply to input feature patterns that may be unlike any other pattern but still fall within the space that is sparsely inhabited by other patterns. The application of the "regular" mapping will depend only weakly or not at all on the amount of the prior experience with similar patterns. In contrast, the "irregular" mappings will be characterized by being strongly dependent on the similarity between the input pattern and previously encountered input patterns, as well as on the amount of prior experience with these patterns. Such a model could develop what may seem like idiosyncratic domain-specific behaviours that may mislead an uninformed observer into believing that there are several distinct domain-specific mechanisms that yield the different behaviours. In domains where the relevant representations form spaces of the "regular" type, the model's behaviour may show no dependence on prior experience with similar inputs and may thus suggest to the uninformed observer that behaviour in this domain is governed by rules. In domains where the relevant representations form "irregular" neighbourhoods, the model's behaviour would be attributed to familiarity with similar experiences. Thus, experience with social interactions may, in theory, result in a regular type neighbourhood where prior experience with individual situations is not important to successful performance as long as sufficiently many general features of the social situation are present to bring the input pattern into the "regular" region of the space.

Obviously, this hypothetical model is at this point speculative and imprecise. But the mere possibility of such a model is enough to show that a nonspecialized mechanism could plausibly yield behaviours that may seem highly domain specific. Importantly, such a mechanism would not encounter the same objections as a specialized cheater-detection module. Its adaptive power lies in its high ability to adapt to varying circumstances and in the availability of information from many domains. It will therefore not be marred by the circumstantial variability problem, as would a highly specialized cheater-detection module. Moreover, the flexibility and domain independence of this mechanism make it likely to survive the variable circumstances of human evolution and thus circumvent the historical variability problem. Natural selection may have resulted in a domain general capacity that can lead to behaviours that are domain specific.

Limited innateness

The Standard Social Sciences Model has been correctly criticized for not allowing innate knowledge to restrict learning and thus making learning impossibly hard, especially in cases where the input seems highly impoverished (Tooby & Cosmides, 1989). Clearly, humans do have an innate capacity for certain domains such as language and are likely to have better innate capacity for reasoning in some areas such as social relations than in others, such as quantum physics. The question is, what form does this innate capacity take? Differences in the innate capacity to acquire skills in different domains do not indicate the existence of domain-specific mechanisms but may be due to some weak biases that determine the trajectory of a learning process that is otherwise domain general. The study of language is a case in point. In a highly influential paper, Chomsky (1959) argued against statistical models of language learning and instead suggested that the child must possess a specialized language-learning device. One reason, Chomsky argued, is that the input to the child is impoverished in several important ways that would make learning a language impossible without a lot of specialized knowledge. Chomsky further argued that the kind of knowledge formed by statistical learning is inadequate and incompatible with the kind of knowledge that language users must have. Recent research has shown that Chomsky was wrong on both counts. First, there is a growing body of research showing that the input to the child is much richer in statistical information than was previously thought (Christiansen, Allen, & Seidenberg, 1998; Mintz, Newport, & Bever, 1995; Morgan & Demuth, 1996; Saffran, 1998). Second, present-day statistical models, and in particular connectionist models, are in fact capable of forming the necessary knowledge representations for language use (Christiansen & Chater, 2001). Finally, it has now been shown that human infants are very good at picking up the statistical properties of the linguistic input they are exposed to (Saffran, Aslin, & Newport, 1996), a finding that makes it all the more plausible that much of the innate knowledge of language is in the input representations to an otherwise domain-general statistical learning mechanism.

In the case of reasoning, certain domains are clearly more important than others at early developmental stages. In particular, social interaction is clearly an important behaviour that, in many forms, develops very early. While this observation certainly necessitates assuming some basic innate social instincts, it does not imply specialized domain-specific reasoning modules. Rather, specialized social knowledge can be reflected in the nature and salience of initial representations. In other words, specialization may be restricted to an initial salience and detail of some basic representations. The prominence of various aspects of social interaction as well as the rich representational repertoire of costs, benefits, and theory of mind may be innate but any processes that utilize these representations, such as cheater detection and perspective-based reasoning, may not. Thus, unlike the Standard Social Science Model, the present proposal allows innate knowledge to have a biasing effect on learning and eventually on behaviour. Unlike current evolutionary psychology theories, the present proposal does not call for any domain specialization beyond an initial biasing that is reflected in some features being more salient than others. As explained above, the behaviour of connectionist-like mechanisms can seem as if it is governed by specialized mechanisms although in fact there is no specialization besides the initial representations. Domain-specific behaviour will be a function of the overlap between different experiences.

Further implications

Although at this stage the connectionist perspective outlined here is too general to make the detailed empirical predictions that an implemented model would, it is nevertheless powerful enough to make several general predictions that could not be made from the specialized modules perspective. These predictions could guide further model development and empirical investigation. In particular, the consistent interaction in connectionist models between the amount of prior experience with a given situation and its regularity, namely its relation to other experiences, leads to specific predictions. One such prediction is that familiarity would play a lesser role in domains that are more "regular" in that many different input situations are mapped to output conclusions similarly than in domains that are more "irregular". The regularity of the domain and the prior experience with the specific input could be assessed independently and reasoning performance with the specific input could be assessed with the selection task. More specifically, this prediction could be tested by examining selection task performance in different domains in relation to the prior experience subjects had with these domains and the consistency of input–output mappings in these domains. Obviously, from a specialized modules perspective there is little reason to expect any consistent relation between performance of one module in one domain and the performance of another module in another domain based on the relative familiarity and regularity of experiences in the two domains.

CONCLUSION

The many specialized modules view held by many evolutionary psychologists is not unequivocally supported by evolutionary logic, nor is it strongly supported by any empirical data. It is further weakened by the observation that domain-specific behaviour can emerge from domain-general mechanisms. Indeed, the combination of a domain-general mechanism and domain-specific information, as in a connectionist network, can have the appearance of a system in which specific behaviours are handled by separate mechanisms. Assuming domain specificity may be useful for describing certain behaviours but this descriptive convenience should not be mistaken for claims about the underlying mental mechanisms. In its current state, evolutionary psychology resembles generative linguistics, which has proved remarkably useful for describing, organizing, and discovering facts about language, but seems to have little psychological relevance. Evolutionary psychology's current distinctions between different content domains may be similarly useful for organizing behavioural observations even if they mean very little for describing the underlying psychological processes. To become a viable *psychological* theory, evolutionary psychology would need to address domain specialization not as an *a priori* assumption but as a legitimate object of study.

ACKNOWLEDGEMENTS

The writing of this chapter was supported by NIH grant RO1 AG-11774-04.

REFERENCES

Almor, A., & Sloman, S.A. (1996). Is deontic reasoning special? *Psychological Review*, *103*(2), 374–380.

Almor, A., & Sloman, S.A. (2000). Reasoning versus text processing in the Wason selection task: A nondeontic perspective on perspective effects. *Memory & Cognition*, *28*(6), 1060–1070.

Axelrod, R.M. (1984). *The evolution of cooperation*. New York: Basic Books.

Axelrod, R.M. (1997). *The complexity of cooperation: agent-based models of competition and collaboration*. Princeton, NJ: Princeton University Press.

Cheng, P.W., & Holyoak, K.J. (1985). Pragmatic reasoning schemas. *Cognitive Psychology*, *17*(4), 391–416.

Chomsky, N. (1959). Review of B.F. Skinner's verbal behavior. *Language*, *35*, 26–58.

Christiansen, M.H., Allen, J., & Seidenberg, M.S. (1998). Learning to segment speech using multiple cues: A connectionist model. *Language and Cognitive Processes*, *13*, 221–268.

Christiansen, M.H., & Chater, N. (Eds.). (2001). *Connectionist psycholinguistics*. Westport, CT: Ablex.

Cosmides, L. (1989). The logic of social exchange: Has natural selection shaped how humans reason? Studies with the Wason selection task. *Cognition, 31*(3), 187–276.

Cosmides, L., & Tooby, J. (1992). Cognitive adaptations for social exchange. In J.H. Barkow, L. Cosmides, et al. (Eds.), *The adapted mind: Evolutionary psychology and the generation of culture* (pp. 163–228). New York: Oxford University Press.

Cosmides, L., & Tooby, J. (1997). The multimodular nature of human intelligence. In A. Schiebel & J.W. Schopf (Eds.), *Origin and evolution of intelligence* (pp. 71–101). Sudbury, MA: Jones and Bartlett Publishers.

Cox, J.R., & Griggs, R.A. (1982). The effects of experience on performance in Wason's selection task. *Memory & Cognition, 10*(5), 496–502.

Cronin, H. (1991). *The ant and the peacock: altruism and sexual selection from Darwin to today.* Cambridge: Press Syndicate of the University of Cambridge.

Dawkins, R. (1989). *The selfish gene* (new ed.). Oxford: Oxford University Press.

Dennett, D.C. (1995). *Darwin's dangerous idea: Evolution and the meanings of life.* New York: Simon & Schuster.

Diamond, J.M. (1997). *Guns, germs, and steel: The fates of human societies* (1st ed.). New York: W.W. Norton & Co.

Fairley, N., Manktelow, K., & Over, D. (1999). Necessity, sufficiency, and perspective effects in causal conditional reasoning. *Quarterly Journal of Experimental Psychology: Human Experimental Psychology, 52A*(3), 771–790.

Fodor, J.A. (1983). *The modularity of mind: An essay on faculty psychology.* Cambridge, MA: MIT Press.

Gigerenzer, G., & Hug, K. (1992). Domain-specific reasoning: social contracts, cheating, and perspective change. *Cognition, 43*(2), 127–171.

Johnson-Laird, P.N. (1983). *Mental models: Towards a cognitive science of language, inference, and consciousness.* Cambridge, MA: Harvard University Press.

Manktelow, K.I., & Over, D.E. (1991). Social roles and utilities in reasoning with deontic conditionals. *Cognition, 39*(2), 85–105.

Manktelow, K.I., & Over, D.E. (1995). Deontic reasoning. In S.E. Newstead & J.St.B.T. Evans (Eds.), *Perspectives on thinking and reasoning: Essays in honour of Peter Wason* (pp. 91–114). Hillsdale, NJ: Lawrence Erlbaum Associates, Inc.

Marchman, V.A. (1997). Children's productivity in the English past tense: The role of frequency, phonology, and neighborhood structure. *Cognitive Science, 21*(3), 283–304.

Mintz, T.H., Newport, E.L., & Bever, T.G. (1995). Distributional regularities of form class in speech to young children. In J. Beckman (Ed.), *Proceedings of the 25th Annual Meeting of the North Eastern Linguistics Society.* Amherst, MA: GLSA.

Morgan, J.L., & Demuth, K. (Eds.). (1996). *Signal to syntax: Bootstrapping from speech to grammar in early acquisition.* Hillsdale, NJ: Lawrence Erlbaum Associates, Inc.

Oaksford, M., & Chater, N. (1996). Rational explanation of the selection task. *Psychological Review, 103*(2), 381–391.

Over, D.E., & Manktelow, K.I. (1993). Rationality, utility and deontic reasoning. In K.I. Manktelow & D.E. Over (Eds.), *Rationality: Psychological and philosophical perspectives* (pp. 231–259). Florence, KY: Taylor & Francis/Routledge.

Pinker, S. (1997). *How the mind works.* New York: W.W. Norton & Co, Inc.

Pinker, S. (1999). *Words and rules: The ingredients of language* (1st ed.). New York: Basic Books.

Pinker, S., & Prince, A. (1988). On language and connectionism: Analysis of a parallel distributed processing model of language acquisition. *Cognition, 28*(1–2), 73–193.

Plotkin, H.C. (1998). *Evolution in mind: An introduction to evolutionary psychology.* Cambridge, MA: Harvard University Press.

Plunkett, K., & Juola, P. (1999). A connectionist model of English past tense and plural morphology. *Cognitive Science, 23*(4), 463–490.

Plunkett, K., & Marchman, V. (1993). From rote learning to system building: Acquiring verb morphology in children and connectionist nets. *Cognition, 48*(1), 21–69.

Plunkett, K., & Marchman, V.A. (1996). Learning from a connectionist model of the acquisition of the English past tense. *Cognition, 61*(3), 299–308.

Prince, A., & Pinker, S. (1988). Rules and connections in human language. *Trends in Neurosciences, 11*(5), 195–202.

Saffran, J.R. (1998). Statistical learning of syntactic structure: Mechanisms and constraints. *Dissertation Abstracts International: Section B: The Sciences & Engineering, 58*(9-B), 5171.

Saffran, J.R., Aslin, R.N., & Newport, E.L. (1996). Statistical learning by 8-month-old infants. *Science, 274*(5294), 1926–1928.

Seidenberg, M.S. (1997). Language acquisition and use: Learning and applying probabilistic constraints. *Science, 275*(5306), 1599–1603.

Shepard, R.N. (1994). Perceptual–Cognitive Universals as Reflections of the World. *Psychonomic Bulletin & Review, 1*(1), 2–28.

Skyrms, B. (1996). *Evolution of the social contract.* Cambridge; New York: Cambridge University Press.

Solomon, R.C., Stearns, P.N., White, G.M., Kemper, T.D., Frijda, N.H., Brown, G.W., Cosmides, L., Tooby, J., & Tan, E.S. (2000). Part I: Interdisciplinary foundations. In M. Lewis & J.M. Haviland-Jones (Eds.), *Handbook of emotions* (2nd ed., pp. 3–134). New York, NY: The Guilford Press.

Sperber, D., Cara, F., & Girotto, V. (1995). Relevance theory explains the selection task. *Cognition, 57*(1), 31–95.

Staller, A., Sloman, S.A., & Ben-Zeev, T. (2000). Perspective effects in nondeontic versions of the Wason selection task. *Memory & Cognition, 28*(3), 396–405.

Symons, D. (1979). *The evolution of human sexuality.* New York: Oxford University Press.

Tooby, J., & Cosmides, L. (1989). Evolutionary psychology and the generation of culture: I, Theoretical considerations. *Ethology & Sociobiology, 10*(1–3), 29–49.

Tooby, J., & Cosmides, L. (1990a). On the universality of human nature and the uniqueness of the individual: The role of genetics and adaptation. *Journal of Personality, 58*(1), 17–67.

Tooby, J., & Cosmides, L. (1990b). The past explains the present: Emotional adaptations and the structure of ancestral environments. *Ethology & Sociobiology, 11*(4–5), 375–424.

Tooby, J., & Cosmides, L. (1992). The psychological foundations of culture. In J.H. Barkow, L. Cosmides & J. Tooby (Eds.), *The adapted mind: Evolutionary psychology and the generation of culture* (pp. 19–136). New York, NY: Oxford University Press.

Wason, P.C. (1966). Reasoning. In B.M. Foss (Ed.), *New horizons in psychology.* Harmondsworth, UK: Penguin.

Wason, P.C., & Shapiro, D. (1971). Natural and contrived experience in a reasoning problem. *Quarterly Journal of Experimental Psychology, 23*, 63–71.

CHAPTER FIVE

From massive modularity to metarepresentation: The evolution of higher cognition

David E. Over
School of Humanities and Social Science, University of Sunderland, UK

Many prominent evolutionary cognitive psychologists (Buss, 1999; Pinker, 1997; Tooby & Cosmides, 1992) have had a view of the mind that has been aptly termed the "Massive Modularity Hypothesis" (Samuels, 1998; Sperber, 1994). They have used tools as vivid metaphors to characterize the mind according to this hypothesis. The mind is like a Swiss army knife, with many blades dedicated to solving particular adaptive problems but no general-purpose blade (Cosmides & Tooby, 1994). Or it is like an adaptive toolbox, with many special tools, but no general one that could be applied to many jobs (Gigerenzer, Todd, & the ABC Research Group, 1999). The dedicated blades, or specialist tools, are modules that some evolutionary psychologists still call instincts (Pinker, 1994). These instinctive modules will not usually be fully fixed at birth but will be the result of a high degree of biological pre-paredness to learn some things, for example, a fear of snakes, much more easily and quickly than others, for example, a fear of flowers (Cummins & Cummins, 1999). The modules will apply only to representations with a specific content about a particular "domain" in the environment, like snakes. Thus we may feel fear if the content of our perception is that of a snake, but not if it is that of a flower. Even if we know that a module is unreliable in some way, as when we realize that some particular snake is harmless, the module may be relatively unaffected, as when we continue to fear the snake. In other words, the modules are to some degree encapsulated, in the sense of Fodor (1983, 2000).

Evolutionary psychology, broadly defined, is not necessarily committed to the Massive Modularity Hypothesis (Bradshaw, 1997). Tooby and Cosmides (1992), however, have been influential not only in supporting the Massive Modularity Hypothesis, but in arguing further that general-purpose, content-independent mechanisms could not possibly have evolved in the environment of evolutionary adaptedness (EEA), when our ancestors faced natural selection. General-purpose mechanisms would supposedly have been ". . . grossly inefficient and easily out competed . . . by content-specific mechanisms" (Cosmides & Tooby, 1992, p. 112). This is an argument, in terms of Cosmides and Tooby's metaphor, that a Swiss army knife could not have a general-purpose blade in it—we would apparently always prefer to buy a knife with only dedicated blades in it, as its screwdriver, for example, would be better for tightening a screw on our backpack than a general purpose blade.

Here we see a difficulty with the Swiss army knife metaphor: real Swiss army knives do include a general-purpose blade, which is often of more use than any content-specific blade. The general-purpose blade does not precisely fit any specific environmental "domain", but can be used to deal with novel problems or old problems in a new way. The Swiss army knife metaphor is really best suited, not to the Massive Modularity Hypothesis, but to dual-process theories of the mind. According to these theories, there are general-purpose cognitive processes as well as content-specific modules (Evans & Over, 1996; Fodor, 1983, 2000; Sloman, 1996; Stanovich & West, 2000; see also Chapter 7). Dual-process theorists make a distinction between Type 1 and Type 2 (Wason & Evans, 1975), or System 1 and System 2 (Stanovich, 1999), mental processes. System 1 (Type 1) mental processes would be found in the content-specific modules that Tooby and Cosmides (1992) argue are so superior to general-purpose or content-independent mental processes, which are classified as being in System 2 (or of Type 2) by dual-process theorists. System 1 processes are modular and encapsulated, and implicitly conform to or comply with rules. System 2 processes are nonmodular and not encapsulated, and explicitly follow rules, including logical and other content-independent rules (Evans & Over, 1996, 1997; Over & Evans, 1997). Another way to state the Massive Modularity Hypothesis is that there are modular System 1 processes but no System 2 processes at all.

Supporters of massive modularity often present their emphasis on the virtues of modularity as if it were a completely new departure in the history of thought. In particular, Gigerenzer (2000) claims that philosophers and psychologists have long wrongly pursued what he calls Leibniz's dream of finding a perspicuous formal system for reasoning. But, in fact, some great philosophers argued strongly that instincts are at least sometimes of more value than reason for effective human thought and action. Hume (1777/1902, Section 45) famously claimed that instinct is better than reason for judgements about causation. But it was Kant (1785/1997) who stated in the strongest form the argument that content-independent reasoning could not be adaptive for the instrumental purpose of reproductive success (as we would now put it). Kant endorsed, in a pre-Darwinian teleological biology, the principle that there will be no instrument for any purpose in a living thing that is not best adapted to it. He then argued against an instrumentalist analysis of reason by claiming that the purpose of reason in any creature cannot be to preserve its life or make it happy, since, in that case (Kant, 1785/1997, p. 395):

> . . . nature would have hit upon a very bad arrangement in selecting the reason of the creature to carry out this purpose. For all the actions of the creature for this purpose . . . would be marked out for it far more accurately by instinct, and that end would have thereby been attained much more surely than it ever can be by reason . . .

Of course, Kant did not have a massively instinctual account of the mind. To use contemporary terms, he was a dual-process theorist (in the widest sense), in that he thought that there are some content-independent cognitive processes as well as instincts, and that people can sometimes follow formal rules. He did not infer that only instincts exist, but rather that reason must have some noninstrumental purpose. His pre-Darwinian biological beliefs allowed him to conclude from his argument that reason does have a purpose, but not the instrumental one of making us happy, preserving our lives, or helping us to reproduce. In contrast to most contemporary dual-process theorists, Kant was an internalist about reason. He held that reason has the intrinsic purpose of allowing human beings to infer *a priori* ethical obligations or duties, independently of what is or is not an effective instrument for yielding happiness, a long life, or reproductive success. Most contemporary dual-process theorists are naturalists as well as externalists, and we cannot follow Kant in holding that content-independent reasoning has a noninstrumental purpose. But if we disagree with massive modularity, we must still have some response to what we can call the Kantian challenge. This challenge is to establish the instrumental value of content-independent reasoning. Put in biological terms, the Kantian challenge is to discover why an increasing ability at content-independent thought in the EEA increased fitness, and hence how this ability evolved by natural selection. To assess this challenge more fully, we must consider in detail the evidence for massive modularity.

MODULARITY ARGUMENTS AND DEONTIC REASONING

Supporters of massive modularity have been most anxious to reject the view that mental processes sometimes follow logical rules, in what would be the best example of general-purpose and content-independent reasoning, and the best possible counterexample to massive modularity. These evolutionary cognitive psychologists have consequently been opposed to psychological theories of mental logic, whether the logical rules are like those of natural deduction (Rips, 1994) or like those of semantic tableaux (Johnson-Laird & Byrne, 1991). Cosmides and Tooby, in particular, have had a clear strategy for trying to get experimental evidence against mental logic and for massive modularity. This strategy is based on arguments with the following structure:

X-type adaptive problems and Y-type nonadaptive problems are of the same clear logical form.

Experiments have shown that people can reliably solve X-type problems but not Y-type problems.

Therefore, people do not have a mental logic that applies equally to X-type and Y-type problems, but rather have an evolved module for content-specific inference about X-type problems and not about Y-type problems.

Let us call any arguments of this structure modularity arguments. It is in the work of Cosmides and Tooby and their collaborators that we find the most explicit modularity arguments, supported by the most stimulating experiments. They have been especially influential in making these arguments about two mental processes: conditional reasoning and probabilistic inference.

Cosmides (1989) was the first evolutionary psychologist to apply a modularity argument to conditional reasoning (but see also Cheng & Holyoak, 1985). Her experiments were on the selection task (Wason, 1966) and presupposed that the following conditionals have the same logical form:

(I)   If a card has an A on one side then it has a 4 on the other side.
(D1) If a man eats cassava root, then he must have a tattoo on his face.

Participants respond differently to selection tasks based on (I) and (D1), in which the object is to choose cards that will show whether (I) is true or whether (D1) has been violated (see Chapter 2 for an introduction to the selection task and more discussion of it). They find it easier to get the right answer in a selection task for (D1), at least if they are told that by eating cassava root one gets a benefit (like an aphrodisiac) for which one must pay a cost (like going through an initiation ceremony to get a tattoo). For an abstract task based on (I) and restricted to four cards, the correct answer is to select the card with A on it and the card with some number other than 4 on it. The former may not have 4 on the other side, and the latter may have A on the other side. Most participants do not select these two cards, which are the only ones that can falsify (I), in this version of the task (Evans & Over, 1996).

Cosmides, however, found that participants do give the correct answer in a selection task based on (D1), given a scenario describing a kind of social

agreement that she called a social contract. As a result of the social agreement, eating cassava root without a tattoo is cheating, which is defined as
taking a benefit (an aphrodisiac) with paying the socially agreed cost (getting
the tattoo). Participants correctly choose the card indicating that a man has
eaten cassava root and the card indicating that a man does not have a tattoo.
The former may reveal on the other side that the man does not have a tattoo,
and the latter may reveal that that man has eaten cassava root. Along with her
experiments, Cosmides employed a modularity argument. She presupposed
that the conditional (I) has the same logical form as the conditional (D1), but
argued that the selection task for (I) has a different content Y from the
content X of the task for (D1). Only the task for (D1) expresses a social
contract, and violators of (D1) are cheaters. Her experiments showed that
people could reliably solve tasks of type X and identify cheaters, but not tasks
of type Y. Cosmides consequently held, relying on a modularity argument,
that there is no mental logic that applies equally to (I) and (D1). Instead, she
concluded that there is only an evolved module for the content-specific purpose of dealing with type X adaptive problems: grasping social contracts and
identifying cheaters. She also took the innovative step of connecting her
claims about conditional reasoning to evolutionary accounts of cooperative
behaviour. Individual human beings could not get the evolutionary benefits
of cooperation, she pointed out, if they could not identify cheaters.

   The problem for Cosmides is that (I) and (D1) are not conditionals of the
same logical form, with the result that the corresponding selection tasks cannot be said to be of the same logical form at a significant level of analysis. All
selections tasks can be thought of as decision problems at the highest level
(Evans & Over, 1996), but still (I) and (D1) are significantly different in
logical form: (I) is an indicative conditional and (D1) a deontic conditional.
The objects of the two versions of the selection tasks are not even the same.
The indicative task for (I) is about the truth or falsity of (I), and finding a
card with A on one side but not a 4 on the other falsifies (I). On the other
hand, the deontic task for (D1) presupposes that (D1) holds as a proper
deontic rule for guiding behaviour in some society, and its object is to find
violators of the rule. A violator who eats cassava root without a tattoo does
not falsify (D1). Cosmides' use of a modularity argument was altogether too
quick in this case. It cannot be applied here as its first premise is false: X and
Y, that is (D1) and (I), are not of the same logical form (see Cummins, 1998,
and Fiddick, Cosmides, & Tooby, 2000, for wider evolutionary arguments
about deontic reasoning).

   There are not yet full psychological theories of how people represent the
meanings of deontic assertions (but see Manktelow & Over, 1995). Nevertheless, people obviously have some grasp of deontic logical form and of the
difference between that and other modal propositions. For example, people
are able to grasp, for any content P, that the logical form:

It is obligatory that P
does not logically imply P
but that the form:
It is causally necessary that P
does logically imply P.

No one gets very far in the world without realizing obligations are not necessarily fulfilled. In addition:

It is obligatory that P
does logically imply
It is permissible that P.

Understanding these and other logical deontic principles requires formal, content-independent thought, and so deontic understanding at this high level cannot be modular. On the other hand, this does not mean that evolutionary psychologists will tell us nothing about lower level deontic thought. Consider this deontic conditional introduced by Manktelow and Over (1990):

(D2) If a man clears up spilt blood, then he must use rubber gloves.

(D1) and (D2) are both deontic conditionals, but (D1) expresses a social contract and (D2) is what has come to be called a conditional precaution. Cosmides (1989) claimed that participants never got a selection task right unless it was based on a social contract and about finding cheaters. This suggested that no such selection task could be constructed, and that is why we based one on (D2), in which participants do get the right answer, although violators of (D2) are not cheaters. Cosmides replied that we had discovered another content-specific module, one for conditional precautions and identifying hazards (Cosmides & Tooby, 1992, p. 205). Later, other researchers were to construct many different selection tasks in which participants got the right answer (Almor & Sloman, 1996; Sperber, Cara, & Girotto, 1995). These responses may be the result of still more content-specific modules, but this cannot be established by a simple application of a modularity argument. The conditionals in these cases are not all of the same logical form and, with many interesting differences between the tasks, much work must be done to try to explain the results by means of the massive modularity hypothesis (Fiddick et al., 2000).

We have already noted that knowledge of deontic logical implications cannot be the result of a content-specific module. That an obligation to perform an action logically implies permission to perform it is a formal relation, not depending on the content of the action. A module that merely identified violators of some kind of rule, whether a social agreement or a precaution, would not even match anything like the range of our thoughts about violations. For example, there can be excuses or mitigating circumstances for cheating or any other type of violation of deontic rules (Manktelow, Fairley, Kilpatrick, & Over, 1999). As every lecturer knows who has ever set an assignment deadline, there appears to be no modular bound to the range of excuses that can plausibly be made relevant to excusing a late submission. There are supposed to be separate modules for identifying cheating and hazards, but a hazard, like dangerous fog on a road, can be a good excuse for not conforming to some social agreement, such as being late for an appointment. Mitigating and aggravating circumstances for a potential violation can depend on high-level cultural, political, and moral notions and be the subject of sophisticated debate in the law, as can our high-level judgements about complementary rights and duties (Holyoak & Cheng, 1995). It is hard to see how the Massive Modularity Hypothesis, with its low-level modules in encapsulated structures for identifying cheating or hazards, could fully explain these points about high-level deontic thought. At that level, deontic reasoning is global, as Fodor (1983, 2000) would put it, rather than encapsulated. No definite bound can be put on the premises that are potentially relevant to it.

Oaksford and Chater (1994) have stimulated much research by applying formal Bayesian concepts to the selection task, and a broad range of responses in different selection tasks can be justified from a Bayesian point of view. These results can be covered by the most general analysis of all, a decision theoretic one (Evans & Over, 1996), but this analysis respects the logical differences between the tasks. People act in the tasks to uncover cases where there is some expected benefit to be gained or loss to be avoided. For an indicative task, these cases are outcomes of relatively high epistemic utility, from confirming or disconfirming the indicative conditional. For a deontic task, the utility results from uncovering instances of cheating or of exposure to a hazard, thereby allowing corrective action to be taken. However, this decision theoretic analysis itself suggests, for all its generality, a necessary place for adaptive modular thought and, more specifically, for modular preferences. The decision theoretic analysis ultimately depends on some basic preferences, for example, for probable truth over probable falsity, and for cooperating with people rather than being cheated by them. There are individual differences in these preferences, but for evolutionary reasons, people will have some strong tendencies to have certain basic preferences tied to some immediate emotional responses.

Fiddick (Chapter 3) presents evidence that people have different emotional responses to violations of social agreements and of precautions. The response to a violation of (D1) would tend to be anger, while the response to a violation of (D2) would tend to be fear. There seem to be solid reasons for holding that these responses originate in content-specific modules, directly reacting to particular external circumstances. There can even be problems at times in modifying such responses in light of high level inferences. Even if we infer that someone had a more or less good excuse for apparently cheating us, we may still feel angry, at least to some extent. Further exploration of such basic-level direct emotions may supply some specific content for different types of obligations and permissions, but that does not mean that, at the highest level, statements about both types do not have the formal property that an obligation logically implies a permission. Dual-process theories, but not massive modularity, can accommodate the fact that we can explicitly follow formal deontic rules as well as implicitly respond in particular emotional ways to what we directly observe. Further progress on the evolutionary psychology of deontic thought will mean moving on from the modularity argument and the massive modularity that it implies.

MODULARITY ARGUMENTS AND PROBABILISTIC REASONING

Probability theory, as a mathematical theory, lays down content-independent rules for assigning probabilities to events or propositions, but supporters of massive modularity have naturally denied that human mental processes follow content-independent rules for probabilistic inference. They have held that probability problems have to have a specific content for people to understand them: the problems supposedly have to be about frequencies.

Cosmides and Tooby (1996) claimed that people only understand how to perform probability inferences from beliefs or propositions having a content to do with objective relative frequencies. Their argument was that it is "theoretically impossible" for people to have the means to detect single-event probabilities, which are "intrinsically unobservable" (Cosmides & Tooby, 1996, p. 15). They held that our human or hominid ancestors, living as hunter–gatherers, were able to observe the frequencies of events in the environment where they evolved, in the EEA. Our ancestors could note how often they had been successful in, say, gathering berries in particular places, and it would have been adaptive for them to be able to recall this information later when making probability judgements in decision-making about foraging. Cosmides and Tooby (1996, p. 16) concluded that we have an adaptive mechanism, in a content-specific module, for probability judgement that works just by taking frequency information as input. Their position is that our adaptive probability judgements are the result of the operation of this mechanism and module alone, without a contribution, however modest, from any ability to follow content-independent rules, which could not have evolved by natural selection.

Cosmides and Tooby (1996) tried to use a modularity argument to get evidence for this view. They compared a single-event version of a medical diagnosis problem (Casscells, Schoenberger, & Grayboys, 1978) with their own frequency form of this problem. Participants in the single-event version were told that 1 in 1000 Americans have a certain disease, and that there is a test for this disease with a false-positive rate of 5 per cent. Few participants gave even a roughly accurate answer (assuming no false negatives) when they were then asked for the single-case probability that an American who tests positive for the disease actually has it. The modal response was the bias of neglecting the base rate, that is, neglecting the prior probability of having the disease, of 1 in 1000, and then giving 95 per cent as the answer. The correct answer, from applying Bayes's theorem (and assuming no false negatives), is almost 2 per cent.

However, Cosmides and Tooby claimed much better performance when this problem was presented to participants in a frequency version (but see Chapter 7). In that version, the information was that 1 out of every 1000 Americans have the disease. A diagnostic test has a positive result for everyone with the disease, but the result is positive as well for 50 out of every 1000 Americans who are healthy. With all this frequency information, participants were asked to imagine the testing of a random sample of 1000 Americans, and then questioned about a relative frequency. How many of these Americans who test positive for the disease will actually have it? Most participants gave the approximately correct answers of 1 in 50 or 1 in 51, although presumably almost no one calculated the exact frequency answer of 1 in 50.95.

Here we have another modularity argument that is clearly laid out. The single-event version of the medical diagnosis problem is formally equivalent to the frequency version used by Cosmides and Tooby. Both versions should be solved using Bayes's theorem, which is implied by the formal rules of probability theory. But Cosmides and Tooby argue that the participants cannot apply these content-independent rules to these versions because they would then get the correct answer to both. According to Cosmides and Tooby, the participants give the right answer to the frequency version because they have an evolved module just for processing frequency information. This supposed module does not apply to the single-event version, and the result is that participants give the wrong answer to that.

However, frequency problems as such are not easy to solve. The medical diagnosis scenario can be made a frequency-hard problem, as opposed to a frequency-easy problem, for participants merely by stating that the test is positive for 1 out of 20 Americans, instead of 50 out of 1000 Americans, and leaving everything else the same. Now it is less easy to infer that the answer is about 1 in 51, although that remains true and the problem is still as much about frequencies as Cosmides and Tooby's easy version. A significant number of participants do have trouble with this new, frequency-hard version of the problem. A modularity argument cannot be applied here. People do not, in general, reliably solve problems with X frequency content while failing at Y single-case versions (Evans, Handley, Perham, Over, & Thompson, 2000; Girotto & Gonzalez, 2001; see also Chapter 6).

Tversky and Kahneman (1983) were the first to discover that expressing a probability problem in terms of frequencies, and then asking about an intuitive set or class of things or events, can sometimes make the problem easier to solve. They did not claim a frequency problem is necessarily easy, but rather that it is easy when its set or class structure is transparent. Now the normative rules for set operations, such as the rule for the transitivity of the subset relation, are content-independent. Grasping these relations is a formal ability, no different from a logical ability like understanding valid syllogisms. Certain formal systems, such as Euler circles, can be used to clarify single-case probability and frequency problems as well as syllogisms (Sloman & Over, Chapter 6).

Tversky and Kahneman studied the extent to which people's judgements are consistent with the conjunction rule of probability theory, which requires the probability of a conjunction to be less than or equal to the probability of each of its conjuncts. As Tversky and Kahneman showed, the application of this rule can be made more or less transparent in particular cases. There are contexts in which the relevance of the rule is obvious, and ones in which it is obscure. Sometimes a frequency version of a problem makes its formal structure particularly clear. These versions allow people to apply content-independent rules, like the conjunction rule, to infer the right answer. However, frequency versions are neither necessary nor sufficient to make the application of the rules transparent (see Chapter 6).

Another point that we should keep in mind is that all of these experiments are about word problems. Solving word problems is nothing like the automatic operation of a dedicated module which might, say, record how often we have found blackberry bushes in places in the woods that had been cleared by fire. So far is it from being the case that Cosmides and Tooby's experiments confirm the massive modularity hypothesis that the opposite is true: their experiments actually support the alternative hypothesis that people can follow some content-independent rules. Their experiments are not evidence that people can accurately recall sample frequencies from their everyday experience. It is rather that people can sometimes do well in certain word problems by grasping content-independent rules about sets and subsets and for whole number arithmetic (Howson & Urbach, 1993; Johnson-Laird, Legrenzi, Girotto, Sonino-Legrenzi, & Caverni, 1999). This ability is a highly bounded one to be sure. The relevance of the rules has to be transparent, but the ability exists nonetheless.

NATURAL SAMPLING

Other psychologists have followed Tversky and Kahneman's lead and found that using frequency information in probability problems sometimes helps participants. Again, it does not always help (Kahneman & Tversky, 1996), but there is some effect to be explained. At least four different explanations have been given, and at least three of these differ from Tversky and Kahneman's explanation in terms of the transparency of subset relations.

First, it has been argued (Gigerenzer, Hoffrage, & Kleinbolting, 1991) that single-case probability judgements differ from frequency judgements in some experiments because the two judgements have different reference classes (but see Griffin & Buehler, 1999).

Second, there is the claim (Hertwig & Gigerenzer, 1999) that the difference exists in Tversky and Kahneman's original experiment on the conjunction rule because the word "probability" is polysemous in natural language. Using frequency information supposedly encourages a mathematical interpretation of the word (but see Mellers, Hertwig, & Kahneman, 2001; and see Chapter 6).

The third and fourth explanations rely on points made by Kleiter (1994). The third is that frequency information in certain formats makes some probability problems, as Kleiter showed, computationally simpler than single-case versions (Gigerenzer & Hoffrage, 1995, 1999). The fourth applies an evolutionary argument to what Kleiter called natural sampling (Gigerenzer & Hoffrage, 1995).

These four explanations do not fit together as a coherent account of the frequency effect, as we can demonstrate by focusing on the third and fourth explanations and bringing out their inconsistency. Word problems about certain frequency formats can be easy, and even utterly trivial, but using natural sampling alone would be difficult under primitive conditions: it would require a massive memory and be prone to damaging biases.

Gigerenzer and Hoffrage (1995) argue that using natural sampling was adaptive in the EEA and remains useful today as a heuristic that everyone employs, thanks to an evolved module. Consider the example they use, for their evolutionary argument, of the natural sampling of a natural frequency in what they term the "standard menu" (Gigerenzer & Hoffrage, 1995, pp. 686–687). They ask us to imagine a physician in an illiterate society who in the course of her long life has "discovered the symptom" of a certain disease. She does this by remembering that she has examined 1000 patients in her life, that 10 of these had the disease, and that 8 of those 10 had the symptom. She also remembers that 95 of the 990 without the disease had the symptom. On that basis her modular mechanism produces the judgement that the probability that someone with the symptom has the disease is 8 out of 8 plus 95, or 8 out of 103. Gigerenzer and Hoffrage lay out the physician's memories in a way that parallels an application of Bayes's theorem, but she, or more strictly her module, has used natural sampling to make an adaptive and useful judgement without following any content-independent rules. She supposedly does not have to attend to the base rate of the disease, of 10 out of 1000, and does not have to normalize the frequencies even implicitly or roughly. Normalizing would mean representing all the frequencies as, for example, numbers out of 100. (Gigerenzer and Hoffrage overlook the fact that it is hard for people to perform calculations with frequencies that are not normalized; see Harries & Harvey, 2000.)

Gigerenzer and Hoffrage's physician would clearly need an incredible memory if she used natural sampling on its own to try to make effective probability judgements. She may have encountered 739 cases of some other disease, and picked 1804 blackberries in one area and 9256 in another, and so on in her long life. She, or her module, would need access to a massive memory to make use of all this data in Gigerenzer and Hoffrage's natural sampling. The Massive Modularity Hypothesis, when applied to probability judgement, leads straight to a Massive Memory Hypothesis. In reality, it would be impossible for the illiterate physician to remember the information she is supposed to be able to call to mind explicitly.

Natural sampling alone, without attending to base rates or normalizing however implicitly and roughly, cannot tell us when two events are independent, and can seriously mislead us about whether one event causes another or is truly diagnostic of it (Over & Green, 2001; see also Chapter 6). Natural sampling, with an unbiased sample, can reveal that one event has a high conditional probability given another, but that is not necessarily adaptive or useful information, as these events can still be independent of each other. For example, the rapid growth of blackberry bushes might have been independent of the occurrence of fire, even though there is a high conditional probability of the former given the latter. To forage for blackberries, what would be adaptive or useful to discover would be that fire causes blackberries to grow vigorously. Is it worth making a special trip to the sight of a fire in recent years to pick blackberries? Is it worth spreading or starting a fire to try to encourage blackberry growth? Natural sampling, as described by Gigerenzer and Hoffrage, cannot answer these questions, but hunter–gatherers are able to do so and must therefore be capable of more than this sampling.

Gigerenzer and Hoffrage slide quickly and without comment from talking about natural sampling as sampling to speaking as if it gives us direct access to natural or objective frequencies. People can supposedly observe objective frequencies but not single-case probabilities. But to observe an objective frequency of 1 in 20 is to observe an objective frequency of 50 in 1000 or 37 in 740, as these are all the same objective frequency. Of course, these would be different sample frequencies, but then it is not so easy to infer that they all refer to the same objective frequency. Our position value number system, with its numeral 0, is a sophisticated cultural invention for helping us with content-independent operations on whole numbers. But even in this system, we can find it difficult to infer that different representations, such as 1 in 20 and 37 in 740, refer to the same objective frequency, number or ratio.

Moreover, we can never be certain that we have observed an objective frequency, rather than a biased sample. We can only record and recall sample frequencies, and then we must use these samples to confirm, or disconfirm, hypotheses about objective frequencies. A module that just recorded sample frequencies would acquire many biased samples under primitive conditions, for example, it would not help us to cope, on its own, with biased samples due to camouflage in the natural world. Supporters of natural sampling point out that it can keep track of sample size, but that is of no help if the sample is biased. We would be very naïve if we only had a module for inferring that 5 out of 6, or 500 out of 600, pheasants are brightly coloured given these as sample frequencies. We only have to observe one female pheasant to become convinced that female pheasants are well camouflaged and to infer that we will see fewer of them than the males. We are then able to predict the biased samples, and not falsely believe that there are five times as many male pheasants as female pheasants.

A severe limitation of massive modularity is that it provides no account of how ordinary people can find hypotheses more or less probable or improbable. That is, it has no notion of the epistemic or inductive probability of hypotheses, nor of the degree of confirmation or disconfirmation of hypotheses about objective frequencies. With massive modularity, evolutionary psychologists cannot explain how people make predictions by content-independent inferences from hypotheses, which are then confirmed if the predictions are true and disconfirmed otherwise. They can have no concept of how people confirm or disconfirm a proposition, expressing a hypothesis, and how this differs from merely recalling a sample frequency of a physical event, like how many successful foraging trips there have been out of a number of attempts. This limitation can be overcome by a proper Bayesian analysis of probabilistic inference (Howson & Urbach, 1993), which is about far more than merely implicitly complying with Bayes's theorem in natural sampling.

A full Bayesian approach can specify what it is to confirm or disconfirm hypotheses about objective frequencies, bias in sample frequencies, independence, and causal relations. To understand confirmation and disconfirmation, one must have some grasp of content-independent relations between propositions (Over & Evans, 1997). For instance, observing that a raven is black strongly confirms the hypothesis that all ravens are black in part because of a logical relation. This hypothesis and the fact that one is looking at a raven logically imply that the raven is black, and knowing this logical relation is part of judging that the hypothesis is strongly confirmed by the observation that this raven is indeed black. Eventually finding a well-camouflaged female pheasant disconfirms the hypothesis that all pheasants are brightly coloured, and that again depends in part on a logical relation. The fact that the female pheasant is not brightly coloured is inconsistent with that hypothesis.

The third explanation above for the frequency effect can also be illustrated by Gigerenzer and Hoffrage's example of the illiterate physician. She would conform to Bayes's theorem by judging, on the basis of the natural frequencies given, that 8 out of 103 people with the symptom have the disease. The third explanation (Gigerenzer & Hoffrage, 1995, 1999) is that solving word problems with natural frequencies is computationally simpler than with single-case probabilities. We must ask to whom this explanation applies. It cannot, in fact, be to their illiterate physician, who could not solve a word problem, and probably would not even have words in her language for numbers like 1000 and 990, but who is supposed to do the natural sampling. As we have already pointed out, she would need a massive memory for that. Far too much is given for free in this story for it to be a realistic example, let alone a believable illustration of what was adaptive under primitive conditions. The illiterate physician has her massive memory for free, although no one could recall what she does explicitly without written records. Any possible problems in diagnosing the disease in the first place are not raised, yet two people have it without the symptom. If we are going to presuppose so much, we may as well imagine that the idealized physician can recall outright what proportion of her patients with the symptom had the disease. In that case, there is not any parallel with the calculations of Bayes's theorem, and the whole process depends on the idealized memory. The point is that such an unbounded memory is irrelevant to the question of what evolved by natural selection.

Clearly, we do not need Bayes's theorem if we are only dealing with physical events A and B and can directly observe and easily recall an unbiased sample frequency of Bs given As. That still leaves us with the problem of biased samples and, to repeat, we do have good reason to fear these in many cases. Physicians are bound to remember some of their patients better than others. Perhaps these would be the younger or more attractive ones, or the ones that complained the least or complained the most. In technical terms, the memory of some of these patients would be more available than the memory of others. With natural sampling, we are right back to the availability heuristic and the problem of the biased samples it can produce (Tversky & Kahneman, 1973). In effect, Gigerenzer and Hoffrage's illiterate physician is employing the availability heuristic, but they do not explain how she can avoid its biases.

Gigerenzer and Hoffrage's example is only easy for those of us who can read it as a word problem. Why is it so easy for us in words? The reason is that it has been expressed in terms that make it clear how to apply elementary content-independent operations on finite sets and subsets, like partitioning these sets and taking their union. The third explanation of the frequency effect returns us to what Tversky & Kahneman (1983) said about transparency. Therefore, the third explanation implies that people are able to grasp content-independent rules, and is inconsistent with the fourth explanation, which is based on massive modularity. Consider using what Gigerenzer and Hoffrage (1995, p. 687) call the "short menu" alternative to the "standard menu" of the word problem. In the "short menu", the illiterate physician would simply recall that 8 people had the symptom and the disease and 95 had the symptom without the disease. Now it could hardly be more trivial for us to infer what proportion of the people with the symptom had the disease, and the relevance of the conjunction rule is totally transparent here (Tversky & Kahneman, 1983). This is a probability problem if the object is to try to predict the disease from the symptom. But problems of this set structure are not necessarily about probability, as we can illustrate by supposing that there are 8 people in a village who ate the berries without helping to gather them and 95 people who ate the berries and did help to gather them. It is again trivial to infer what proportion of people who ate the berries did not help to gather them, and the object of this could be not to make a probability judgement, but to infer how serious a problem of cheating there is in the village. For "short menu" problems like these, we simply take the union of two sets and then infer that one of these sets is a subset of the union, and do not even partition sets as in the "standard menu". Gigerenzer and Hoffrage contend that the adaptive value of natural sampling explains why their word problems are so easy. But obviously this claim about sampling in the EEA cannot account for the lack of computational complexity in the set operations of any of these word problems, whatever their content or object.

A simple use of the modularity argument does not establish that there is a special module for processing frequency information and solving probability problems given in terms of frequencies. There is an effect to be explained, but it is even misleading to call it a frequency effect, as frequency information is neither necessary nor sufficient for people to find a probability problem easy. What makes a probability problem easy is putting it in a form that makes grasping content-independent relations easy, just as Tversky and Kahneman (1983) first pointed out. In recent years, some psychologists (Gigerenzer, 2000) have claimed again and again that problems are easier to solve when they are given a realistic content, but this is certainly a mistaken interpretation of the frequency studies. These really show that some problems are easier when their formal structure is made transparent, and that is sometimes when abstract logical or mathematical constructions are used, such as Euler circles (see Chapter 6).

Brase, Cosmides, and Tooby (1998) make an additional claim about whole objects based on a modularity argument. They argue, on evolutionary grounds, that it should be easier for people to make probability judgements about whole objects than arbitrary parts of these. Of course, as Brase et al.

point out, other researchers have pointed out that people more easily notice and recall certain types of object, like apple trees and their apples, than arbitrary parts of these, like random lengths of a branch or the trunk. But Brase et al. make the specific claim about probability judgements and provide some experimental support for it. In one experiment, they compared responses to a probability problem about whole candy canes, which were either peppermint or lemon, with responses to the same problem about candy canes including some that were half peppermint and half lemon, with the flavour and colour changing in the middle of the canes. The result was that the percentage of correct solutions for the condition about only whole candy canes was significantly higher than for the condition including some candy canes that were half peppermint and half lemon.

The results of Brase et al. are very interesting and should stimulate more research. However, these results do not imply that people do not follow content-independent rules about set relations when solving frequency-easy word problems. We know anyway that such explicit rule following is bounded by important cognitive constraints (Evans & Over, 1996, 1997). It may well be easier for people to grasp the logical form of a problem when it is about whole objects and not their arbitrary parts. In any case, we have helped ourselves to grasp content-independent forms by sophisticated cultural inventions designed for that very purpose, like Euler circles. Such abstract representations do not allow us to be distracted by any content or unnatural partitioning of objects. They partly solve for us the problem of extracting logical form from irrelevant content, and thus help us to apply content-independent rules that depend on form and not content.

METAREPRESENTATION

Recently, some supporters of the Massive Modularity Hypothesis have developed accounts of metarepresentation that are in considerable tension with any reasonable interpretation of the hypothesis. Sperber (2000, p. 136) argues for the existence ". . . of an ability to check for consistency and to filter incoming information on this basis". He has been influenced by Cosmides' argument about the adaptive value of being able to identify cheaters. Human beings depend greatly on communication but this exposes us to possible cheating by deception, misinformation, and lying. To uncover this kind of cheating, we must do more than pick-out people who have taken some physical benefit without paying the appropriate physical cost. What would be additionally advantageous, Sperber holds, is to be able to check what we are told for logical inconsistencies. It is notoriously difficult for liars and deceivers to be wholly consistent in what they say.

Sperber's argument for a logical ability might be part of an effective reply to the Kantian challenge. Kant does not appear to have considered that logical reasoning may have an instrumental value through enabling us to understand other minds or, more specifically, helping us to infer when other minds are trying to mislead us. But Sperber's proposal must be given empirical support if it is to be an adequate response to the Kantian challenge. An ability to uncover inconsistencies in communication may have increased fitness in the EEA, but whether it really did so is a challenging empirical question, as of course Sperber realizes.

Sperber combines his view of logical reasoning with notions of content-specific or domain-specific modularity by suggesting that there is a logical module. His point is that the capacity for logical thought is "... a highly domain-specific metarepresentational ability: its domain is some specific properties of abstract representations" (Sperber, 2000, p. 134). But logical thought could not be anything but modular and domain specific in these senses, since this "module" is no more than the set of computational processes that identify logical forms, and the domain is identical with the set of logical forms. These sets necessarily exist. In these senses, a capacity for identifying the logical forms in just elementary propositional logic would be even more narrowly "modular" with an even more restricted domain. It is not difficult to programme a present-day computer to identify propositional logical forms, such as conjunctions and disjunctions, in fragments of natural language, and then to produce valid inferences from these. It is tautological to describe such a computer as having a logical "module" in Sperber's sense, and its valid inferences would be content-independent, and not modular, in the senses in which we have used, and will continue to use, these terms in this chapter. The existence of such inferences as a natural part of the human mind is what is ruled out by the Massive Modularity Hypothesis.

Sperber is right that grasping the logical form of arguments in natural language is a special ability, and it is one that can fail us surprisingly easily at times. But this very fact helps us to bring out again a limitation of the modularity arguments that have been used to try to support the massive modularity hypothesis. The conclusions of these arguments have been too strong. Assume that people do have a module that helps them to get the correct answer for X problems but not Y problems, when X and Y can be shown to be of the same logical form. That does not mean that people have no ability at all to recognize that these problems are of the same logical form and to solve them equally well with content-independent inferences. Perhaps the logical form of Y is not sufficiently transparent for people to apply easily their mental logic to it. We have seen evidence above that making logical form transparent can help people to solve problems with content-independent inferences. Dual-process theorists explain the fragile nature of logical ability by the slow sequential nature and limited processing capacity, particularly in working memory, of explicit thought or System 2 (Evans & Over, 1996, 1997). These limitations have encouraged, as we noted above, technically advanced peoples to create abstract means of displaying logical forms clearly, as when symbols are used in syllogisms, or their premises represented in Euler circles. The whole purpose of these technical means is to help facilitate content-independent thought. It is also necessary to stress that there are individual differences in people's abilities to recognize logical forms and to solve problems on that basis. Some people are better able to do this than others, but almost everyone appears to have this ability to some extent. These facts can also be explained by dual-process theory, but not by massive modularity (Stanovich, 1999; Stanovich & West, 2000; see also Chapter 7).

Cosmides and Tooby (2000) have developed their position in a way that goes far beyond an unrestricted massive modularity hypothesis. They no longer claim that general-purpose mechanisms would have been ". . . grossly inefficient and easily out competed . . . by content-specific mechanisms" (Tooby & Cosmides, 1992, p. 112). Mechanisms for logical thought evolved by natural selection, they now accept, and were adaptive in the EEA. They do not believe this happened merely because of social competition. They have a much more general account of why it was adaptive, having to do with the capacity of suppositional reasoning to make inferences about possibilities and cope with uncertainty and novelty in the world.

Cosmides and Tooby's present position is close in substance to dual-process theories, and their arguments for it are similar to those used by dual-process theorists. A logical reasoning ability, on top of dedicated modules, can help us to deal with novel problems, for which past conditioning, learning, and evolution have not fully prepared us (Evans & Over, 1996, 1997; Over & Evans, 1997). Cosmides and Tooby (2000, p. 108) say that mental logics ". . . have been empirically rejected by many on the assumption that the only licensed inferences are logical". In contrast, they now believe in both modules for content-specific thought and what can only be described as a mental logic. Their view has become very close indeed to what many dual-process theorists have held for a long time. Perhaps the only difference has become one of degree, with Cosmides and Tooby claiming that relatively more modules are content-specific capacities for which there is a high degree of biological preparedness. These capacities would result from a content-specific tendency to learn some things much more quickly and easily than others. Most early dual-process theorists probably held that modules for content-specific inference above the level of input systems, like those for vision, arise from a more general and flexible learning process. Many would continue to claim, for example, that people have a general ability for deontic reasoning that develops through general learning (see Chapter 4), while admitting that there may be much more biological preparedness at a lower level, as in the affective response of anger at being cheated. In contrast, Cosmides and Tooby still argue that deontic reasoning is mainly the result of separate content-specific capacities, like the ability to identify cheaters, for which there is a great deal of biological preparedness.

Cosmides and Tooby's evolving views should not make us forget the seriousness of the Kantian challenge, which, to their credit, they independently pressed in contemporary terms in their earlier work. It is one thing to point out the advantages of content-independent reasoning in the contemporary world, and another to establish exactly why this reasoning, in a dual process system, was adaptive in the EEA. Why exactly were human actions more effective in the EEA when they were sometimes the result of content-independent reasoning on top of instincts, rather than the output of instincts alone? Dual-process theorists have themselves argued that it is often best to reply on instincts or, more generally, on implicit and automatic processes in System 1 to achieve everyday purposes. But they have also pointed out that sometimes people can only achieve a goal in a novel situation by overriding System 1, after inferring what is best in System 2 with the help of explicit content-independent reasoning (Evans & Over, 1996, 1997; Over & Evans, 1997). The fact that it is sometimes better for System 2 to override System 1, and sometimes not, makes it even more difficult to answer the Kantian challenge. What is needed to begin with is a better understanding of how System 1 and System 2 work together, and of when it is, and is not, advantageous for System 2 to override System 1. Note also that, in a way, System 1 can override System 2 by means of weakness of the will, when people give in to a basic drive against what they have explicitly inferred that they ought to do. Perhaps some balance has been achieved between System 1 and System 2 that reflects facts about what was adaptive in the EEA, but it is not easy to understand the subtle relation between the systems, let alone to explain its evolution by natural selection.

Some dual-process theorists, in particular Fodor (2000), argue that what we are calling System 2 may not be an adaptation, but that it may have arisen indirectly, or as a side-effect, as the brain increased in size for other, unknown reasons. This view implies that the Kantian challenge cannot be met. If this is true then nonmodular, System 2 thought, as part of a dual-process mind, had no natural instrumental purpose or function, and increasing steps towards it did not increase reproductive success for any reason. Such an extreme view is not widely supported by dual-process theorists but it can only be countered decisively by meeting the Kantian challenge, and that means answering the question of why System 2 combined with System 1 was better than System 1 on its own for reproductive success. Why did it increase fitness in the EEA to combine content-independent thought with modular processes in the way that they are combined in human beings?

The difficulty of this question about dual processes can be brought most sharply into focus by considering the epistemological distinction between constructive and nonconstructive reasoning. Suppose that someone openly cheats us by calling on our help but not paying us back later. An example of constructive thought would be to identify this person as a cheater, perhaps going so far as to point him out for all to see. In the non-constructive case, there would be no open cheating, but we would be able to infer explicitly, from our general beliefs, that someone or other was cheating us. Perhaps we could infer this after doing some sums and finding that our books do not balance. We might not be able, at first anyway, to say who this person was or to point him or her out. In this case, we have nonconstructive knowledge, inferred top-down, that someone or other is cheating us. In the former case, we had constructive knowledge of a particular person who was cheating us, acquired bottom-up from our perception of this person's actions. The purest example of constructive thought comes from the implicit lower-level operation of a System 1 perceptual module, to observe that a certain object has a property. Nonconstructive inference is the purest example of an explicit higher-level, or metalevel if one prefers, System 2 reasoning process to acquire knowledge. In general, following content-independent rules is a necessary part of nonconstructive reasoning, which is the best possible example of reasoning that is nonmodular and not encapsulated.

There are philosophical problems about how nonconstructive reasoning can be normatively justified (Dummett, 1978), but these are demands for an internalist justification. From the externalist point of view, we can relatively easily point out the usefulness of nonconstructive reasoning in the contemporary world. That does not necessarily help us to discover why increasing steps towards it were adaptive in the EEA, and there are not, in fact, any hypotheses about this.

More specific questions must be asked as well. Cosmides and Tooby (2000, pp. 61–62) state that there is a "primary workplace" that operates like a natural deduction system, with introduction and elimination rules for logical constants such as "if". In other words, there is a mental logic, but Cosmides and Tooby are vague about its set of valid rules. This is understandable: any hypothesis about that would have to take account of myriad results in the psychology of reasoning and would be highly controversial. Trying to give the valid rules for the indicative conditional alone would be to enter into deep controversies in philosophical logic and debates about what the many psychological experiments on conditionals tell us (Edgington, 1995; Evans, Handley, & Over, 2002). The first step should be to distinguish, in the natural deduction system, deontic and indicative conditionals, which have different logical forms, as we have pointed out above. Eventually, given a possible mental logic, evolutionary psychologists should develop hypotheses about how the ability to follow its set of valid rules arose by natural selection. Why do people follow those rules, in the bounded way that they do, and not some others in the type of dual-process system that they have? Some people can follow content-independent rules in abstract thought significantly better than

others, and how are we to account for these individual differences in evolutionary terms (Stanovich, 1999; Stanovich & West, 2000, Chapter 8; Over &
Evans, 2000)? Evolutionary psychology has not yet even begun to offer
answers to these questions, and many others that it must now ask, as it moves
beyond the Massive Modularity Hypothesis.

CONCLUSION

There are numerous problems with an unrestricted Massive Modularity
Hypothesis, and therefore it is not surprising that some former supporters of
it have moved significantly towards a dual-process theory, in which they can
still have the advantages of modularity but add those of content-independent
thought. This step should, however, make them re-examine their early use of
modularity arguments. If we agree that people have a mental logic, or a
primary workplace where they follow logical rules, then they should have the
ability to follow these rules to solve problems of the same clear logical form.
If people do not do this then perhaps the problems are not really of the same
logical form, as they are not in indicative and deontic selection tasks. Another
possibility is that the logical forms are not sufficiently clear, but we can sometimes correct this with some formal techniques, such as Euler circles. Modularity arguments may still establish that certain modules exist, but these
arguments should be used more carefully, with weaker conclusions. People
may have some content-specific mechanism for solving a problem, but some
of them, or all of them, may also be capable of solving it just as naturally
with content-independent means. However, supporters of the Massive Modularity Hypothesis, and especially Cosmides and Tooby, were initially justified
in pressing a contemporary version of the Kantian challenge of explaining
why content-independent reasoning was adaptive in the EEA. This challenge
raises difficult, but fundamental questions that evolutionary psychology
should now start to address.

REFERENCES

Almor, A., & Sloman, S. (1996). Is deontic reasoning special? *Psychological Review, 103*, 374–378.
Bradshaw, J.L. (1997). *Human evolution: A neuropsychological approach.* Hove, UK: Psychology
    Press.
Brase, G.L., Cosmides, L., & Tooby, J. (1998). Individuation, counting, and statistical inference:
    The role of frequency and whole-object representations in judgment under uncertainty.
    Journal of Experimental Psychology, 127, 3–21.
Buss, D. (1999). *Evolutionary psychology: The new science of the mind.* Boston, MA: Allyn &
    Bacon.
Casscells, W., Schoengerger, A., & Grayboys, T. (1978). Interpretation by physicians of clinical
    laboratory results. *New England Journal of Medicine, 299*, 999–1000.
Cheng, P., & Holyoak, K. (1985). Pragmatic reasoning schemas. *Cognitive Psychology, 17*,
    391–416.

Cosmides, L. (1989). The logic of social exchange: Has natural selection shaped how humans reason? Studies with the Wason selection task. *Cognition, 31*, 187–276.

Cosmides, L., & Tooby, J. (1992). Cognitive adaptations for social exchange. In J.H. Barkow, L. Cosmides, & J. Tooby (Eds.), *The adapted mind: Evolutionary psychology and the generation of culture*. New York: Oxford University Press.

Cosmides, L., & Tooby, J. (1994). Beyond intuition and instinct blindness: Toward an evolutionarily rigorous cognitive science. *Cognition, 50*, 41–77.

Cosmides, L., & Tooby, J. (1996). Are humans good intuitive statisticians after all? Rethinking some conclusions from the literature on judgment under uncertainty. *Cognition, 58*, 1–73.

Cosmides, L., & Tooby, J. (2000). Consider the source: The evolution of adaptations for decoupling and metarepresentations. In D. Sperber (Ed.), *Metarepresentations: A multidisciplinary perspective*. Oxford: Oxford University Press.

Cummins, D.D. (1998). Social roles and other minds: The evolutionary roots of higher cognition. In D.D. Cummins & C. Allen (Eds.), *The evolution of mind*. New York: Oxford University Press.

Cummins, D.D., & Cummins, R. (1999). Biological preparedness and evolutionary explanation. *Cognition, 73*, B37-B53.

Dummett, M. (1978). *Truth and other enigmas*. London: Duckworth.

Edgington, D. (1995). On conditionals. *Mind, 104*, 235–329.

Evans, J.St.B.T., Handley, S.H., & Over, D.E. (2002). *Conditionals and conditional probability*. University of Plymouth manuscript.

Evans, J.St.B.T., Handley, S.H., Perham, N., Over, D.E., & Thompson, V.A. (2000). Frequency versus probability formats in statistical word problems. *Cognition, 77*, 197–213.

Evans, J.St.B.T., & Over, D.E. (1996). *Rationality and reasoning*. Hove, UK: Psychology Press.

Evans, J.St.B.T., & Over, D.E. (1997). Rationality in reasoning: The case of deductive competence. *Current Psychology of Cognition, 16*, 3–38.

Fiddick, L., Cosmides, L., & Tooby, J. (2000). No interpretation without representation: The role of domain-specific representations and inferences in the Wason selection task. *Cognition, 77*, 1–79.

Fodor, J. (1983). *Modularity of mind*. Cambridge, MA: The MIT Press.

Fodor, J. (2000). *The mind doesn't work like that*. Cambridge, MA: The MIT Press.

Gigerenzer, G. (2000). *Adaptive thinking*. New York: Oxford University Press.

Gigerenzer, G., & Hoffrage, U. (1995). How to improve Bayesian reasoning without instruction: Frequency formats. *Psychological Review, 102*, 684–704.

Gigerenzer, G., & Hoffrage, U. (1999). Overcoming difficulties in Bayesian reasoning: A reply to Lewis and Keren (1999) and Mellers and McGraw (1999). *Psychological Review, 106*, 425–430.

Gigerenzer, G., Hoffrage, U., & Kleinbolting, H. (1991). Probabilistic mental models: A Brunswikian theory of confidence. *Psychological Review, 98*, 506–528.

Gigerenzer, G., Todd, P., & the ABC Research Group (1999). *Simple heuristics that make us smart*. New York: Oxford University Press.

Girotto, V., & Gonzalez, M. (2001). Solving probabilistic and statistical problems: A matter of information structure and question form. *Cognition, 78*, 247–276.

Griffin, D., & Buehler, R. (1999). Frequency, probability, and prediction: Easy solutions to cognitive illusions? *Cognitive Psychology, 38*, 48–78.

Harries, C., & Harvey, N. (2000). Are absolute frequencies, relative frequencies, or both effective in reducing cognitive biases? *Journal of Behavioral Decision Making, 13*, 431–444.

Hertwig, R., & Gigerenzer, G. (1999). The conjunction fallacy revisited: How intelligent inferences look like reasoning errors. *Journal of Behavioral Decision Making, 12*, 275–305.

Holyoak, K.J., & Cheng, P.W. (1995). Pragmatic factors in deontic reasoning. *Thinking & Reasoning, 1*, 289–313.

Howson, C., & Urbach, P. (1993). *Scientific reasoning: The Bayesian approach* (2nd ed.). La Salle, IL: Open Court.

Hume, D. (1902). *Enquiries concerning the human understanding and concerning the principles of morals*. Edited by L.A. Selby Bigge (2nd ed.). Oxford: Oxford University Press (Original published in 1777).

Johnson-Laird, P.N., & Byrne, R.M.J. (1991). *Deduction*. Mahwah, NJ: Lawrence Erlbaum Associates.

Johnson-Laird, P.N., Legrenzi, P., Girotto, V., Sonino-Legrenzi, M., & Caverni, J-P. (1999). Naive probability: A mental model theory of extensional reasoning. *Psychological Review*, *106*, 62–88.

Kahneman, D., & Tversky, A. (1996). On the reality of cognitive illusions: A reply to Gigerenzer's critique. *Psychological Review*, *103*, 582–591.

Kant, I. (1997). *Groundwork of the metaphysics of morals*. Translated by M. Gregor. Cambridge: Cambridge University Press (Original published in 1785).

Kleiter, G. (1994). Natural sampling: Rationality without base rates. In G.H. Fisher & D. Laming (Eds.), *Contributions to mathematical psychology, psychometrics, and methodology*. New York: Springer-Verlag.

Manktelow, K.I., Fairley, N., Kilpatrick, S.G., & Over, D.E. (1999). Pragmatics and strategies for practical reasoning. In G. De Vooght, G. D'Ydewalle, W. Schaeken, & A. Vandierendonck (Eds.), *Deductive reasoning and strategies*. Mahwah, NJ: Lawrence Erlbaum Associates, Inc.

Manktelow, K.I., & Over, D.E. (1990). Deontic thought and the selection task. In K.J. Gilhooly, M. Keane, R.H. Logic, & G. Erdos (Eds.), *Lines of thinking* (Vol. 1). Chichester: Wiley.

Manktelow, K.I., & Over, D.E. (1995). Deontic reasoning. In S.E. Newstead & J.St.B.T. Evans (Eds.), *Perspectives on thinking and reasoning*. Hove, UK: Lawrence Erlbaum Associates.

Mellers, B., Hertwig, R., & Kahneman, D. (2001). Do frequency representations eliminate conjunction effects? An exercise in adversarial collaboration. *Psychological Science*, *12*, 269–275.

Oaksford, M., & Chater, N. (1994). A rational analysis of the selection task as optimal data selection. *Psychological Review*, *101*, 608–631.

Over, D.E. & Evans, J.St.B.T. (1997). Two cheers for deductive competence. *Current Psychology of Cognition*, *16*, 255–278.

Over, D.E., & Evans, J.St.B.T. (2000). Rational distinctions and adaptations. *Behavioral and Brain Sciences*, *23*, 693–694.

Over, D.E., & Green, D.W. (2001). Contingency, causation, and adaptive inference. *Psychological Review*, *108*, 682–684.

Pinker, S. (1994). *The language instinct*. New York: HarperCollins.

Pinker, S. (1997). *How the mind works*. New York: The Penguin Press.

Rips, L.J. (1994). *The psychology of proof*. Cambridge, MA: MIT Press.

Samuels, R. (1998). Evolutionary psychology and the massive modularity hypothesis. *British Journal for the Philosophy of Science*, *49*, 575–602.

Sloman, S. (1996). The empirical case for two systems of reasoning. *Psychological Bulletin*, *119*, 3–22.

Sperber, D. (1994). The modularity of thought and the epidemiology of representations. In L.A. Hirschfeld & S.A. Gelman (Eds), *Mapping the mind: Domain specificity in cognition and culture*. Cambridge: Cambridge University Press.

Sperber, D. (2000). Metarepresentations in an evolutionary perspective. In D. Sperber (Ed.), *Metarepresentations: A multidisciplinary perspective*. Oxford: Oxford University Press.

Sperber, D., Cara, F., & Girotto, V. (1995). Relevance theory explains the selection task. *Cognition*, *57*, 31–95.

Stanovich, K.E. (1999). *Who is rational? Studies in individual differences in reasoning*. Mahwah, NJ: Lawrence Erlbaum Associates.

Stanovich, K.E., & West, R.F. (2000). Individual differences in reasoning: Implications for the rationality debate? *Behavioral and Brain Sciences*, *23*, 645–726.

Tooby, J., & Cosmides, L. (1992). The psychological foundations of culture. In J.H. Barkow, L. Cosmides, & J. Tooby (Eds.), *The adapted mind: Evolutionary psychology and the generation of culture.* New York: Oxford University Press.

Tversky, A., & Kahneman, D. (1973). Availability: A heuristic for judging frequency and probability. *Cognitive Psychology, 5*(2), 207–232.

Tversky, A., & Kahneman, D. (1983). Extensional versus intuitive reasoning: The conjunction fallacy in probability judgment. *Psychological Review, 90,* 293–315.

Wason, P.C. (1966). Reasoning. In B.M. Foss (Ed.), *New horizons in psychology I.* Harmondsworth: Penguin.

Wason, P.C., & Evans, J.St.B.T. (1975). Dual processes in reasoning? *Cognition, 13,* 141–154.

CHAPTER SIX

Probability judgement from the inside and out

Steven A. Sloman
Brown University, Providence, RI, USA

David E. Over
University of Sunderland, UK

One outcome of the study of judgement and decision making's heuristics and biases programme is that it has become conventional wisdom that people make systematic errors when judging probability. To take just one example: Judgements are sometimes guided by beliefs about causality, and these beliefs on occasion compete with sound probabilistic principles (Tversky & Kahneman, 1983). Some errors of this type can be reduced by changing the object of judgement. For example, Tversky and Kahneman (1983) showed that the incidence of the conjunction fallacy—cases in which the probability of a conjunction is judged greater than the probability of one of its constituents—can be reduced by asking people to imagine a finite set of individuals and to make a frequency judgement about that set rather than a probability judgement about a single individual. Since then, as we shall see below, parallel reductions induced by frequency frames have been observed for other fallacies and biases.

Some theorists have used this effect of frequency as the empirical basis for the argument that the heuristics and biases programme is deeply flawed because it fails to understand behaviour in its ecological context. The reason, on this view, that the programme has uncovered so much error is because it has primarily asked people to make judgements of single-event probabilities, that is, the probability of one-time occurrences. This is inappropriate, detractors have argued, because people did not evolve to make single-event probability judgements; they evolved to make judgements using natural frequencies. Ask people to judge the "natural frequency" of events and many errors disappear.

Proponents of some form of the "Natural Frequency Hypothesis" include Gigerenzer and Hoffrage (1995, p. 697) who claim, "An evolutionary point of view suggests that the mind is tuned to frequency formats, which is the information format humans encountered long before the advent of probability theory". Gigerenzer (1998, p. 14) states, "If there are mental algorithms that perform Bayesian-type inferences from data to hypotheses, these are designed for natural frequencies acquired by natural sampling, and not for probabilities or percentages". The view is echoed by Cosmides and Tooby (1996, p. 16): "[Humans] evolved mechanisms that took frequencies as input, maintained such information as frequentist representations, and used these frequentist representations as a database for effective inductive reasoning".

Cosmides and Tooby (1996) make the evolutionary argument for the hypothesis most clearly. Our hominid ancestors in the Pleistocene, they say, were able to remember and share specific events that they had encountered and, indeed, this was all they had available to make judgements under uncertainty. Single-case probability estimators did not evolve because the "probability" of a single event is intrinsically unobservable. Hence, what evolved, according to Cosmides and Tooby, was an algorithm for computing ratios of counts of specific events.

Cosmides and Tooby's (1996) argument has the virtue of implying a strong claim: Probability judgements are coherent when they concern frequencies, but not when they concern one-time events. More recently, Brase, Cosmides, and Tooby (1998) have followed Kleiter (1994) in making the weaker claim that people are able to conform to Bayesian prescriptions when solving probability word problems that are in a very specific format. This format is called "natural frequency via natural sampling" by Gigerenzer and Hoffrage (1999). Gigerenzer and Hoffrage (1995) argue, also following Kleiter (1994), that a critical virtue of natural frequency representations of numerical information is that Bayesian conclusions can be reached with fewer computational steps than they can with (normalized) relative frequencies or single-case probabilities.

Some of the evidence favoured by natural frequency proponents is encapsulated in the claim that certain cognitive illusions "disappear" when frequency judgements are substituted for single-event probability judgements. Gigerenzer (1994), for example, claims that the illusion of control, the conjunction fallacy, and base-rate neglect all disappear when questions are asked concerning natural frequencies rather than probabilities. One reason that natural frequency formats produce more coherent judgements, according to Hertwig and Gigerenzer (1999), is that the word "probability" is polysemous whereas the natural language sense of "frequency" is primarily mathematical. Gigerenzer, Hoffrage, and Kleinbolting (1991) argue that overconfidence can be manipulated by varying the representativeness of the sample of questions that are used. These claims have been disputed (Brenner, Koehler, Liberman, & Tversky, 1996; Griffin & Buehler, 1999). A general argument against the hypothesis was advanced by Kahneman and Tversky (1996), who pointed out that biases have been demonstrated with frequency judgements since the onset of the heuristics and biases programme.

An alternative hypothesis, the Nested-Sets Hypothesis, was proposed by Tversky and Kahneman (1983) to explain how frequency judgements could show greater coherence than corresponding single-case probability judgements. Several other authors have echoed these ideas (Ayton & Wright, 1994; Evans, Handley, Perham, Over, & Thompson, 2000; Girotto & Gonzalez, 2001; Johnson-Laird, Legrenzi, Girotto, Legrenzi, & Caverni, 1999; Kahneman & Tversky, 1982; Mellers & McGraw, 1999). The Nested-Sets Hypothesis assumes that people can take two different perspectives on the structure of a category or class. They can think about the category or class in terms of its instances, by mentally enumerating them, or at least generating several. Call this an outside view of category structure. Alternatively, people can think about the internal structure of their concept of a category, the parts and properties of a canonical instance and how the parts and properties relate to one another. Call this an inside view of the category. The outside/inside distinction is related, but not identical, to the philosophical distinction between the extension versus the intension of a word. Unlike the philosophical distinction, the outside/inside dichotomy is psychological in nature, does not necessarily concern word meaning, and does not refer to different descriptions of the same reference class. The sets of relevant category members may differ depending on whether one adopts an outside or an inside view. Indeed, the distinction can help to explain the frequency effect only on the assumption that the two perspectives do lead to different construals of a reference category. The Nested-Sets Hypothesis makes three assumptions:

(1) Frequency descriptions induce a representation of category instances (an outside view), rather than category properties (an inside view).
(2) All else being equal, people prefer an inside view.
(3) Representing instances makes their set inclusion relations transparent.

The idea is that people normally represent a category being judged from the inside. Hence, they tend to make probability judgements by appealing to relations like representativeness that rely on similarity and categorization processes, both of which involve comparison of internal structures. However, such a representation does not necessarily afford coherent probability judgement. The frequency frame induces an outside perspective by asking participants to think about multiple instances of the category. This reveals relations amongst instances that would otherwise not be observed, for example it can reveal when one to-be-judged category is composed of a superset of another, as in cases of the conjunction fallacy. Armed with this perception, people are more likely to make judgements consistent with it.

The Nested-Sets Hypothesis is that certain frequency frames increase coherent probabilistic responding by eliciting a representation in terms of nested sets and that other frames can too. Gigerenzer and Hoffrage (1995) argue that we have a special ability to understand the natural sampling of natural frequencies because this was adaptive under primitive conditions. They contend that this claim explains why certain word problems about natural frequencies are easier for people than problems about single-case probabilities. Yet they also hold that the set structure of the word problems about natural frequencies makes them less computationally complex than the problems about single-case probabilities. Although we agree with the latter assertion, we do not see how the two claims fit together as a consistent account of the evidence (see Chapter 5). The Nested-Sets Hypothesis explains the lack of computational complexity simply in terms of elementary set operations, such as taking partitions and unions of sets, which place the sets and their subsets in a nested relationship.

BASE-RATE NEGLECT

We first compare the hypotheses using a problem that has shown base-rate neglect. The following problem was first posed by Casscells, Schoenberger, and Grayboys (1978) to 60 students and staff at Harvard Medical School:

Original probability problem:
If a test to detect a disease whose prevalence is 1/1000 has a false-positive rate of 5 per cent, what is the chance that a person found to have a positive result actually has the disease, assuming you know nothing about the person's symptoms or signs?

Assuming that the probability of a positive result given the disease is 1, the Bayesian answer to this problem is approximately 2 per cent. Casscells et al. found that only 18 per cent of participants gave this answer. The modal response was 95 per cent, presumably on the supposition that, because the reported error rate of the test is 5 per cent, it must get 95 per cent of results correct.

We have replicated this result using a similar problem:

Modified original probability problem:
Consider a test to detect a disease that a given American has a 1/1000 chance of getting. An individual that does not have the disease has a 50/1000 chance of testing positive. An individual who does have the disease will definitely test

positive. What is the chance that a person found to have a positive result actually has the disease, assuming that you know nothing about the person's symptoms or signs? ____ per cent.

Unlike the original problem, this one makes explicit that the probability of testing positive is 1 if the individual does have the disease. Also, this problem, expresses uncertainty values as fractions (e.g. 1/1000). The natural frequency hypothesis does not state that Bayesian facilitation is merely a result of simpler arithmetic, so it is important to control the difficulty of the arithmetic demanded by different problems. A fraction is itself neither a frequency nor a probability; it is the interpretation of the value that classifies it.

Define a response as "Bayesian" if it is between 1.8 per cent and 2.2 per cent (written in any format). Despite the changes we made to the problem, our results closely replicated those of Casscells et al. (1978). We found that only 20 per cent of Brown University undergraduates gave the Bayesian response.

To test the natural frequency hypothesis, Cosmides and Tooby (1996) constructed several versions of a formally identical problem. One version used the following wording that states the problem in terms of relative frequencies and asks for a response in terms of frequencies:

Frequency version:
1 out of every 1000 Americans has disease X. A test has been developed to detect when a person has disease X. Every time the test is given to a person who has the disease, the test comes out positive. But sometimes the test also comes out positive when it is given to a person who is completely healthy. Specifically, out of every 1000 people who are perfectly healthy, 50 of them test positive for the disease. Imagine that we have assembled a random sample of 1000 Americans. They were selected by lottery. Those who conducted the lottery had no information about the health status of any of these people.

Given the information above, on average, how many people who test positive for the disease will *actually* have the disease? ____ out of ____.

Cosmides and Tooby found that a large majority of Stanford University students got the Bayesian answer to this problem (of the 50 or 51 people who test positive, only 1 has the disease), 72 per cent in their Experiment 2, Condition 1 and 80 per cent in their Experiment 3, Condition 2. They interpret this high performance as evidence that people have an adaptation for making inferences about frequencies.

We tried to replicate this effect using Brown undergraduates. Like Stanford, Brown is a highly selective undergraduate institution. We used the identical problem, but, to our surprise, found that only 51 per cent of our students gave the Bayesian response. To make sure this was not a fluke, we did it again. This time, only 31 per cent of our students gave the Bayesian answer. In sum, we failed to replicate the size of the frequency effect reported by Cosmides and Tooby (1996), although we too found that the frequency formulation increased Bayesian responding. The increase was only statistically significant in one of our two comparisons (the 51 per cent case), but it was in the predicted direction both times.

The explanation for this increase provided by the natural frequency hypothesis is obvious. The nested-sets hypothesis explains it by assuming that:

- Participants can represent people who have been tested for a disease from a perspective that gives access to the category's internal structure—relations amongst its features or properties—perhaps by considering a prototypical instance.
- This is our participants' default representation.
- The frequency frame induces an outside perspective by asking participants to think about multiple instances of the category.

An effective representation of the three relevant categories of the medical diagnosis problem should be isomorphic to the Euler circles of Fig. 6.1. In particular, the representation should make explicit that the set of possibilities

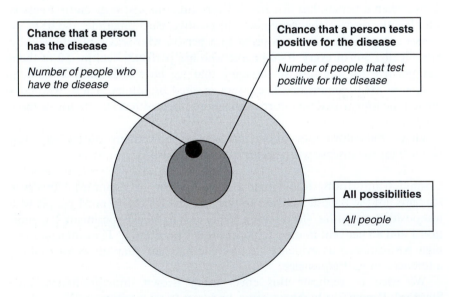

Figure 6.1   Euler circles for the medical diagnosis problem. Bold text appeared in the single-case probability condition; italicized text in the frequency condition.

in which a person tests positive is a subset of all possibilities and the set corresponding to having the disease is a subset of the positive tests. Once these nested-set relations are understood, the Bayesian answer can more easily be seen to reflect the degree to which the subset corresponding to having the disease covers the set corresponding to a positive test, obtained by calculating the ratio of the two magnitudes. The hypothesis implies that the advantage of frequency over single-case probability formats should disappear when nested-set relations are also made transparent in the single-case probability format (cf. Johnson-Laird et al., 1999).

Consider the following probability problem:

Clarified single-case probability version 1:
The prevalence of disease X among Americans is 1/1000. A test has been developed to detect when a person has disease X. Every time the test is given to a person who has the disease, the test comes out positive. But sometimes the test also comes out positive when it is given to a person who is completely healthy. Specifically, the chance is 50/1000 that someone who is perfectly healthy would test positive for the disease.

Imagine that we have given the test to a random sample of Americans. They were selected by lottery. Those who conducted the lottery had no information about the health status of any of these people.

What is the chance that a person found to have a positive result actually has the disease? ____ per cent.

This problem comes almost word for word from Cosmides and Tooby (1996; Experiment 6, Condition 1), who labelled it a non-frequentist problem. The only difference is that, like Casscells et al., Cosmides and Tooby described the false-positive rate by saying "5% of all people who are . . ." To ease calculations and to maintain focus on a single individual, we instead said, "the chance is 50/1000 that someone who is . . ." The text of this problem seems to make the nested-sets relation just as transparent as the frequency version, while providing identical information. The only difference is that it concerns single-event probabilities rather than frequencies. Therefore, the nested-sets hypothesis predicts that it should show just as much Bayesian facilitation as the frequency version.

Forty-eight per cent of our participants gave the Bayesian response to this problem, essentially the same proportion giving the Bayesian response to the frequency problem. Apparently, the determinant of facilitation is not the use of a frequency format *per se*, but the use of any format that clarifies the set relations amongst the events.

Although this transparent probability problem considers a single individual and the probability that that individual has the disease, one could argue that people represent the problem in terms of frequency, rather than single-case probability. The problem uses the term "prevalence", and the phrase "every time", and asks participants to imagine a random sample of Americans, all aspects that could conceivably cue a frequency representation. That is, a proponent of the natural frequency hypothesis could claim that, even though Cosmides and Tooby (1996) themselves characterized essentially the same question as a single-case probability problem, it might really induce a frequency set, or induce one in the group of people we tested. To make sure that our results hold even with a problem that is not susceptible to these concerns, we tested the following version of a probability problem with transparent nested sets that in every sense concerns the probability that a single individual has the disease, and not the frequency of the disease in a group:

Clarified single-case probability version 2:
The probability that an average American has disease X is 1/1000. A test has been developed to detect if that person has disease X. If the test is given and the person has the disease, the test comes out positive. But the test can come out positive even if the person is completely healthy. Specifically, the chance is 50/1000 that someone who is perfectly healthy would test positive for the disease. Consider an average American. Assume you know nothing about the health status of this person.

What is the probability that if this person is tested and found to have a positive result, the person would actually have the disease? ____.

Forty per cent of respondents to this problem gave the Bayesian response, a percentage not significantly different than the Bayesian percentages in the frequency or other clarified probability problems. Thus, this version of the problem, that concerns single-case probability and not frequency in every respect, leads to just as much Bayesian responding as the problem framed in frequency terms merely by stating the problem clearly and making the structure of the situation transparent. To the extent that the frequency hypothesis differs from the Nested-Sets Hypothesis, this is strong evidence in favour of nested sets.

The Nested-Sets Hypothesis predicts that any manipulation that increases the transparency of the nested-sets relation should increase Bayesian responding. As a further test of this prediction, we gave two different groups of participants the modified original probability problem of Casscells et al. (1978) and the frequency version along with a diagram using Euler circles (see Fig. 6.1). The diagram was intended to increase transparency by making the nested-set relations explicit, a manipulation also used by Cosmides and Tooby (1996, Experiment 4). Instructions were to use the diagram to help reason through the problem.

The diagram brought performance up to the level seen with the frequency and clarified single-case probability problems (all percentages of Bayesian responding are shown in Table 6.1). The diagram facilitated Bayesian responding in the modified original probability condition to 48 per cent but had no effect on performance in the frequency condition. Making the nested-set relations transparent facilitated performance if and only if they were not already clear; the diagram provided no added benefit once the set structure had already been exposed. Similar results are reported by Cosmides and Tooby (1996). In Condition 2 of their Experiment 4, they found that 76 per cent of participants gave a Bayesian response, a percentage comparable to that in their standard frequency conditions. In our study, the problems remained difficult for just over half the participants for reasons of calculation or conceptual mapping despite transparent nested-sets structure.

Another implication of the Nested-Sets Hypothesis is that a problem should be more difficult if the relevant relations are not nested. If the facilitation in Bayesian responding observed on this problem is due to transparent nested-sets relations, then a slightly modified problem whose set representation is not nested should not be facilitated in either a single-case probability or a frequency frame. To create such a problem, we changed the false-negative rate from 0 to 1/1000. This is equivalent to changing the hit rate from 1 to 999/1000. The critical set relations are no longer nested because the chance of having the disease is not nested within the chance of testing positive; there is a small chance of having the disease even without testing positive. The Nested-Sets Hypothesis predicts that few participants will arrive at the Bayesian solution to this problem. The natural frequency hypothesis predicts that more people should get the Bayesian answer under a frequency than under a single-case probability frame.

One problem we tested, the single-case probability version with positive false-negative rate, was identical to the clarified single-case probability version 1 except that the sentence "Every time the test is given to a person who

TABLE 6.1
Percentage Bayesian responses on various versions of the medical diagnosis problem

	Single-case probability problems		Frequency problems
Modified original	20	Cosmides & Tooby replication	51/31
Clarified 1	48		
Clarified 2	40		
With Euler circles	48	With Euler circles	45
Unnested: positive false-negative rate	15	Unnested: positive false-negative rate	21

has the disease, the test comes out positive" was replaced with "The test is almost sure to come out positive for a person who has the disease. Specifically, the chance is 999/1000 that someone who has the disease will test positive." A frequency version with positive false-negative rate was also tested. In this version, the corresponding sentence was replaced with, "The test almost always comes out positive for someone who has the disease. Specifically, out of every 1000 people who have the disease, the test comes out positive 999 times." The Bayesian answer to these problems is almost identical to all previous problems, about 2 per cent.

Performance on both versions was low. Fifteen per cent of those given the single-case probability version with positive false-negative rate gave the Bayesian response; 21 per cent of those given the frequency version with positive false-negative rate gave the Bayesian response. These do not statistically differ from each other, or from the proportions getting the original problem correct.

In conclusion, the critical variable for generating Bayesian responses with the medical diagnosis problem is not whether the problem is framed in terms of frequency rather than single-case probability, but whether the problem can be represented using nested sets and the nested-set relations are made transparent by the statement of the problem. Facilitation is observed with both single-case probability and frequency problems when relations are transparent. Facilitation is observed with neither kind of problem when relations are not nested.

CONJUNCTION FALLACY

A second cognitive illusion of probability judgement that has been claimed to "disappear" under a frequency frame (Gigerenzer, 1994) is the conjunction fallacy of Tversky and Kahneman (1983). Their most famous example begins with the description:

> Linda is 31 years old, single, outspoken and very bright. She majored in philosophy. As a student, she was deeply concerned with issues of discrimination and social justice, and also participated in antinuclear demonstrations.

and asks participants to judge the relative likelihood of the following two statements:

> Linda is a bank teller. (A)
> Linda is a bank teller and is active in the feminist movement. (A&B)

Because proposition A is logically implied by proposition A&B, the probability of A is necessarily greater than or equal to the probability of A&B (the conjunction rule of probability). In this case, the rule follows from common sense. No commitment to Bayesianism or any other theory of the foundations of probability is required to see that, if one has to make a guess about Linda, choosing the more general statement is sensible. But, as Tversky and Kahneman (1983) showed and many others have replicated (Bar-Hillel & Neter, 1993; Johnson, Hershey, Meszaros, & Kunreuther, 1993), people fail to do so consistently. Rather, most people judge Linda more likely to be a feminist bank teller because she sounds like a feminist. That is, people reason from the inside, in terms of properties, not in accordance with the fact that the set of bank tellers includes the set of feminist bank tellers.

Evidence that judgements on this problem can respect nested-set relations—greater certainty being assigned to more inclusive sets—is provided by Fiedler (1988). He asked people either to evaluate the relative probability that Linda was a bank teller versus a feminist bank teller (he asked them to rank order the statements according to their probability) or about relative frequency ("To how many out of 100 people who are like Linda do the statements apply?"). Fiedler found that 91 per cent of participants violated the conjunction rule in the probability condition but only 22 per cent violated it in the frequency condition.

Tversky and Kahneman (1983) interpreted their own demonstration of frequency debiasing with the conjunction fallacy in terms of the Nested-Sets Hypothesis: Presenting the options as concrete classes made the inclusion relation between the two sets more transparent. Specifically, single-case probability frames tend to encourage people to think about events in terms of properties; one naturally considers the match between the properties of Linda and the properties of bank tellers. These frames elicit a focus on intensional structure, a perspective on events that causes people to rely on the representativeness of outcomes and obscures the set relations between instances. In contrast, frequency frames induce a representation in terms of multiple instances, so that problem solvers can "see" the embedding of one set of instances inside another. When the correct logical relation between categories (all feminist bank tellers are bank tellers) is evident, participants are more likely to generate judgements of probability that respect it. Hence, the incidence of the conjunction fallacy is reduced.

Both Fiedler (1988) and Tversky and Kahneman (1983) found significant effects for frequency frames; at most 20–25 per cent of participants violated the conjunction rule in both frequency conditions. However, Tversky and Kahneman found markedly different results than Fiedler in the single-case probability condition: Tversky and Kahneman found that only 65 per cent of participants committed the conjunction fallacy; Fiedler found that 91 per cent did. The difference may be a result of different tasks. Fiedler's single-case probability question asked participants to rank-order each alternative. This forced a choice between events by not offering the option to judge both alternatives as equally probable. Without this option, some people may have committed the conjunction fallacy despite the (perfectly reasonable) conviction that the two options were equally likely. Tversky and Kahneman asked for probability ratings—not rankings—and obtained far fewer conjunction fallacies, possibly because ratings allowed people to assign equal probabilities to the two events. Whereas the question was held constant in Tversky and Kahneman's study, Fiedler used a ranking question in the single-case probability condition and a rating question for frequency. This confound was repeated and the issue extensively discussed by Hertwig and Gigerenzer (1999). They attribute about half of the difference between their single-case probability and frequency conditions to the difference between rating and ranking.

To contrast the Natural Frequency and Nested-Sets hypotheses, the effect of frequency was measured on two conjunction fallacy problems in the absence of a transparent nested-set relation. The Natural Frequency Hypothesis presumably predicts a stable frequency effect. In contrast, the Nested-Sets Hypothesis predicts that a frequency format would not reduce the conjunction fallacy if the relation between the critical statements is opaque. To make it opaque, we hid the nested-sets relation by inserting statements between the conjunction and its constituent. We expected that spacing the critical statements would obscure their inclusion relation so that they would be judged independently. We attempted to reconcile Tversky and Kahneman's (1983) and Fiedler's (1988) findings by using both ranking and rating tasks. We expected that ranking would lead to more conjunction errors, because it forces a choice between the critical statements. This effect could be attenuated because ranking also forces a comparison of statements, a process that could increase the likelihood of discovering the critical set inclusion relation. However, ratings are usually also made in relation to other statements and so could involve just as much comparison, at least when statements with similar terms are in close proximity. In sum, we predict that performance in the single-case probability and frequency frames should not differ for either task.

Two problems were tested: "Linda" and "Bill the accountant" (see Tversky & Kahneman, 1982). All conditions in the Linda problem used the description above. All participants were asked to rate or rank-order a set of 11 statements concerning Linda (or Bill). The nested-sets relations were made opaque by separating the critical statements (the conjunction and its constituent) by seven unrelated items. The format of the Bill problem was identical. In the single-case probability version, participants were asked either to "Please rank order the following items from most to least likely" (ranking), or "Using the information above, estimate the probability that:" (rating). Frequency frames were analogous.

Table 6.2 shows the percentages of correct responses for frequency and single-case probability judgements in the rating and ranking conditions for

TABLE 6.2
Percentages of correct responses for frequency and single-case probability frames in rating and ranking conditions and percentages of responses that assigned equal values to conjunction and constituent in rating condition

	Ranking	Rating	Equal ratings
Linda: Probability	25.0	65.2	34.8
Linda: Frequency	30.1	66.7	19.0
Bill: Probability	17.2	45.5	18.2
Bill: Frequency	20.1	54.2	29.2

each problem as well as percentages of ratings that assigned equal values to conjunction and constituent. As predicted, single-case probability and frequency frames did not differ in either the rating or ranking conditions for either problem. These results suggest that frequency frames do not improve performance over probability frames unless the nested-sets structure of the problem is exposed. By making it opaque in the frequency condition, we eliminated the enhancement typically seen in relation to single-event probability judgements. Notice that more than two-thirds of ranking participants (80 per cent for the Bill problem) produced conjunction fallacies, even with a frequency format. Conjunction fallacies were less common in the rating conditions, where participants were not forced to rank order statements.

As shown in the third column of Table 6.2, a substantial number of participants chose to assign equal values to the conjunction and its constituent when rating. These responses largely account for differences between rating and ranking tasks. Hertwig and Chase (1998) argue that the difference between the tasks emanates from different strategies: They hold that people rate by making independent evaluations of evidential support and integrate across cues using rules. In contrast, people rank by making pairwise comparisons of evidential support using single cues. Such a theory cannot be ruled out by these data. Our suggestion is simpler, but the important point here is that ranking produces more conjunction fallacies than rating.

SUMMARY OF STUDIES

The studies reported support the Nested-Sets Hypothesis over the Natural Frequency Hypothesis. They found that, first, the facilitation observed with a frequency frame on the medical diagnosis task was also induced by a clearly stated single-event probability frame. Second, comparable facilitation was obtained with a diagram that clarified the critical nested-set relations of the problem. Third, the effect of frequency framing has been overstated. It can be eliminated by using a problem that does not involve nested sets. We also found the effect size with the original medical diagnosis task was smaller than that reported by Cosmides and Tooby (1996). And the effect on the conjunction fallacy, as reported by Fiedler (1988) and Hertwig and Gigerenzer (1999), was exaggerated by a confound with rating versus ranking. Fourth, the benefit of frequency in reducing the conjunction fallacy was eliminated by making the critical nested-set relation opaque by spacing the conjunction and its constituent.

Taken together, the data suggest that greater coherence in probabilistic responding on word problems is not a direct consequence of presenting problems in a frequency format, but rather of making the structure of the problem apparent by inducing participants to represent the problem in a way that highlights how relevant instances relate to one another. Our claim is decidedly not that frequency formats never help to make nested-set relations clear. Indeed, they can very effectively by cueing a representation that makes subset relations transparent. But not all situations can meaningfully be construed in terms of multiple instances. For instance, the probability of a defendant's guilt or of nuclear war cannot meaningfully be framed in terms of frequency. Some events can only occur once. Worse, some probability judgements reflect beliefs about things that can never happen. What is the probability that your car would have started yesterday if it were in Antarctica? Counterfactual questions like this are well formed, even if you do not have a car.

TYPES OF PROBABILITY JUDGEMENT

Philosophers of science have long distinguished two different concepts of probability (Carnap, 1950): on one hand, epistemic or inductive probability, and on the other hand, objective probability. We follow Bayesians in interpreting epistemic or inductive probabilities as degrees of belief or confidence, that can be based, to a greater or lesser extent, on evidence (Howson & Urbach, 1993). Our judgement that it is likely that all giraffes have aortic arches attaches a probability to our state of belief, not to giraffes. Giraffes either do or do not have aortic arches; any uncertainty is due to ignorance, lack of confidence, or inadequate evidence. Objective probability can be defined in a number of ways. One definition is in terms of relative frequency, but what does it mean to hold that the relative frequency that a coin will come up heads is 1 out of 2? It cannot mean that any sample frequency, from actually spinning the coin, will necessarily be 1 out of 2, or 5 out of 10, or 50 out of 100. Many probability theorists have therefore characterized the objective probability that a fair coin will come up heads as the relative frequency of heads in the long run or, more technically, as the limiting value in a certain kind of infinite sequence. But other theorists have argued that statements about what would happen in the long run have no observable counterparts. They have proposed instead that an objective probability is a theoretical property, a propensity: in our example, a property of fairness in the coin. This analysis also faces problems, and the whole question is one of lively debate among philosophers of science (Howson & Urbach, 1993). However, we do not see how resolving this matter can be relevant to what was adaptive in probability judgement under primitive conditions. The fact is that people cannot observe infinite sequences of possible outcomes, nor theoretical propensities. The only access that people could have to them is indirect, by way of the sample frequencies that they collect or through probabilistic models. Cosmides and Tooby and Gigerenzer make no attempt to resolve any of the problems in the philosophy of science about objective probability. Their arguments about primitive people refer only to sample frequencies, yet objective probabilities cannot be naively reduced to these samples. Nevertheless, we can make our points using sample frequencies alone and will not have to enter into a philosophical debate about what is objective beyond the samples.

Gigerenzer and Hoffrage (1995) and Cosmides and Tooby (1996) appear to presuppose that a single-case probability is simply a percentage or fraction applied to a singular proposition, for example, a proposition about a specific man or giraffe rather than all men or all giraffes. That is fine as far as the experiments are concerned, but it masks problems in their evolutionary argument. They claim that it would be useless for a primitive person to think and communicate about single-case probabilities in the sense that they discuss them. But primitive people would have benefited from expressing and understanding degrees of belief or confidence about singular propositions, and one way to justify these single-case probabilities is through sample frequencies. Suppose that some primitive people have hunted 50 giraffes and failed in 40 of these attempts to kill one, and that they remember this sample frequency. Suppose also that they face the question one morning whether to hunt some specific giraffe in front of them. What is the good of recalling the sample frequency if they cannot use it that morning to justify the single-case judgement that they will probably fail in hunting this giraffe?

Brase et al. (1998) rightly stress the advantage of keeping track of sample size. But that is only an advantage if the hunters in our example make a more confident single-case judgement about the specific giraffe than they would have when they only had a sample of 4 failures in 5 giraffe hunts. Thus people need to understand how to make good single-case probability judgements that are sensitive to sample size. Brase et al. (1998) also note that new reference classes can be extracted from remembered samples, and suggest that the availability heuristic of Tversky and Kahneman (1973) might serve this function. To extend our example, the hunters might observe that the giraffe in front of them is lame, and use the availability heuristic to recall that they successfully hunted 4 out of 5 lame giraffes in the past. This is certainly a worthwhile suggestion, as long as we do not take it to imply that people can always make unbiased single-case probability judgements.

Now let us assume that some other people under primitive conditions have no experience of hunting giraffes. Using a mental model, they can still make the epistemic single-case judgement that they will probably fail in hunting a specific giraffe when they finally come across one. This might be the result of guessing the distance from which the giraffe will be able to see them coming, and that in turn might depend on thinking of the giraffe's vision as similar to their own when they are up a tree. They will then decide not to hunt the giraffe and go off in search of easier prey. Perhaps they will never sample giraffe hunting, yet their model of giraffe hunting will always enable them to make a useful single-case judgement that they will probably fail in a hunt of any particular giraffe.

Moreover, what would be the point of making inductive inferences to beliefs about all giraffes if there were no effective probability inferences in turn from these general propositions to singular propositions? In fact, Gigerenzer and Hoffrage (1995) and Cosmides and Tooby (1996) do not propose any account of epistemic or inductive probabilities, and appear to presuppose that this is unnecessary. But people must work with some notion of epistemic or inductive probability if they are to make effective inferences from observations of the world and of sample frequencies within it, including when those sample frequencies may be biased.

Regardless of the concept of probability at issue, the formal structure of normative probability theory associates a measure of uncertainty with sets and subsets. For the frequency concept, the members of the sets and subsets are of course physical events. For the epistemic or inductive concept, the sets and subsets are propositions or possible states of affairs that are believed with some degree of confidence (Jeffrey, 1983). Any coherent probability judgements can be given a set and subset structure, but of course people do not always make coherent judgements, and even when they do, they do not always themselves represent these with a set and subset structure. They instead tend to take an inside view. Still, any experimental manipulation that affords perception of a transparent set and subset structure for a probability problem has the potential to increase the coherence of judgements. Frequency formats can sometimes do that but they are not necessary, because single-case probabilities and set-theoretic relations between propositions can also be made transparent (as shown here and in, for example, Ajzen, 1977; Evans et al., 2000; Johnson-Laird et al., 1999; Mellers & McGraw, 1999). And they are not sufficient, because other criteria must be satisfied to ensure a veridical representation. These include the nesting of relevant sets (see Table 6.1), and the transparency of nesting (see Table 6.2), as well as representative sampling and accurate working and long-term memory retrieval (Bar-Hillel & Neter, 1993;

Gigerenzer et al., 1991; Gluck & Bower, 1988; Lewis & Keren, 1999; Tversky & Kahneman, 1974).

Hence, the success of some frequency formats for some problems provides no support for the psychological reality of a specific "sort of instinct" for frequency representations that allows people to solve the problems (as concluded by Gigerenzer & Hoffrage, 1995, p. 701). Perhaps the strongest evidence for this point is a thought experiment. If the Linda problem were given along with Euler circles that exposed its logical structure, hardly anyone would commit the conjunction fallacy even in a single-event probability context, and in fact, we found that only 2 of 39 people did. Gigerenzer (2000) dismisses what he calls Leibniz's dream and the goal of his followers in the Enlightenment and later, which is to create a system in which formal relations are as clear as possible. Ironically, Euler, a great Enlightenment figure, devised his circle system by following Leibniz's lead (Kneale & Kneale, 1962, p. 349), and this system does enable people to avoid biases by helping them to grasp logical and set theoretic relations.

The nested-sets hypothesis is the general claim that making nested-set relations transparent will increase the coherence of probability judgement (at the cost, in some cases, of changing the object of judgement). Note again that making set relations transparent is not the same as inducing a frequency frame. Epistemic probabilities can also be given a set structure, and subset and set membership relations can represent probabilities even for single-case probability judgements. Nested-set relations are more general than frequency representations. This is most obvious with the Linda problem. Consider the theory of Johnson-Laird et al. (1999), in which people sometimes use coherent mental models rather than heuristics to make probability judgements. When they do, their set of mental models of A&B is a subset of their set of mental models of A. The relation between A&B and A is epistemic and indeed logical, and not any kind of frequency.

MORE ON THE NATURAL FREQUENCY HYPOTHESIS

The natural frequency via natural sampling hypothesis suffers from several inadequacies. Gigerenzer and Hoffrage (1995) illustrate natural sampling with an example of an old physician in an illiterate society who recalls 10 people with a certain disease out of 1000 people she has seen in her life. She can also remember that 8 of these 10 had some symptom of the disease, and that 95 also had this symptom out of the 990 without the disease. It is then easy for her to infer, in conformity with Bayesian inference, that 8 people have the disease out of 103 with the symptom.

The transparency of the set relations in this example, and the initial plausibility of the working memory requirements, depends on using numbers, like 10 and 1000, that are easy to recall and operate on in our number system. But this system is a convention that was created by sophisticated mathematicians precisely to help us in these ways. This is most obvious in the case of the use of the numeral 0, which was not even present in Greek and Roman mathematics. No primitive hominids or human beings had such a conventional number system when they were feeling the effects of natural selection.

In its stronger form, the natural sampling hypothesis fails to explain why the errors obtained with single-case probability judgement are systematic; if they arise simply because people do not understand single-case probabilities, such errors should be random. In its weaker form (Brase et al. 1998; Gigerenzer & Hoffrage, 1999), it makes unsupportable assumptions about the process of probability judgement. It requires massive memories to maintain counts of all relevant experiences. Not many of us can recall the total number of first-year essays we have marked. Still less can we say how many of these got a C or less, how many of those showed a problem with spelling, and how many of those with a higher mark than C showed these signs. An illiterate physician would presumably not have much better memory for a disease and its symptom. Unfortunately, the experiments offered as evidence for the hypothesis require no memory because handy counts are always provided.

Another problem is that the purported frequency module lacks critical capabilities. It fails to indicate qualitative characteristics like independence. The frequency module would not know if data provided no information about a hypothesis. This could be fatal to a user of such an inductive mechanism for it would not indicate whether or not a symptom were diagnostic of a disease. Natural sampling may tell us that 800 out of 1000 people have some disease, and that 640 of the 800 people with the disease show some symptom. But if 160 out of the 200 without the disease also show the symptom, and if these are unbiased samples, then the symptom and the disease are independent, because 80 per cent of people have the disease if they show the symptom and 80 per cent have the disease if they do not. This concern is particularly acute for Gigerenzer and Hoffrage (1995, 1999) because they stress that a virtue of natural sampling is that samples are not normalized. But normalization is necessary to see that the symptom and disease are independent (Over, 2000a, 2000b; Over & Green, 2001).

Gigerenzer and Hoffrage (1995, 1999) also confuse sample frequencies with objective frequencies. They presuppose in their examples that natural sampling does not produce biased samples; but avoiding bias even in apparently well-designed experiments is notoriously difficult. Therefore, they and Cosmides and Tooby (1996) are mistaken that objective frequencies are more observable than single-case probabilities. In both cases, an inference is required to have some rational confidence that a sample frequency is unbiased and a single-case probability judgement is justified. These theorists all beg the question by concluding, on the basis of responses to idealized word problems, that cognitive illusions disappear in the real world. They assume what they should be arguing for: That people are not prone to biases and cognitive illusions about a sampling process and what to infer from it (Over, 2000a, 2000b, Chapter 5).

FRAMES FOR PROBABILITY JUDGEMENT

People use multiple representational formats to make probability judgements. Each is more or less useful in different situations and each reveals different aspects of the situations being judged.

Nested sets

Probability judgements can reflect proportions read off of a real or imagined surface that contains regions corresponding to one or more subsets of the sample space. These regions obey two constraints: (1) their size is proportional to the perceived coverage of the sample space by the corresponding subset; (2) the overlap of regions respects perceived subset relations within the sample space. Such a representation can be constructed only when people think about the problem at hand from the outside. People are more likely to think this way when asked a question about a frequency, but other formats can also elicit this perspective. Nested-sets frames are easiest to construct when judgements directly concern objective probabilities about multiple events. If the size of the symbolic regions are not normalized and correspond to counts of the relevant events, and no sampling bias is in question, then the ratio calculation recommended by Kleiter (1994) is simple and accurate for generating conditional probabilities. The limitation of this calculation is that it abstracts from sampling problems and presupposes a detailed understanding of the structure of the sample space, an understanding that a probability judge often lacks.

Strength of evidence

A complete understanding of a probability judgement requires knowledge of the task that participants think they are performing. People may not always be judging the axiomatized senses of probability, but might construe problems otherwise (Hilton, 1995). For example, instead of probability, people sometimes judge the strength of evidence in favour of a hypothesis (cf. Briggs & Krantz, 1992). Judgements of evidential strength need not satisfy the axioms of probability. The normative issue of whether or not participants' judgements should conform to the axioms of probability is an interesting one, but not really relevant here (see Vranas, 2000, for an enlightening normative analysis). A question that might be more pertinent is whether the manipulations in the current experiments changed the task that participants assigned themselves. In particular, manipulations that facilitate performance may operate by replacing a non-extensional task interpretation, like evidence strength, with an extensional one. Note that such a construal of the effects we have shown just reframes the questions that our studies address: Under what conditions are people's judgements extensional, and what aspects of their judgements correspond to the prescripts of probability theory?

Representativeness

One way to estimate a probability is by analogy to other, similar events or propositions. The effectiveness of this kind of similarity-based heuristic is the motivation for the representativeness heuristic (Kahneman & Tversky, 1972). Linda is more likely to be a feminist bankteller because she is similar to other feminists. Such a heuristic may be all one has for some single-case probability judgements. An accurate judgement of the probability that a particular leaf is an oak leaf would seem to depend on an assessment of similarity between the leaf and other oak leaves. Conceiving of a population of identical oak leaves would not shed any light on this problem.

Categorical inductive inference is a special case of this kind of analogical inference. On learning that robins have sesamoid bones, most people will conclude that sparrows are likely to have sesamoid bones too, and that they are certainly more likely than penguins to have sesamoid bones, because robins and sparrows are more similar than robins and penguins (Osherson, Smith, Wilkie, Lopez, & Shafir, 1990; Sloman, 1993). Frequency relations are simply no help here, and not merely because few people have any experience with instances of the bone types of various birds. After all, having sesamoid bones is a highly projectible property: If one sparrow (or penguin) has them, then presumably all do. So the issue is not the proportion of birds with the property. The matter is one of inductive probability and degrees of belief. Evidence about robins increases one's degree of belief in the hypothesis about sparrows more than the hypothesis about penguins because robins and sparrows have relatively more in common, not because the fact about robins adds to some sparrow frequency count. As a general rule, a frequency representation is useless for determining a degree of belief that a hypothesis is true or false. Obviously, this is not to say that sample size or particular instances are not useful. It is merely to say the relation between evidence and hypothesis is an epistemic one between propositions, and not a relative frequency between physical events. Epistemic relations themselves can sometimes have a transparent set structure and sometimes not. For example, if you believe that all sparrows are birds and you learn that all birds have sesamoid bones, then you should conclude that all sparrows do. But people do not always make this inference, relying instead on similarity (Sloman, 1998), suggesting that people prefer an inside view, and that the outside view of set structure is not always transparent to them.

Causal models

Another way to estimate a probability in the absence of detailed knowledge of the structure of the sample space is to rely on a causal model. Many (if not all) causal relations are probabilistic (e.g. working hard increases the chance of success but, unfortunately, does not guarantee it). Probabilistic causal models have proven popular in the form of Bayesian graphical networks (Pearl, 1988). However, in their usual formulation, such networks are merely representations of observed data. More recent formulations (Pearl, 2000) have succeeded in giving graphical networks a true causal interpretation by introducing an operator that allows for the representation of action as opposed to just observation. Representing an action requires intervening on the network to set an independent variable to some value. The availability of an operator to do so gives us the ability to model an experiment, by manipulating the value of an independent variable and inferring the resulting effect on a dependent variable. It also gives us the ability to make a counterfactual inference, by setting a variable to a value that does not correspond to the current state and inferring the effect on other variables. Moreover, the ability to model an experiment enables us to model causal induction. Pearl (2000) also proposes to infer causal relations from correlational data. Whether or not his approach is valid, the framework does offer a powerful and plausible normative model of causal and counterfactual reasoning that might turn out to help explain how people learn about causal relations through their own and others' actions. People's more sophisticated causal models of objects and events may be learned through an iterative process of experiment, instruction, and observation that could bootstrap off of the micro-experiments that infants conduct when they manipulate their environments by reaching, kicking, or screaming, thus learning about the physical and social relations in their environments.

Evidence in favour of the psychological validity of models of this sort can be found in Cheng (1997) and Waldmann, Holyoak, and Fratianne (1995). People can be exquisitely sensitive to the structure of a causal model (Rehder & Hastie, 1997; Waldmann, 1996), responding differently if, for example, a variable is labelled a cause as opposed to an effect. Other evidence shows that people choose causal over correlational facts to explain an event (Ahn, Kalish, Medin, & Gelman, 1995) and that evidence is more influential if it is presented in the form of a causal story than if it is not (Pennington & Hastie, 1988). Tversky and Kahneman (1983) argued that some instances of the conjunction fallacy are due to attributions of causality.

To sum up, powerful causal models exist to make probabilstic inferences. Such models assume an inside view: They represent relations between parts and properties of objects and events (causes and effects), not between instances. The evidence suggests that people show a preference for information that relates to a causal model, and that they are responsive to such information in predictable ways. Causal models provide a powerful frame for people to use to make judgements of probability, a frame that is quite different from nested sets.

CONCLUSION

Proponents of the Natural Frequency Hypothesis claim that it can be grounded in evolutionary theory, but there is no reason why evolutionary psychology should be committed to such a hypothesis, for it is less credible than its antithesis. This is an evolutionary account of why people should be good, although far from perfect, at making epistemic and inductive probability judgements as well as single-case judgements. After all, most events that we have to think about, rather than automatically react to, are one-offs. When we engage in battle, an interpersonal relationship, an intellectual enterprise, or many other endeavours, judgements must be made in at least partly novel contexts. The conditions we find ourselves in change regularly because human environments produce varied, complex interactions that we must respond to intelligently to survive. We cannot naïvely rely only on counts of previous experiences that we recall, or imagine we recall, to deal with such novelty and complexity. We must also rely on our theories and causal and explanatory models of previous experience. Such theories and models allow us to make judgements and predictions on the basis of our understanding of the unfolding structure of a situation, rather than on the sole basis of what we may, or may not, accurately remember of our past samples of frequencies. They allow us to make accurate pre- and post-dictions about unique events, and help us to assign reliable degrees of belief to uncertain singular propositions. This is true now; this was true of our evolutionary ancestors when they confronted challenging new environments.

ACKNOWLEDGEMENTS

This chapter is based on Sloman, Slovak, and Over, Frequency Illusions and Other Fallacies. We would like to thank Ralph Hertwig for helpful comments and Lila Slovak for helping to run the studies and analyse the data. This work was supported by Grant IS-01-S2H-070 from NASA.

REFERENCES

Ahn, W., Kalish, C.W., Medin, D.L., & Gelman, S.A. (1995). The role of covariation versus mechanism information in causal attribution. *Cognition, 54*, 299–352.

Ajzen, I. (1977). Intuitive theories of events and the effects of base-rate information on prediction. *Journal of Personality and Social Psychology, 35*, 303–314.

Ayton, P., & Wright, G. (1994). Subjective probability: What should we believe? In G. Wright & P. Ayton (Eds.), *Subjective probability* (pp. 163–183). Chichester, UK: John Wiley & Sons.

Bar-Hillel, M., & Neter, E. (1993). How alike is it versus how likely is it: A disjunction fallacy in probability judgments. *Journal of Personality and Social Psychology, 65*, 1119–1131.

Brase, G.L., Cosmides, L., & Tooby, J. (1998). Individuals, counting, and statistical inference: The role of frequency and whole-object representations in judgment under uncertainty. *Journal of Experimental Psychology: General, 127*, 3–21.

Brenner, L.A., Koehler, D.J., Liberman, V., & Tversky, A. (1996). Overconfidence in probability and frequency judgments: A critical examination. *Organizational Behavior and Human Decision Processes, 65*, 212–219.

Briggs, L., & Krantz, D. (1992). Judging the strength of designated evidence. *Journal of Behavioral Decision Making, 5*, 77–106.

Carnap, R. (1950). *Logical foundations of probability*. Chicago: University of Chicago Press.

Casscells, W., Schoenberger, A., & Grayboys, T. (1978). Interpretation by physicians of clinical laboratory results. *New England Journal of Medicine, 299*, 999–1000.

Cheng, P.W. (1997). From covariation to causation: A causal power theory. *Psychological Review, 104*, 367–405.

Cosmides, L., & Tooby, J. (1996). Are humans good intuitive statisticians after all? Rethinking some conclusions from the literature on judgment under uncertainty. *Cognition, 58*, 1–73.

Evans, J.St.B.T., Handley, S.H., Perham, N., Over, D.E., & Thompson, V.A. (2000). Frequency versus probability formats in statistical word problems. *Cognition, 77*, 197–213.

Fiedler, K. (1988). The dependence of the conjunction fallacy on subtle linguistic factors. *Psychological Research, 50*, 123–129.

Gigerenzer, G. (1994). Why the distinction between single-event probabilities and frequencies is important for psychology (and vice versa). In G. Wright & P. Ayton (Eds.), *Subjective probability* (pp. 129–162). Chichester: John Wiley & Sons.

Gigerenzer, G. (1998). Ecological intelligence: An adaptation for frequencies. In D.D. Cummins & C. Allen (Eds.), *The evolution of mind*. New York: Oxford University Press.

Gigerenzer, G. (2000). *Adaptive thinking*. New York: Oxford University Press.

Gigerenzer, G., & Hoffrage, U. (1995). How to improve Bayesian reasoning without instruction: Frequency formats. *Psychological Review, 102*, 684–704.

Gigerenzer, G., & Hoffrage, U. (1999). Overcoming difficulties in Bayesian reasoning: A reply to Lewis and Keren (1999) and Mellers and McGraw (1999). *Psychological Review, 106*, 425–430.

Gigerenzer, G., Hoffrage, U., & Kleinbolting, H. (1991). Probabilistic mental models: A Brunswikian theory of confidence. *Psychological Review, 98*, 506–528.

Girotto, V., & Gonzalez, M. (2001). Solving probabilistic and statistical problems: A matter of information structure and question form. *Cognition, 78*, 247–276.

Gluck, M.A. & Bower, G.H. (1988). From conditioning to category learning: An adaptive network model. *Journal of Experimental Psychology: General, 117*, 227–247.

Griffin, D., & Buehler, R. (1999). Frequency, probability, and prediction: Easy solutions to cognitive illusions? *Cognitive Psychology, 38*, 48–78.

Hertwig, R., & Chase, V.M. (1998). Many reasons or just one: How response mode affects reasoning in the conjunction problem. *Thinking and Reasoning, 4*, 319–352.

Hertwig, R., & Gigerenzer, G. (1999). The "conjunction fallacy" revisited: How intelligent inferences look like reasoning errors. *Journal of Behavioral Decision Making, 12*, 275–305.

Hilton, D.J. (1995). The social context of reasoning: Conversational inference and rational judgment. *Psychological Bulletin, 118*, 248–271.

Howson, C., & Urbach, P. (1993). *Scientific reasoning* (2nd ed.). Chicago: Open Court.

Jeffrey, R.C. (1983). *The logic of decision* (2nd ed.). Chicago: University of Chicago Press.

Johnson, E.J., Hershey, J., Meszaros, J., & Kunreuther, H. (1993). Framing, probability distortions, and insurance decisions. *Journal of Risk and Uncertainty, 7*, 35–51.

Johnson-Laird, P.N., Legrenzi, P., Girotto, V., Legrenzi, M., & Caverni, J-P. (1999). Naive probability: A mental model theory of extensional reasoning. *Psychological Review, 106*, 62–88.

Kahneman, D., & Tversky, A. (1972). Subjective probability: A judgment of representativeness. *Cognitive Psychology, 3*, 430–454.

Kahneman, D., & Tversky, A. (1982). Variants of uncertainty. In D. Kahneman, P. Slovic, & A. Tversky (Eds.), *Judgment under uncertainty: Heuristics and biases* (pp. 509–520). Cambridge: Cambridge University Press.

Kahneman, D., & Tversky, A. (1996). On the reality of cognitive illusions. *Psychological Review, 103*, 3, 582–591.

Kleiter, G. (1994). Natural sampling: Rationality without base rates. In G.H. Fisher & D. Laming (Eds). *Contributions to mathematical psychology, psychometrics, and methodology*. New York: Springer-Verlag.

Kneale, W., & Kneale, M. (1962). *The development of logic*. Oxford: Oxford University Press.

Lewis, C., & Keren, G. (1999). On the difficulties underlying Bayesian reasoning: A comment on Gigerenzer and Hoffrage (1995). *Psychological Review, 106*, 2, 411–416.

Mellers, B.A., & McGraw, P.A. (1999). How to improve Bayesian reasoning: Comment on Gigerenzer and Hoffrage (1995). *Psychological Review, 106*, 2, 417–424.

Osherson, D., Smith, E.E., Wilkie, O., Lopez, A., & Shafir, E. (1990). Category-based induction. *Psychological Review, 97*, 185–200.

Over, D.E. (2000a). Ecological rationality and its heuristics. *Thinking and Reasoning, 6*, 182–192.

Over, D.E. (2000b). Ecological issues: A Reply to Todd, Fiddick, & Krauss. *Thinking and Reasoning, 6*, 385–388.

Over, D.E., & Green, D.W. (2001). Contingency, causation, and adaptive inference. *Psychological Review, 108*, 682–684.

Pearl, J. (1988). *Probabilistic reasoning in intelligent systems: networks of plausible inference*. San Mateo: Morgan Kaufmann.

Pearl, J. (2000). *Causality*. Cambridge: Cambridge University Press.

Pennington, N. & Hastie, R. (1988). Explanation-based decision making: Effects of memory structure on judgment. *Journal of Experimental Psychology: Learning, Memory, and Cognition, 14*, 521–533.

Rehder, B., & Hastie, R. (1997). The roles of causes and effects in categorization. In M.G. Shafto & P. Langley (Eds.), *Proceedings of the Nineteenth Annual Conference of the Cognitive Science Society* (pp. 650–655). Mahwah, NJ: Lawrence Erlbaum Associates.

Sloman, S.A. (1993). Feature-based induction. *Cognitive Psychology, 25*, 231–280.

Sloman, S.A. (1998). Categorical inference is not a tree: The myth of inheritance hierarchies. *Cognitive Psychology, 35*, 1–33.

Tversky, A., & Kahneman, D. (1973). Availability: A heuristic for judging frequency and probability. *Cognitive Psychology, 5*(2), 207–232

Tversky, A., & Kahneman, D. (1974). Judgment under uncertainty: Heuristics and biases. In D. Kahneman, P. Slovic, & A. Tversky (Eds.), *Judgment under uncertainty: Heuristics and biases*. Cambridge: Cambridge University Press.

Tversky, A., & Kahneman, D. (1982). Judgments of and by representativeness. In D. Kahneman, P. Slovic, & A. Tversky (Eds.) *Judgment under uncertainty: Heuristics and biases*. Cambridge: Cambridge University Press.

Tversky, A., & Kahneman, D. (1983). Extensional versus intuitive reasoning: The conjunction fallacy in probability judgment. *Psychological Review, 90*, 293–315.

Vranas, P.B.M. (2000). Gigerenzer's normative critique of Kahneman and Tversky, *Cognition, 76*, 179–193.

Waldmann, M.R. (1996). Knowledge-based causal induction. *The Psychology of Learning and Motivation, 34*, 47–88.

Waldmann, M.R., Holyoak, K., & Fratiannea, A. (1995). Causal models and the acquisition of category structure. *Journal of Experimenal Psychology: General, 124*, 181–206.

CHAPTER SEVEN

Evolutionary versus instrumental goals: How evolutionary psychology misconceives human rationality

Keith E. Stanovich
University of Toronto, Canada

Richard F. West
James Madison University, Harrisonburg, Virginia, USA

An important research tradition in the cognitive psychology of reasoning—called the heuristics and biases approach—has firmly established that people's responses often deviate from the performance considered normative on many reasoning tasks. For example, people assess probabilities incorrectly, they display confirmation bias, they test hypotheses inefficiently, they violate the axioms of utility theory, they do not properly calibrate degrees of belief, they overproject their own opinions onto others, they display illogical framing effects, they uneconomically honour sunk costs, they allow prior knowledge to become implicated in deductive reasoning, and they display numerous other information processing biases (for summaries of the large literature, see Baron, 1998, 2000; Dawes, 1998; Evans, 1989; Evans & Over, 1996; Kahneman & Tversky, 1972, 1984, 2000; Kahneman, Slovic, & Tversky, 1982; Nickerson, 1998; Shafir & Tversky, 1995; Stanovich, 1999; Tversky, 1996).

It has been common for these empirical demonstrations of a gap between descriptive and normative models of reasoning and decision making to be taken as indications that systematic irrationalities characterize human cognition. However, over the last decade, an alternative interpretation of these findings has been championed by various evolutionary psychologists, adaptationist modellers, and ecological theorists (Anderson, 1990, 1991; Chater & Oaksford, 2000; Cosmides & Tooby, 1992, 1994b, 1996; Gigerenzer, 1996a; Oaksford & Chater, 1998, 2001; Rode, Cosmides, Hell, & Tooby, 1999; Todd & Gigerenzer, 2000). They have reinterpreted the modal response in most of the classic heuristics and biases experiments as indicating an optimal information processing adaptation on the part of the subjects. It is argued by these investigators that the research in the heuristics and biases tradition has not demonstrated human irrationality at all and that a Panglossian position (see Stanovich & West, 2000), which assumes perfect human rationality, is the proper default position to take.

It will be argued in this chapter that although the work of the evolutionary psychologists has uncovered some fundamentally important things about human cognition, these theorists have misconstrued the nature of human rationality and have conflated important distinctions in this domain. What these theorists have missed (or failed to sufficiently emphasize) is that definitions of rationality must coincide with the level of the entity whose optimization is at issue. This admonition plays out most directly in the distinction between evolutionary rationality and instrumental rationality—necessitated by the fact that the optimization procedures for replicators and for vehicles (to use Dawkins' (1976) terms) need not always coincide. The distinction follows from the fact that the genes—as subpersonal replicators—can increase their fecundity and longevity in ways that do not necessarily serve the instrumental goals of the vehicles built by the genome (Skyrms, 1996; Stanovich, 1999). Despite their frequent acknowledgements that the conditions in the environment of evolutionary adaptedness (EEA) do not match those of modern society, evolutionary psychologists have a tendency to background potential mismatches between genetic interests and personal interests.

We will argue below that dual-process models of cognitive functioning provide a way of reconciling the positions of the evolutionary psychologists and researchers in the heuristics and biases tradition. Such models acknowledge the domain specificity of certain modular processes emphasized by the evolutionary psychologists. But importantly, they also posit general, interactive, nonautonomous, and central serial-processing operations of executive control and problem solving that serve to guarantee instrumental rationality by overriding the responses generated by autonomous modules when the latter threaten optimal outcomes at the personal level.

DEBATES ABOUT THE NORMATIVE RESPONSE IN HEURISTICS AND BIASES TASKS: SOME EXAMPLES

The empirical data pattern that provoked our attempted reconciliation of the positions of the evolutionary psychologists and researchers in the heuristics and biases tradition is the repeated finding in our research (Stanovich & West, 1998a, 1998b, 1998c, 1998d, 1999, 2000) that the modal response was different from the response given by the more cognitively able subjects. We have related this finding to the disputes about which response is normative in various heuristics and biases tasks. An example is provided by the most investigated task in the entire reasoning and problem solving literature—Wason's (1966) selection task. The participant is shown four cards lying on a table; two show letters and two show numbers (A, D, 3, 8). They are told that each card has a number on one side and a letter on the other and that the experimenter has the following rule (of the "if P, then Q" type) in mind with respect to the four cards: "If there is a vowel on one side of the card, then there is an even number on the other side". The participants are then told that they must turn over whichever cards are necessary to determine whether the experimenter's rule is true or false. Performance on such abstract versions of the selection task is extremely low (Evans, Newstead, & Byrne, 1993; Manktelow, 1999; Newstead & Evans, 1995). Typically, less than 10 per cent of participants make the correct selections of the A card (P) and 3 card (not-Q)—the only two cards that could falsify the rule. The most common incorrect choices made by participants are the A card and the 8 card (P and Q) or the selection of the A card only (P).

Numerous alternative explanations for the preponderance of incorrect PQ and P responses have been given (see Evans et al., 1993; Hardman, 1998; Johnson-Laird, 1999; Liberman & Klar, 1996; Margolis, 1987; Newstead & Evans, 1995; Oaksford & Chater, 1994; Sperber, Cara, & Girotto, 1995; Stanovich & West, 1998a). What is important in the present context is that several of these alternative theories posit that the incorrect PQ response results from the operation of efficient and optimal cognitive mechanisms. For example, Oaksford and Chater (1994, 1996; see also Nickerson, 1996) argue that rather than interpreting the task as one of deductive reasoning (as the experimenter intends), many people interpret it as an inductive problem of probabilistic hypothesis testing (see Evans & Over, 1996). They show that the P and Q response is actually the expected one if an inductive interpretation of the problem is assumed along with optimal data selection (which they modeled with a Bayesian analysis). Although their model is different, Sperber et al. (1995) stress that selection task performance is driven by optimized cognitive mechanisms. They explain selection task performance in terms of inferential comprehension mechanisms that are "geared towards the processing of optimally relevant communicative behaviors" (Sperber et al., 1995, p. 90).

Our second example of theorists defending as rational the response that heuristics and biases researchers have long considered incorrect is provided by the much-investigated Linda Problem (Tversky & Kahneman, 1983):

> Linda is 31 years old, single, outspoken, and very bright. She majored in philosophy. As a student, she was deeply concerned with issues of discrimination and social justice, and also participated in anti-nuclear demonstrations. Please rank the following statements by their probability, using 1 for the most probable and 8 for the least probable.

(a) Linda is a teacher in an elementary school
(b) Linda works in a bookstore and takes Yoga classes
(c) Linda is active in the feminist movement
(d) Linda is a psychiatric social worker
(e) Linda is a member of the League of Women Voters
(f) Linda is a bank teller
(g) Linda is an insurance salesperson
(h) Linda is a bank teller and is active in the feminist movement

Because alternative (h) (Linda is a bank teller and is active in the feminist movement) is the conjunction of alternatives (c) and (f), the probability of (h) cannot be higher than that of either (c) (Linda is active in the feminist movement) or (f) (Linda is a bank teller), yet 85 per cent of the participants in Tversky and Kahneman's (1983) study rated alternative (h) as more probable than (f), thus displaying the so-called conjunction fallacy. Those investigators argued that logical reasoning on the problem (all feminist bank tellers are also bank tellers, so (h) cannot be more probable than (f)) was trumped by a heuristic based on so-called representativeness that primes answers to problems based on an assessment of similarity (a feminist bank teller seems to overlap more with the description of Linda than does the alternative "bank teller"). Of course, logic dictates that the subset (feminist bank teller)/superset (bank teller) relationship should trump assessments of representativeness when judgements of probability are at issue.

However, several investigators have suggested that rather than illogical cognition, it is rational pragmatic inferences that lead to the violation of the logic of probability theory in the Linda Problem (see Adler, 1991; Dulany & Hilton, 1991; Politzer & Noveck, 1991; Slugoski & Wilson, 1998). Hilton (1995, p. 264) summarizes the view articulated in these critiques by arguing that "the inductive nature of conversational inference suggests that many of the experimental results that have been attributed to faulty reasoning may be reinterpreted as being due to rational interpretations of experimenter-given information".

In short, these critiques imply that displaying the conjunction fallacy is a rational response triggered by the adaptive use of social cues, linguistic cues, and background knowledge (see Hilton, 1995). For example, Macdonald and Gilhooly (1990, p. 59) argue that it is possible that subjects will:

> ... usually assume the questioner is asking the question because there is some reason to suppose that Linda might be a bank teller and the questioner is interested to find out if she is ... If Linda were chosen at random from the electoral register and "bank teller" was chosen at random from some list of occupations, the probability of them corresponding would be very small, certainly less than 1 in 100 ... the question itself has suggested to the subjects that Linda could be a feminist bank teller. Subjects are therefore being asked to judge how likely it is that Linda is a feminist bank teller when there is some

unknown reason to suppose she is, which reason has prompted the question itself.

Hilton (1995; see Dulany & Hilton, 1991) provides a similar explanation of subjects' behaviour on the Linda Problem. Under the assumption that the detailed information given about the target means that the experimenter knows a considerable amount about Linda, then it is reasonable to think that the phrase "Linda is a bank teller" does not contain the phrase "and is not active in the feminist movement" because the experimenter already knows this to be the case. If "Linda is a bank teller" is interpreted in this way, then rating (h) as more probable than (f) no longer represents a conjunction fallacy.

Several investigators have suggested that pragmatic inferences lead to seeming violations of the logic of probability theory in the Linda Problem (see Adler, 1984, 1991; Hertwig & Gigerenzer, 1999; Politzer & Noveck, 1991; Slugoski & Wilson, 1998). Most of these can be analysed in terms of Grice's (1975) norms of rational communication (see Hilton & Slugoski, 2000; Sperber & Wilson, 1986; Sperber et al., 1995), which require that the speaker be cooperative with the listener—and one of the primary ways that speakers attempt to be cooperative is by not being redundant. The key to understanding the so-called Gricean maxims of communication is to realize that to understand a speaker's meaning the listener must comprehend not only the meaning of what is spoken but also what is implicated in a given context assuming that the speaker intends to be cooperative. And Hilton (1995) is at pains to remind us that these are rational aspects of communicative cognition. They are rational heuristics as opposed to the suboptimal shortcuts as emphasized in the heuristics and biases literature. Thus, they are not to be seen as processing modes that are likely to be given up for more efficient processing modes when the stakes become high (Hilton, 1995, pp. 265–266):

> However, it is not clear why increasing the financial stakes in an experiment should cause respondents to abandon an interpretation that is pragmatically correct and rational . . . Incentives are not going to make respondents drop a conversationally rational interpretation in favor of a less plausible one in the context . . . the conversational inference approach does not predict that increased incentives lead respondents to change an interpretation that seems rational in the context.

Clearly, in the view of these theorists, committing the conjunction fallacy in such contexts does not represent a cognitive error.

Many theorists have linked their explanation of Linda-problem performance to the automatic linguistic socialization of information. These theorists commonly posit that the socialization tendency reflects evolutionary adaptations in the domain of social intelligence. This linkage stems from many theories that, although varied in their details, all posit that much of human intelligence has foundations in social interaction (Baldwin, 2000; Barton & Dunbar, 1997; Brothers, 1990; Bugental, 2000; Byrne & Whiten, 1988; Caporael, 1997; Cosmides, 1989; Cummins, 1996; Dunbar, 1998; Humphrey, 1976; Jolly, 1966; Kummer, Daston, Gigerenzer, & Silk, 1997; Mithen, 1996; Tomasello, 1999; Whiten & Byrne, 1997).

In a seminal essay that set the stage for this hypothesis, Nicholas Humphrey (1976) argued that the impetus for the development of primate intelligence was the need to master the social world. Based on his observation of nonhuman primates, Humphrey (1976) concluded that the knowledge and information processing necessary to engage efficiently with the physical world seemed modest compared with the rapidly changing demands of the social world. Humphrey (1976) posited that the latter was the key aspect of the environment that began to bootstrap higher intelligence in all primates.

This social, or interactional, intelligence forms that substrate upon which all future evolutionary and cultural developments in modes of thought are overlaid. That such social intelligence forms the basic substrate upon which all higher forms of intelligence must build leads to the important assumption that a social orientation toward problems is always available as a default processing mode when computational demands become onerous. The cognitive illusions demonstrated by three decades of work in problem solving, reasoning, and decision making (Evans, 1989; Kahneman, Slovic, & Tversky, 1982; Kahneman & Tversky, 1996, 2000; Stanovich, 1999) seem to bear this out. As in the Linda Problem and four-card selection task discussed above, the literature is full of problems where an abstract, decontextualized—but computationally expensive—approach is required for the normatively appropriate answer. However, often, alongside such a solution, resides a tempting social approach ("Oh, yeah, the author of this knows a lot about Linda") that with little computational effort will prime a response.

Since our theme has now been established with the selection-task and Linda-problem examples, our final two examples of theorists defending as rational the response that heuristics and biases researchers have long considered incorrect will be described only briefly.

Covariation detection

The 2×2 covariation detection task is run in a variety of different formats (Levin, Wasserman, & Kao, 1993; Stanovich & West, 1998d; Wasserman, Dorner, & Kao, 1990). In one, for example, subjects are asked to evaluate the efficacy of a drug based on a hypothetical well-designed scientific experiment. They are told that:

150 people received the drug and were cured.
150 people received the drug and were not cured.
300 people did not receive the drug and were cured.
 75 people did not receive the drug and were not cured.

These data correspond to four cells of the 2 × 2 contingency table traditionally labelled A, B, C, and D (see Levin et al., 1993). Subjects are asked to
evaluate the effectiveness of the drug on a scale. In this case, they have
to detect that the drug is ineffective. In fact, not only is it ineffective, it is
positively harmful. Only 50 per cent of the people who received the drug were
cured (150 out of 300), but 80 per cent of those who did *not* receive the drug
were cured (300 out of 375).

Much previous experimentation has produced results indicating that subjects weight the cell information in the order cell A > cell B > cell C > cell D—
cell D receiving the least weight and/or attention (see Arkes & Harkness,
1983; Kao & Wasserman, 1993; Schustack & Sternberg, 1981). The tendency
to ignore cell D is non-normative, as indeed is any tendency to differentially
weight the four cells. The normatively appropriate strategy (see Allan, 1980;
Kao & Wasserman, 1993; Shanks, 1995) is to use the conditional probability
rule—subtracting from the probability of the target hypothesis when the
indicator is present the probability of the target hypothesis when the indicator is absent. Numerically, the rule amounts to calculating the Δp statistic:
$[A/(A + B)] - [C/(C + D)]$ (see Allan, 1980). For example, the Δp value for the
problem presented above is −.300, indicating a fairly negative association.

Despite the fact that it is a nonnormative strategy, the modal subject in
such experiments underweights (sometimes markedly underweights, see
Stanovich & West, 1998d) cell D. However, Anderson (1990) has modelled
the 2 × 2 contingency assessment experiment using a model of optimally
adapted information processing and come to a startling conclusion. He demonstrates that an adaptive model can predict the much-replicated finding that
the D cell (cause absent and effect absent) is vastly underweighted (but see
Over & Green, 2001) and concludes that "this result makes the point that
there need be no discrepancy between a rational analysis and differential
weighting of the cells in a 2 × 2 contingency table" (Anderson, 1990, p. 160).
Thus, here again in another task is the pattern where the modal response is
nonnormative—but that response has been defended from the standpoint of
an adaptationist analysis.

Probability matching

The probabilistic contingency experiment has many versions in psychology
(Gal & Baron, 1996; Tversky & Edwards, 1966). In one, the subjects sit in
front of two lights (one red and one blue) and are told that they are to predict

which of the lights will be flashed on each trial and that there will be several dozen of such trials (subjects are often paid money for correct predictions). The experimenter has actually programmed the lights to flash randomly, with the provision that the red light will flash 70 per cent of the time and the blue light 30 per cent of the time. Subjects do quickly pick up the fact that the red light is flashing more, and they predict that it will flash on more trials than they predict that the blue light will flash. Most often, they switch back and forth, predicting the red light roughly 70 per cent of the time and the blue light roughly 30 per cent of the time.

This strategy of probability matching is suboptimal because it insures that, in this example, the subject will correctly predict only 58 per cent of the time ($.7 \times .7 + .3 \times .3$) compared with the 70 per cent hit rate achieved by predicting the more likely colour on each trial. In fact, much experimentation has indicated that animals and humans often fail to maximize expected utility in the probabilistic contingency experiment[1] (Estes, 1964, 1976; Gallistel, 1990; Tversky & Edwards, 1966). Nevertheless, Gigerenzer (1996b; see also Cooper, 1989) shows how probability matching could, under some conditions, actually be an evolutionarily stable strategy (see Skyrms, 1996, for many such examples). Thus, we have in probability matching our final example of how a non-normative response tendency is defended on an evolutionary or adaptationist account.

DISSOCIATIONS BETWEEN COGNITIVE ABILITY AND THE MODAL RESPONSE IN HEURISTICS AND BIASES TASKS

We will argue in this chapter that, in each of these examples, evolutionary rationality has dissociated from normative rationality—where the latter is viewed as utility maximization for the individual organism (instrumental rationality) and the former is defined as survival probability at the level of the gene (Dawkins, 1976, 1982). Our conceptualization of these findings explicitly acknowledges the impressive record of descriptive accuracy enjoyed by a variety of adaptationist and evolutionary models in predicting the modal response (Anderson, 1990, 1991; Gigerenzer, 1996b; Oaksford & Chater, 1994, 1996; Rode et al., 1999), but our account attempts to make sense of another important empirical fact—that cognitive ability often dissociates from the response deemed adaptive on an evolutionary analysis

---

[1] In probability learning, or choice situations, both animals and humans generally approximate probability matching when reinforcement is delivered on variable-interval schedules. However, things appear to be more complex when reinforcement is delivered on variable-ratio schedules. Although humans still tend to approximate probability matching (Estes, 1964, 1976, 1984), animals often maximize (Herrnstein & Loveland, 1975; MacDonall, 1988; but see Gallistel, 1990; Graf, Bullock, & Bitterman, 1964; Sutherland & Mackintosh, 1971).

(Stanovich, 1999; Stanovich & West, 2000). Specifically, we have repeatedly found that in cases where the normative response is not the modal response, the subjects in the sample who were the highest in cognitive ability gave the normative response rather than the modal response. This is true for each of the four tasks described above.

For example, Table 7.1 presents the results from an investigation of ours (Stanovich & West, 1998a) using a selection task with a nondeontic rule, the so-called Destination rule (in this instance: If "Baltimore" is on one side of the ticket, then "plane" is on the other side of the ticket). The table presents the mean SAT scores for several of the dominant choices on this selection rule (the SAT test is a test used for university admissions in the United States that is highly loaded on psychometric g). From the table, it is clear that respondents giving the deductively correct P and not-Q response had the highest SAT scores, followed by the subjects choosing the P card only. All other responses, including the modal P and Q response (chosen by 49 per cent of the sample), were given by subjects having SAT scores almost 100 points lower than those giving the correct response under a deductive construal. It is to the credit of models of optimal data selection (Oaksford & Chater, 1994) that they predict the modal response. But we are left with the seemingly puzzling finding that the response deemed optimal under such an analysis (PQ) is given by subjects of substantially lower general intelligence than the minority giving the response deemed correct under a strictly deductive interpretation of the problem (PNQ).

A similar puzzle surrounds findings on the Linda conjunction problem. Gricean analyses assume that those subjects committing the conjunction fallacy in such a contrived problem are reflecting the evolved use of sociolinguistic cues. Because this group is in fact the vast majority in most studies—and because the use of such pragmatic cues and background knowledge is often interpreted as reflecting adaptive information processing (Hilton, 1995)—it might be expected that these individuals would be the subjects of higher cognitive ability. We found the contrary. In our study

TABLE 7.1
Mean SAT total scores as a function of response given on a selection task using the destination rule (number of subjects in parentheses)

Response	SAT score	
P, NQ (correct)	1190	(24)
P	1150	(38)
All	1101	(21)
P, Q	1095	(144)
P, Q, NQ	1084	(14)
Other	1070	(53)

(Stanovich & West, 1998b), we examined the performance of 150 subjects on the Linda Problem. Consistent with the results of previous experiments on this problem (Tversky & Kahneman, 1983), 80.7 per cent of our sample committed the conjunction effect—they rated the feminist bank teller alternative as more probable than the bank teller alternative. However, the mean SAT score of the 121 subjects who committed the conjunction fallacy was 82 points *lower* than the mean score of the 29 who avoided the fallacy. This difference was highly significant and it translated into an effect size of .746 (which Rosenthal & Rosnow, 1991, classify as large). Thus, the pragmatic interpretations of why the conjunction effect is the modal response on this task might well be correct, but the modal response happens not to be the one given by the most intelligent subjects in the sample.

Likewise, in the 2 × 2 covariation detection experiment, we have found (Stanovich & West, 1998d) that it is those subjects weighting cell D more *equally* (not those underweighting the cell in the way that the adaptationist model dictates) who are higher in cognitive ability and who tend to respond normatively on other tasks. Again, Anderson (1990, 1991) might well be correct that a rational model of information processing in the task predicts underweighting of cell D by most subjects, but more severe underweighting is in fact associated with *lower* cognitive ability in our individual differences analyses.

Finally, we found a similar pattern in several experiments on probability matching using a variety of different paradigms (West & Stanovich, in press). For example, in one experiment involving choices among general strategies for approaching the probabilistic prediction task, subjects were given the following task description:

> A die with 4 red faces and 2 green faces will be rolled 60 times. Before each roll you will be asked to predict which color (red or green) will show up once the die is rolled. You will be given one dollar for each correct prediction. Assume that you want to make as much money as possible. What strategy would you use in order to make *as much money as possible* by making the most correct predictions?

They were asked to choose from among the following five strategies:

Strategy A: Go by intuition, switching when there has been too many of one color or the other.

Strategy B: Predict the more likely color (red) on most of the rolls but occasionally, after a long run of reds, predict a green.

Strategy C: Make predictions according to the frequency of occurrence (4 of 6 for red and 2 of 6 for green). That is, predict twice as many reds as greens.

Strategy D: Predict the more likely color (red) on all of the 60 rolls.

Strategy E: Predict more red than green, but switching back and forth depending upon "runs" of one color or the other.

The probability matching strategy corresponds to Strategy C here, and the normatively optimal strategy is Strategy D, which maximizes expected utility. Table 7.2 presents the number of subjects choosing each of the five strategies and their mean SAT scores. The probability matching and maximizing strategies were both preferred over the three foil strategies, with the former being the modal choice. Again, the choice defensible on evolutionary grounds (probability matching, see Gigerenzer, 1996b), is the modal choice. But again, as before, it is the maximizing, normatively dictated choice that is the choice of the subjects with the highest intellectual ability. The mean SAT scores of those choosing the maximizing choice was 55 points higher than those who preferred probability matching ($p < .001$).

RECONCILING THE TWO DATA PATTERNS WITHIN A TWO-PROCESS VIEW

We see in the results just reviewed two basic patterns that must be reconciled. The evolutionary psychologists and optimal data selection theorists correctly predict the modal response in a host of heuristics and biases tasks. Yet in all of these cases—despite the fact that the adaptationist models predict the modal response quite well—individual differences analyses demonstrate associations that also must be accounted for. Correct responders on the nondeontic selection task (P and not-Q choosers—not those choosing P and Q) are higher in cognitive ability. Despite conversational implicatures cuing the opposite response, individuals of higher cognitive ability disproportionately tend to adhere to the conjunction rule. In the 2 × 2 covariation detection experiment, it is those subjects weighting cell D more *equally* who are higher in cognitive ability. Finally, subjects of higher intelligence

TABLE 7.2
Mean SAT total scores as a function of strategy choice on a probabilistic contingency problem (number of subjects in parentheses)

Strategy choice	SAT score
Strategy A	1151 (15)
Strategy B	1163 (64)
Strategy C*	1160 (168)
Strategy D**	1215 (150)
Strategy E	1148 (48)

* = The probability matching response; ** = The normatively correct utility maximizing response.

disproportionally *avoid* the evolutionarily justified probability matching tendency.

We believe that a useful framework for incorporating both of these data patterns is provided by two-process theories of reasoning (Epstein, 1994; Evans, 1984, 1996; Evans & Over, 1996; Sloman, 1996; Stanovich, 1999). Such a framework can encompass both the impressive record of descriptive accuracy enjoyed by a variety of evolutionary/adaptationist models as well as the fact that cognitive ability sometimes dissociates from the response deemed optimal on an adaptationist analysis.

A summary of terms used by several two-process theorists and the generic properties distinguished by several two-process views is presented in Table 7.3. Although the details and technical properties of these dual-process theories do not always match exactly, nevertheless there are clear family resemblances (for discussions, see Evans & Over, 1996; Gigerenzer & Regier, 1996; Sloman, 1996). To emphasize that his concept of these two processes involved the synthesis of a prototype of the different models in the literature (rather than to attempt to defend the specific and unique properties of any one view), Stanovich (1999) adopted the generic labels System 1 and System 2.

The key differences in the properties of the two systems are listed in Table 7.3. System 1 processes are characterized as automatic, heuristic-based, and relatively undemanding of computational capacity. Thus, System 1 processes conjoin properties of automaticity, modularity, and heuristic processing as these constructs have been variously discussed in the literature. There is a sense in which the term System 1 is a misnomer in that it implies that it is referring to a single system. In fact, we intend the term System 1 to refer to a (probably large) *set* of systems in the brain (partially encapsulated modules in some views) that operate autonomously—in response to their own triggering stimuli and not under the control of a central processing structure (System 2).

System 2 conjoins the various characteristics that have been viewed as typifying controlled processing—serial, rule-based, language-biased, computationally expensive cognition. System 2 encompasses the processes of analytic intelligence that have traditionally been studied by information processing theorists trying to uncover the computational components underlying intelligence. Evans and Over (1999) argue that the function of the explicit processes of System 2 is to support hypothetical thinking. In their view, hypothetical thinking involves representing possible states of the world rather than actual states of affairs; for example, "deductive reasoning is hypothetical when its premises are not actual beliefs, but rather assumptions or suppositions ... Consequential decision making consists of forecasting a number of possible future world states and representing the possible actions available ... Scientific thinking is itself hypothetical when entertaining hypotheses about the way the world might be and deducing their consequences for making predictions" (Evans & Over, 1999, p. 764). Evans and

TABLE 7.3

The terms for the two systems used by a variety of theorists and the properties of dual-process theories of reason

	System 1 (TASS)	*System 2 (Analytic system)*
Dual-process theories		
Sloman (1996)	Associative system	Rule-based system
Evans & Over (1996)	Tacit thought processes	Explicit thought processes
Evans (1984, 1989)	Heuristic processing	Analytical processing
Evans & Wason (1976)	Type 1 processes	Type 2 processes
Reber (1993)	Implicit cognition	Explicit learning
Levinson (1995)	Interactional intelligence	Analytic intelligence
Epstein (1994)	Experiential system	Rational system
Pollock (1991)	Quick and inflexible modules	Intellection
Klein (1998)	Recognition-primed decisions	Rational choice strategy
Johnson-Laird (1983)	Implicit inferences	Explicit inferences
Fodor (1983)	Modular processes	Central processes
Chaiken, Liberman, & Eagly (1989)	Heuristic processing	Systematic processing
Gibbard (1990)	Animal control system	Normative control system
Norman & Shallice (1986)	Contention scheduling	Supervisory attentional
Shiffrin & Schneider (1977)	Automatic processing	Controlled processing
Posner & Snyder (1975)	Automatic activation	Conscious processing
Properties	Associative	Rule-based
	Holistic	Analytic
	Automatic	Controlled
	Relatively undemanding of cognitive capacity	Demanding of cognitive capacity
	Relatively fast	Relatively slow
	Acquisition by biology, exposure, and personal experience	Acquisition by cultural and formal tuition
	Highly contextualized	Decontextualized
Goal structure	Short-leash genetic goals that are relatively stable	Long-leash goals that are utility-maximizing for the organism and constantly updated because of changes in environment

TASS = The Autonomous Set of Systems.

Over (1999) posit that hypothetical thought involves representing assumptions—and these necessarily must be represented as such; otherwise content would be confounded with belief. Linguistic forms such as conditionals provide a medium for such representations—and the serial manipulation of this type of representation seems to be largely a System 2 function. Language provides the discrete representational tools that fully exploit the computational power of the serial manipulations of which System 2 is capable (following Dennett, 1991, we think that System 2 processing is computationally demanding because the serial processes must be simulated by a largely parallel network).

The two systems tend to lead to different types of task construals. Construals triggered by System 1 are highly contextualized, personalized, and socialized. They are driven by considerations of relevance and are aimed at inferring intentionality by the use of conversational implicature even in situations that are devoid of conversational features (see Hilton, 1995). These properties characterize what Levinson (1995) has termed interactional intelligence—a system composed of the mechanisms that support a Gricean theory of communication that relies on intention–attribution. The primacy of these mechanisms leads to what has been termed the fundamental computational bias[2] in human cognition (Stanovich, 1999, in press)—the tendency or predilection toward automatic contextualization of problems. In contrast, the more controlled processes of System 2 serve to decontextualize and depersonalize problems. This system is more adept at representing in terms of rules and underlying principles. It can deal with problems without social content and is not dominated by the goal of attributing intentionality nor by the search for conversational relevance.

Using the distinction between System 1 and System 2 processing, Stanovich and West (2000) argued that in order to observe large cognitive ability differences in a problem situation, the two systems must strongly cue *different* responses. One reason that this outcome is predicted is that it is assumed that individual differences in System 1 processes (interactional intelligence) are smaller and bear little relation to individual differences in System 2 processes (analytic intelligence; see McGeorge, Crawford, & Kelly, 1997; Reber, 1993; Reber, Walkenfeld, & Hernstadt, 1991). If the two systems cue opposite responses, rule-based System 2 will tend to differentially cue those of high analytic intelligence and this tendency will not be diluted by System 1 nondifferentially drawing subjects to the same response. For example, in nondeontic selection tasks there is ample opportunity for the two systems to cue different responses. A deductive interpretation conjoined with an exhaustive search for

---

[2] We strongly caution that the term "bias" is used throughout this chapter to denote "a preponderating disposition or propensity" (*The Compact Edition of the Oxford Short English Dictionary*, p. 211) and not a processing *error*. That a processing bias does not necessarily imply a cognitive error is a point repeatedly emphasized by the critics of the heuristics and biases literature (Funder, 1987; Gigerenzer, 1996a; Hastie & Rasinski, 1988; Kruglanski & Ajzen, 1983), but in fact it was always the position of the original heuristics and biases researchers themselves (Kahneman, 2000; Kahneman & Tversky, 1973, 1996; Tversky & Kahneman, 1974). Thus, the use of the term bias here is meant to connote "default value" rather than "error". Under the assumption that computational biases result from evolutionary adaptations of the brain (Cosmides & Tooby, 1994b), it is likely that they are efficacious in most situations.

falsifying instances yields the response P and not-Q. This interpretation and processing style is likely associated with the rule-based System 2. In contrast, within the heuristic-analytic framework of Evans (1984, 1989, 1996), the matching response of P and Q reflects the heuristic processing of System 1 (in Evans' theory, a linguistically cued relevance response).

The sampling of experimental results reviewed here (see Stanovich, 1999, for further examples) indicates that the alternative responses favoured by the critics of the heuristics and biases literature were the choices of the subjects of lower analytic intelligence. We will explore the possibility that these alternative construals may have been triggered by heuristics that make evolutionary sense—as the evolutionary psychologists argue—but that subjects higher in a more flexible type of analytic intelligence (and those more cognitively engaged, see Smith & Levin, 1996; Stanovich & West, 1999) are more prone to follow normative rules that maximize personal utility.

EVOLUTIONARY RATIONALITY IS NOT INSTRUMENTAL RATIONALITY

The argument depends on the distinction between evolutionary adaptation and instrumental rationality (utility maximization given goals and beliefs). The key point is that for the latter (variously termed practical, pragmatic, or means/ends rationality), maximization is at the level of the individual person. Adaptive optimization in the former case is at the level of the genes. In Dawkins' (1976, 1982) terms, evolutionary adaptation concerns optimization processes relevant to the so-called replicators (the genes), whereas instrumental rationality concerns utility maximization for the so-called vehicle (or interactor, to use Hull's, 1982, term), which houses the genes. Anderson (1990, 1991) emphasizes this distinction in his treatment of adaptationist models in psychology. Anderson (1990) accepts Stich's (1990; see also Skyrms, 1996) argument that evolutionary adaptation (hereafter termed evolutionary rationality) does not guarantee perfect human rationality in the instrumental sense that is focused on goals of the whole organism. As a result, a descriptive model of processing that is adaptively optimal could well deviate substantially from a normative model of instrumental rationality (Skyrms, 1996, spends an entire book demonstrating just this) because there may be different models characterizing optimization at the subpersonal and personal levels, respectively.[3]

A key aspect of our framework is the assumption that the goal structures

---

[3] It should be noted that the distinction between evolutionary and instrumental rationality is different from the distinction between rationality$_1$ and rationality$_2$ utilized by Evans and Over (1996). They define rationality$_1$ as reasoning and acting "in a way that is generally reliable and efficient for achieving one's goals" (p. 8). Rationality$_2$ concerns reasoning and acting "when one

that are keyed to primarily the genes' interests and the goal structures keyed primarily to the organism's interests are differentially represented in Systems 1 and 2 (see Reber, 1992, 1993, for a theoretical and empirical basis for this claim). It is hypothesized that the features of System 1 are designed to very closely track increases in the reproduction probability of genes. System 2, while also clearly an evolutionary product, is primarily a control system focused on the interests of the whole person. It is the primary maximizer of an individual's *personal* utility. Maximizing the latter will occasionally result in sacrificing genetic fitness (Barkow, 1989; Cooper, 1989; Skyrms, 1996). Because System 2 is more attuned to instrumental rationality than is System 1, System 2 will seek to fulfil the individual's goals in the minority of cases where those goals conflict with the responses triggered by System 1.

Thus, the last difference between Systems 1 and 2 listed in Table 7.3 is that System 1 instantiates short-leashed genetic goals, whereas System 2 instantiates a flexible goal hierarchy that is oriented toward maximizing goal satisfaction at the level of the whole organism. We borrow the short- /long-leash terminology by way of another metaphor used by Dawkins (1976), Dennett (1984), and Plotkin (1988)—the "Mars Explorer" analogy. Dennett (1984) describes how, when controlling a device such as a model airplane, one's sphere of control is only limited by the power of the equipment, but when the distances become large, the speed of light becomes a non-negligible factor. NASA engineers responsible for the Mars Explorer vehicle knew that direct control was impossible because "the time required for a round trip signal was greater than the time available for appropriate action . . . Since controllers on Earth could no longer reach out and control them, they had to *control themselves*" (Dennett, 1984, p. 55, italics in the original). The NASA engineers had to move from the "short-leash" direct control, as in the model airplane case, to the "long-leash" control of the Mars Explorer case where the vehicle is not given moment-by-moment instructions on how to act, but instead is given a more flexible type of intelligence plus some generic goals.

As Dawkins (1976), in his similar discussion of the Mars Explorer logic in the science fiction story *A for Andromeda* notes, there is an analogy here to the type of control exerted by the genes when they build a brain: "The genes

---

has a reason for what one does sanctioned by a normative theory" (p. 8). Because normative theories concern goals at the personal level, not the genetic level, both of the rationalities defined by Evans and Over (1996) fall within what has been termed here instrumental rationality. Both concern goals at the personal level. Evans and Over (1996) wish to distinguish the explicit (i.e. conscious) following of a normative rule (rationality$_2$) from the largely unconscious processes "that do much to help them achieve their ordinary goals" (p. 9). Their distinction is between two sets of algorithmic mechanisms that can both serve instrumental rationality. The distinction we draw is in terms of *levels* of optimization (at the level of the replicator itself—the gene—or the level of the vehicle); whereas theirs is in terms of the *mechanism* used to pursue personal goals (mechanisms of conscious, reason-based rule-following versus tacit heuristics).

can only do their best in *advance* by building a fast executive computer for themselves . . . Like the chess programmer, the genes have to 'instruct' their survival machines not in specifics, but in the general strategies and tricks of the living trade . . . The advantage of this sort of programming is that it greatly cuts down on the number of detailed rules that have to be built into the original program" (Dawkins, 1976, pp. 55, 57). Human brains represent, according to Dawkins (1976, pp. 59–60) "the culmination of an evolutionary trend towards the emancipation of survival machines as executive decision-makers from their ultimate masters, the genes . . . By dictating the way survival machines and their nervous systems are built, genes exert ultimate power over behavior. But the moment-to-moment decisions about what to do next are taken by the nervous system. Genes are the primary policy-makers; brains are the executives . . . The logical conclusion to this trend, not yet reached in any species, would be for the genes to give the survival machine a single overall policy instruction: do whatever you think best to keep us alive".

The type of long-leash control that Dawkins is referring to is built in *addition* to (rather than as a replacement for) the short-leash genetic control mechanisms that earlier evolutionary adaptation has installed in the brain. That is, the different types of brain control that evolve do not replace earlier ones but are layered on top of them (and of course perhaps alter the earlier structures as well, see Badcock, 2000, pp. 27–29). Dennett (1996), in his short but provocative book *Kinds of Minds* (see also, Dennett, 1975), describes the overlapping short-leashed and long-leashed strategies embodied in our brains by labelling them as different "minds"—all lodged within the same brain in the case of humans—and all simultaneously operating to solve problems.

One key distinction between Dennett's kinds of minds is how directly the various systems code for the goals of the genes. Dennett (1996) distinguishes four different kinds of minds, the Darwinian mind, the Skinnerian mind, the Popperian mind, and Gregorian mind (Fig. 7.1). The minds reflect increasingly powerful mechanisms for predicting the future world. As Dennett (1991) notes, brains are anticipation machines. The four minds he proposes reflect increasingly sophisticated modes of anticipation. It will be argued here that the minds, in the order listed above, also reflect decreasing degrees of direct genetic control.

The different minds control in different ways how the vehicle will react to stimuli in the environment. The Darwinian mind uses prewired reflexes and thus produces hardwired phenotypic behavioural patterns (the genes have "said" metaphorically "do *this* when x happens because it is best"). The Skinnerian mind uses operant conditioning to shape itself to an unpredictable environment (the genes have "said" metaphorically "learn what is best as you go along"). The Popperian mind (after the philosopher Karl Popper) can represent possibilities and test them internally before responding (the genes have "said" metaphorically "think about what is best before you do it"). The

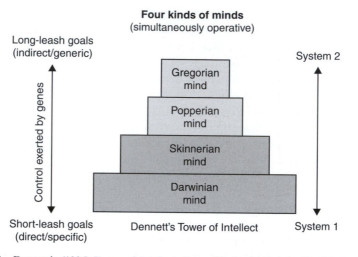

Figure 7.1 Dennett's (1996) Tower of Intellect. From *Kinds of Minds* by Daniel C. Dennett. Copyright © 1997 by Daniel C. Dennett. Reprinted by permission of Basic Books, a member of Perseus Books, L.L.C.

Gregorian mind (after the psychologist Richard Gregory) exploits the mental tools (see Clark, 1997) discovered by others (the genes have "said" metaphorically "imitate and use the mental tools used by others to solve problems"). In humans, all four "minds" are simultaneously operative (Fig. 7.1). The Darwinian and Skinnerian minds have short-leash goals installed ("when this stimulus appears, do *this*"). In contrast, the Popperian and Gregorian minds are characterized by long-leash goals ("operate with other agents in your environment so as to increase your longevity").

When confronted with a problem, all these parts of the brain contribute potential solutions. It is variable which one will dominate. We have argued (Stanovich, 1999; Stanovich & West, 2000) that measures of psychometric intelligence are measures of current computational capacity instantiated at the algorithmic level of System 2. This computational capacity is available to be deployed in a System 1 override function if the intentional-level goals of System 2 dictate that this will achieve goal maximization (Fig. 7.2). This override of System-1-triggered responses will not always be successful and thus it is predicted that on tasks where Systems 1 and 2 are triggering different responses, the instrumentally optimal response will be made by individuals with higher psychometric intelligence. It is precisely this that accounts for the pattern of results we reviewed earlier. In short, we argue that high analytic intelligence may lead to task construals that track instrumental rationality; whereas the alternative construals of subjects low in analytical intelligence (and hence more dominated by System 1 processing) might be more likely to track evolutionary rationality in situations that put the two

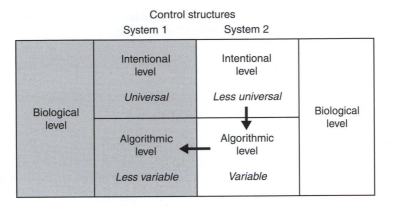

Figure 7.2 Nature of processing control when a System 1 response is overridden by System 2.

types of rationality in conflict, as is conjectured to be the case with the problems discussed previously. It is the failure to recognize the possibility of goal conflict between the two systems that we feel plagues the treatment of human rationality in the evolutionary psychology literature.

WHERE EVOLUTIONARY PSYCHOLOGY GOES WRONG

Consider the bee. As a Darwinian creature, it has a goal structure as indicated in Fig. 7.3. The area labelled A indicates the majority of cases where the

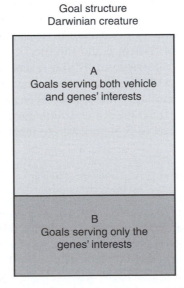

Figure 7.3 Goal structure of a Darwinian creature. The areas indicate overlap and nonoverlap of vehicle and genetic "interests".

replicator and vehicle goals coincide. Not flying into a brick wall serves both the interests of the replicators (the bee has a function in the hive that will facilitate replication) and of the bee itself as a coherent organism. Of course, the exact area represented by A is nothing more than a guess. The important point is the existence of a nonzero area B—a set of goals that serve only the interests of the replicators and that are antithetical to the interests of the vehicle itself.[4] A given bee will sacrifice itself as a vehicle if there is greater benefit to the same genes by helping other individuals (for instance, causing its own death when it loses its sting while protecting its genetically related hive-queen). There are no conflicting goals in a Darwinian creature. Its goals are the genes' goals pure and simple. It is just immaterial as far as evolutionary rationality is concerned how much genetic goals overlap with vehicle goals. Perfect rationality for the bee means local fitness optimization for its genes, because for the bee the only relevant rationality *is* evolutionary rationality.

The error that evolutionary psychologists tend to make is that they stop right there, with an implicit assumption that evolutionary rationality is all there is; that there is no instrumental rationality (no maximization issue at the level of the whole organism—the vehicle). Evolutionary psychologists, in effect, treat humans as if they were bees. This error comes about for two reasons. First, despite emphasizing in their writings that the EEA was different from the modern environment, evolutionary psychologists have been reluctant to play out the implications of this fact. Second, because of their advocacy of a strictly modular view of mind and their tendency to eschew domain-general mechanisms (Cosmides & Tooby, 1992, 1994b; Tooby & Cosmides, 1992), evolutionary psychologists de-emphasize the utility of the flexible goal structures of System 2 and the functions of the serial, systematically analytic processes carried out by that system. In short, evolutionary psychologists take issue with the characterization of the algorithmic level of System 2 (that it can instantiate domain-general procedures), but in doing so they miss the important function of the flexible goal structure that rides on top of the algorithmic level of System 2 (at the intentional level of analysis;

---

[4] We will continue the practice here of using the metaphorical language about genes having "goals" or "interests" in confidence that the reader understands that this is a shorthand only. As Blackmore (1999, p. 5) notes, "the shorthand 'genes want X' can always be spelled out as 'genes that do X are more likely to be passed on'." but that, in making complicated arguments, the latter language becomes cumbersome. Thus, we will follow Dawkins (1976, p. 88) in "allowing ourselves the licence of talking about genes as if they had conscious aims, always reassuring ourselves that we could translate our sloppy language back into respectable terms if we wanted to". Dawkins points out that this is "harmless unless it happens to fall into the hands of those ill-equipped to understand it" (Dawkins, 1976, p. 278) and then proceeds to quote a philosopher smugly and pedantically admonishing biologists that genes can't be selfish any more than atoms can be jealous. We trust, Dawkins' philosopher aside, that no reader needs this pointed out.

see Stanovich, 1999). They are so focused on denying domain generality in algorithmic-level mechanisms (in part because they mistakenly believe that it is meant by theorists to *displace* the modular mind, see below) that they miss the functionality (and implications for rationality) of the goal structure at the intentional level of System 2.

With the advent of the higher-level System 2 minds (of the Popperian and Gregorian type), evolution has inserted into the architecture of the brain a flexible system that is somewhat like the ultimate long-leash goal suggested by Dawkins: "Do whatever you think best". But "best for whom?" is the critical question here. The key point is that for a creature with a flexible intelligence, long-leash goals, and a Popperian/Gregorian mind, we have the possibility of genetic optimization becoming dissociated from the vehicle's goals. For the first time, we have the possibility of a goal structure like that displayed in Fig. 7.4. Here, although we have area A (where gene and vehicle goals coincide) and area B (goals serving the genes' interests but not the vehicle's) as before, we have a new area, C (again, the sizes of these areas in all diagrams in this chapter are pure conjecture). In humans, we have the possibility of goals that serve the vehicle's interests but not those of the genes.

Why does area C come to exist only in creatures with long-leash goals? When they started building Popperian and Gregorian minds, the genes were giving up on the strategy of coding moment-by-moment responses and moving to a long-leash strategy that at some point was the equivalent of saying "Things will be changing too fast out there, brain, for us to tell you exactly

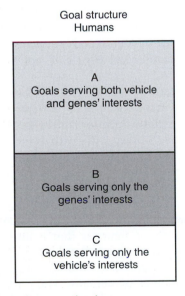

Figure 7.4   The logic of the goal structure in a human.

what to do—you just go ahead and do what you think is best given the general goals (survival, sexual reproduction) that we (the genes) have inserted". And there is the rub. In long-leash brains, genetically coded goals can be represented only in the most general sense. There is no goal of "mate with person X at 6:57pm on Friday, June 13" but instead "have sex because it is pleasurable". But once the goal has become this general, a potential gap has been created whereby behaviours that might serve the vehicle's goal might not serve that of the genes. We need not go beyond the obvious example of sex with contraception—an act that serves the vehicle's goal of pleasure without serving the genes' goal of reproduction. What is happening here is that the flexible brain is coordinating multiple long-term goals—including its own survival and pleasure goals—and these multiple long-term goals come to overshadow its reproductive goal. From the standpoint of the genes, the human brain can sometimes be like a Mars Explorer run amok. It is so busy coordinating its secondary goals (master your environment, engage in social relations with other agents, etc.) that it sometimes ignores the primary goal of replicating the genes that the secondary ones were supposed to serve.

Ironically, what from an evolutionary design point of view could be considered design defects actually make possible instrumental rationality—optimizing the utility of the person rather than the fitness of subpersonal units called genes. That is, inefficient design (from an evolutionary point of view) in effect creates the possibility of a divergence between organism-level goals and gene-level goals, which is an implication of Millikan's (1993, p. 67) point that "there is no reason to suppose that the design of our desire-making systems is itself optimal. Even under optimal conditions these systems work inefficiently, directly aiming, as it were, at recognizable ends that are merely roughly correlated with the biological end that is reproduction. For example, mammals do not, in general, cease efforts at individual survival after their fertile life is over".

Our framework integrates the insight of the possibility of vehicle/replicator goal mismatch in the direction of the vehicle (although the possibility of area B has been acknowledged for some time, the implications of area C have been incompletely worked out) with some assumptions about the intentional-level properties of Systems 1 and 2 drawn largely from Reber (1992, 1993). The integrated framework is displayed in Fig. 7.5 (of course, the exact size of the areas of overlap are mere guesses). Again, an assumption reflected in the figure is that, in the vast majority of real-life situations, evolutionary rationality *also* serves the goals of instrumental rationality. But the most important feature of the figure is that it illustrates the asymmetries in the "interests" served by the goal distribution of the two systems. The remnants of the Darwinian creature structure (see Fig. 7.3) are present in the System 1 brain structures of humans. Many of the goals instantiated in this system were acquired nonreflectively—they have not undergone an evaluation in terms of whether they served the *person's* interests. They have in fact been evaluated, but by a different set of criteria entirely: whether they enhanced the longevity and fecundity of the replicators. From the standpoint of the individual person (the vehicle) these are the dangerous goals, the ones that sacrifice the vehicle to the goals of replicators—the ones that lead the bee to sacrifice itself for its genetically related queen. As Pinker (1997, p. 370) notes, "the problem with emotions is not that they are untamed forces vestiges of our animal past; it is that they are designed to propagate copies of the genes that built them rather than to promote happiness, wisdom, or moral values. We often call an act 'emotional' when it is harmful to the social group, damaging to the actor's happiness in the long run, uncontrollable and impervious to persuasion, or a product of self-delusion. Sad to say, these outcomes are not malfunctions but precisely what we would expect from well-engineered emotions".

What the right side of Fig. 7.5 (indicating the goal structure of System 2) indicates is that a bee with a Popperian/Gregorian intelligence might well decide that it would rather forgo the sacrifice! It is the reflective processes embodied in System 2 that derive the flexible long-leash goals that often have utility for the organism but thwart the goals of the genes (sex with contraception, resource use after the reproductive years have ended, etc.). These are the goals at the top of the right side of Fig. 7.5 that overlap with vehicle interests but not genetic interests.

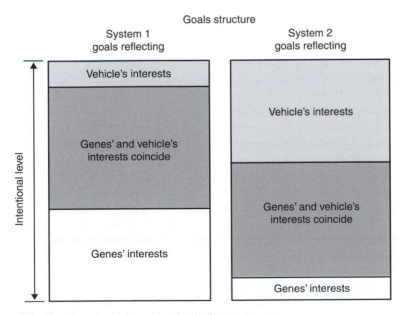

Figure 7.5   Genetic and vehicle goal overlap in the two systems.

Failure to acknowledge the divergence of "interests" (see footnote 4, p. 190) between replicators and their vehicles is an oversight that sociobiologists were certainly guilty of (see Symons, 1992, on the "genetic fallacy") and that evolutionary psychologists are sometimes guilty of. For example, evolutionary psychologists are fond of pointing to the optimality of cognitive functioning—of showing that certain reasoning errors that cognitive psychologists have portrayed as a characteristic and problematic aspect of human reasoning (Kahneman & Tversky, 1984, 1996, 2000) have in fact a logical evolutionary explanation (Brase, Cosmides, & Tooby, 1998; Cosmides & Tooby, 1996; Gigerenzer, 1996b; Rode et al., 1999). The connotation, or unspoken assumption, is that therefore there is nothing to worry about—that since human behaviour is optimal from an evolutionary standpoint, the concern for cognitive reform that has been characteristic of many cognitive psychologists (termed "Meliorists" by Stanovich, 1999) has been misplaced. But this sanguine attitude too readily conflates genetic optimization with goal optimization for the vehicle. To avoid the error, the different "interests" of the replicators and vehicles must be recognized—and we must keep evaluations of efficiency consistent with the entity whose optimization is at issue. The bee, as a Darwinian creature, needs no cognitive reform because it has no "interests" other than its genes' interests. Humans, with Gregorian minds, have interests as vehicles and thus might benefit from cognitive reform in situations where vehicle interests conflict with genetic interests and their Darwinian minds are siding with the latter. In such a case, it is imperative that System 2 carry out its override function (as depicted in Fig. 7.2), and suppress the System 1 response and substitute one more congruent with vehicle well-being.

Situations where evolutionary and instrumental rationality dissociate might well be rare, but the few occasions on which they occur might be important ones. This is because knowledge-based, technological societies often put a premium on abstraction and decontextualization, and they sometimes require that the fundamental computational bias of human cognition toward contextualization of problems (see Stanovich, 1999, in press; Stanovich & West, 2000) be overridden by System 2 processes.

Evolutionary psychologists are prone to emphasize situations where genetic goals and personal goals coincide. They are not wrong to do so, because this is most often the case. Accurately navigating around objects in the natural world was adaptive during the EEA, and it similarly serves our personal goals as we carry out our lives in the modern world. Likewise, with other evolutionary adaptations: It is a marvel that humans are exquisite frequency detectors (Hasher & Zacks, 1979), that they infer intentionality with almost supernatural ease (Levinson, 1995), and that they acquire a complex language code from impoverished input (Pinker, 1994). All of these mechanisms serve personal goal fulfilment in the modern world. But none of this means that the overlap is necessarily 100 per cent.

Unfortunately, the modern world tends to create situations where some of the default values of evolutionarily adapted cognitive systems are not optimal. Modern technological societies continually spawn situations where humans must decontextualize information—where they must deal abstractly (Adler, 1984) and in a depersonalized manner with information rather than in the context-specific way assumed by proponents of the massive modularity thesis (Samuels, 1998). Such situations require the active suppression of the personalizing and contextualizing styles that characterize the fundamental computational biases (Stanovich, 1999, in press). Such biases directly conflict with the demands for decontextualization that a highly bureaucratized society puts on its citizens. Indeed, this is often why schools have to explicitly teach such skills of cognitive decontextualization. Increasingly, modern society is demanding such skills (Dickens & Flynn, 2001; Frank & Cook, 1995; Gottfredson, 1997; Hunt, 1995, 1999) and, in some cases, it is rendering economically superfluous anyone who does not have them (Bronfenbrenner, McClelland, Wethington, Moen, & Ceci, 1996; Frank & Cook, 1995). For example, many aspects of the contemporary legal system put a premium on detaching prior belief and world knowledge from the process of evidence evaluation. There has been understandable vexation at odd jury verdicts rendered because of jury theories and narratives concocted during deliberations that had nothing to do with the evidence but that instead were based on background knowledge and personal experience.

The need to decontextualize also characterizes many work settings in contemporary society. Consider the common admonition in the retail service sector of "the customer is always right". This admonition is often interpreted to include even instances where customers unleash unwarranted and sometimes astonishingly vitriolic verbal assaults. The service worker is supposed to remain polite and helpful under this onslaught, despite the fact that such emotional social stimuli are no doubt triggering evolutionarily instantiated modules of self defence and emotional reaction. All of this emotion, all of these personalized attributions—all fundamental computational biases—must be set aside by the service worker and instead an abstract rule that "the customer is always right" must be invoked in this special, socially constructed domain of the market-based transaction. The worker must realize that he or she is not in an *actual* social interaction with this person (which, if true, might call for socking them on the nose!), but in a special, indeed "unnatural", realm where different rules apply.

Concerns about the real-world implications of the failure to engage in necessary cognitive abstraction (see Adler, 1984) were what led Luria (1976) to warn against minimizing the importance of decontextualizing thinking styles. In discussing the syllogism he notes that "a considerable proportion of our intellectual operations involve such verbal and logical systems; they comprise the basic network of codes along which the connections in discursive human thought are channeled" (Luria, 1976, p. 101). Einhorn and Hogarth (1981) highlight the importance of decontextualized environments in their discussion of the optimistic and pessimistic views of the cognitive biases revealed in laboratory experimentation. Einhorn and Hogarth (1981, p. 82) note that "the most optimistic asserts that biases are limited to laboratory situations which are unrepresentative of the natural ecology", but they go on to caution that "in a rapidly changing world it is unclear what the relevant natural ecology will be. Thus, although the laboratory may be an unfamiliar environment, lack of ability to perform well in unfamiliar situations takes on added importance" (p. 82).

Critics of the abstract content of most laboratory tasks and standardized tests have been misguided on this very point. Evolutionary psychologists have singularly failed to understand the implications of Einhorn and Hogarth's (1981) warning. They regularly bemoan the "abstract" problems and tasks in the heuristics and biases literature and imply that since these tasks are not like "real life" we need not worry that people do poorly on them. The issue is that, ironically, the argument that the laboratory tasks and tests are not like "real life" is becoming less and less true. "Life", in fact, is becoming more like the tests! Try using an international automated cash dispenser with which you are unfamiliar; or try arguing with your health maintenance organization/ insurance company about a disallowed medical procedure. In such circumstances, we invariably find out that our personal experience, our emotional responses, our stimulus-triggered intuitions about social justice are all worthless—all are for naught when talking over the phone to the representative looking at a computer screen displaying a spreadsheet with a hierarchy of branching choices and conditions to be fulfilled. The social context, the idiosyncrasies of individual experience, the personal narrative—all are abstracted away as the representatives of modernist technological-based services attempt to "apply the rules".

Modern mass communication technicians have become quite skilled at implying certain conclusions without actually stating those conclusions (for fear of lawsuits, bad publicity, etc.). Advertisements rely on the fundamental computational bias (particularly its enthymematic processing feature) to fill in the missing information. Margolis (1987; see also Margolis, 1996) warns of the ubiquitousness of this situation in modern society: "We can encounter cases where the issue is both out-of-scale with everyday life experience and contains important novelties, so that habitual responses can be highly inappropriate responses. The opportunity for unrecognized contextual effects akin to the scenario effects ... [demonstrated in the laboratory] can be something much more than an odd quirk that shows up in some contrived situation" (Margolis, 1987, p. 168).

Evolutionary psychologists have argued that some problems can be solved more efficiently if represented to coincide with how various brain modules represent information.[5] Nevertheless, they often seem to ignore the fact that the world will not always *let* us deal with representations that are optimally suited to our evolutionarily designed cognitive mechanisms. For example, in a series of elegant experiments, Gigerenzer, Hoffrage, and Kleinbolting (1991) have shown how at least part of the overconfidence effect in knowledge calibration studies is due to the unrepresentative stimuli used in such experiments—stimuli that do not match the participants' stored cue validities, which are optimally tuned to the environment. But there are many instances in real life when we are suddenly placed in environments where the cue validities have changed. Metacognitive awareness of such situations and strategies for suppressing incorrect confidence judgements generated by automatic responses to cues will be crucial here. Every high school musician who aspires to a career in music has to recalibrate when he or she arrives at university and sees large numbers of talented musicians for the first time. If they persist in their old confidence judgements they may not change to a different specialty area when this would be advisable. Many real-life situations where accomplishment yields a new environment with even more stringent performance requirements share this logic. Each time we "ratchet up" in the competitive environment of a capitalist economy (Frank & Cook, 1995) we are in a situation just like the overconfidence knowledge calibration experiments with their unrepresentative materials. It is important to have learned strategies that will temper one's overconfidence in such situations (Koriat, Lichtenstein, & Fischhoff, 1980).

HOW EVOLUTIONARY PSYCHOLOGY GOES WRONG

Dawkins (1976, p. 234) notes that there is an "uneasy tension . . . between gene and individual body as fundamental agent of life". Many evolutionary psychologists have missed this essential tension by focusing on parallels between the evolutionary optimization of humans and other animals. But humans are vehicles with interests beyond those of their genes' replication. Humans aspire to be more than mere survival machines serving the "ends" of their genes (which are replication pure and simple). Only humans *really* turn

---

[5] Frequency representations of probabilistic information are one example. However, although it is claimed that frequentist representations can eliminate cognitive illusions (Gigerenzer, 1991), this claim remains controversial. Over (Chapter 6), for example, presents evidence suggesting that the favourable evidence with respect to frequentist representations may have resulted from the use of problems with transparent logical forms. Furthermore, even if frequency representations sometimes attenuate cognitive illusions, they do not remove them entirely (Evans, Handley Perham, Over, & Thompson, 2000; Girotto & Gonzalez, 2001; Harries & Harvey, 2000; Macchi, 1998; Mellers et al., 2001; Sloman, Over, & Slovak (in press); Tversky & Kahneman, 1983; see also Chapter 6).

the tables (or at least have the potential to) by occasionally ignoring the interests of the genes in order to further the interests of the vehicle. Evolutionary psychology, for all its important insights about human behaviour, has failed to develop this profound insight. By failing to highlight the interests of the vehicle in discussions of optimal cognitive functioning, evolutionary psychology has colluded with the genes in delivering their most sophisticated vehicle (human beings) over to them, as if this vehicle—like the bee—had no interests other than replication.

As argued above, evolutionary psychologists relegate the evolutionary/ instrumental rationality distinction to the background because many are: (1) wedded to a cognitive architecture that displays massive modularity; (2) as a result, they eschew domain-general System 2 mechanisms; and (3) they conjoin these two theoretical assumptions with a tendency to ignore the implications of mismatches between the EEA and the cognitive requirements of technological societies.

To the extent that modern society increasingly requires the fundamental computational biases to be overridden, then dissociations between evolutionary and individual rationality will become more common, and System 2 overrides will be more essential to personal well-being. Cosmides and Tooby (1996, p. 15) argue that "in the modern world, we are awash in numerically expressed statistical information. But our hominid ancestors did not have access to the modern accumulation which has produced, for the first time in human history, reliable, numerically expressed statistical information about the world beyond individual experience. Reliable numerical statements about single event probabilities were rare or nonexistent in the Pleistocene". "It is easy to forget that our hominid ancestors did not have access to the modern system of socially organized data collection, error checking, and information accumulation . . . In ancestral environments, the only external database available from which to reason inductively was one's own observations" (Brase et al., 1998, p. 5).

Although this may be entirely correct (but see footnote 5, p. 197), let us carry through with the implications of this point. We are living in a technological society where we must: decide which health maintenance organization to join based on just such statistics; figure-out whether to invest in an individual retirement account or personal pension plan; decide what type of mortgage to purchase; figure-out what type of insurance policy to buy; decide whether to trade-in a car or sell it ourselves; decide whether to lease or to buy; think about how to apportion our retirement funds; and decide whether we would save money by joining a book club—to simply list a random set of the plethora of modern-day decisions and choices. And we must make all of these decisions based on information represented in a manner for which our brains may not be adapted (in none of these cases have we coded individual frequency information from our own personal experience). To reason normatively in all of these domains (to maximize our personal utility) we are going to have to deal with probabilistic information represented in nonfrequentistic terms—in representations that the evolutionary psychologists have argued are different from our adapted algorithms for dealing with frequency information (Cosmides & Tooby, 1996; Gigerenzer & Hoffrage, 1995).

Consider the work of Brase et al. (1998), who improved performance on a difficult probability problem (Bar-Hillel & Falk, 1982; Falk, 1992; Granberg, 1995) by presenting the information as frequencies and in terms of whole objects—both alterations designed to better fit the posited frequency-computation systems of the brain. In response to a query about why the adequate performance observed was not even higher given that our brains contain such well-designed frequency-computation systems, Brase et al. (1998, p. 13) replied that "in our view it is remarkable that they work on paper-and-pencil problems at all. A natural sampling system is designed to operate on actual events". The problem is that in a symbol-oriented postindustrial society, we are presented with paper-and-pencil problems all the time, and much of what we know about the world comes not from the perception of actual events but from abstract information preprocessed, prepackaged, and condensed into symbolic codes such as probabilities, percentages, tables, and graphs (the voluminous statistical information routinely presented in *USA Today* and *Social Trends* comes to mind).

What we are attempting to combat here is a connotation implicit in some discussions of findings in evolutionary psychology and indeed in the situated cognition literature as well (see Anderson, Reder, & Simon, 1996) that there is nothing to be gained from being able to understand a formal rule at an abstract level (the conjunction rule of probability, etc.), and no advantage in flexibly overriding the fundamental computational biases. We can see the tendency of evolutionary psychologists to fall into this trap in the following statement (Tooby & Cosmides, 1992, p. 79):

> In actuality, adaptationist approaches offer the explanation for why the psychic unity of humankind is genuine and not just an ideological fiction; for why it applies in a privileged way to the most significant, global, functional, and complexly organized dimensions of our architecture; and for why the differences among humans that are caused by genetic variability that geneticists have found are so overwhelmingly peripheralized into architecturally minor and functionally superficial properties.

This statement provides an example of how and why evolutionary psychology goes off the rails. Let us see what is in some of that "genetic variability that geneticists have found" and let us ask ourselves, *seriously*, whether it does reflect "functionally superficial properties".

Well, for starters, some of that "genetic variability that geneticists have found" is in general intelligence (*g*), which virtually everyone who has looked at the evidence agrees is at least 40–50 per cent heritable (Deary, 2000; Grigorenko, 1999; Neisser et al., 1996; Plomin & Petrill, 1997). Is *g* a "functionally superficial" individual difference property of human cognition? No responsible psychologist thinks so. It is, indeed, the single most potent psychological predictor of human behaviour in both laboratory and real-life contexts that has ever been identified (Lubinski, 2000; Lubinski & Humphreys, 1997). It is a predictor of real-world outcomes that are critically important to the maximization of personal utility (to instrumental rationality) in a modern technological society. Objective measures of the requirements for cognitive abstraction have been increasing across most job categories in technological societies throughout the past several decades (Gottfredson, 1997). This is why measures of the ability to deal with abstraction such as *g* remain the best employment predictor and the best earnings predictor in postindustrial societies (Brody, 1997; Gottfredson, 1997; Hunt, 1995). The psychometric literature contains numerous indications that cognitive ability is correlated with the avoidance of harmful behaviours and with success in employment settings, as well as social status attainment (MacDonald & Geary, 2000), independent of level of education (Brody, 1997; Gottfredson, 1997; Hunt, 1995; Lubinski & Humphreys, 1997).

We view individual differences in *g* as indicating differences in the current computational capacity of the algorithmic level of System 2. It is critically related to the override function of System 2 discussed above—the override function necessary to trump the fundamental computational biases of System 1 when they lead to a response that is antithetical to the interests of the vehicle.

Our algorithmic-level understanding of System 2 borrows from Dennett (1991), who conceives of System 2 as a serial von Neumann computer simulated by the massively parallel computational network of the brain. It is language-based, rule-based, and at least *more* logic-based than System 1 (Evans & Over, 1996, 1997)—and is the focus of our awareness (it is the system we use to construct a model of the self). As mentioned previously, Evans and Over (1999) discuss the fundamental importance of System 2 as the mechanism that supports hypothetical thinking. In contrast to the holistic/associative nature of System 1, System 2 is analytic in operation, and it is demanding in terms of computational capacity. We view general intelligence to encompass two fundamental classes of property (that perhaps map into the fluid/crystallized distinction from the Horn/Cattell model, Horn, 1982; Horn & Cattell, 1967). First, there is the computational power of the parallel network to sustain the serial simulation[6] (this is probably closer to

---

[6] Deary (2000) has written a book summarizing the evidence on the relationship between reaction time and other speeded tasks and intelligence. It turns out to be difficult to explain why

fluid intelligence in the Horn/Cattell model of intelligence). The second major factor is the power of the cultural tools used during serial simulation—the Gregorian mind in Dennett's (1991) Tower of Intellect model (individual differences in this factor might relate to variance in crystallized intelligence in the Horn/Cattell model).

Intelligence is not the only type of "genetic variability that geneticists have found" that is manifestly *not* "functionally superficial". Similar stories could be told about many personality variables (reflective of intentional-level cognitive variability, see Stanovich, 1999) that have been shown to be heritable but also important predictors of behavioural outcomes (see p. 394 of Buss, 1999; Matthews & Deary, 1998). Indeed, this stance by some evolutionary psychologists against heritable cognitive traits with demonstrable linkages to important real-world behaviours has become an embarrassment even to some evolutionary theorists. Buss (1999, p. 394) characterizes the view of Tooby and Cosmides as the notion that "heritable individual differences are to species-typical adaptations, in this view, as differences in the colors of the wires in a car engine to the engine's functional working components", and points to some of the same embarrassing empirical facts noted above. For example, heritable personality traits such as conscientiousness and impulsivity have been related to important life goals such as work, status attainment, mortality, and faithfulness in partnerships. Buss's (1999) alternative interpretation is in terms of genetic concepts such as frequency-dependent selection. But whether or not one accepts such explanations, the point is that many evolutionary theorists have mistakenly downplayed cognitive constructs that are heritable (intelligence, personality dimensions, thinking styles) and that have demonstrated empirical relationships to behaviours that relate to utility maximization for the individual (job success, personal injury, success in relationships, substance abuse).

Despite Buss's (1999) more nuanced position on individual differences, other influential evolutionary psychologists repeat like a mantra the view that any psychological processes with genetic variation lack any importance (and presumably lack any relevance for rationality, since this is obviously important to the vehicle):

---

elementary information processing tasks correlate with intelligence at all. Stanovich (2001) conjectured that it is not because they measure some inherent "mental speed" (Deary reviews evidence indicating that the RT–IQ relationship is virtually unchanged when differences in nerve conduction speed are partialled out). But the speed component of these IP tasks may not be the critical thing. Rather, they all may serve as indirect indicators of the computational power available in the brain's connectionist network—computational power that is available to sustain the simulation of a serial processor. Of course, there are other more direct indicators of the computational power available to sustain serial simulation, such as working memory, and not surprisingly these indicators show larger correlations with intelligence.

> Human genetic variation . . . is overwhelmingly sequestered into functionally superficial biochemical differences, leaving our complex functional design universal and species typical.
>
> (Tooby & Cosmides, 1992, p. 25)

> Humans share a complex, species typical and species-specific architecture of adaptations, however much variation there might be in minor, superficial, nonfunctional traits.
>
> (Tooby & Cosmides, 1992, p. 38)

One boggles at general intelligence—one of the most potent psychological predictors of life outcomes—being termed "nonfunctional". But then one realizes what is motivating these statements—a focus on the gene. Even if one buys the massive-modularity-of-adaptations line of the evolutionary psychologist and views general intelligence as some kind of spandrel or byproduct,[7] from the standpoint of the *vehicle's* interests, it is certainly not nonfunctional. Only a focus on the subpersonal replicators would spawn such a statement—one that relegates important cognitive traits such as intelligence and conscientiousness to the background (Lubinski, 2000; Matthews & Deary, 1998). As soon as one focuses on the organismic level of optimization rather than genetic optimization, the "nonfunctional" traits spring to the foreground as the System 2 algorithmic-level (intelligence) and intentional-level (conscientiousness, openness) constructs that explain individual differences in attaining one's goals (Baron, 1993, 1994; Stanovich, 1999).

The downplaying of the importance of a heritable cognitive indicator such as general intelligence by evolutionary psychologists often results from their tendency to caricature cognitive theories that stress a domain-general mechanism (like the type of analytical processing hypothesized for System 2 by many dual-process theorists). The evolutionary theorists purport to dispute theories that view the evolutionary history of human cognition as the replacement of context-dependent modules with context-independent general intelligence mechanisms. For example, in attacking the so-called Standard Social Science Model (SSSM), Tooby and Cosmides (1992, p. 113) argue that this default social science model "views an absence of content-specific structure as a precondition for richly flexible behavior". Their view of the standard cognitive model in psychology is that general processing mechanisms *replace* domain-specific ones. Actually, as the long history of dual-process models attests (see Table 7.3), the standard view in psychology is

---

[7] Although the outcome of disputes about whether general intelligence is a byproduct or adaptation does not alter our argument, it should be noted that theorists such as LaCerra and Bingham (1998) and Foley (1996) argue that the changing online requirements of the ancestral hominid environment would, unlike the massive modularity thesis, have required a flexible general intelligence (see also, Nozick, 1993, p. 120, for a philosophically oriented version of a similar argument).

much more similar to the evolutionary psychology view than Tooby and Cosmides want to admit. As in Dennett's (1996) "Tower of Intellect" model, all of the two-process views listed in Table 7.3 conceive of analytical processes developing in *conjunction* with domain-specific mechanisms (see Mithen, 1996). Analytical processing mechanisms develop *in addition to* System 1 modules—they do not replace them.

Evolutionary psychologists also tend to misleadingly minimize the consequences of mismatches between the EEA and the modern environment. Tooby and Cosmides (1992, p. 72) approvingly paraphrase Shepard's (1987) point that evolution insures a mesh between the principles of the mind and the regularities of the world. But this "mesh" concerns regularities in the EEA, not in the modern world—with its unnatural requirements for decontextualization (requirements that do not "mesh" with the fundamental computational biases toward comprehensive contextualization of situations). One page later in their chapter, Tooby and Cosmides (1992, p. 73) reveal the characteristic bias of evolutionary psychologists—the belief that "often, but not always, the ancestral world will be similar to the modern world (e.g. the properties of light and the laws of optics have not changed)". We largely agree. However, although the laws of optics haven't changed, the type of one-shot, abstract, probabilistic, and symbolically represented decision situations a modern human being must deal with are certainly unprecedented in human history. Think of insurance decisions, retirement decisions, investment decisions, home-buying decisions, relocation decisions, and school choices for children. These are not the highly practised, frequency-coded, time-pressured, recognition-based situations (Klein, 1998) where evolutionary heuristics work best. Instead, these are all the types of situation that invoke just the type of representativeness, availability, sunk cost, confirmation bias, overconfidence, and other effects that the heuristics and biases researchers have studied (see the many real-life examples in Kahneman & Tversky, 2000). We can walk and navigate among objects as well as we ever did, but no evolutionary mechanism has sculpted my brain to estimate the type of insurance policy we need or how we should evaluate the cost of a disability policy to cover salary loss.

Tooby and Cosmides (1992) seem to take a completely one-sided message from the potential mismatch between the EEA and modern conditions, when in fact the mismatch has more than one implication. Using the example of how our colour constancy mechanisms fail under modern sodium vapour lamps, they warn that "attempting to understand color constancy mechanisms under such unnatural illumination would have been a major impediment to progress" (Tooby & Cosmides, 1992, p. 73)—a fair enough point. But our purpose here is to stress a different corollary point that one might have drawn. The point is that if the modern world *were* structured such that making colour judgements under sodium lights was critical to our well-being, then this would be troublesome for us because our evolutionary mechanisms have not naturally equipped us for this. One might be given impetus to search for a cultural invention that would circumvent this defect (relative to the modern world, not the EEA) in our cognitive apparatus.

We argue that humans in the modern world are in just this situation *vis-à-vis* the mechanisms needed for fully rational action in industrial and bureaucratized societies. The processing of probabilistic information provides a case in point. We argued above that it is critical to many tasks faced by a full participant in a First World society. Of course, the heuristics and biases literature is full of demonstrations of the problems that people have in dealing with probabilistic information. Evolutionary psychologists have done important work that suggests that the human cognitive apparatus may be more adapted to dealing with frequencies than with probabilities (Brase et al., 1998; Cosmides & Tooby, 1996; Gigerenzer & Hoffrage, 1995; but see footnote 5 and Chapter 5). For example, it has been found that when tasks such as the Linda Problem, knowledge calibration tasks, and base-rate tasks are revised in terms of estimating the frequency of categories rather than judging probabilities that performance is improved (see Cosmides & Tooby, 1996; Fiedler, 1988; Gigerenzer, 1991, 1993; Gigerenzer & Hoffrage, 1995; Tversky & Kahneman, 1983; but see Mellers, Hertwig, & Kahneman, 2001). As useful as this research has been (and, indeed, it can usefully be adapted to tell us how to more understandably present probabilistic information in real-life settings, see Gigerenzer, Hoffrage, & Ebert, 1998), it will not remove the necessity of being able to process probabilistic information when it *is* presented in the real world.

The evolutionary psychologists and ecological rationality theorists are sometimes guilty of implying just this—that if the human cognitive apparatus can be shown to have been adapted during evolution to some *other* representation (other than that required for a problem in modern society) then somehow it has been shown that there really is no cognitive problem. For example, in the titles and subheadings of several papers on frequency representations, Gigerenzer (1991, 1993, Gigerenzer et al., 1991) has used the phrasing "how to make cognitive illusions disappear". This is a strange way to phrase things, because the original illusion has of course not "disappeared". As Kahneman and Tversky (1996) note, the Muller–Lyer illusion is removed when the two figures are embedded in a rectangular frame, but this does not mean that the *original* illusion has "disappeared" in this demonstration (see also Samuels, Stich, & Tremoulet, 1999). The cognitive illusions in their original form still remain (although their explanation has perhaps been clarified by the different performance obtained in the frequency version), and the situations (real-life or otherwise) in which these illusions occur have not been eliminated. Banks, insurance companies, medical, and many other institutions of modern society are still exchanging information using linguistic terms like "probability" and applying that term to singular events. Our physician may on occasion give us a migraine prescription (Imitrex, for instance) with the assurance that he is 90 per cent certain it will work in our case. As many Bayesian investigators in the calibration literature have pointed out, it is likely that we would be quite upset if we found out that for 50 per cent of his patients so advised the medication did not work.

Drawing on Sperber's (1994) distinction between the actual domain and the proper domain (the modern environment versus the EEA), Samuels et al., (1999, p. 114) argue that "we suspect that those Panglossian-inclined theorists who describe Darwinian modules as 'elegant machines' are tacitly assuming that normative evaluation should be relativized to the proper domain, while those who offer a bleaker assessment of human rationality are tacitly relativizing their evaluations to the actual domain, which, in the modern world, contains a vast array of information-processing challenges that are quite different from anything our Pleistocene ancestors had to confront" (see also Davies, 1996; Looren de Jong & van der Steen, 1998). Perhaps both groups are guilty of some disproportionate emphasis here. Evolutionary theorists err by emphasizing the proper domain so much that they seem to forget about the actual domain, and the Meliorists in the heuristics and biases camp are so prone to emphasize the errors occurring in the actual domain that they fail to acknowledge that humans really are optimally designed for a proper domain.

Buss (1999, p. 378) shows the former tendency when he asks the question: "If humans are so riddled with cognitive mechanisms that commonly cause errors and biases, how can they routinely solve complex problems that surpass any system that can be developed artificially?"—and answers it by quoting an unpublished paper by Tooby and Cosmides where the argument is made that our criteria for recognizing sophisticated performance "have been parochial" (Buss, 1999, p. 378). Buss seems to be calling our natural privileging of the present environment—the one we actually have to operate in—unnecessarily parochial. The devaluing of the actual decontextualized environment in which we must operate in modern technological society continues as Buss (1999) repeatedly minimizes rational thinking errors by pointing out that they occur in "artificial or novel" (p. 378) situations. The latter seems damning to his own argument (that these errors are trivial) because novel symbolic situations are exactly what bureaucratically immersed workers and citizens in technological societies must constantly deal with.

With respect to the "artificial situations" criticism, Buss (1999, p. 379) trots out the old sodium vapour lamps example, saying that the experiments have used "artificial, evolutionarily unprecedented experimental stimuli analogous to sodium vapour lamps". Like Tooby and Cosmides (1992), Buss (1999) takes exactly the wrong message from the potential mismatch between EEA and modern conditions. It is *a very serious worry* that we are essentially in situations where we must work under sodium vapour lamps! The cognitive equivalent of the sodium vapour lamps are: the probabilities we must deal with; the causation we must infer from knowledge of what *might* have happened; the vivid advertising examples we must ignore; the unrepresentative sample we must disregard; the favoured hypothesis we must not privilege; the rule we must follow that dictates we ignore a personal relationship; the narrative we must set aside because it does not square with the facts; the pattern that we must infer, which is not there because we know a randomizing device is involved; the sunk cost that must not affect our judgement; the judge's instructions we must follow despite their conflict with common sense; the contract we must honour despite its negative affects on a relative; the professional decision we must make because we know it is beneficial in the aggregate even if unclear in this case. These are all the "sodium vapour lamps" that modern society presents to our cognitive apparatus and, if evolution has not prepared us to deal with them, so much the worse for our rational behaviour in the modern world (Stanovich, 1999, in press). Luckily, the Gregorian tools of rational thought, running as virtual machines on our System 2 serial simulator are there to help us in situations such as this.

THE SLIPPERY NOTION OF ECOLOGICAL RATIONALITY

Many of the foregoing arguments about matching conceptions of rationality to the level of the entity being optimized apply to the concept of ecological rationality as well, and the work of those who have championed this concept. But the concept itself is not straightforward. A textual analysis of its usage reveals that it is a slippery concept indeed.

Typical of these confusions is a statement at the end of a volume summarizing the work of one of the laboratories responsible for popularizing the term: "Ultimately, ecological rationality depends on decision making that furthers an organism's adaptive goals in the physical or social environment" (Gigerenzer & Todd, 1999, p. 364). In statements such as this we see a double ambiguity, which makes the ecological rationality term devilishly difficult to pin down and hence to evaluate. First, the phrasing "organism's adaptive goals" makes it unclear what level of analysis we are talking about. The word "adaptive" suggests we are talking, in the technical sense, about evolutionary (hence genetic) goals—that ecological rationality is about how organisms are optimized to achieve the goals of their genes. On the other hand, one looks at the same phrase and wonders whether the word "organism" is not key here— that the word adaptive is actually being used more colloquially—and that we are to put a stress on it (as in the "*organism's* adaptive goals") and view the ecological rationality concept as akin to instrumental rationality (as maximizing the vehicle's utility). This ambiguity in the "organism's adaptive goals" phrase introduces a second ambiguity into the second part of the quote. Because we are unsure whether adaptive goals refer to the genes' goals or the vehicle's goals it becomes unclear whether "the physical or social environment" is meant to refer to the current (modern) environment or to the EEA.

These two interpretations of the phrase "organism's adaptive goals" slip in and out throughout the 400 pages of the book by Gigerenzer and Todd (1999) and the Adaptive Behavior and Cognition Group at the Max Planck Institute in Berlin (see also, Todd & Gigerenzer, 2000). On page 335 of the book, they draw tight links between work in behavioural ecology and ecological rationality ("ecological rationality is what behavioral ecology is all about"), which suggest that genetic fitness maximization is, likewise, what ecological rationality is all about. This view is reinforced in other parts of the book where we are told that "the collection of specialized cognitive mechanisms that evolution has built into the human mind for specific domains of inference and reasoning" (p. 30) include the fast and frugal heuristics that are the focus of a dozen chapters in the Gigerenzer and Todd (1999) book. Elsewhere, we are told that "evolution would seize upon informative environmental dependencies such as this one and exploit them with specific heuristics if they would give a decision-making organism an adaptive edge" (Gigerenzer & Todd, 1999, p. 19).

Buss (1999), discussing Tooby and Cosmides' use of the term ecological rationality in an unpublished manuscript, likewise links the term to fitness in the evolutionary sense: "Over evolutionary time, the human environment has had certain statistical regularities . . . These statistical regularities are called ecological structure. Ecological rationality consists of evolved mechanisms containing design features that utilize this ecological structure to facilitate adaptive problem solving" (Buss, 1999, p. 378). Thus, Buss, like Gigerenzer and Todd (1999), seems to clearly imply that what ecological rationality is designed to optimize is genetic fitness in the EEA.

After all this emphasis on evolution being the superstructure on which ecological rationality sits, it is a surprise to hear Todd, Fiddick, and Krauss (2000) reply to a critique of Over (2000) by saying that although evolutionary psychology is grounded in ecological rationality the converse is not true. Unlike Buss's (1999) emphasis on the human environment "over evolutionary time," Todd et al. (2000, p. 379), in a complete theoretical reversal from the quotes above, instead assert that ecological rationality "encompasses decision making in present environments without privileging problems with fitness consequences".

In short, there is considerable inconsistency in the writings of the ecological rationality theorists about whether ecological rationality is optimization to the EEA or to the modern environment—in short, about whether ecological rationality is maximizing for the genes or for the vehicle. The term needs to be explicitly identified with what Stanovich has termed evolutionary rationality (Stanovich, 1999) or with what has traditionally been viewed as instrumental rationality—rationality for the whole organism (see Over, 2000). Instead, these theorists seem to slip back and forth in their usage, adopting whichever stance is most convenient for the argument being made. Ecological rationality theorists seem to want the imprimatur of evolution (and the biological plausibility that evolutionary adaptation provides) without accepting other inconvenient implications of evolutionary explanations. One implication is that we cannot assume that System 1 heuristics (adapted for the EEA) are optimal for achieving rationality in the modern world (Stanovich, 1999, in press). Many important decisions in life are nearly "one shot" affairs (job offers, pension decisions, investing decisions, housing decisions, marriage decisions, reproductive decisions, etc.). Some of these decisions were not present at all in the EEA, and we have had no time nor learning trials to acquire extensive personal frequency information about them. Instead, we need to make certain logical and probabilistic inferences using various rules of inference and, most importantly, we must decouple myriad sources of information that our autonomously functioning modules might be detecting and feeding into the decision ("No, the likeability of this salesperson should not be a factor in my deciding on this $25,000 car").

In fact, some of the System 1 heuristics that are in place might seriously subvert instrumental goals in a modern technological society. For example, one chapter in the Gigerenzer and Todd (1999) book (see Goldstein & Gigerenzer, 1999) is devoted to the so-called recognition heuristic—the chapter subheading being "How Ignorance Makes us Smart". The idea behind such "ignorance-based decision making" as they call it, is that the fact that some items of a subset are unknown can be exploited to aid decision making. The yes/no recognition response can be used as a frequency estimation cue. With ingenious simulations, Goldstein and Gigerenzer (1999) demonstrate how certain information environments can lead to such things as less-is-more effects: where those who know less about an environment can display more inferential accuracy in it.

One is certainly convinced after reading material like this that the recognition heuristic is certainly efficacious in *some* situations. But then one immediately begins to worry when we ponder how it relates to a market environment specifically designed to exploit it. If the first author of this chapter left his home—located in the middle of the financial and industrial capital of a developed country—and relied solely on the recognition heuristic, he could easily be led to:

(1) Buy a $3 coffee when in fact a $1.25 one would satisfy him perfectly.
(2) Eat in a single snack the number of grammes of fat he should have in an entire day.
(3) Pay the highest bank fees (because the highest fees are charged by the most recognized banks in Canada).

(4) Incur credit card debt rather than pay cash.

(5) Buy a mutual fund with a 6% sales charge rather than a no-load fund.

None of these behaviours serves his long-term instrumental goals at all—none of them help get him towards his reflectively acquired aspirations. Yet the recognition heuristic triggers these and dozens more that will trip him up while trying to make his way through the maze of modern society.

The proponents of ecological rationality refuse to acknowledge this downside of the ecological approach. For example, Borges, Goldstein, Ortmann, and Gigerenzer (1999) take curious pride in the finding that a portfolio of stocks recognized by a group of Munich pedestrians beat two benchmark mutual funds over a 6-month period during the mid-1990s. This finding is of course a pure artifact of an extraordinary short period in the 1990s when large capitalization stocks outperformed small capitalization stocks (Over, 2000). The adaptive heuristics investigated by Borges et al. (1999) haven't repealed the basic laws of investing. Risk is still related to reward, and over longer time periods small capitalization stocks outperformed their less-risky large capitalization counterparts. Obviously, the Munich pedestrians had better recognition for the large companies—precisely those enjoying a good run in that particular 6-month period (which is, of course, too short for various risk/reward relationships to show themselves).

Borges et al. (1999) might alternatively have focused on another well-known finding in the domain of personal finance discussed by Bazerman (2001)—that consumers of financial services overwhelmingly purchase high-cost products that underperform in terms of investment return the low-cost strategies recommended by true experts (e.g. dollar-cost averaging into no-load index mutual funds). The reason is, of course, that the high-cost fee-based products and services are the ones with high immediate recognizability in the marketplace, whereas the low-cost strategies must be sought out in financial and consumer publications.

One leaves the writings of the ecological rationality theorists—whatever they take the term to mean—thinking that they, like the evolutionary psychologists, are being much too sanguine about the ability of System 1 processes to achieve instrumental rationality—to optimize the broad and reflective goals of System 2 rather than the short-leash evolutionary goals of System 1.

THE UNACKNOWLEDGED IMPORTANCE OF THE MEME

Why do the evolutionary psychologists and ecological theorists show such a tendency to misconstrue human rationality—to fail to distinguish the interests of the replicators from the interests of the vehicle? Our conjecture is that the error follows from a particular overgeneralization that is encouraged by the evolutionary psychologists' attack on what Tooby and Cosmides (1992) call the Standard Social Science Model (SSSM). These evolutionary psychologists believe that the SSSM stands in the way of a fully articulated evolutionary psychology based on the assumption that the human brain is composed of content-specific information-processing mechanisms that have evolved as adaptions. Instead, the SSSM has become the default model of most social scientists in their view, and the SSSM contains many misleading assumptions about human cognition, including the assumption that the human mind is structured as a general, unbiased learning mechanism. Among the many assumptions of the SSSM that are wrong according to Tooby and Cosmides (1992), are its assumptions about culture. Tooby and Cosmides (1992) feel that the default assumptions of the SSSM of most social scientists are that "the individual is the more or less passive recipient of her culture and is the product of that culture" (p. 32) and that "human nature is an empty vessel, waiting to be filled by social processes" (p. 29).

The idea of free-floating cultural products—those totally unconditioned by and unadapted to evolved mental mechanisms (what Tooby & Cosmides, 1992 call epidemiological culture)[8]—is an anathema to many evolutionary psychologists. In fact, Tooby and Cosmides (1992, p. 119) labour hard to convince the reader that even epidemiological culture "is also shaped by the details of our evolved psychological organization". To use Dawkins' (1976) term, evolutionary psychologists are hostile to the concept of the meme. But because human rationality is in large part a memetic product—a set of cultural tools for the Gregorian mind—evolutionary psychologists are prone to miss or denigrate its importance.

Dawkins (1976) introduced the term meme to refer to a unit of cultural information that is meant to be understood in rough (rather than one-to-one) analogy to a gene. Blackmore (1999) defines the meme as the instructions for behaviours and communications that can be learned by imitation broadly defined (in the sense of copying by the use of language, memory, or any other mechanism) and that can be stored in brains (or other storage devices). Collectively, genes contain the instructions for building the bodies that carry them. Collectively, memes build the culture that transmits them. Like the gene, the meme is a true replicator in the sense of the distinction made in theoretical biology between replicators and interactors (Dawkins, 1976; Hull, 1988; Sterelny, 2001; Sterelny & Griffiths, 1999; Williams, 1985, 1992). Replicators are entities that pass on their structure relatively intact after copying and interactors or vehicles are "those entities that interact as cohesive wholes

---

[8] This is opposed to what they call evoked culture, which to Tooby and Cosmides (1992) is merely domain-specific mechanisms being triggered by local circumstances (culture on a short-leash as Lumsden & Wilson, 1981, have argued; see also Sperber, 1996).

with their environments in such a way as to make replication differential" (Hull, 1988, p. 27).

The key idea in memetic theory is that the meme is a true selfish replicator in the same sense that a gene is—it acts only in its own "interests". The anthropomorphic language about genes and memes having interests is short-hand for the complicated description of what is actually the case: that genes/ memes that perform function X make more copies of themselves, copy with greater fidelity, or have greater longevity—and hence will leave more copies in future generations. Or, as Blackmore (1999, p. 5) states it, "the shorthand 'genes want X' can always be spelled out as 'genes that do X are more likely to be passed on.' This is the only power they have—replicator power. And it is in this sense that they are selfish".

Memes are independent replicators. They do not necessarily exist in order to help the vehicle (those who hold the belief), they exist because through memetic evolution they have displayed the best fecundity, longevity, and copying fidelity—the defining characteristics of successful replicators. The fundamental insight triggered by memetic theory is that a meme may display fecundity and longevity *without necessarily being true or helping the vehicle (the human being holding the belief) in any way*. Memetic theorists often use the example of a chain letter. Here is a meme: "If you do not pass on this message to five people you will experience misfortune". This is an instruction for a behaviour that can be copied and stored in brains. It survives because of its *own* self-replicating properties (it is neither good for the genes or for the vehicle). Dawkins (1976, p. 27) argues that "what we have not previously considered is that a cultural trait may have evolved in the way it has, simply because it is *advantageous to itself*". Memetic theory asks instead what is it about certain memes that leads them to collect many "hosts" for themselves. Indeed, this type of language was suggested by Dawkins (1976, p. 192) himself who, paraphrasing Nick Humphrey, said that "when you plant a fertile meme in my mind you literally parasitize my brain, turning it into a vehicle for the meme's propagation in just the way that a virus may parasitize the genetic mechanism of a host cell" (p. 192).

With Dawkins' point in mind we are now in a position to extract from the writings of the memetic theorists (Aunger, 2000; Blackmore, 1999; Dawkins, 1993; Dennett, 1991, 1995; Lynch, 1996) a taxonomy of reasons for meme survival:

(1) Memes survive and spread because they are helpful to the interactors that store them (most memes that reflect true information in the world would be in this category).
(2) Memes become frequent because they fit genetic predispositions, or domain-specific evolutionary modules (this is the evoked culture that

is emphasized by evolutionary psychologists; see Cosmides & Tooby, 1992; Sperber, 1996).

(3) Memes spread because they facilitate the spread of the genes that make good hosts for these particular memes (religious beliefs that urge people to have more children would be in this category, see Lynch, 1996).

(4) Memes survive and spread because of the self-perpetuating properties of the memes themselves.

We must consider these categories in the context of the fact that many of the intentional-level goals that humans have are meme-installed: they are the products of our culture, rather than installed by the genes that built the vehicle. A schematic that helps to understand our conception of the intentional-level goal structure of System 1 and System 2 in terms of which replicator is a source of the goal is portrayed in Figure 7.6 (again, absolute areas are guesses—for illustrative purposes only). The goal structure of System 1 is dominated by gene-installed goals. These are the short-leash goals discussed earlier—nearly universal in the sense that they are shared by most humans and not the result of the environmental history of the organism. They are not flexible or generic goals, but instead are content specific, situation specific, and hard-wired to trigger (disgust and repulsion to noxious smells and substances, and fear responses to animals like snakes, would be examples; see Buss, 1999; Rozin, 1996; Rozin & Fallon, 1987).

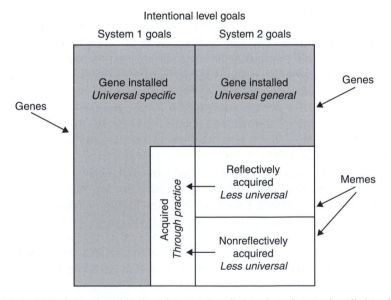

Figure 7.6 Hypotheses about the way that gene-installed goals and meme-installed goals are distributed across System 1 and System 2.

System 2, with its more general, flexible goals is more evenly balanced with genetic goals shared by most humans (e.g. rise in the dominance hierarchy of your conspecifics) and with meme-installed goals that are the result of the specific environmental experience (and culture) of the individual. In Fig. 7.6 we distinguish between mimetically acquired goals that are "caught" like viruses (as in the Dawkins quote above)—what we call nonreflectively acquired memetic goals—and memetic goals that an individual takes on reflectively, with full awareness of their effects on the organism. The nonreflectively acquired goals are perhaps the equivalent of the parasites that Dawkins refers to. They may not actually be good for the individual but, just like the vehicle-sacrificing genes discussed previously, these memes use the vehicle merely to propagate themselves.

The figure also indicates that meme-acquired goals need not be barred from becoming System 1 goals (automatic, autonomous, and rapidly triggering). Through practice, memetically installed goals can become lodged in the goal hierarchy of System 1. "Branding" and other advertising gimmicks aspire to do just this—to have a logo for X trigger the "must have X" response without much thought. These then become especially pernicious memes— parasites that, because they are not part of the reflective mind, become difficult to dislodge.

Of course, meme-derived goals that become part of System 1 can be good for the vehicle too. A reflectively acquired meme—one that was reflectively acquired because it served vehicle ends (perhaps even vehicle ends that thwart the genes' interests)—can become part of System 1 as well. This fact explains a part of Fig. 7.5 that might have seemed perplexing when that figure was first presented. Why is there a small section of area in System 1 representing goals that serve the vehicle's interests only? One might have thought that all of the goals instantiated in System 1 would reflect the genes' interests whether or not they were serving the interests of the vehicle—rather like that of the Darwinian creature represented in Fig. 7.3. However, the possibility of the higher-level goal states of System 2 becoming installed in the more rigid and inflexible System 1 through practice opens up a new possibility. Reflectively acquired goal-states might be memes that were taken on for their unique advantages to the vehicle (advantages that might accrue because they trump contrary gene-installed goals—"don't flirt with your boss's wife"). Those particular memes becoming instantiated in System 1 through practice would create the area depicted in Fig. 7.5—System 1 goal-states serving the vehicle's interests only. We might say that in situations such as this, System 1 in humans reflects the outcome of residing in a brain along with a reflective System 2. This is why the goal structure of System 1 in humans does not simply recapitulate the structure of a Darwinian creature depicted in Fig. 7.3.

What evolutionary psychologists do not like about the previous conceptualization is the notion of memes becoming completely "unglued" from genetic control. Instead, evolutionary psychologists prefer Lumsden and Wilson's (1981) notion that the genes hold culture on a leash (see Sperber, 1996). What they do not like is the idea, which we are advancing here, that at a certain level of recursiveness a Gregorian mind populated with cultural tools in the form of memeplexes designed for the evaluation of other meme-plexes (science; logic; some notions from decision science such as consistency, transitivity, etc.) acquires some autonomy from genetic control. But it is just such autonomy that we are arguing for. We are in fact arguing that the cul-tural tools of logic and decision science, when reflectively used in conjunction with the potent cultural insight that there can be a conflict of interest between replicators and vehicle, have the potential to create a creature with a uniquely critical and discerning type of self reflection. In short, we are arguing that understanding the full implications of the replicator/vehicle distinction may be a cultural tool that could foster even greater levels of self reflection than humans have heretofore achieved.

Combined with the tools of decision science, the vehicle/replicator distinc-tion can spawn thoughts and new tools for the restructuring of human goals—new memes that further sever the connection between memeplexes resident in some brains and genetic goals installed by the replicators. Indeed, we propose that this cultural change is already underway. There are already memeplexes in the air (of which this book is one) that will, contrary to the emphasis in the writings of evolutionary psychologists, further background the role of the genes in human culture.[9]

Evolutionary psychologists resist this extrapolation, falling back on their "culture on a leash" notion. For example, Tooby and Cosmides (1992, p. 119) insist that "epidemiological culture is also shaped by the details of our evolved psychological organization" and, even more strongly, that "our developmental and psychological programs evolved to invite the social and cultural worlds in, but only the parts that tended, on balance, to have adap-tively useful effects" (p. 87). But the evolutionary psychologists seem to have underestimated the power of the memes to break this linkage. What they have neglected is the recursive power of evaluative memes in the context of an organism that has become *aware* of the replicator/vehicle distinction. Science writer Robert Wright (1994) paraphrases the Tooby and Cosmides statement above about "our developmental and psychological programs evolved . . ."

---

[9] Indeed, genetic engineering for purposes of human health and longevity is perhaps the ultimate triumph of Dawkins' (1976) so-called "survival machines" (the human vehicles) over their creators—the replicators. With the technology of genetic engineering, we, who were built by the replicators to serve as their survival machines, use *them* for our *own* goals—goals that are not the genes' goals (e.g. survival past our reproductive years). Williams (1988) uses such an example to counter Stent's (1978) argument against Dawkins (1976) that rebelling against one's own genes is a contradiction. Williams (1988, p. 403) notes that Stent "apparently missed the relevance of major technologies (hair dyeing, tonsillectomy, etc.) based on such rebellion".

into the more readable notion that ideas must "have a kind of harmony with the brains they settle into" (Wright, 1994, p. 366). However, unlike Tooby and Cosmides (1992), Wright (1994) realizes that there are implications that follow from becoming aware of this fact *in the context of replicator/vehicle distinction*. So, after noting that ideas must have a kind of harmony with the brains they settle into, Wright (1994, p. 366) warns that *"that doesn't mean they're good for those brains in the long run"*.

A brain that realizes this startling (and still underappreciated) fact might begin the (admittedly difficult) process of slipping culture off the leash of the genes when the culture is dysfunctional for the person.[10] A brain aware of the replicator/vehicle distinction and in the possession of evaluative memeplexes such as science, logic, and decision theory might begin a process of pruning vehicle-thwarting goals from intentional-level psychology and reinstalling memetic structures that serve the vehicle's interests more efficiently (of course, this is exactly what the canons of normative instrumental rationality—largely a product of the twentieth century—were designed to accomplish).

This might seem like a Promethean goal but, in fact, a rich tradition in cognitive science has emphasized how cultural changes and increased scientific knowledge result in changes in folk psychology. For example, Churchland (1989, 1995) has long emphasized how a mature neuroscience might change our folk language of the mental and of behaviour. Other theorists have emphasized how moral notions change as general knowledge of the deterministic explanatory power of neuroscience becomes more widespread (Wright, 1994). Already, among educated citizens of the twenty-first century, violations of transitivity and independence of irrelevant alternatives can be a cause of cognitive sanction in ways that are probably historically unprecedented. A full appreciation of the implications of the replicator/ vehicle distinction, with its emphasis that differing optimization criteria apply to the personal and subpersonal levels of analysis (utility maximization versus genetic fitness), could have equally profound cultural implications.

Of course, we do not mean to imply that all evolutionary psychologists are guilty of committing a sophisticated version of the genetic fallacy (inferring current function from ancestral function, see Dennett, 1995, p. 465). For example, Pinker (1997, p. 401) does not endorse the culture-on-a-short-leash view and explicitly recognizes the implications of the differing interests of the replicators and the vehicle: "Genes are not puppetmasters; they acted as the recipes for making the brain and body and then they got out of the way. They live in a parallel universe, scattered among bodies, with their own agendas".

---

[10] Those not committed *a priori* to a relativistic denial of the notion of cultural advance might well argue that the history of civilization reflects just this trend (the emancipation of women and the control of our reproductive lives come immediately to mind).

Clearly, not all evolutionary psychologists miss the implication of replicator/vehicle distinction for conceptions of rationality. But some evolutionary theorists do—quite egregiously. In an astonishing essay titled "How Evolutionary Biology Challenges the Classical Theory of Rational Choice", Cooper (1989) basically argues that when choosing between your own goals and those of your genes, you should opt for the latter! After a marvellous discussion of why a probability-matching strategy (Estes, 1964, 1976) might be a fitness-optimizing rather than the utility-maximizing strategy (picking the most frequent option each time), Cooper (1989, p. 459) implies that this outcome undermines the prescriptive force of the utility maximizing strategy: "The upshot is that one is faced with a dilemma. Either rationality is not always the fittest policy, or else classical decision analysis is not as universally rational as is commonly claimed. If the latter horn of the dilemma is seized (and I shall argue that that is indeed the lesser of the evils) . . .". Of course, early in the article one feels that this is a verbal slip. But, ten pages on, we find out that the author does indeed want to argue that we should follow goals that satisfy our genes rather than ourselves as individual organisms. The ordinary application of the logic of decision science is termed "naïvely applied" when interpreted "with the individual treated as an isolated locus of decision making and with the role of the genotype ignored" (Cooper, 1989, p. 473). The instability in preference orderings that signal the failure of individual utility maximization (Dawes, 1998; Kahneman & Tversky, 2000; Slovic, 1995) are defended because "perhaps some of the observed instability is due to adaptive strategy mixing. If so, instability would have to be reevaluated; when one is acting as an agent of one's genotype, it could sometimes be a sound strategy" (Cooper, 1989, p. 473). But who in the world would want to act as an agent of one's genotype rather than in the service of one's own life goals! This is precisely the choice Cooper (1989) is posing when he pits the concerns of genetic fitness against those of instrumental rationality.

Lest the reader worry that we caricature, Cooper (1989) leaves us in no doubt because he concludes his paper with replies to possible criticisms of his view. In this section he makes it clear that his view is that "all adequate choice rules are seen as mere extensions of evolutionary principles" (p. 475) because "the maximization of fitness is a ubiquitous goal" (p. 475). A ubiquitous goal of the genes no doubt, but—completely ignoring the individual organism as a potential critical locus of utility maximization—Cooper (1989, p. 475) proposes that we "revise the classical theory [utility theory] itself at its mathematical core, letting biologically motivated decision rules . . . replace or supplement the traditional ones as basic decision rules".

In his summary statement, Cooper (1989, p. 479) makes it clear that the proposition he wishes to defend is that "the traditional theory of rationality is invalid as it stands, and in need of biological repair", and acknowledges that this is "a stance not likely to be popular with confirmed classical decision theorists, but perhaps understandable to evolutionists, psychologists, philosophers, and others that have been impressed by the pervasive explanatory power of the modern evolutionary perspective" (p. 479). The view explicitly championed is the notion that "behavioral rationality [be] interpreted in terms of fitness" (p. 480) and that any dissent from this policy be viewed as "biologically naive" (p. 480). Like the sociobiologists before him, Cooper (1989) seems to have taken the defence of the genes as his brief!

Cooper's (1989) view may well seem extreme, and few evolutionary psychologists so explicitly throw out the vehicle with the bathwater. But many evolutionary psychologists and proponents of ecological rationality (Cosmides & Tooby, 1994a; Gigerenzer, 1996a; Gigerenzer & Todd, 1999) actually do do it implicitly in the way that they echo Cooper's (1989, p. 479) contention that "the traditional theory of rationality is invalid as it stands, and in need of biological repair". For example, in a paper discussing economics and evolutionary psychology, Cosmides and Tooby (1994a) quite closely mimic Cooper's (1989) view when they argue that "evolutionary considerations suggest that traditional normative and descriptive approaches to rationality need to be reexamined" (Cosmides & Tooby, 1994a, p. 329). Throughout this essay they repeat the odd declaration that "despite widespread claims to the contrary, the human mind is not worse than rational (e.g. because of processing constraints)—but may often be better than rational" (p. 329).

It is, in fact, relatively common for the traditional normative rules of rational thought to be denigrated in the literature critical of the heuristics and biases approach. Gigerenzer and Goldstein (1996) adopt exactly Cooper's (1989) extreme position in their argument that in their view "questions classical rationality as a universal norm and thereby questions the very definition of 'good' reasoning on which both the Enlightenment and the heuristics-and-biases views were built" (p. 651). The classical norms are referred to as just so much useless "baggage" in quotes such as the following: "A bit of trust in the abilities of the mind and the rich structure of the environment may help us to see how thought processes that forgo the baggage of the laws of logic and probability can solve real-world adaptive problems quickly and well" (Gigerenzer & Todd, 1999, p. 365).

Likewise, as noted in our discussion above, Gigerenzer's repeated refrain that cognitive illusions (violations of the canons of normative rationality) "disappear" with more evolutionarily propitious problem representations implies that these normative violations are of no concern. Since we know that they (the normative violations) are of concern to the vehicle (a vehicle who does not follow them does not maximize utility), we can only conclude that what these authors want us to imply is that evolutionary rationality is the only rationality that need concern us—precisely Cooper's (1989) point (although the point is much more subtle and somewhat hidden in the writings of the ecological theorists).

Cosmides and Tooby (1994a), in an essay directed at economists, ignore completely the role of memetic evolution and culture in determining human preferences. In a series of points laid out like a series of axioms they argue that because "natural selection built the decision-making machinery in human minds" (p. 328) and because "this set of cognitive devices generates all economic behavior", "therefore . . . the design features of these devices define and constitute the human universal principles that guide economic decision making" (p. 328).

These postulates lead Cosmides and Tooby (1994a, p. 311) to the grandiose claim that "evolutionary psychology should be able to supply a list of human universal preferences, and of the procedures by which additional preferences are acquired or reordered". But to the extent that the claim is true, it is only because the grain-size of the predictions will be all wrong. The economic literature is not full of studies debating whether humans who are dying of thirst prefer water or shelter—or whether men prefer 23-year-old females over 75-year-old ones. Instead, the literature is full of studies trying to determine the rationale for such fine-grained judgements as, for example, whether a poor briefcase produced by an athletic shoe company will adversely affect the family brand name (Ahluwalia & Gurhan-Canli, 2000). Economists and psychologists are not debating the reasons for preferences among basic biological needs. Instead, they are debating the reasons for fine-grained preferences among highly symbolic products embedded in a complex, information-saturated, "attention-based" (Davenport & Beck, 2001) economy. Even after we grant evolutionary assumptions like, for example, that people use clothes purchases for some type of modern dominance display or sexual display, we have not progressed very far in explaining how brand names wax and wane in the fashion world, or how price elastic such purchases will be, and/or what kind of substitutability there will be among these types of goods.

This essay by Cosmides and Tooby (1994a) directed to economists serves to reinforce all of the worst Panglossian tendencies in the latter discipline. For example, Kahneman, Wakker, and Sarin (1997) discuss why experienced utility is essentially ignored in modern economics despite psychological studies showing that experienced utility is not identical to expected utility. They argue that experienced utility is ignored by economists on the grounds that "choices provide all necessary information about the utility of outcomes because rational agents who wish to do so will optimize their hedonic experience" (Kahneman et al., 1997, p. 375). Two-process theories of cognition—in conjunction with the assumptions that we have made about goal structures—help to explain why this assumption might not hold. The choices triggered by the goal structures of System 1 might not always be oriented towards the optimization of hedonic experience for the individual agent. The hedonic experience is just a means to an end for most of the goals lodged in System 1 (largely genetic goals). This System will readily sacrifice the vehicle's hedonic pleasure if ultimate fitness goals are achievable without it.

CHOOSING THE VEHICLE RATHER THAN THE REPLICATORS: EVOLUTIONARY PSYCHOLOGY WITHOUT GREEDY REDUCTIONISM

What the evolutionary psychologists and ecological rationality theorists have occasionally been guilty of in the domain of rationality is what Dennett (1995, p. 82) has termed "greedy reductionism". According to Dennett (1995), in their "zeal to explain too much too fast", greedy reductionists tend to "skip whole layers or levels of theory in their rush to fasten everything securely and neatly to the foundation" (p. 82). Like Dennett (1995), we applaud reductionist efforts in the behavioural sciences. We are impressed with the seminal achievements of evolutionary psychology (see Table 1 of Buss, Haselton, Shackelford, Beske, & Wakefield, 1998, for a long list of important behavioural relationships that were in large part uncovered because of applications of the theoretical lens of evolutionary psychology) and consider its emergence as a dominant force in psychology during the 1990s (Barkow, Cosmides, & Tooby, 1992; Buss, 1999, 2000; Cartwright, 2000; Cosmides & Tooby, 1994b; Geary & Bjorklund, 2000; Pinker, 1997; Plotkin, 1998) to be a salutary development. But in the area of rationality, the evolutionary psychologists have built a bridge too far. They too easily gloss over the important issue of replicator/vehicle goal mismatches and their implications. They too easily dismiss the role of general intelligence and/or general computational power in overriding deleterious System 1 responses (Stanovich, 1999; Stanovich & West, 2000). Because many of the tools of instrumental and epistemic rationality are cultural inventions (memes) and not biological modules, their usefulness in technological societies is too readily dismissed by evolutionary psychologists.

In the extreme, evolutionary theorists begin to sound as if they are siding with genetic interests against those of people. Cooper (1989), in the essay quoted extensively above, admits that "nonclassical behaviors such as betting against the probabilities are detrimental to the reasoner's own welfare" (p. 477), but argues that this is justified because "what if the individual identifies its own welfare with that of its genotype?" (p. 477). Well, what if? Then yes, maybe they should probability match. But who are these people with such loyalty to the random shuffle of genes that is their genotype? Which alleles, for example, do *you* have particularly emotional feelings for? Beyond a few scientists too narrowly focused on the promised explanatory power of evolutionary psychology, we doubt that there are such people.[11]

Gibbard (1990, pp. 28–29) offers the more reasoned view:

> It is crucial to distinguish human goals from the Darwinian surrogate of purpose in the "design" of human beings . . . The Darwinian evolutionary surrogate for divine purpose is now seen to be the reproduction of one's genes. That has not, as far as I know, been anyone's goal, but the biological world looks as if someone quite resourceful had designed each living thing for that purpose . . . A person's evolutionary *telos* explains his having the propensities in virtue of which he develops the goals he does, but his goals are distinct from this surrogate purpose. My evolutionary *telos*, the reproduction of my genes, has no straightforward bearing on what it makes sense for me to want or act to attain . . . A like conclusion would hold if I knew that I was created by a deity for some purpose of his: his goal need not be mine . . . Likewise, if I know that my evolutionary *telos* is to reproduce my genes, that in itself gives me no reason for wanting many descendants.

In short, "human moral propensities were shaped by something it would be foolish to value in itself, namely multiplying one's own genes" (p. 327)

Gibbard's (1990) view is shared by distinguished biologist George Williams, who feels that "there is no conceivable justification for any personal concern with the interests (long-term average proliferation) of the genes we received in the lottery of meiosis and fertilization. As Huxley was the first to recognize, there is every reason to rebel against any tendency to serve such interest" (Williams, 1988, p. 403).

Dennett (1995) discusses this point in a different way—by making the astonishing observation that, until quite recently, the genes were the only beneficiary of all of the selective forces on the planet. That is, "there were no forces whose principal beneficiary was anything else. There were accident and catastrophes (lightning bolts and tidal waves), but no steady forces acting systematically to favor anything but genes" (Dennett, 1995, p. 328). But now *we* are here. There exist in the universe, for the first time, another set of interests because, unlike Darwinian creatures, our interests are not necessarily those of our genes. Rationality is the meme that trumps genetic interests in cases such as this. The remarkable cultural project to advance human rationality concerns how to best advance human interests whether or not they coincide with genetic interests. Its emancipatory potential is lost if we fail to

---

[11] To be precise, we are doubting whether there are people who say they value their genome *and have an accurate view of what they are valuing* when they say this. For example, in such a case, the person would have to be absolutely clear that valuing your own genome is not some proxy for valuing your children; be clear that having children does not replicate one's genome; and be clear about the fact that the genome is a *subpersonal* entity.

see the critical divergence of interests that creates the distinction between evolutionary and instrumental rationality.

ACKNOWLEDGEMENTS

Preparation of this chapter was supported by a grant from the Social Sciences and Humanities Research Council of Canada to Keith E. Stanovich.

REFERENCES

Adler, J.E. (1984). Abstraction is uncooperative. *Journal for the Theory of Social Behaviour, 14*, 165–181.

Adler, J.E. (1991). An optimist's pessimism: Conversation and conjunctions. In E. Eells & T. Maruszewski (Eds.), *Probability and rationality: Studies on L. Jonathan Cohen's philosophy of science* (pp. 251–282). Amsterdam: Editions Rodopi.

Ahluwalia, R., & Gurhan-Canli, Z. (2000). The effects of extensions on the family brand name: An accessibility–diagnosticity perspective. *Journal of Consumer Research, 27*, 371–381.

Allan, L.G. (1980). A note on measurement of contingency between two binary variables in judgment tasks. *Bulletin of the Psychonomic Society, 15*, 147–149.

Anderson, J.R. (1990). *The adaptive character of thought.* Hillsdale, NJ: Erlbaum.

Anderson, J.R. (1991). Is human cognition adaptive? *Behavioral and Brain Sciences, 14*, 471–517.

Anderson, J.R., Reder, L.M., & Simon, H.A. (1996). Situated learning and education. *Educational Researcher, 25*(4), 5–11.

Arkes, H.R., & Harkness, A.R. (1983). Estimates of contingency between two dichotomous variables. *Journal of Experimental Psychology: General, 112*, 117–135.

Aunger, R. (2000). *Darwinizing culture: The status of memetics as a science.* New York: Oxford University Press.

Badcock, C. (2000). *Evolutionary psychology: A critical introduction.* Cambridge: Polity Press.

Baldwin, D.A. (2000). Interpersonal understanding fuels knowledge acquisition. *Current Directions in Psychological Science, 9*, 40–45.

Bar-Hillel, M., & Falk, R. (1982). Some teasers concerning conditional probabilities. *Cognition, 11*, 109–122.

Barkow, J.H. (1989). *Darwin, sex, and status: Biological approaches to mind and culture.* Toronto: University of Toronto Press.

Barkow, J., Cosmides, L., & Tooby, J. (Eds.) (1992). *The adapted mind.* New York: Oxford University Press.

Baron, J. (1993). *Morality and rational choice.* Dordrecht: Kluwer.

Baron, J. (1994). Nonconsequentialist decisions. *Behavioral and Brain Sciences, 17*, 1–42.

Baron, J. (1998). *Judgment misguided: Intuition and error in public decision making.* New York: Oxford University Press.

Baron, J. (2000). *Thinking and deciding* (3rd ed.). Cambridge, MA: Cambridge University Press.

Barton, R.A., & Dunbar, R. (1997). Evolution of the social brain. In A. Whiten & R.W. Byrne (Eds.), *Machiavellian intelligence II: Extensions and evaluations* (pp. 240–263). Cambridge: Cambridge University Press.

Bazerman, M. (2001). Consumer research for consumers. *Journal of Consumer Research, 27*, 499–504.

Blackmore, S. (1999). *The meme machine.* New York: Oxford University Press.

Borges, B., Goldstein, D.G., Ortmann, A., & Gigerenzer, G. (1999). Can insurance beat the stock market? In G. Gigerenzer & P.M. Todd (Eds.), *Simple heuristics that make us smart* (pp. 59–72). New York: Oxford University Press.

Brase, G.L., Cosmides, L., & Tooby, J. (1998). Individuation, counting, and statistical inference: The role of frequency and whole-object representations in judgment under uncertainty. *Journal of Experimental Psychology: General, 127,* 3–21.

Brody, N. (1997). Intelligence, schooling, and society. *American Psychologist, 52,* 1046–1050.

Bronfenbrenner, U., McClelland, P., Wethington, E., Moen, P., & Ceci, S.J. (1996). *The state of Americans.* New York: Free Press.

Brothers, L. (1990). The social brain: A project for integrating primate behaviour and neuro-psychology in a new domain. *Concepts in Neuroscience, 1,* 27–51.

Bugental, D.B. (2000). Acquisitions of the algorithms of social life: A domain-based approach. *Psychological Bulletin, 126,* 187–219.

Buss, D.M. (1999). *Evolutionary psychology: The new science of the mind.* Boston, MA: Allyn and Bacon.

Buss, D.M. (2000). The evolution of happiness. *American Psychologist, 55,* 15–23.

Buss, D.M., Haselton, M.G., Shackelford, T., Beske, A., & Wakefield, J. (1998). Adaptations, exaptations, and spandrels. *American Psychologist, 53,* 533–548.

Byrne, R.W., & Whiten, A. (Eds.) (1988). *Machiavellian intelligence: Social expertise and the evolution of intellect in monkeys, apes, and humans.* Oxford: Oxford University Press.

Caporael, L.R. (1997). The evolution of truly social cognition: The core configurations model. *Personality and Social Psychology Review, 1,* 276–298.

Cartwright, J. (2000). *Evolution and human behavior.* Cambridge, MA: MIT Press.

Chaiken, S., Liberman, A., & Eagly, A.H. (1989). Heuristic and systematic information within and beyond the persuasion context. In J.S. Uleman & J.A. Bargh (Eds.), *Unintended thought* (pp. 212–252). New York: Guilford Press.

Chater, N., & Oaksford, M. (2000). The rational analysis of mind and behaviour. *Synthese, 122,* 93–131.

Churchland, P.M. (1989). *A neurocomputational perspective: The nature of mind and the structure of science.* Cambridge, MA: MIT Press.

Churchland, P.M. (1995). *The engine of reason, the seat of the soul.* Cambridge, MA: MIT Press.

Clark, A. (1997). *Being there: Putting brain, body, and world together again.* Cambridge, MA: MIT Press.

Cooper, W.S. (1989). How evolutionary biology challenges the classical theory of rational choice. *Biology and Philosophy, 4,* 457–481.

Cosmides, L. (1989). The logic of social exchange: Has natural selection shaped how humans reason? Studies with the Wason selection task. *Cognition, 31,* 187–276.

Cosmides, L., & Tooby, J. (1992). Cognitive adaptations for social exchange. In J. Barkow, L. Cosmides, & J. Tooby (Eds.), *The adapted mind* (pp. 163–228). New York: Oxford University Press.

Cosmides, L., & Tooby, J. (1994a). Better than rational: Evolutionary psychology and the invisible hand. *American Economic Review, 84,* 327–332.

Cosmides, L., & Tooby, J. (1994b). Beyond intuition and instinct blindness: Toward an evolutionarily rigorous cognitive science. *Cognition, 50,* 41–77.

Cosmides, L., & Tooby, J. (1996). Are humans good intuitive statisticians after all? Rethinking some conclusions from the literature on judgment under uncertainty. *Cognition, 58,* 1–73.

Cummins, D.D. (1996). Evidence for the innateness of deontic reasoning. *Mind & Language, 11,* 160–190.

Davenport, T., & Beck, J. (2001). *The attention economy.* Cambridge, MA: Harvard Business School Press.

Davies, P.S. (1996). Discovering the functional mesh: On the methods of evolutionary psychology. *Minds and Machines, 6,* 559–585.

Dawes, R.M. (1998). Behavioral decision making and judgment. In D.T. Gilbert, S.T. Fiske, &

G. Lindzey (Eds.), *The handbook of social psychology* (Vol. 1, pp. 497–548). Boston, MA: McGraw-Hill.

Dawkins, R. (1976). *The selfish gene* (New edition, 1989). New York: Oxford University Press.

Dawkins, R. (1982). *The extended phenotype*. New York: Oxford University Press.

Dawkins, R. (1993). Viruses of the mind. In B. Dahlbom (Ed.), *Dennett and his critics* (pp. 13–27). Cambridge, MA: Blackwell.

Deary, I.J. (2000). *Looking down on human intelligence: From psychometrics to the brain*. Oxford: Oxford University Press.

Dennett, D.C. (1975). Why the law of effect will not go away. *Journal of the Theory of Social Behavior, 2*, 169–187.

Dennett, D.C. (1984). *Elbow room: The varieties of free will worth wanting*. Cambridge, MA: MIT Press.

Dennett, D.C. (1991). *Consciousness explained*. Boston, MA: Little Brown.

Dennett, D.C. (1995). *Darwin's dangerous idea: Evolution and the meanings of life*. New York: Simon & Schuster.

Dennett, D.C. (1996). *Kinds of minds: Toward an understanding of consciousness*. New York: Basic Books.

Dickens, W.T., & Flynn, J.R. (2001). Heritability estimates versus large environmental effects: The IQ paradox resolved. *Psychological Bulletin, 108*, 346–369.

Dulany, D.E., & Hilton, D.J. (1991). Conversational implicature, conscious representation, and the conjunction fallacy. *Social Cognition, 9*, 85–110.

Dunbar, R. (1998). Theory of mind and the evolution of language. In J.R. Hurford, M. Studdert-Kennedy, & C. Knight (Eds.), *Approaches to the evolution of language* (pp. 92–110). Cambridge: Cambridge University Press.

Einhorn, H.J., & Hogarth, R.M. (1981). Behavioral decision theory: Processes of judgment and choice. *Annual Review of Psychology, 32*, 53–88.

Epstein, S. (1994). Integration of the cognitive and the psychodynamic unconscious. *American Psychologist, 49*, 709–724.

Estes, W.K. (1964). Probability learning. In A.W. Melton (Ed.), *Categories of human learning* (pp. 89–128). New York: Academic Press.

Estes, W.K. (1976). The cognitive side of probability learning. *Psychological Review, 83*, 37–64.

Estes, W.K. (1984). Global and local control of choice behavior by cyclically varying outcome probabilities. *Journal of Experimental Psychology: Learning, Memory, and Cognition, 10*, 258–270.

Evans, J.St.B.T. (1984). Heuristic and analytic processes in reasoning. *British Journal of Psychology, 75*, 451–468.

Evans, J.St.B.T. (1989). *Bias in human reasoning: Causes and consequences*. London: Lawrence Erlbaum Associates.

Evans, J.St.B.T. (1996). Deciding before you think: Relevance and reasoning in the selection task. *British Journal of Psychology, 87*, 223–240.

Evans, J.St.B.T., Newstead, S.E., & Byrne, R.M.J. (1993). *Human reasoning: The psychology of deduction*. Hove, UK: Lawrence Erlbaum Associates.

Evans, J.St.B.T., & Over, D.E. (1996). *Rationality and reasoning*. Hove, UK: Psychology Press.

Evans, J.St.B.T., & Over, D.E. (1997). Rationality in reasoning: The problem of deductive competence. *Cahiers de Psychologie Cognitive (Current Psychology of Cognition), 16*, 3–38.

Evans, J.St.B.T., & Over, D.E. (1999). Explicit representations in hypothetical thinking. *Behavioral and Brain Sciences, 22*, 763–764.

Evans, J.St.B.T., Handley, S.J., Perham, N., Over, D.E., & Thompson, V.A. (2000). Frequency versus probability formats in statistical word problems. *Cognition, 77*, 197–213.

Evans, J.St.B.T., & Wason, P.C. (1976). Rationalization in a reasoning task. *British Journal of Psychology, 67*, 479–486.

Falk, R. (1992). A closer look at the probabilities of the notorious three prisoners. *Cognition, 43*, 197–223.

Fiedler, K. (1988). The dependence of the conjunction fallacy on subtle linguistic factors. *Psychological Research, 50*, 123–129.

Fodor, J. (1983). *Modularity of mind*. Cambridge, MA: MIT Press.

Foley, R. (1996). The adaptive legacy of human evolution: A search for the EEA. *Evolutionary Anthropology, 4*, 194–203.

Frank, R.H., & Cook, P.J. (1995). *The winner-take-all society*. New York: Free Press.

Funder, D.C. (1987). Errors and mistakes: Evaluating the accuracy of social judgment. *Psychological Bulletin, 101*, 75–90.

Gal, I., & Baron, J. (1996). Understanding repeated simple choices. *Thinking and Reasoning, 2*(1), 81–98.

Gallistel, C.R. (1990). *The organization of learning*. Cambridge, MA: MIT Press.

Geary, D.C., & Bjorklund, D.F. (2000). Evolutionary developmental psychology. *Child Development, 71*, 57–65.

Gibbard, A. (1990). *Wise choices, apt feelings: A theory of normative judgment*. Cambridge, MA: Harvard University Press.

Gigerenzer, G. (1991). How to make cognitive illusions disappear: Beyond "heuristics and biases". *European Review of Social Psychology, 2*, 83–115.

Gigerenzer, G. (1993). The bounded rationality of probabilistic mental models. In K. Manktelow & D. Over (Eds.), *Rationality: Psychological and philosophical perspectives* (pp. 284–313). London: Routledge.

Gigerenzer, G. (1996a). On narrow norms and vague heuristics: A reply to Kahneman and Tversky (1996). *Psychological Review, 103*, 592–596.

Gigerenzer, G. (1996b). Rationality: Why social context matters. In P.B. Baltes & U. Staudinger (Eds.), *Interactive minds: Life-span perspectives on the social foundation of cognition* (pp. 319–346). Cambridge: Cambridge University Press.

Gigerenzer, G., & Goldstein, D.G. (1996). Reasoning the fast and frugal way: Models of bounded rationality. *Psychological Review, 103*, 650–669.

Gigerenzer, G., & Hoffrage, U. (1995). How to improve Bayesian reasoning without instruction: Frequency formats. *Psychological Review, 102*, 684–704.

Gigerenzer, G., Hoffrage, U., & Ebert, A. (1998). AIDS counselling for low-risk clients. *AIDS Care, 10*, 197–211.

Gigerenzer, G., Hoffrage, U., & Kleinbolting, H. (1991). Probabilistic mental models: A Brunswikian theory of confidence. *Psychological Review, 98*, 506–528.

Gigerenzer, G., & Regier, T. (1996). How do we tell an association from a rule? Comment on Sloman (1996). *Psychological Bulletin, 119*, 23–26.

Gigerenzer, G., & Todd, P.M. (1999). *Simple heuristics that make us smart*. New York: Oxford University Press.

Girotto, V., & Gonzalez, M. (2001). Solving probabilistic and statistical problems: A matter of information structure and question form. *Cognition, 78*, 247–276.

Goldstein, D.G., & Gigerenzer, G. (1999). The recognition heuristic: How ignorance makes us smart. In G. Gigerenzer & P.M. Todd, *Simple heuristics that make us smart* (pp. 37–58). New York: Oxford University Press.

Gottfredson, L.S. (1997). Why g matters: The complexity of everyday life. *Intelligence, 24*, 79–132.

Graf, V., Bullock, D.H., & Bitterman, M.E. (1964). Further experiments on probability-matching in the pigeon. *Journal of the Experimental Analysis of Behavior, 7*, 151–157.

Granberg, D. (1995). The Monte Hall dilemma. *Personality and Social Psychology Bulletin, 31*, 711–723.

Grice, H.P. (1975). Logic and conversation. In P. Cole & J. Morgan (Eds.), *Syntax and semantics: Vol. 3, Speech acts* (pp. 41–58). New York: Academic Press.

Grigorenko, E.L. (1999). Heredity versus environment as the basis of cognitive ability. In R.J. Sternberg (Ed.), *The nature of cognition* (pp. 665–696). Cambridge, MA: MIT Press.

Hardman, D. (1998). Does reasoning occur on the selection task? A comparison of relevance-based theories. *Thinking and Reasoning, 4*, 353–376.

Harries, C., & Harvey, N. (2000). Are absolute frequencies, relative frequencies, or both effective in reducing cognitive biases? *Journal of Behavioral Decision Making, 13*, 431–444.

Hasher, L., & Zacks, R.T. (1979). Automatic processing of fundamental information: The case of frequency of occurrence. *Journal of Experimental Psychology: General, 39*, 1372–1388.

Hastie, R., & Rasinski, K.A. (1988). The concept of accuracy in social judgment. In D. Bar-Tal & A. Kruglanski (Eds.), *The social psychology of knowledge* (pp. 193–208). Cambridge: Cambridge University Press.

Herrnstein, R.J., & Loveland, D.H. (1975). Maximizing and matching on concurrent ratio schedules. *Journal of the Experimental Analysis of Behavior, 24*, 107–116.

Hertwig, R., & Gigerenzer, G. (1999). The conjunction fallacy revisited: How intelligent inferences look like reasoning errors. *Journal of Behavioral Decision Making, 12*, 275–305.

Hilton, D.J. (1995). The social context of reasoning: Conversational inference and rational judgment. *Psychological Bulletin, 118*, 248–271.

Hilton, D.J., & Slugoski, B.R. (2000). Judgment and decision making in social context: Discourse processes and rational inference. In T. Connolly, H.R. Arkes, & K.R. Hammond (Eds.), *Judgment and decision making: An interdisciplinary reader (2nd ed.)* (pp. 651–676). Cambridge, MA: Cambridge University Press.

Horn, J.L. (1982). The theory of fluid and crystallized intelligence in relation to concepts of cognitive psychology and aging in adulthood. In F.I.M. Craik & S. Trehub (Eds.), *Aging and cognitive processes* (pp. 847–870). New York: Plenum Press.

Horn, J.L., & Cattell, R.B. (1967). Age differences in fluid and crystallized intelligence. *Acta Psychologica, 26*, 1–23.

Hull, D.L. (1982). The naked meme. In H.C. Plotkin (Eds.), *Learning, development, and culture: Essays in evolutionary epistemology* (pp. 273–327). Chichester, England: John Wiley.

Hull, D.L. (1988). *Science as a process: An evolutionary account of the social and conceptual development of science.* Chicago: University of Chicago Press.

Humphrey, N. (1976). The social function of intellect. In P.P.G. Bateson & R.A. Hinde (Eds.), *Growing points in ethology* (pp. 303–317). London: Faber & Faber.

Hunt, E. (1995). *Will we be smart enough? A cognitive analysis of the coming workforce.* New York: Russell Sage Foundation.

Hunt, E. (1999). Intelligence and human resources: Past, present, and future. In P. Ackerman, P. Kyllonen, & R. Richards (Eds.), *Learning and individual differences: Process, trait, and content determinants* (pp. 3–28). Washington, DC: American Psychological Association.

Johnson-Laird, P.N. (1983). *Mental models.* Cambridge, MA: Harvard University Press.

Johnson-Laird, P.N. (1999). Deductive reasoning. *Annual Review of Psychology, 50*, 109–135.

Jolly, A. (1966). Lemur social behaviour and primate intelligence. *Science, 153*, 501–506.

Kahneman, D. (2000). A psychological point of view: Violations of rational rules as a diagnostic of mental processes. *Behavioral and Brain Sciences, 23.*

Kahneman, D., Slovic, P., & Tversky, A. (Eds.) (1982). *Judgment under uncertainty: Heuristics and biases.* Cambridge: Cambridge University Press.

Kahneman, D., & Tversky, A. (1972). Subjective probability: A judgment of representativeness. *Cognitive Psychology, 3*, 430–454.

Kahneman, D., & Tversky, A. (1973). On the psychology of prediction. *Psychological Review, 80*, 237–251.

Kahneman, D., & Tversky, A. (1984). Choices, values, and frames. *American Psychologist, 39*, 341–350.

Kahneman, D., & Tversky, A. (1996). On the reality of cognitive illusions. *Psychological Review, 103*, 582–591.

Kahneman, D., & Tversky, A. (Ed.). (2000). *Choices, values, and frames*. Cambridge: Cambridge University Press.

Kahneman, D., Wakker, P.P., & Sarin, R. (1997). Back to Bentham? Explorations of experienced utility. *The Quarterly Journal of Economics, 112*(2), 375–405.

Kao, S.F., & Wasserman, E.A. (1993). Assessment of an information integration account of contingency judgment with examination of subjective cell importance and method of information presentation. *Journal of Experimental Psychology: Learning, Memory, and Cognition, 19*, 1363–1386.

Klein, G. (1998). *Sources of power: How people make decisions*. Cambridge, MA: MIT Press.

Koriat, A., Lichtenstein, S., & Fischhoff, B. (1980). Reasons for confidence. *Journal of Experimental Psychology: Human Learning and Memory, 6*, 107–118.

Kruglanski, A.W., & Ajzen, I. (1983). Bias and error in human judgment. *European Journal of Social Psychology, 13*, 1–44.

Kummer, H., Daston, L., Gigerenzer, G., & Silk, J.B. (1997). The social intelligence hypothesis. In P. Weingart, S.D. Mitchell, P.J. Richerson, & S. Maasen (Eds.), *Human by nature: Between biology and the social sciences* (pp. 157–179). Mahwah, NJ: Lawrence Erlbaum Associates.

LaCerra, P., & Bingham, R. (1998). The adaptive nature of the human neurocognitive architecture: An alternative model. *Proceeds of the National Academy of Sciences, 95*, 11290–11294.

Levin, I.P., Wasserman, E.A., & Kao, S.F. (1993). Multiple methods of examining biased information use in contingency judgments. *Organizational Behavior and Human Decision Processes, 55*, 228–250.

Levinson, S.C. (1995). Interactional biases in human thinking. In E. Goody (Eds.), *Social intelligence and interaction* (pp. 221–260). Cambridge: Cambridge University Press.

Liberman, N., & Klar, Y. (1996). Hypothesis testing in Wason's selection task: Social exchange cheating detection or task understanding. *Cognition, 58*, 127–156.

Looren de Jong, H., & van der Steen, W.J. (1998). Biological thinking in evolutionary psychology: Rockbottom or quicksand? *Philosophical Psychology, 11*, 183–205.

Lubinski, D. (2000). Scientific and social significance of assessing individual differences: "Sinking shafts at a few critical points". *Annual Review of Psychology, 51*, 405–444.

Lubinski, D., & Humphreys, L.G. (1997). Incorporating general intelligence into epidemiology and the social sciences. *Intelligence, 24*, 159–201.

Lumsden, C.J., & Wilson, E.O. (1981). *Genes, mind and culture*. Cambridge, MA: Harvard University Press.

Luria, A.R. (1976). *Cognitive development: Its cultural and social foundations*. Cambridge, MA: Harvard University Press.

Lynch, A. (1996). *Thought contagion*. New York: Basic Books.

Macchi, L. (1998). Computational features vs frequentist phrasing in the base-rate fallacy. *Swiss Journal of Psychology, 57*, 79–85.

MacDonald, K., & Geary, D.C. (2000). g and Darwinian algorithms. *Behavioral and Brain Sciences, 23*, 685–686.

Macdonald, R.R., & Gilhooly, K.J. (1990). More about Linda *or* conjunctions in context. *European Journal of Cognitive Psychology, 2*, 57–70.

MacDonall, J.S. (1988). Concurrent variable-ratio schedules: Implications for the generalized matching law. *Journal of the Experimental Analysis of Behavior, 50*, 55–64.

Manktelow, K.I. (1999). *Reasoning & Thinking*. Hove, UK: Psychology Press.

Margolis, H. (1987). *Patterns, thinking, and cognition*. Chicago: University of Chicago Press.

Margolis, H. (1996). *Dealing with risk*. Chicago: University of Chicago Press.

Matthews, G., & Deary, I.J. (1998). *Personality traits*. Cambridge: Cambridge University Press.

McGeorge, P., Crawford, J., & Kelly, S. (1997). The relationships between psychometric intelligence and learning in an explicit and an implicit task. *Journal of Experimental Psychology: Learning, Memory, and Cognition, 23*, 239–245.

Mellers, B., Hertwig, R., & Kahneman, D. (2001). Do frequency representations eliminate conjunction effects? An exercise in adversarial collaboration. *Psychological Science, 12,* 269–275.

Millikan, R.G. (1993). *White Queen psychology and other essays for Alice.* Cambridge, MA: The MIT Press.

Mithen, S. (1996). *The prehistory of mind: The cognitive origins of art and science.* London: Thames and Hudson.

Neisser, U., Boodoo, G., Bouchard, T., Boykin, A.W., Brody, N., Ceci, S.J., et al. (1996). Intelligence: Knowns and unknowns. *American Psychologist, 51,* 77–101.

Newstead, S.E., & Evans, J.St.B.T. (Eds.) (1995). *Perspectives on thinking and reasoning.* Hove, UK: Lawrence Erlbaum Associates.

Nickerson, R.S. (1996). Hempel's paradox and Wason's selection task: Logical and psychological puzzles of confirmation. *Thinking and Reasoning, 2,* 1–31.

Nickerson, R.S. (1998). Confirmation bias: A ubiquitous phenomenon in many guises. *Review of General Psychology, 2,* 175–220.

Norman, D.A., & Shallice, T. (1986). Attention to action: Willed and automatic control of behavior. In R.J. Davidson, G.E. Schwartz, & D. Shapiro (Eds.), *Consciousness and self-regulation* (pp. 1–18). New York: Plenum.

Nozick, R. (1993). *The nature of rationality.* Princeton, NJ: Princeton University Press.

Oaksford, M., & Chater, N. (1994). A rational analysis of the selection task as optimal data selection. *Psychological Review, 101,* 608–631.

Oaksford, M., & Chater, N. (1995). Theories of reasoning and the computational explanation of everyday inference. *Thinking and Reasoning, 1,* 121–152.

Oaksford, M., & Chater, N. (1996). Rational explanation of the selection task. *Psychological Review, 103,* 381–391.

Oaksford, M., & Chater, N. (1998). *Rationality in an uncertain world.* Hove, UK: Psychology Press.

Oaksford, M., & Chater, N. (2001). The probabilistic approach to human reasoning. *Trends in Cognitive Sciences, 5,* 349–357.

Over, D.E. (2000). Ecological rationality and its heuristics. *Thinking and Reasoning, 6,* 182–192.

Over, D.E., & Green, D.W. (2001). Contingency, causation, and adaptive inference. *Psychological Review, 108,* 682–684.

Pinker, S. (1994). *The language instinct.* New York: William Morrow.

Pinker, S. (1997). *How the mind works.* New York: Norton.

Plomin, R., & Petrill, S.A. (1997). Genetics and intelligence: What's new? *Intelligence, 24,* 53–77.

Plotkin, H.C. (1988). Behavior and evolution. In H.C. Plotkin (Ed.), *The role of behavior in evolution* (pp. 1–17). Cambridge, MA: MIT Press.

Plotkin, H. (1998). *Evolution in mind: An introduction to evolutionary psychology.* Cambridge, MA: Harvard University Press.

Politzer, G., & Noveck, I.A. (1991). Are conjunction rule violations the result of conversational rule violations? *Journal of Psycholinguistic Research, 20,* 83–103.

Pollock, J.L. (1991). OSCAR: A general theory of rationality. In J. Cummins & J.L. Pollock (Eds.), *Philosophy and AI: Essays at the interface* (pp. 189–213). Cambridge, MA: MIT Press.

Posner, M.I., & Snyder, C.R.R. (1975). Attention and cognitive control. In R.L. Solso (Eds.), *Information processing and cognition: The Loyola Symposium* (pp. 55–85). New York: Wiley.

Reber, A.S. (1992). An evolutionary context for the cognitive unconscious. *Philosophical Psychology, 5,* 33–51.

Reber, A.S. (1993). *Implicit learning and tacit knowledge.* New York: Oxford University Press.

Reber, A.S., Walkenfeld, F.F., & Hernstadt, R. (1991). Implicit and explicit learning: Individual differences and IQ. *Journal of Experimental Psychology: Learning, Memory, and Cognition, 17,* 888–896.

Rode, C., Cosmides, L., Hell, W., & Tooby, J. (1999). When and why do people avoid unknown probabilities in decisions under uncertainty? Testing some predictions from optimal foraging theory. *Cognition, 72*, 269–304.

Rosenthal, R., & Rosnow, R.L. (1991). *Essentials of behavioral research: Methods and data analysis (2nd ed.)*. New York: McGraw-Hill.

Rozin, P. (1996). Towards a psychology of food and eating: From motivation to module to model to marker, morality, meaning and metaphor. *Current Directions in Psychological Science, 5*(1), 18–24.

Rozin, P., & Fallon, A.E. (1987). A perspective on disgust. *Psychological Review, 94*, 23–41.

Samuels, R. (1998). Evolutionary psychology and the massive modularity hypothesis. *British Journal for the Philosophy of Science, 49*, 575–602.

Samuels, R., Stich, S.P., & Tremoulet, P.D. (1999). Rethinking rationality: From bleak implications to Darwinian modules. In E. Lepore & Z. Pylyshyn (Eds.), *What is cognitive science?* (pp. 74–120). Oxford: Blackwell.

Schustack, M.W., & Sternberg, R.J. (1981). Evaluation of evidence in causal inference. *Journal of Experimental Psychology: General, 110*, 101–120.

Shafir, E., & Tversky, A. (1995). Decision making. In E.E. Smith & D.N. Osherson (Eds.), *Thinking (Vol. 3)* (pp. 77–100). Cambridge, MA: The MIT Press.

Shanks, D.R. (1995). Is human learning rational? *Quarterly Journal of Experimental Psychology, 48A*, 257–279.

Shepard, R.N. (1987). Evolution of a mesh between principles of the mind and regularities of the world. In J. Dupre (Eds.), *The latest on the best: Essays on evolution and optimality* (pp. 251–275). Cambridge, MA: MIT Press.

Shiffrin, R.M., & Schneider, W. (1977). Controlled and automatic human information processing: II. Perceptual learning, automatic attending, and a general theory. *Psychological Review, 84*, 127–190.

Skyrms, B. (1996). *The evolution of the social contract*. Cambridge: Cambridge University Press.

Sloman, S.A. (1996). The empirical case for two systems of reasoning. *Psychological Bulletin, 119*, 3–22.

Sloman, S.A., Over, D., & Slovak, L. (in press). Frequency illusions and other fallacies. *Organizational Behavior and Human Decision Processes*.

Slovic, P. (1995). The construction of preference. *American Psychologist, 50*, 364–371.

Slugoski, B.R., & Wilson, A.E. (1998). Contribution of conversation skills to the production of judgmental errors. *European Journal of Social Psychology, 28*, 575–601.

Smith, S.M., & Levin, I.P. (1996). Need for cognition and choice framing effects. *Journal of Behavioral Decision Making, 9*, 283–290.

Sperber, D. (1994). The modularity of thought and the epidemiology of representations. In L.A. Hirschfeld & S.A. Gelman (Eds.), *Mapping the mind: Domain specificity in cognition and culture* (pp. 39–67). Cambridge: Cambridge University Press.

Sperber, D. (1996). *Explaining culture: A naturalistic approach*. Oxford: Blackwell Publishers.

Sperber, D., Cara, F., & Girotto, V. (1995). Relevance theory explains the selection task. *Cognition, 57*, 31–95.

Sperber, D., & Wilson, D. (1986). *Relevance: Communication and cognition*. Cambridge, MA: Harvard University Press.

Stanovich, K.E. (1999). *Who is rational? Studies of individual differences in reasoning*. Mahwah, NJ: Lawrence Erlbaum Associates, Inc.

Stanovich, K.E. (2001). Reductionism in the study of intelligence: Review of "Looking Down on Human Intelligence" by Ian Deary. *Trends in Cognitive Sciences, 5*(2), 91–92.

Stanovich, K.E. (in press). The fundamental computational biases of human cognition: Heuristics that (sometimes) impair reasoning and decision making. In J.E. Davidson & R.J. Sternberg (Eds.), *The psychology of problem solving*. New York: Cambridge University Press.

Stanovich, K.E., & West, R.F. (1998a). Cognitive ability and variation in selection task perform- ance. *Thinking and Reasoning, 4*, 193–230.

Stanovich, K.E., & West, R.F. (1998b). Individual differences in framing and conjunction effects. *Thinking and Reasoning, 4*, 289–317.

Stanovich, K.E., & West, R.F. (1998c). Individual differences in rational thought. *Journal of Experimental Psychology: General, 127*, 161–188.

Stanovich, K.E., & West, R.F. (1998d). Who uses base rates and P(D/~H)? An analysis of individual differences. *Memory & Cognition, 28*, 161–179.

Stanovich, K.E., & West, R.F. (1999). Discrepancies between normative and descriptive models of decision making and the understanding/acceptance principle. *Cognitive Psychology, 38*, 349–385.

Stanovich, K.E., & West, R.F. (2000). Individual differences in reasoning: Implications for the rationality debate? *Behavioral and Brain Sciences, 23*, 645–726.

Stent, G.S. (1978). Introduction. In G.S. Stent (Eds.), *Morality as a biological phenomenon* (pp. 1–18). Berkeley, CA: University of California Press.

Sterelny, K. (2001). *The evolution of agency and other essays*. Cambridge: Cambridge University Press.

Sterelny, K., & Griffiths, P.E. (1999). *Sex and death: An introduction to philosophy of biology*. Chicago: University of Chicago Press.

Stich, S.P. (1990). *The fragmentation of reason*. Cambridge, MA: MIT Press.

Sutherland, N.S., & Mackintosh, N.J. (1971). *Mechanisms of animal discrimination learning*. New York: Academic Press.

Symons, D. (1992). On the use and misuse of Darwinism in the study of human behavior. In J. Barkow, L. Cosmides, & J. Tooby (Eds.), *The adapted mind* (pp. 137–159). New York: Oxford University Press.

Todd, P.M., Fiddick, L., & Krauss, S. (2000). Ecological rationality and its contents. *Thinking and Reasoning, 6*, 375–384.

Todd, P.M., & Gigerenzer, G. (2000). Precis of simple heuristics that make us smart. *Behavioral and Brain Sciences, 23*, 727–780.

Tomasello, M. (1999). *The cultural origins of human cognition*. Cambridge, MA: Harvard University Press.

Tooby, J., & Cosmides, L. (1992). The psychological foundations of culture. In J. Barkow, L. Cosmides, & J. Tooby (Eds.), *The adapted mind* (pp. 19–136). New York: Oxford University Press.

Tversky, A. (1996). Contrasting rational and psychological principles of choice. In R. Zeck- hauser, R. Keeney, & J. Sebenius (Eds.), *Wise choices* (pp. 5–21). Boston, MA: Harvard Business School Press.

Tversky, A., & Edwards, W. (1966). Information versus reward in binary choice. *Journal of Experimental Psychology, 71*, 680–683.

Tversky, A., & Kahneman, D. (1974). Judgment under uncertainty: Heuristics and biases. *Science, 185*, 1124–1131.

Tversky, A., & Kahneman, D. (1983). Extensional versus intuitive reasoning: The conjunction fallacy in probability judgment. *Psychological Review, 90*, 293–315.

Wason, P.C. (1966). Reasoning. In B. Foss (Eds.), *New horizons in psychology* (pp. 135–151). Harmonsworth, UK: Penguin.

Wasserman, E.A., Dorner, W.W., & Kao, S.F. (1990). Contributions of specific cell information to judgments of interevent contingency. *Journal of Experimental Psychology: Learning, Memory, and Cognition, 16*, 509–521.

West, R.F., & Stanovich, K.E. (in press). Is probability matching smart? Associations between probabilistic choices and cognitive ability. *Memory and Cognition*.

Whiten, A., & Byrne, R.W. (Eds.) (1997). *Machiavellian intelligence II: Extensions and evaluations*. Cambridge: Cambridge University Press.

Williams, G.C. (1985). A defense of reductionism in evolutionary biology. *Oxford Surveys in Evolutionary Biology*, *2*, 1–27.

Williams, G.C. (1988). Huxley's *Evolution and Ethics* in sociobiological perspective. *Zygon*, *23*, 383–407.

Williams, G.C. (1992). *Natural selection: Domains, levels and challenges*. Oxford: Oxford University Press.

Wright, R. (1994). *The moral animal: Evolutionary psychology and everyday life*. New York: Vintage Books.

Author Index

Abbey, A. 22
ABC Research Group, The 4, 88, 121
Abell, F. 77
Adler, J.E. 174–175, 195
Adolphs, R. 75–76, 87, 89, 91
Aggleton, J.P. 76
Ahluwalia, R. 218
Ahn, W. 165
Aiello, L.C. 77
Ajzen, I. 160, 184
Alexander, M.P. 75–76
Allan, L.G. 177
Allen, J. 116
Allison, T. 75, 77
Allman, J. 76
Almor, A. 6, 35, 49, 50–52, 111–112, 126
Amaral, D.G. 76–77
Anderson, A. 76
Anderson, J.R. 171, 177–178, 180, 185, 199

Anderson, S. 76
Archer, J. 1
Arkes, H.R. 177
Ashburner, J. 77
Ashwin, C. 76
Atkinson, A.P. 6, 26, 61–63, 65, 70–71, 73, 86, 90
Atkinson, R.C. 12
Aunger, R. 211
Axelrod, R.M. 34, 81, 88, 104
Ayton, P. 147

Badcock, C. 2, 187
Baizer, J.S. 69
Baldwin, D.A. 176
Bargh, J.A. 19
Bar-Hillel, M. 155, 160, 199
Barkow, J.H. 1, 2, 186, 219
Baron, J. 171, 177, 202
Baron-Cohen, S. 62, 64, 75–76, 78
Barrett, L. 2

Bartlett, F.C. 28
Barton, R.A. 75, 176
Bazerman, M. 209
Bechara, A. 75–76, 87, 89
Bechtel, W. 71
Beck, J. 218
Benson, P.J. 76–77
Ben-Zeev, T. 111
Berkowitz, L. 20
Beske, A. 219
Bevan, R. 76–77
Bever, T.G. 116
Bilger, R.C. 15
Bingham, R. 202
Bitterman, M.E. 178
Bjorklund, D.F. 219
Black, F.W. 75
Blackmore, S. 190, 210–211
Blair, R.J.R. 76
Blalock, H. 43
Blaye, A. 35–36
Bloom, P. 57, 61
Bock, G.R. 25
Bonda, E. 76

Boodoo, G. 199–200
Borges, B. 209
Boring E.G. 16
Bouchard, T. 199–200
Bower, G.H. 161
Boykin, A.W. 199–200
Bradshaw, J.L. 4, 122
Brammer, M. 76
Brase, G.L. 5, 18, 22, 28, 135–136, 146, 159, 162, 194, 198–199, 204
Brenner, L.A. 146–147
Briggs, L. 163
Brody, N. 199–200
Broennimann, R. 76–77
Broks, P. 76
Bronfenbrenner, U. 195
Brothers, L.A. 75–76, 176
Brown, G.W. 101
Buchel, C. 76
Buehler, R. 131, 146–147
Bugental, D.B. 176
Bullmore, E.T. 76
Bullock, D.H. 178
Bullock, P.R. 75
Buss, D.M. 1–2, 11, 22, 27, 62, 74, 80, 121, 201, 205, 207, 212, 219
Byrne, R.M.J. 124, 173
Byrne, R.W. 77–78, 176

Calder, A.J. 76
Call, J. 78
Campbell, A. 1, 4
Caporael, L.R. 176
Cara, F. 37, 49, 50, 52–53, 57, 111, 126, 173, 175
Cardew, G. 25
Carey, D.P. 77
Carmichael, S.T. 77

Carnap, R. 158
Cartwright, J. 219
Casscells, W. 129, 148–149, 151–152
Cattell, R.B. 200–201
Caverni, J-P. 130, 147, 151, 160–161
Ceci, S.J. 195, 199–200
Cezayirli, E. 76
Chaiken, S. 183
Chalmers, M. 87
Chase, V. M. 157
Chater, N. 49–50, 55–56, 86, 107, 116, 127, 171, 173, 178–179
Cheney, D.L. 15–16, 87
Cheng, P.W. 5–6, 12, 26, 35–36, 38–42, 49–50, 53, 83, 110, 124, 127, 165
Cherry, S. 75, 89
Cherubini, P. 39, 41–42, 49
Chitty, A.J. 76–77
Chomsky, N. 116
Christiansen, M.H. 116
Churchland, P.M. 215
Churchland, P.S. 85
Cialdini, R.B. 21
Clark, A. 188
Coffey, P.J. 76
Cohen, J. 43
Cook, M. 3
Cook, P.J. 195, 197
Cooper, W.S. 178, 186, 216–217, 219
Cosmides, L. 1–3, 5–7, 11–12, 14, 16–18, 21–22, 26–27, 33–37, 39–41, 44–45, 47, 49–50, 53–57, 61–62, 70, 73, 79–84, 88–90, 101–103, 106–108, 110, 114, 116,

121–122, 124–126, 128–130, 135–136, 138–141, 146, 149–153, 158–160, 162, 171, 176, 178, 184, 190, 194, 198–199, 201–205, 207, 209–212, 214–215, 217–219
Cox, J.R. 34, 110
Crawford, J. 184
Cronin, H. 106
Cummins, D.D. 3, 6–7, 37–38, 49–50, 55, 57, 61, 63, 86–90, 121, 125, 176
Cummins, R. 3, 61, 63, 121

Damasio, A.R. 75–77, 87, 89
Damasio, H. 75–76, 87, 89
Dasser, V. 87
Daston, L. 176
Davenport, T. 218
Davidson, B.J. 15
Davies, P.S. 205
Davis, M. 76
Dawes, R.M. 171, 216
Dawkins, R. 13, 23, 25, 79, 104, 172, 178, 185–187, 190–191, 197, 210–211, 213–214
Deary, I.J. 199–202
Demuth, K. 116
Dennett, D.C. 101, 183–184, 186–188, 200–201, 203, 211, 215, 219–220
Desimone, R. 69
Deyoe, E. 69
Diamond, J.M. 108
Dickens, W.T. 195
Dolan, R.J. 75–76

Dorner, W.W. 176
Doty, R.L. 15
Drain, M. 27
Dulany, D.E. 174–175
Dummett, M. 140
Dunbar, R.I.M. 1–2, 4,
    75, 77, 176
Duncan, J. 75

Eagly, A.H. 183
Ebert, A. 204
Edgington, D. 140
Edwards, W. 177–178
Einhorn, H.J. 196
Ekman, P. 46
Ellis, A.W. 69
Emery, N.J. 76–77
Emshoff, J.R. 88
Epstein, S. 182–183
Epstein, W. 63
Estes, W.K. 178, 216
Etcoff, N. L. 76
Evans, A. 76
Evans, D. 1–2
Evans, J.St.B.T. 7,
    34, 37, 51, 122,
    124–125, 127,
    129–130, 133,
    136–141, 147, 160,
    171, 173, 176,
    182–183, 185–186,
    197, 200

Fadiga, L. 77
Fairley, N. 111–112
Falk, R. 199
Fallon, A.E. 212
Farah, M.J. 27
Farioli, F. 36
Fiddick, L. 4–5, 17–18,
    35–37, 41, 44–45,
    47, 53–54, 79,
    83–84, 88–90,
    125–127, 207
Fiedler, K. 155–156,
    158, 204

Fine, C. 76
Fischhoff, B. 197
Flynn, J.R. 195
Fodor, J.A. 2, 12, 25,
    54, 108, 121–122,
    127, 139, 183
Fogassi, L. 77
Foley, R. 202
Frackowiak, R. 77
Frank, R.H. 195, 197
Fratiannea, A. 165
Frijda, N.H. 101
Friston, K.J. 77
Frith, C.D. 76–77
Frith, U. 76–77
Fukuda, H. 76
Funder, D.C. 184

Gal, I. 177
Gallese, V. 77
Gallistel, C.R. 178
Gallup, G.G. 75–76
Garnham, A. 13
Geary, D.C. 200, 219
Gelman, S.A. 165
Gentner, D. 24
Gentner, D.R. 24
Ghaffer, O. 75
Gibbard, A. 183, 220
Gigerenzer, G. 4, 7, 18,
    23–24, 35, 50, 54,
    57, 62, 79, 82, 88,
    102, 110–112,
    121–122, 131–132,
    134–135, 146, 148,
    154, 156, 158–162,
    171, 175–176, 178,
    181–182, 184, 194,
    197, 199, 204,
    206–209, 217
Gilhooly, K.J. 7, 174
Gillian, D.J. 87
Gilly, M. 36
Girotto, V. 35–39,
    41–42, 49–50,
    52–53, 57,

110–111, 126,
    129–130, 147, 151,
    160–161, 173, 175,
    197
Gluck, M.A. 160–161
Goldman, A. 77
Goldman-Rakic, P.S.
    75
Goldstein, D.G.
    208–209, 217
Gonzalez, M. 129–130,
    147, 197
Goodale, M.A. 69
Gottfredson, L.S. 195,
    200
Gould, J.L. 16
Graf, V. 178
Granberg, D. 199
Grayboys, T. 148–149,
    151–152
Green, D.M. 14
Green, D.W. 7, 132,
    162, 177
Grice, H.P. 175, 179,
    184
Griffin, D. 131,
    146–147
Griffiths, P.E. 5–6,
    63–70, 72–73, 79,
    90, 210
Griggs, R.A. 34–35, 39,
    40–42, 49, 110
Grigorenko, E.L.
    199–200
Gurhan-Canli, Z. 218

Hadley, D. 76
Haidt, J. 44
Hamann, S. 76
Hamilton, W.D. 1, 34,
    81, 88
Handley, S.H. 129–130,
    140, 147, 160, 197
Hanley, J.R. 76
Happe, F. 77
Hardman, D. 173

Harkness, A.R. 177
Harries, C. 132, 197
Harries, M.H. 76–77
Harris, P.L. 87
Harvey, N. 132, 197
Haselton, M.G. 27, 219
Hasher, L. 194
Hastie, R. 165, 184
Hatano, K. 76
Hayashi, N. 88
Head, A.S. 76–77
Hebb, D.O. 75
Heberlein, A.S. 76
Hell, W. 171, 178, 194
Hellawell, D.J. 76
Henson, R.N.A. 75
Hernstadt, R. 184
Herrnstein, R.J. 178
Hershey, J. 155
Hertwig, R. 131, 146,
    156–158, 166, 175,
    204
Heyes, C. 4
Heyes, C.M. 78
Hietanen, J.K. 76–77
Higgins, E.T. 19
Hill, K. 4
Hilton, D.J. 163,
    174–175, 179, 184
Hodges, J.R. 76
Hoeksta, J. 88
Hoffrage, U. 7,
    131–132, 134–135,
    146, 148, 159–162,
    197, 199, 204
Hogarth, R.M. 196
Holway A.H. 16
Holyoak, K.J. 5–6, 12,
    26, 35–42, 49–50,
    53, 83, 110, 124,
    127, 165
Horn, J.L. 200–201
Howson, C. 130, 133,
    158, 159
Hrdy, S.B. 23
Huang, S.-C. 75, 89

Hug, K. 35, 49–50,
    57, 79, 82, 102,
    110–112
Hull, D.L. 185,
    210–211
Hume, D. 122
Humphrey, N. 4, 77,
    176, 211
Humphreys, L.G. 200
Hunt, E. 195, 200
Hurvich, L.M. 22

Imada, S. 44
Isaac, C.L. 76
Ito, K. 76

Jackson, S. 39–42, 49
Jameson, D. 22
Jamieson, D.G. 15
Jeeves, M.A. 76–77
Jeffrey, R.C. 160
Jellema, T. 76–77
Johnson, E.J. 155
Johnson, M. 76
Johnson-Laird, P.N. 34,
    112, 124, 130, 147,
    151, 160–161, 173,
    183
Jolly, A. 176
Juola, P. 113–114

Kahneman, D. 7,
    18–19, 23,
    130–131, 134–135,
    145, 147, 154–156,
    159–161, 164–165,
    171, 173–174, 176,
    180, 184, 194, 197,
    203–204, 216, 218
Kalish, C.W. 165
Kant, I. 122–123,
    136–137, 139, 141
Kao, S.F. 176–177
Karmiloff-Smith, A. 12
Kato, T. 76
Katsuki, J. 15

Kawashima, R. 76
Keil, F.C. 25
Kelly, S. 184
Kemmerer, D. 76
Kemper, T.D. 101
Keren, G. 160–161
Kessler, C. 36, 52–53
Kilpatrick, S.G. 127
King, G.A. 19
Kirby, K. 55–56
Kitcher, P. 1
Klar, Y. 52–53, 173
Klein, G. 183, 203
Kleinbolting, H. 131,
    146, 160–161, 197,
    204
Kleiter, G. 131, 146,
    163
Kling, A.S. 76
Kneale, M. 161
Kneale, W. 161
Knight, N. 84
Knight, R.T. 75
Koehler, D.J. 146–147
Kojima, S. 76
Koriat, A. 197
Krams, M. 77
Krantz, D. 163
Krauss, S. 57, 207
Krebs, J.R. 23
Kroger, K. 39–42, 49
Kroll, R. 84
Kruglanski, A.W. 185
Kudo, H. 77
Kummer, H. 176
Kunreuther, H. 155

La Bar, K.S. 76
LaCerra, P. 202
Lazarus, R. 45, 56–57
Le Doux, J.E. 76
Lee, G.P. 76
Legrenzi, M. 34, 130,
    147, 151, 160–161
Legrenzi, P. 34, 130,
    147, 151, 160–161

LePage, A. 20
Lepage, M. 75
Leslie, A.M. 64
Levin, D.T. 27
Levin, I.P. 176–177, 185
Levinson, S.C. 183–184, 194
Lewis, C. 160–161
Lewontin, R.C. 69, 79
Liberman, A. 183
Liberman, N. 52–53, 173
Liberman, V. 146–147
Lichtenstein, S. 197
Liebrand, W.B. 88
Light, P. 36
Linder, D.E. 15
Loftus, E.F. 28
Looren de Jong, H. 205
Lopez, A. 164
Love, R. 36, 52–53
Loveland, D.H. 178
Lowery, L. 44
Lubinski, D. 200, 202
Lucassen, M.P. 22
Lumsden, C.J. 210, 214
Lumsden, J. 76
Luria, A.R. 75, 195–196
Lycett, J. 1–2
Lynch, A. 211–212
Lynch, J. 37

Macchi, L. 197
MacDonald, K. 200
Macdonald, R.R. 174
MacDonall, J.S. 178
Mackintosh, N.J. 178
Mahapatra, M. 49
Manktelow, K.I. 6–7, 12, 34–38, 49–50, 55–56, 83, 88, 107, 111–112, 125–127, 173
Maratos, E.J. 76

Marchman, V.A. 113–115
Margolis, H. 173, 196
Marler, P. 15–16
Marr, D. 14, 33, 70–72, 74, 80
Matsumoto, D. 46
Matthews, G. 201–202
Maunsell, J.H.R. 69
Mavin, G.H. 19
Mayes, A.R. 76
Mazzocco, A. 39, 41–42, 49
McAuslan, P. 22
McCarthy, G. 75, 77
McClamrock, R. 71
McClelland, P. 195
McDermott, K.B. 28
McDuffie, D. 22
McGeorge, P. 184
McGonigle, B.O. 22
McGraw, P.A. 147, 160
McGuire, M. 75, 89
Medin, D.L. 165
Melega, W. 75, 89
Mellers, B. 131, 197, 204
Mellers, B.A. 147, 160
Messick, D.M. 88
Meszaros, J. 155
Miller, E.K. 75
Miller, J. 49
Miller, R.L. 18
Millikan, R.G. 192
Milner, A.D. 69, 76–77
Milner, B. 75
Mineka, S. 3
Mintz, T.H. 116
Mishkin, M. 69
Mistlin, A.J. 76–77
Mithen, S. 176, 203
Moen, P. 195
Montaldi, A. 21, 27
Montaldi, D. 76
Morgan, J.L. 116
Morris, J.S. 76

Morris, R.G. 75
Mowen, J.C. 16
Mulder, M.B. 4
Murphy, D. 12

Nakamura, A. 76
Nakamura, K. 76
Nauta, D. 88
Neisser, U. 199–200
Neter, E. 155, 160–161
Newport, E.L. 116
Newsome, W.T. 69
Newstead, S.E. 173
Nguyen-Xuan, A. 35–36
Nickerson, R.S. 171, 173
Norman, D.A. 183
Noveck, I. 39, 41–42, 49–50, 174–175
Nozick, R. 202
Nunez, M. 87
Nyberg, L. 75

O'Brien, D. 39, 41–42, 49–50
O'Guinn, T.C. 19–20
Oakhill, J.V. 13
Oaksford, M. 49–50, 55–56, 86, 107, 127, 171, 173, 178–179
Oram, M.W. 76–77
Ortega, J.E. 76–77, 209
Ortmann, A. 209
Osherson, D. 164
Ostry, D. 76
Over, D.E. 4–7, 12, 28, 35–38, 49–50, 55–57, 83, 88, 91, 107, 111–112, 122, 124–127, 129–130, 132–133, 136–137, 139–141, 147, 160, 162–163, 166, 171,

173, 177, 182–183,
185–186, 197, 200,
207–209

Passingham, R. 77
Passingham, R.E. 75
Pastore, R.E. 15
Payne, B.K. 20
Pearl, J. 165
Penner, S.B. 15
Pennington, N. 165
Perham, N. 129–130,
147, 160, 197
Perrett, D.I. 76–77
Petrides, M. 75–76
Petrill, S.A. 199–200
Phelps, E.A. 76
Phelps, M. 75, 89
Pinker, S. 2–3, 11, 57,
62, 101, 112–114,
121, 193–194, 215,
219
Pitkanen, A. 77
Platt, R. 35
Plomin, R. 199–200
Plotkin, H.C. 1–2, 102,
104, 186, 219
Plunkett, K. 113–114
Politzer, G. 35–36,
174–175
Polkey, C.E. 75
Pollock, J.L. 183
Posner, M.I. 15, 183
Potter, D.D. 76–77
Povinelli, D.J. 78
Pratto, F. 19
Premack, D. 78
Preuss, T.M. 78
Price, J.L. 77
Prince, A. 114
Prince, C.G. 78
Puce, A. 75, 77

Raleigh, M. 75, 89
Ramachandran, V.S. 62
Rasinski, K.A. 184

Reber, A.S. 183–186,
192
Reder, L.M. 199
Regier, T. 182
Rehder, B. 165
Reicher, G.M. 26–27
Richardson, R.C. 71
Ring, B. 76
Ring, H.A. 76
Rips, L.J. 124
Rizzolatti, G. 77
Roackland, C. 76
Roberts, N. 76
Rode, C. 171, 178,
194
Roe, A.W. 69
Roediger, H.L. 28
Rolls, E.T. 76
Rose, H. 1
Rose, S. 1
Rosenthal, R. 180
Rosnow, R.L. 180
Ross, L.T. 22
Rowe, A.D. 75
Rowland, D. 76
Rozin, P. 44, 212
Russell, J.A. 76

Saffran, J.R. 116
Salmon, C. 2–3
Samuels, R. 2, 5, 12–13,
18–19, 22–23, 61,
63, 121, 195,
204–205
Sarin, R. 218
Sawaguchi, T. 77
Scheirer, C.J. 15
Schneider, W. 183
Schoenberger, A.
128–129, 148–149,
151–152
Schustack, M.W. 177
Scott, S. 76
Segal, L. 1
Seidenberg, M.S. 112,
116

Seyfarth, R.M. 15–16,
87
Shackelford, T. 219
Shafir, E. 164, 171
Shallice, T. 75, 183
Shanks, D.R. 177
Shapiro, D. 34, 110
Shapiro, L. 63
Shepard, R.N. 101,
203
Shiffrin, R.M. 12, 183
Shrum, L.J. 20
Shweder, R. 49
Silk, J.B. 176
Simmons, A. 76
Simon, H.A. 199
Skyrms, B. 104–106,
172, 178, 185–186
Sloman, S.A. 7, 35,
49–52, 110–112,
122, 126, 130,
164–166, 182–183,
197
Slovak, L. 166, 197
Slovic, P. 171, 176, 216
Slugoski, B.R. 174–175
Smith, E.A. 4
Smith, E.E. 164
Smith, M.L. 75
Smith, P.A. 76–77
Smith, S.M. 185
Snyder, C.R.R. 15,
183
Solomon, R.C. 101
Sonino-Legrenzi, M.
130
Speaks, C.E. 15
Spencer, D.D. 76
Sperber, D. 2, 12, 37,
49–50, 52–53, 57,
62–63, 110–111,
121, 126, 136–137,
173, 175, 205,
210–212, 214
Staller, A. 111

Stanovich, K.E. 7, 122, 138, 140–141, 171–173, 176–180, 182, 184–185, 188, 190–191, 194–195, 201–202, 206–208, 219, 221

Stearns, P.N. 101

Stent, G.S. 214

Sterelny, K. 5–6, 12, 63–73, 90, 210

Sternberg, R.J. 177

Stich, S.P. 5, 12–13, 18–19, 22–23, 185, 204–205

Stone, V.E. 75–76, 84

Stuss, D.T. 75–76

Sugiura, M. 76

Sutherland, N.S. 178

Swets, J.A. 14

Symons, D. 2–3, 61–62, 101, 106, 194

Tan, E.S. 101

Tanaka, J.N. 27

Thomas, S. 76–77

Thompson, S.C. 21

Thompson, V.A. 129–130, 147, 160, 197

Thrall, N. 21, 27

Todd, P.M. 4, 88, 121, 171, 206–208, 217

Tomasello, M. 78, 176

Tooby, J. 1–3, 5–7, 11–13, 16–18, 21–22, 25–27, 34–37, 41, 45, 47, 53–55, 57, 61–62, 70, 73, 79, 80–84, 88–90, 101–103, 106–108, 114, 116, 121, 122, 124–126, 128–130, 135–136, 138–141, 146, 149–153, 157–160, 162, 171, 178, 184, 190, 194, 198–199, 201–205, 207, 209–212, 214–215, 217–219

Tranel, D. 75–76, 87, 89

Tremoulet, P.D. 5, 13, 18–19, 22–23, 204–205

Trivers, R.L. 1, 34–35, 81

Ts'o, D.Y. 69

Tulving, E. 75

Tversky, A. 7, 18–19, 23, 130–131, 134–135, 145–147, 154–156, 159–161, 164–165, 171, 173–174, 176–178, 180, 184, 194, 197, 203–204, 216

Ungerleider, L.G. 69

Urbach, P. 130, 133, 158, 159

Van De Wal, C. 76

van der Steen, W. J. 205

Van Essen, D.C. 69

Vranas, P.B.M. 163–164

Wakefield, J. 219

Wakker, P.P. 218

Waldmann, M.R. 165

Walkenfeld, F.F. 184

Walvaren, J. 22

Wason, P.C. 5, 33, 34, 109–110, 122, 124, 173, 183

Wasserman, E.A. 176–177

Watanabe, Y. 88

Weiskrantz, L. 76

West, R.F. 7, 122, 138, 140–141, 172–173, 176–180, 184–185, 188, 194, 219

Wethington, E. 195

Whalen, P. 76

Wheeler, M. 6, 26, 61–63, 65, 70–71, 73, 86, 90

Wheelwright, S. 76

White, G.M. 101

Whiten, A. 77–78, 176

Wilkie, O. 164

Williams, G.C. 79, 210, 214, 220

Williams, S.C.R. 76

Wilson, A.E. 174–175

Wilson, D. 57, 175

Wilson, D.S. 2, 4

Wilson, E.O. 210, 214

Wilson, K.D. 27

Woodruff, G. 78

Wright, G. 147

Wright, R. 214–215

Yamagishi, T. 88

Young, A.W. 76, 69

Zacks, R.T. 194

Zarate, O. 1–2

Subject Index

Abstract reasoning 136–141, 176
  as required for instrumental
    rationality 194–197, 199–200, 203
  as suspension of allocation 24
  see also decontextualised reasoning;
    metarepresentation
Adaptation
  as accommodation vs.
    transformation 68–69
  cognitive/psychological 11–13,
    25–26, 54, 62–63
  see also modules, mental
Adaptationist, adaptationism 61,
    66, 68, 72, 171–172, 177–178,
    180–182, 185, 199
'Adaptive rules' 41–43, 46, 55
  see also precaution, social contract
'Adaptive toolbox' 121
Advertising 196, 206, 213
  see also branding; fundamental
    computational bias
Algorithms, cognitive/Darwinian – *see*
    modules, mental
Algorithmic level 71–72, 74, 79–80, 82,
    88, 188–191, 200, 202
  see also analysis, levels of; System 2

Allocation
  error(s) 18–24
  see also base-rate bias, initial; context
    bias; formulation errors;
    instigation errors; personality
    biases
  manipulation/suspension of 23–24
  system 5, 13–14, 16–18,
    24–28
Altruism, reciprocal 1, 5, 34, 77–78,
    80–81, 104
  see also cooperation; social contract
    theory
Amygdala 73–74, 76–78
Analysis, levels of 70–74, 78, 80,
    84–85
  see also algorithmic level; biological
    level; computational/ecological
    level; intentional level;
    implementation level
Analytic
  intelligence – *see* intelligence,
    analytic
  system/process(es) 183, 190, 200,
    202–203
  see also System 2

Anger, as indicative of social contract
    violation 5, 45–49, 54–56,
    127–128, 138
'Arms race', co-evolutionary 67–68,
    77–78
Availability heuristic 19–20, 134,
    159–160, 203
    see also base-rate bias, initial;
    heuristics and biases

Base forms, of words – see inflection
Base-rate
    bias, initial 19–20
    neglect 129, 132, 146, 148–154
Bayes' theorem, Bayesian reasoning
    19, 127, 129, 131–134, 146,
    148–155, 158–161, 165, 173, 205
Bias – see also heuristics and biases
    base-rate – see base-rate bias, initial
    context – see context bias
    fundamental computational – see
        fundamental computational bias
    personality – see personality biases
Biological level 189
    see also analysis, levels of
Biological preparedness 3–4, 121,
    138–139
    see also canalisation
Branding 213, 218
    see also advertising

Calibration 171, 197, 204–205
    see also overconfidence
Canalisation 3–5
    see also biological preparedness
Category instances vs. properties,
    category structure (inside/outside
    view) 147–148, 150
Causal models, of probability
    judgement 145, 165–166
Cheater detection/identification 5–6,
    12, 17, 26, 33–34, 45–46, 57, 67,
    80–82, 88–89, 102, 104–112,
    114–117, 125–127, 136, 138–139
    see also 'look for cheaters'
    algorithm

Chronically accessible schemas 19
    see also base-rate bias, initial
Cognitive
    ability, differential 172–173,
        178–182, 184, 200
    see also individual differences in
        reasoning
    illusions 146, 154, 162–163, 176, 197,
        204–205, 217–218
    neuroscience 63, 72–78, 84–85,
        87–89
    traits 202
    see also thinking styles
Communication, Gricean maxims of
    175, 184
    see also conversational implicature;
    relevance theory
Computational
    capacity/power 182–184, 188,
        200–201, 219
    demands, simplicity/complexity 131,
        134–135, 146, 148, 176, 182–184,
        200
    level 14, 33, 70–71
    see also analysis, levels of; ecological
    level
Conditional probability 132, 163, 177
Conditional rules/reasoning 5, 12,
    34, 38, 44, 51–52, 81–83, 112,
    124–127, 140
    see also deontic reasoning; selection
    task
Confirmation-seeking strategy 80,
    86–87
Conjunction
    fallacy 145–148, 154–158, 161, 165,
        174–175, 179–180
    see also Linda problem
    rule 130–131, 135, 154–155, 181,
        199
Connectionism 6, 102, 112–118, 201
Consistency-checking ability
    136–137
Construal(s), task – see task construal
Constructive/nonconstructive thought
    139–140

Content
    see also domain-general/specific
        effects 33–36, 53–54, 87
    see also facilitation, thematic
    -general/independent reasoning 2,
        6–7, 122–126, 128–130, 132–141
    see also metarepresentation
    -specific reasoning 2–7, 121–122,
        124–128, 137–139, 141, 202, 210,
        212
Context bias 20–21
Contextualised thinking 183–184,
    194–195, 203
    see also fundamental computational
        bias
Controlled processing 23, 172,
    182–184, 186
Conversational implicature/inference/
    pragmatics 52, 174–175, 181, 184
    see also communication, Gricean
        maxims of; relevance theory
Cooperation 34–35, 53–55, 57, 77–78,
    86, 104–109, 125, 127
    see also altruism, reciprocal; social
        contract theory; social exchange
Cost/benefit reasoning 6, 12–13, 17,
    26–27, 34–36, 39–42, 50, 56,
    81–83, 104–109, 117, 124–125, 136
    see also social contract theory; social
        exchange
Counterfactual reasoning 158, 165
Covariation detection 176–177,
    180–181
Criterion, for signal detection 14–15,
    27
    bias 15, 20–21
Cue(s), for signal detection/allocation
    14, 16–17, 20–21, 25
Cutting score – see criterion

Decision theory/science 55–57, 127,
    214–217
    see also Bayes' theorem; Bayesian
        response/reasoning
Decontextualised thinking 176,
    183–184, 194–196, 203, 205

Degrees of belief/confidence 158–160,
    164, 166, 171
    see also probability, epistemic/
        inductive
Deontic logic 26, 125–126
Deontic rules/reasoning 5–7, 35,
    37–44, 46–47, 49–50, 79–84,
    86–90, 123–128, 138–141
    see also permission; obligation;
        selection task; social contract
        theory
'Deontic rules' (as contrasted with
    'adaptive rules') 41–44, 46–50
    semantic analysis of 56–57
Determinism, cultural/genetic 3–4
Disease problem 128–129, 131–132,
    134–135, 148–154, 161–162
    see also medical diagnosis task
Domain
    actual/proper 205
    see also environment of evolutionary
        adaptedness; modern society
    -general 62, 88, 90, 102, 112–113,
        116, 118, 190–191, 198, 202
    -specific 12, 37, 41–42, 50, 54,
        62–63, 67–68, 86, 88, 90, 102–104,
        107, 109–110, 112–118, 137, 172,
        202, 210–212
Dominance theory 55–56, 80, 86–90,
    213
Dual process theory of reasoning 2, 7,
    122–123, 128, 137–141, 172,
    182–183, 202
    see also system 1; system 2

Ecological level 70–72, 74, 78–81,
    87–88
    see also analysis, levels of;
        computational level
Ecological rationality – see rationality,
    ecological
Economics 81, 217–218
Elimination rules – see introduction
    and elimination rules
Emotions 44–49, 54–57, 74–76, 87,
    101, 127–128, 193, 195–196

Encapsulation 12, 107–108, 121–122, 127–128
Engineering analysis 79
Environment of evolutionary adaptedness (EEA) 62, 70–72, 78–81, 122–123, 128, 131, 135–141, 172, 190, 194, 198, 203–205, 207–208
  see also domain, proper
Epidemiological culture 210, 214
Equilibrium, evolutionary 105
Error(s)
  allocation – *see* allocation error
  formulation – *see* formulation error
  instigated – *see* instigated error
  type I/II – *see* type I/II error
Euler circles 130, 135–136, 138, 141, 150–153, 161
Evidence, strength of, as a frame for probability judgement 163–164
Evolutionary biology 1, 33, 61, 81–82, 85, 101
Extensional vs. intensional interpretation 147, 164
  see also category structure
Externalism (regarding reason) 123, 140
Eye gaze, perception of 64, 74, 76–78

Facilitation, thematic 12–13, 18, 40, 83, 151, 153–154, 157
  see also content effects; selection task
False belief task 74–76, 78
Fear
  as indicative of precautionary violation 5, 45–48, 54, 127
  as innate vs. learned 3–4, 121, 212
Fitness, maximisation of 61–62, 123, 137, 139, 186, 191–192, 207, 215–217, 219
Formal logic, rules, reasoning 24, 122–123, 126, 128–130, 135, 141, 160–161, 199
  see also logical rules, reasoning
Formulation errors 22–23

Frequency
  definitions of 158–160
  effect, frames/formats, frequentist reasoning 7, 18, 22–23, 128–136, 145–166, 197–199, 203–204
  natural/objective 128, 131–134, 145–146, 148–150, 152–154, 156–162, 166
  normalised 132, 146
  sample 130, 133–134, 158–162, 165–166
Fundamental computational bias 184, 194–196, 198–200, 203

g 200
  see also intelligence, general; cognitive ability
Game theory 81–82
Gaze – *see* eye gaze, perception of
General-purpose (cognitive processes, etc) 2–3, 12, 103, 122, 138
  see also domain-general
Genetic
  coding 25, 106
  determinism – *see* determinism, genetic
  fallacy 194, 215
  goals/interests – *see* goals, genetic
  variability – *see* variability, genetic
'Genocentric logic' of selection 104
Genome, genotype 216, 219–220
Goals
  see also 'leash', short/long-; interests, of genes/vehicles
  conflict, mismatch 172, 186, 189–190, 192–194
  genetic, subpersonal 185–187, 190, 192–194, 212
  individual, intentional-level, personal, vehicle's 172, 185–186, 188, 191–194
  structure 183, 185–186, 189–193
Grain problem 5–6, 54–55, 72–73, 90–91
  solution to 84–86

Sterelny & Griffiths' (one-dimensional) 63, 69–70
two-dimensional 63–69

Hazard (management theory) 5–6, 36–37, 39, 41, 45, 47, 53–55, 57, 79, 83–84, 86, 88–89, 126–127
see also precaution
Heuristic
availability – *see* availability heuristic
'fast and frugal' 88, 207
processing 182–183, 185, 208
recognition – *see* recognition heuristic
representativeness – *see* representativeness heuristic
'Heuristics and biases' research programme 145, 147, 171–173, 175–176, 181, 184–285, 196, 203–205, 217
Hypothetical thinking 133–134, 182–183, 200

Implementation (hardware) level 71–72, 74, 78–80, 88
see also analysis, levels of
Implicature, conversational – *see* conversational implicature
Independence
criterion (of explanatory argument) 66–69
of events, as significant for hypothesis evaluation 132–133, 162
Indicative reasoning 86–87, 125, 127, 140–141
see also selection task
Individual differences in reasoning 7, 138, 141, 180–181, 184, 200–202
see also cognitive ability, differential
Individual goals/interests – *see* goals, individual
Inflection 113–115
Information-processing system 62, 69–73, 82, 103, 171–172, 176–177, 179–180, 182, 201, 205, 210

Innateness, limited 116–117
Instigated errors 23
Instincts 3, 7, 25, 37, 39, 117, 121–123, 139, 161
see also modules
Intelligence
see also cognitive ability
analytic, general, psychometric 179, 182–185, 188, 200, 202, 219
crystallised/fluid 200–201
interactional, Machiavellian, social 73–74, 77–80, 87–88, 176, 183–184
Intension – *see* extensional vs. intensional interpretation
Intentional level 188–193, 212
see also analysis, levels of
Interactional intelligence – *see* intelligence, interactional
Interactor 185, 211
see also vehicle
Interests
see also goals
of genes, replicators 7, 185–196, 189–191, 193–194, 197–198, 209, 213–215, 219–221
of individuals, persons, vehicles 7, 185–186, 189–194, 197–198, 200, 202, 209, 213–215, 219–221
Internalism (regarding reason) 123, 140
Introduction and elimination rules 140

Kantian challenge 122–123, 136–137, 139, 141

Labelling effect 20–21
see also context bias
Learning, as a content-general mechanism/process 3, 104, 112, 114, 116, 138, 210
'Leash'
culture on a 210, 214–215
short- 7, 183, 186–188, 209, 212
long- 7, 183, 186–188, 191–193
see also goals, conflict/genetic/individual

'Leibniz's dream' 122, 161
Lexical processing 112–113
Linda problem 156, 161, 173–176,
    179–180, 204
    see also conjunction fallacy
Logic
    deontic – *see* deontic logic
    formal – *see* formal logic, rules,
        reasoning
    mental – *see* mental logic
Logical rules, reasoning 6, 33–38, 57,
    122–128, 130, 133–138, 140–141,
    154–155, 161, 174–175, 197, 200,
    208, 214–217
    see also 'primary workplace'
'Look for cheaters' algorithm 34–35,
    39–40
    see also cheater detection

Machiavellian intelligence hypothesis –
    see intelligence, Machiavellian
'Mars explorer' analogy 186, 192
    see also 'leash', long-
Massive
    memory, *see* memory, massive
    modularity, *see* modularity, massive
Matching, probability – *see* probability
    matching
Medical diagnosis task 128–129,
    148–154, 157–158
    see also disease problem
Meliorist position 194, 205
Memes 209–215, 218–220
Memory
    for individuals 27
    massive 131–132, 134
    neural substrate of 75
    retrieval 160–161
    system, models of 12, 15, 28,
        113–114
    working 75, 137, 160–161, 201
Mental
    disorders 21–22
    see also personality biases
    logic 124–125, 137–138, 140–141
    models 112, 160–161

organs 25, 107
    see also modules
'Menu', short/standard 131, 135
Metaphor
    neural substrate for understanding
        of 76
    use of 23–24
    see also allocation, manipulation/
        suspension of
Metarepresentation 7, 136–141
    see also abstract reasoning
'Mindreading' 65
    see also theory of mind
Minds, kinds of
    Darwinian 187–190, 192, 194, 213,
        220
    Gregorian 187–188, 191, 193–194,
        201, 206, 210, 214
    Popperian 187–188, 191, 193
    Skinnerian 187–188
Misallocation – *see* allocation error(s)
Modal
    response 48, 129, 148, 171–172,
        177–181
    operators, terms 42, 57, 125
Modern society, as different from EEA
    172, 190, 194–196, 198–200,
    203–209
    see also domain, actual/proper;
        environment of evolutionary
        adaptedness
Modules (mental), modularity
    cost/benefit evaluation – *see* cost/
        benefit reasoning
    cheater detection – *see* cheater
        detection
    Massive Modularity Hypothesis
        (MMH) 2–7, 12–13, 26, 63, 68,
        121–124, 126–128, 130, 132–133,
        135–138, 141, 195, 198, 202
    modularity arguments 6, 123–126,
        128–130, 135, 137, 141
    multimodularity 2, 5, 11–14, 16–17,
        23–26, 35
    theory of mind – *see* theory of
        mind

Motion, biological, perception of 25–26, 74, 76–78

Natural
  deduction – *see* mental logic
  frequency – *see* frequency, natural
  sampling – *see* sampling, natural
  selection 62, 68, 71, 102, 104–105, 107–109, 116, 122–123, 128, 134, 138–140, 162, 218
Naturalism 123
Nested sets hypothesis 147–148, 150–158, 160–161, 163, 166
  see also set relations
'Noise' 14–16
Nonconstructive thought – *see* constructive/nonconstructive thought
Normalised frequencies – *see* frequency, normalised
Normative reasoning/response 22, 51–52, 130, 160, 165, 171, 179–181, 185–186, 199, 215
  debate surrounding 140, 163–164, 171–178, 205, 217

Obligation 38, 41–44, 46–49, 55, 79, 87–88, 126, 128
Orbitofrontal cortex (OFC) 74–77, 89
  see also ventromedial prefrontal cortex
Overconfidence 146, 197, 203
  see also calibration

'Panglossian' position 172, 205, 218
Parallel processing 17, 25, 184, 200–201
  see also connectionism; System 1
Permission 38–50, 55–56, 79, 88, 126–128
Personality
  biases 21–22
  traits, heritable 201
  see also cognitive traits; thinking styles

Phenotype, phenotypic feature/ solution/trait 11, 61, 66, 69–70, 72, 74, 79–80, 82, 84–85, 188
Pragmatic reasoning schemas theory (PRST) 26, 38–41, 44, 46–50, 55
Precaution 5, 18, 21–23, 36–39, 41–48, 51, 53–57, 79, 83–84, 88–90, 126–127
  see also hazard
Preparedness, biological – *see* biological preparedness
'Primary workplace' 140–141
  see also logical rules, reasoning; mental logic
Probability
  as polysemous 131, 146
  concepts/types of 158–161
  conditional 132, 163, 177
  epistemic/inductive 133, 158, 160–161, 164, 166
  matching 177–178, 180–182, 216, 219
  objective 158–159, 163
  prior 129
  see also base rate
  ranking/rank-ordering vs. rating of 156–157, 173–174
  single-case/event 18, 22, 128–129, 131–132, 134, 145–146, 148, 151–154, 156–157, 159–162, 164, 198
  theory 24, 129–130, 133, 145–146, 154–155, 158, 160, 163–164, 174–175, 217
Probabilistic reasoning 6–7, 19, 124, 128–136, 145–166, 171, 173–175, 180, 199, 203–206, 208
Psychometric intelligence – *see* intelligence, psychometric

Ranking/rank-ordering of probabilities – *see* probabilities, ranking/rank-ordering of
Rating of probabilities – *see* probabilities, rating of

Rationality 7, 18–19, 21–22, 162,
    171–172, 175, 180, 183, 191, 201,
    204–206, 209–210, 216, 218–221
  see also normative reasoning/
    response
  debate surrounding 173–177,
    205–206, 209–210, 216–217
  ecological 7, 88, 204, 206–209, 217,
    219
  evolutionary 7, 172, 178, 185–189,
    190, 192, 194, 198, 207–208,
    217–218, 220–221
  instrumental 7, 172, 178, 185–189,
    190, 192, 194, 198, 200, 206–209,
    215, 219–221
Recognition heuristic 208–209
Reductionism, greedy 219–221
Relativism, cultural 28, 215
Relevance theory 52–55, 173,
    184–185
  see also communication, Gricean
    maxims of; conversational
    implicature
Replication
  genetic, replicator 104–105, 172,
    185–186, 189–190, 192–194,
    197–198, 202, 209, 212, 214–216,
    219–221
  see also genetic
  memetic 210–211
Representativeness heuristic 147, 155,
    164–165
  see also conjunction fallacy;
    heuristics and biases
Rule-based processing 113–115,
    182–185, 200
  see also abstract reasoning; formal
    rules/reasoning

Sample, sampling
  biased vs. representative 132–134,
    160–163, 206
  frequency – *see* frequency, sample
  natural 131–136, 146, 148, 161–162,
    199
  size 133, 159, 164

Scholastic Aptitude Test (SAT)
    179–181
  see also g
Selection task 5, 12, 33–34, 36–37, 44,
    54–57, 82, 109–111, 117, 127, 173,
    176
  deontic 6, 37–39, 41–42, 50–54,
    124–125, 141
  see also deontic rules/reasoning
  emotion 46, 48–49, 556
  see also emotions
  indicative/nondeontic 38, 50–54,
    124–125, 141, 179, 181, 184–185
  obligation 41–43
  permission 38, 41–43, 45
  see also permission
  precaution 36–38, 41–43, 45, 83–84,
    126
  see also hazard; precaution
  social contract 34–38, 41–43, 75, 89,
    126
  see also social contract theory; social
    exchange
Selection, natural – *see* natural
    selection
Selection pressure 5, 11, 13, 55 ,61,
    63–64, 72–73, 77–79, 81–83,
    85–90
  hierarchical/nested 69–70
Serial processing 57, 172, 182–184,
    190, 200–201, 206
  see also System 2
Set relations/structure 7, 130–131,
    134–136, 147–148, 150–158,
    160–165, 174
  see also nested sets hypothesis
Sex differences 21–22, 107
  see also personality biases
Sexual
  harassment, construal of 18
  opportunity, detection of 17, 20, 22,
    26
Signal detection
  parameters, constant/variable
    26–28
  theory (SDT) 5, 14–28

Social
    cognition 63, 72–73, 75–77
    contract theory (SCT) 12, 33–50,
        54–57, 79–84, 86–90, 124–127
    exchange 5, 12–13, 18, 20–21, 23,
        26–28, 34–35, 57, 79, 81–83
    intelligence – *see* intelligence, social
    reasoning 70, 73–74, 77–78, 80–81,
        86–87, 89, 102, 107
Socialisation of information 175–176,
    184
Sociobiology 1–2, 194, 217
Sodium vapour lamps
    as example of actual/proper domain
        mismatch 203, 205–206
    as source of formulation errors 22
Standard Social Science Model
    (SSSM) 3–4, 103–104, 116–117,
    202, 210
Stereotypes 27–28
    see also categorisation of individuals
Superior temporal sulcus (STS) 73–74,
    76–77, 79
'Swiss army knife' metaphor 2,
    121–122
System 1 7, 122, 139–140, 182–186,
    188–189, 192, 194, 200, 203,
    208–209, 212–213, 218–219
System 2 7, 122, 137, 139–140,
    182–186, 188–189, 190–194, 198,
    200, 202, 206, 209, 212–213

Task construal, differential 184,
    188–189
Theory of mind 12, 26, 74–78, 117
    see also mindreading
Thinking styles 195–196, 201
    see also cognitive traits
Threat, detection of/representation as
    17–18, 20–21, 23, 26, 28, 46, 76
Type
    I/II errors 15
    see also signal detection theory

1/2 processes 122, 183
    see also dual process theory of
        reasoning; system 1/2

Uncertainty, judgement under 16, 18,
    138, 146
    see also frequentist/probabilistic
        reasoning
Universal features of human cognition
    2, 4–5, 28, 189, 202, 212, 218
Utility
    expected vs. experienced 218
    maximisation of personal/subjective
        56, 178, 181, 183, 185–186, 192,
        199–201, 206, 215–217
    see also decision theory
    theory 171

Variability
    circumstantial 106–109, 116
    genetic 105, 199–201
    historical 108–109, 116
Vehicles 7, 172, 185–187, 189–194,
    197–198, 200–202, 206–207,
    209–217, 219–221
    see also goals, individual
Ventromedial prefrontal cortex
    (VMPFC) 73–78, 87, 89
    see also orbitofrontal cortex

Wason selection task – *see* selection
    task
Weakness of the will 139
Weapons effect 20
    see also context bias
Whole
    preferred mental representation of
        18, 135–136, 199
    system considered as 71, 74
    see also ecological level
Word problems 130–131, 134–136, 146,
    148, 158, 162–163
Word superiority effect 26–27